Prose
in the Age of Poets

*Romanticism and
Biographical Narrative
from Johnson to De Quincey*

Annette Wheeler Cafarelli

upp

University of Pennsylvania Press
Philadelphia

Library of Congress Cataloging-in-Publication Data

Cafarelli, Annette.
    Prose in the age of poets: romanticism and biographical narrative from Johnson to
De Quincey / Annette Wheeler Cafarelli.
        p.   cm.
    Includes bibliographical references.
    ISBN 0-8122-8198-5
    1. English prose literature—19th century—History and criticism. 2. English prose
literature—18th century—History and criticism. 3. Biography (as a literary form)
4. Authors, English—Biography—History and criticism. 5. Romanticism—England.
6. Johnson, Samuel, 1709–1784. Lives of the poets. 7. Hazlitt, William, 1778–1830. Spirit
of the age. 8. De Quincey, Thomas, 1785–1859. Literary reminiscences. I. Title.
PR778.B56C34 1990
828'.60809—dc20   89-40396
                                                                                CIP

Contents

Acknowledgments

This book is indebted to the advice and assistance of A. Walton Litz, Thomas McFarland, Paul Korshin, Michael Goldman, Alvin B. Kernan, David R. Coffin, and the editors at the University of Pennsylvania Press. Final research for this book was completed with the assistance of grants from the Columbia University Council on Research and Faculty Development. I also would like to thank the staff of the Rare Book Division of the Princeton University Library; the Astor, Lenox and Tilden Foundations of the New York Public Library for permission to quote from De Quincey's letter to Thomas Noon Talfourd, held in the Carl H. Pforzheimer, Shelley & His Circle Collection; and the Special Collections Division of Van Pelt Library of the University of Pennsylvania, for permission to quote Byron's marginalia in his copy of Isaac D'Israeli's *The Literary Character,* held in the Meyer Davis, Jr., Collection. Portions of Chapters III and V appeared earlier in "Johnson's *Lives* and the Romantic Canon," *Age of Johnson* 1 (1987): 403–35, and "De Quincey and Wordsworthian Narrative," *Studies in Romanticism* 28 (1989): 121–47.

Chapter I

Introduction: Biography as Symbolic Narrative

The chronological periodization of literature has long been recognized as an impediment in the study of the movement we call Romanticism. Nowhere is the artificial barrier between the eighteenth and nineteenth centuries clearer than in assessing the Romantic reaction to the complex prose legacy of Johnson. The common belief is that Johnson represents the zenith of eighteenth-century prose, a genre largely abandoned by the Romantics in favor of poetry; and that Johnson, the culminating figure as writer and subject of biography, is best represented in Boswell's *Life of Johnson,* the chief legacy of British biography and the central model for the subsequent development of the genre.[1] From the critical inattention given to the forces of Romanticism in biography, one might wrongly conclude that biography was either immune to the sweeping trends of literature or went unwritten for several generations. The biographical historian John A. Garraty utters the prevalent view when he declares, "Romanticism might have been expected to contribute a new dimension to biography. In fact, though it rose to prominence at a time when biography was flowering as never before, it added little to the form."[2]

In truth, Romantic experimentation in prose is part of the complex matrix of generic redefinition and experimentation that characterizes the early nineteenth century. Biography was an essential Romantic vehicle of thought, and it was Johnson who called attention to the genre and who initiated Romantic exploration of the formal qualities of biography and biography as a critical methodology. Rather than considering failed Boswellian imitations as anticlimactic specimens of an uncharacteristic genre in an age of inferior prose, we must look for biographical innovation in the characteristically Romantic prose form, the fragmented and subjective narrative of the genre René Wellek has named collective biography.[3]

Virtually every major prose writer of the Romantic age experimented with collective biography. Yet the twentieth-century emphasis on Boswell has eclipsed Johnsonian biography and generated the common misconception that all biography aspires to the condition of Boswell. It was not, however, the massive Boswellian *Life of Johnson* compiled of letters and raw documents, but rather the short, anecdotal, sequenced biographies of Johnson's *Lives of the Poets* that provided the central model for Romantic biography in shape, interpretive authority, and critical ambition. Boswell, like Rousseau, encouraged intimacy and iconoclastic detail. But lives composed on the Johnsonian model—interpretive, subjective, fragmentary, allusive, iconographic—constitute the Romantic mainstream in prose. The brief sequenced lives of collective biography epitomize Romantic discourse in their emphasis on subjectivity rather than objectivity, heuristic inference rather than proof, paratactic innuendo rather than univocal interpretation, and truth rather than accuracy. Post-Johnsonian biography overturned the panegyrical and factual confines of the genre through juxtaposition of incident rather than explicit editorial intrusion, symbolic economy of anecdote rather than exhaustive antiquarianism, and exegetical reading of the life as if it were a literary text.

The conventional image of the Romantics as autobiographers has obscured autobiography's position as a part of a wider cultural interest in biography. William Spengemann echoes the current bias in calling autobiography "the prime instrument of Romantic knowledge";[4] yet what we call autobiography was regarded in the early nineteenth century as a subgenre of biography. Although one hesitates to say there is any single expression of Romanticism, certainly biographical modes of inquiry were at the core of Romantic intellectual pursuits, fundamental to the investigation of society, texts, and the human mind. Biographical writing was at the root of what Coleridge called the "AGE OF PERSONALITY,"[5] the Romantic interest in literature as an expression of the self. For the Romantics, collective biography provided a way to allegorize their lives and the life of their times. To understand the movement of Romanticism, it is necessary to recontextualize autobiography into biography and nonfictional prose into the literary mainstream. This study will use the favored status of biography in the late eighteenth and early nineteenth centuries, evident in the profusion of biographical methodologies and narratives in both poetry and prose, as an instrument for discussing the transmission and redefinition of genre, and for examining nonfictional narrative as part of the main current of Romantic composition.

Prose was the salient genre of the eighteenth century, and for the British Romantics, the most monumental intellectual figure of the eighteenth century was Johnson, foremost a biographer and a subject of biography. The colossus of the *Lives of the Poets* and Boswell's *Life* asserted a formidable prose tradition that every Romantic prose writer was obliged to confront. The centrality of Johnson in shaping prose discourse posed both a precedent and a target for his successors; yet the ubiquitous challenges and fulminations against Johnson signify the fundamental and pervasive influence of eighteenth-century biography on the Romantic intellectual tradition. No writer after Johnson in either poetry or prose could ignore the presence of Johnson, for he engaged not only a generic dialogue, but a critical dialogue. In the wake of Johnson's *Lives of the Poets,* prose writers became aware of critical biography as a literary form; and in the wake of Johnson's *Life,* authors became aware of their potential role as subjects of literary biography.

The cultural rise of interest in the individual gave rise to a complex critical dialogue in the field of biography. It is in this perspective that literary biography emerges as a crucial index for identifying the continuities and discontinuities of the movement from Neoclassicism to Romanticism. We tend to think of British Romanticism chiefly in terms of poetry, but there has been a growing realization that the great poets were also important prose writers. It is a mistake to privilege poetry while overlooking the new economic importance assumed by prose in the literary marketplace of the later eighteenth and early nineteenth centuries. Immense expansion of periodical publication arose from advances in print and distribution technology, accompanied by the increase in readership and book purchasing which followed rising availability of texts, lowered costs, and increasing leisure (in at least some social classes). Alongside this print revolution arose a vast community of writers. Even those writers fortunate enough to win the few available patrons and sinecures turned to nonfictional prose for income. With so many contributors, nonfictional prose assumed new importance in the scope of intellectual discourse.

The most familiar view of the Romantic attitude toward Johnson is the rebellion from his critical dominance. The goal of this study, however, is to bring to light unstated Johnsonian subtexts in Romanticism, particularly in his enduring presence on a narrative level despite the ostensible rejection of his critical principles as outmoded. Johnson's last major project was the *Lives of the Poets,* and for Romantic readers, it was his most recent and his most important work, the one that defined him most fully as the critical arbiter of the preceding generation. It is in the rebellion from this text that we see Johnson's most ubiquitous legacy, for the era that prided itself on its resistance to Johnson insured his continuing presence by animating in new directions the narrative forms and biographical theories of reading most closely identified with him. Their writing of biographical sequences, their revision of Johnsonian valuations and expropriation of Johnson critical issues, pay the unwitting homage of rebellion.

In the wake of Johnson, collective biography—a genre dating back to Cornelius Nepos, Plutarch, Suetonius, and Christian hagiography—was revived as an instrument for literary discourse. The early biographical historian Wilbur Cross wisely observed that the kinds of biographical sequences composed in an era provide a clue to the mind of an age.[6] Plutarch collected rulers of the world in an era of statecraft; saints' lives were common in a time of theological dominion; Vasari collected lives of artists at a time when the visual arts assumed aesthetic preeminence. The abundance of Romantic biographical collections of literary figures reflects the Romantic concern with guarding the claims of literature in an age troubled by mechanistic and utilitarian assaults on art.

Before Johnson there had been a number of encyclopedic collections of literary lives. Edward Phillips's *Theatrum Poetarum* (1675) was a directory of poets divided into Ancients and Moderns, accompanied by paragraph-long descriptions of the works. William Winstanley's derivative *Lives of the Most Famous English Poets* (1687) also assembled poets without critiques of their works. Gerard Langbaine's *Account of the English Dramatic Poets* (1691) had longer, valuative entries ranging from one paragraph to several pages on Dryden (who, reflecting the tastes of the age, received far more space than Shakespeare). The *Lives of the Poets of Great Britain and Ireland to the Time of Dean Swift* (1753), prepared by Theophilus Cibber and Robert Shiels, provided an eclectic collection of literary biographies by various hands, including Johnson himself. Horace Walpole's *Catalogue of the Royal and Noble Authors of England* (1758) offered a more limited directory circumscribed by social class.[7]

One of Johnson's major sources, however, the *Biographia Britannica* (first printed in 1747–66), distinguished itself from mere encyclopedic compilations by calling attention to a French precedent, Pierre Bayle's *Dictionnaire historique et critique* (first published in 1697 and revised in 1702). The second edition of the *Biographia* advertised itself as "digested in the Manner of Mr. Bayle's Historical and Critical Dictionary," its lives being written, not merely assembled from documents.[8] Although compilers of encyclopedic sequences objected to Bayle's idiosyncratic collection, later anecdotalists preferred his subjective and selective narratives. Johnson himself said in tribute, "Bayle's Dictionary is a very useful work for those to consult who love the biographical part of literature, which is what I love most."[9]

Indifferent editorial collectivism—prosopographic or alphabetically encyclopedic grouping of lives—does not concern us in this study.[10] Nor shall we be looking at the relatively uncommon composite biographies, exampled by the four gospels, which assemble multiple biographies of a single individual by different hands. Our interest here is in the tradition of subjective sequencing of lives in which a sustained ideological program emerges. On a narrative level, perhaps the truest antecedents to collective biography lie not in biography proper, but in collections of pseudobiographical sketches such as the prologue to *The Canterbury Tales,* or *A Mirror for Magistrates.* Secular biographies, such as those by Izaak Walton, Thomas Fuller, Anthony Wood, John Aubrey, and Roger North, contributed to a tradition of collecting literary lives—some appeared individually and were later collected, some were only published in the wake of Johnson.[11] It was Johnson's vindication of the importance of literary lives that widely revived the form of collective literary biography as an instrument of critical discourse: the genre assumed new significance as an agent for discussing theories of creativity, canon, and the place of the poet in society.[12] Johnson's critical essays and the *Lives of the Poets* together elevated the status of biography and provided a theoretical context for its evaluation.[13] What Suetonius said of Augustus, and Johnson said of Dryden, we may say of Johnson and collective biography: he found it brick, and he left it marble.

We may distinguish two basic time structures unifying sequences: the synchronic history of an age and the diachronic history through time. Synchronic collectivity, usually associated with notions of *Zeitgeist,* appears in texts such as Hazlitt's *The Spirit of the Age,* De Quincey's *Literary Reminiscences,* and Pater's *The Renaissance.* Diachronic collectivity, usually associated with literary or intellectual history, appears in such texts as Suetonius's *Lives of the Caesars,* Johnson's *Lives of the Poets,* and Hazlitt's *Lectures on the English Poets.* Thematic groupings may or may not incorporate a systematic chronology; Plutarch's leaders span time, but Scott's *Lives of the Novelists* clusters the generations just preceding Scott's life. The objective of this study is not merely to establish a classifying vocabulary, however, but to explore more complex developmental sequences that arose in the wake of Johnson. In taking this narratological approach toward biographical sequencing, we must distinguish between collective biography as a linear but discontinuous narrative based on a specifically ordered sequence and collective biography as an episodically random but intellectually cumulative narrative. In treating Johnson's *Lives* and many of its successors, the latter kind of collection is of chief importance in examining narrative experimentation.

What concerns us here is reading these lives as collective units. It does not matter whether such sequences arose by force of convention or by authorial selection. An example of the former is Plutarch, whose pairings have come down to us in a form known as the traditional order, but which is evidently not the original order.[14] An example of the latter is *The Spirit of the Age,* a sequence deliberately readjusted by Hazlitt for British and for Continental audiences. Between the extremes of accident and intentionality lies a blurred spectrum of serendipity and cognition; therefore, any study of these texts must concern itself with the institutions that govern reading.

For this reason we will be considering collective biography in terms of print culture: how the books appeared in print and were read as sequences, whether in periodical serials or bound within covers. Recent critical approaches to the poetic book provide a useful analogue for our discussion of textual coherence. James Averill, for example, has discussed the *Lyrical Ballads* as a unified text.[15] Even as a collaboration, this crucial Romantic document operated as a cumulative and, it can be argued, linear sequence. Discontinuous narrative in poetry and prose emerged in the context of an age that evolved an aesthetic of fragmentation.[16] It is particularly significant to our discussion of Romantic collective biography that the great landmark of Romanticism, the *Lyrical Ballads,* assembled disjunctive lyrics into a collective narrative unity. Similarly, biographical collections assembled and juxtaposed discrete biographical essays—sometimes separately composed, usually only truncated fragments of the life—to achieve a kind of heuristic collectivity.

Print culture was as much or even more responsible for such collective formulations than was authorial intention. The readiness and willingness of readers to accept discontinuous narratives between covers as unified texts was a trait of the Romantic era. The practice of serializing articles in periodicals contributed to the aesthetic of fragmentation by ingraining strategies of reading discontinuous narrative. The prevalence of such narratives in Reviews and Magazines encouraged the acceptance of reading practices in nonfictional narrative that were already established in books of lyric poetry and in fictional texts such as Rousseau's *Nouvelle Héloïse* and Mackenzie's *Man of Feeling*.

The popularity of biography in the early nineteenth century and the many editions of individual biographies indicate that biography was (as it continues to be) a genre attesting to the collaboration of an intellectual and a popular craving. The nineteenth-century prose masters were able to develop narrative forms spanning a wide and diverse audience. The revival of collective biography was a particularly commercial venture: prose writers were largely dependent on serial publication in periodicals, and the discontinuous narrative of collective biography offered a versatile narrative form. Johnson brought a canonical legitimacy to biography by subjecting it to literary inspection, and by practicing it himself; as he said in *Rambler* 60, "No species of writing seems more worthy of cultivation than biography."

Johnsonian authority drew attention to the potential of collective biography as a narrative form, and to the potential of biographical criticism as a strategy for reading. Johnson's institutionalization of critical biography encouraged the ascendancy of the critic over the text. The *Lives* illustrates what Geoffrey Hartman has said of the blurring of relations between primary and secondary texts in twentieth-century criticism: literary commentary became literature.[17] Johnsonian biographical readings, ignited by the Romantic emphasis on the subjectivity of perception, led to a new emphasis on the reader and textual reception. In the post-Johnsonian age, increasing interest in the use of biographical commentaries to decode literature not only elevated the prestige of the critic, but implicitly called into question the primacy of the poetic text. The biographical critic in the Romantic era became responsible for interpreting the oracular but misunderstood utterance of the poet; indeed, literary biographies came to be privileged over the works they were to illuminate.

As a historical phenomenon, the popularity of literary biography seems to disrupt conventional hierarchies of reading, for it suggests widespread acceptance of not only biographical approaches to literature but also a kind of literary voyeurism that subordinated the text to the author. The fact that readers in the early nineteenth century unhesitatingly equated Childe Harold with Byron and Prospero with Shakespeare raises the issue of whether the life of the poet was being used to read the works or the works to read the life. If understanding the life was deemed essential to bringing meaning to the text, the phenomenon of Byron hints at an infatuation with biography and poetic identity in which the literary text itself was only a means of gaining information about the life.

Considering the Romantics as prose writers and biographers enables us to better understand the theories of reading and writing implicit in Romantic poetry, and sheds new light on conventional boundaries of genre, periodization, and factual license. It has been difficult in the past to account for many works of literature by major authors in the Romantic period. Indeed, Romantic prose has remained largely unfamiliar because of the difficulty of placing it in a generic tradition; its innovations ultimately have brought about its inaccessibility. Writings by De Quincey, Hazlitt, and Wordsworth appear to fall outside the usual critical and generic approaches to Romanticism. Works by major prose writers of the age, Isaac D'Israeli, Scott, Southey, Hunt, Wilson, Lockhart, and others, have entirely fallen from critical visibility because they have hitherto resisted generic classification. The examination of Johnson's *Lives* in the following chapters will help us to position and understand major Romantic nonfictional prose works in the context of generic history, narratology, and the emergence of Romanticism.

"You Shall Know Their Fate No Further"

Biographical Judgment and the "Atoms of Probability"

Nowhere do we more willingly suspend our disbelief than in the reading of nonfictional prose. Implicit in the term nonfiction is a trust in the veracity of the text; at most we measure the reliability of the author before engaging the contract of belief. Such generic assumptions encourage readers to regard nonfictional prose as exempt from the subjectivity of narrative and possessing an inevitability of meaning arising from a literal use of language. But as Jacques Derrida and others have observed, there is no writing entirely free of figuration.[18] Biography, like all nonfictional genres, is a form of symbolic discourse and benefits from being read as we do fictional genres—as a narrative construct.

The mystery of the orange peel in Boswell's *Life of Johnson* can provide a demonstration of the polyvalency of meaning in nonfictional prose. The episode illustrates the instability of both language and biographical interpretation.

> "O, Sir, (said I,) I now partly see what you do with the squeezed oranges which you put into your pocket at the Club." JOHNSON. "I have a great love for them." BOSWELL. "And pray, Sir, what do you do with them? You scrape them, it seems, very neatly, and what next?" JOHNSON. "I let them dry, Sir." BOSWELL. "And what next?" JOHNSON. "Nay, Sir, you shall know their fate no further." BOSWELL. "Then the world must be left in the dark. It must be said (assuming a mock solemnity,) he scraped them, and let them dry, but what he did with them next, he never could be prevailed upon to tell." JOHNSON. "Nay, Sir, you should say it more emphatically:—he could not be prevailed upon, even by his dearest friends, to tell."[19] (1775)

As presented in the text, Boswell reintroduced the mystery eight years later during a series of conversations illustrating Johnson's technical knowledge:

> BOSWELL. "Do you know, Sir, I have discovered a manufacture to a great extent, of what you only piddle at,—scraping and drying the peel of oranges. At a place in Newgate-street, there is a prodigious quantity prepared, which they sell to the distillers." JOHNSON. "Sir, I believe they make a higher thing out of them than a spirit; they make what is called orange-butter, the oil of the orange inspissated, which they mix perhaps with common pomatum, and make it fragrant. The oil does not fly off in the drying."[20] (1783)

Finally, a decade later Boswell returned to the mystery when preparing the second edition of the *Life,* adding a footnote to the unresolved passage:

> It is suggested to me by an anonymous Annotator on my Work, that the reason why Dr. Johnson collected the peels of squeezed oranges, may be found in the 558th Letter in Mrs. Piozzi's Collection, where it appears that he recommended "dried orange-peel, finely powdered," as a medicine.[21] (1793)

On the surface of the Boswellian text, the episode is one of a number of self-referential moments in the *Life of Johnson,* resembling other appropriative passages where Boswell quotes earlier biographical theorists as precedents or cites his subject's approval of his method.[22] Ostensibly the episode testifies to the resourcefulness and perseverance of the biographer in finding documentation; and it offers a paradigm of the cooperation and resistance between biographer and subject in first-generation biography. The medicinal solution becomes a methodological touchstone, proving that research can disclose more than the subject has said.

But is the biographer alone decoyed into thinking he has found a resolution? The apparent closure is deceptive, for within the episode is inscribed a Johnsonian subtext that questions the extent to which a biographer ever can control a subject and suggests the impossibility of ever knowing. Johnson's mystification of the orange peel—what Boswell represents as comic agreement, "not even his closest friends"—parodies the biographical vice Johnson ridiculed in *Cowley* as the "propagation of wonder." Yet it also suggests a parable of the elusiveness of meaning and the elusiveness of biographical understanding. The biographer's futile attempt to sift and resolve documentation is an allegory of the inherently uncertain act of interpretation for any reader or listener.

The enigma of the orange peel is ultimately, of course, a parable of the impossibility of understanding not just individual lives but human life. In its largest sense, "You shall know their fate no further" reverberates beyond the inquisitiveness of the biographer to the mystery of the human condition. Biography poses certain unuttered questions that arise in contemplating the ephemerality of human life; like the unanswered questions posed by Keats to the Grecian urn, "not a soul to tell . . . can e'er return," the final questions of human life remain unanswerable.

Let us look in more detail, however, at the passage's troubling methodological implications for the biographer reading the text of life. Boswell's hermeneutic quest for a univocal and fixed interpretation is confronted with opacity even in the collaborative subject's own explanations. Johnson responds to Boswell's empiric gestures with dispersal and irresolution: the condition of biography is only to guess, never to know. Even in first-generation biography, where the biographer knows the subject and may even have Boswell's opportunity of testing his hypotheses, irrecoverable mysteries persist. Some issues remain imponderable because of lost information, others from the willful equivocation of the subject; and almost all are obscured by the lapse of time in second- and third-generation biography. In the mystery of the orange peels, Johnson creates an emblem of the enigmatic situation of biography—its inevitable irresolution, its approximation of truth, its narrative appropriation of incidents.

Moreover, Johnson's control of the episode allegorizes the way in which the individual prepares a public image for posterity. His comic rebuffs of Boswell implicitly confirm what Johnson states in his own writings about the unreliability of documentation. Indeed, their dialogue over the oranges not only illustrates their fundamental methodological polarity (Boswell hunts for documentation, Johnson comments upon it), but demonstrates the basic division in biographical form, Johnsonian composition and Boswellian compilation. Boswell uncovers information, Johnson analyzes it; Boswell lets the documents speak for themselves, Johnson distrusts unmediated documents; biographical insight in Boswell comes from recording unstintingly; in Johnson, from recording knowingly.

Such distinctions are not new; Herodotus differentiated logographers and historians,[23] those who merely wrote down current stories and those who provided an investigation or inquiry. In biography, the dichotomy has been variously described as compiled and composed, scientific and literary, antiquarian and interpretive; perhaps most germane for studying the Romantics is the denotation Boswellian and Johnsonian.

The distinction between the two forms entails matters of length, tone, and methodology. The fundamental and irreconcilable difference in approach may be seen most clearly in the biographers' comments on the matter of factual verification. Boswell prides himself on a meticulous scientific perseverance and accuracy: "Let me only observe, as a specimen of my trouble, that I have sometimes been obliged to run half over London, in order to fix a date correctly."[24] In contrast, Johnson complains of the nuisance of ascertaining the dates of Dryden's plays: "To adjust the minute events of literary history is tedious and troublesome; it requires indeed no great force of understanding." Johnson's privileging of the "great force of understanding" over "running half over London" is the exact opposite of the antiquarian tradition, which had been embodied in biographers such as Thomas Fuller, Anthony Wood, and John Aubrey, whose short lives epitomized accuracy and research, before Boswell added the precedent of length. Wilbur Cross accurately assesses composed biography in saying "the aim is not new knowledge, but a new interpretation of facts already known."[25] Johnson's *Lives* did entail research because many of the figures had no previous biographies, but Johnson's brevity and indifference to factual thoroughness set a tradition in short anecdotal biography of relying on convenient or available information. When Boswell urged Johnson to do research on Pope by interviewing Lord Marchmont, Johnson refused:

JOHNSON. "I shall not be in town to-morrow. I don't care to know about Pope." MRS. THRALE: (surprized as I was, and a little angry.) "I suppose, Sir, Mr. Boswell thought, that as you are to write Pope's Life, you would wish to know about him." JOHNSON. "Wish! why yes. If it rained knowledge I'd hold out my hand; but I would not give myself the trouble to go in quest of it."[26]

Johnson's unconcern with facts so riled Boswell throughout the *Life* that he here enlisted his rival biographer, Hester Thrale Piozzi, to refute Johnson.[27]

As Johnson declared of his critical judgments in *Dryden*, "Of all this however if the proof be demanded I will not undertake to give it; the atoms of probability, of which my opinion has been formed, lie scattered over all his works." In biographical judgment, there can be no solutions, only probabilities. The fundamental task of the biographer is to give weight to the "atoms of probability": to select, to assess, to sequence, to emphasize, to problematize. Boswell's boast, "I trace as distinctly as I can, year by year" the chronology of Johnson's life,[28] contrasts sharply with Johnson's uninterest in chronology—in *Rambler* 60 he dismisses those who think to write a biography by exhibiting "a chronological series of actions." Even the *Dictionary*, in defining biography, named chronology as only one possible narrative strategy: "In writing the lives of men, which is called *biography,* some authors place everything in the precise order of time when it occurred." Johnson's indifference to verification extended to his critical evaluations—John Nichols, the printer of the *Lives*, reports that Johnson gave him the manuscript of *Rowe* and "complacently observed that the criticism was tolerably well done, considering that he had not read one of Rowe's plays for thirty years." Nichols himself merely accepts it as "a very remarkable instance of the uncommon strength of Dr. Johnson's memory."[29] Johnson's anti-antiquarianism was in good company: the historians Clarendon, Fielding, and Hume were harsh on mere chronology and disregarded meticulous accuracy; Gibbon permitted anachronism before dullness; and Bolingbroke objected to "mere antiquaries" who failed to perceive the biographical incidents of history as instruments of "public and private virtue."[30]

Although Boswell quoted Johnson's belief that the *Lives of the Poets* was "'written, I hope, in such a manner as may tend to the promotion of piety,'"[31] Johnsonian biography is equally uncomfortable with the traditional hagiographic didacticism often associated with early antiquarianism. Boswell's example of Johnson's uncertainty on the judiciousness of discussing Addison's vice in biography has become proverbial of Johnson's fallibility. But Johnson's difficulty deciding whether Addison's example were more likely to encourage drunkenness or produce an "instructive caution" is an example of how Johnson habitually problematizes issues that others merely polarize. The trait Boswell describes as "varying from himself in talk"—Johnson's seeming inconsistencies on the depiction of vice—is part of the Johnsonian climate of irresolution in the face of conflicting claims and difficulties.[32] No biographer can resolve the ambiguities of the human condition; any attempt to weigh moral utility against factual accuracy merely speculates on the unquantifiable relationships between text, reader, and praxis.

Johnson rejected not only antiquarian methods but also the available philosophical genres for talking about the mind. The eighteenth-century philosophical interest in genius and a science of the mind is surely more than coincidental with the rise of biographical theory. But as Lawrence Lipking argues, citing Johnson's ridicule of philosophical jargon in *Idler* 36 ("these dreadful sounds"), Johnson's decision to write biography represented a deliberate choice of a nonphilosophical format for his observations on human nature, and he and other biographical anecdotalists of his century rejected schematization and philosophical conventions of discourse.[33] The Romantics followed Johnson in seeing biography as individualized portraiture rather than as an empirical tool for systematizing human science; in the wake of mechanistic theories of the mind, the Romantics were as wary of theories of intellectual determinism as Johnson had been of hagiographic theories of moral determinism. The prominence of literary biography in the Romantic era was in itself an expression of new values that rejected nonmechanistic approaches to the mind and creativity.

Johnson's choice of nonphilosophical discourse, his "varying from himself," his disinclination to systemization, his irritable refusal to reach for facts—"If it rained knowledge I'd hold out my hand"—were all tendencies compatible with the mainstream of Romantic thought. The Romantics found a congenial theory of reading lives and works in Johnsonian irresolution—in his willingness to remain in uncertainties, mysteries, doubts, in what Roland Barthes calls the irreducible "plurality of meaning," and what Geoffrey Hartman calls "indeterminacy as a 'speculative instrument.'"[34] The Romantics saw in Johnsonian biography the same traits of textual irresolution that twentieth-century critics saw in their study of Romanticism, the study that gave rise to deconstructive practices in American literary theory. Indeed, the Romantic interest in biography generated many theories of reading and writing that adumbrate twentieth-century deconstructive and affectivist approaches. Moreover, the conviction that life itself is a text to be read, an idea implicit in the *Lives* (Johnson praises Addison, "He had read with critical eyes the important volume of human life"), is made explicit in Romantic biographical strategies of reading literature and exegetical approaches to what Keats called the "life of allegory."

In contrast, the Boswellian compiler, a mere Herodotan logographer who records words without doubt or understanding, had no sense of the subjectivity of narrative or the mutability of meaning. John Gibson Lockhart, reviewing Croker's edition of the *Life of Johnson*, was astonished that Boswell could tell a story yet "leave so strong an impression that he did not himself understand it,"[35] and concluded Boswell's chief asset as a biographer was an "intellectual inferiority" which removed all threat of rivalry or envy. Macaulay concurred in calling Boswell "a slave proud of his servitude," an "inspired idiot" whose strength as a biographer was in his "weaknesses" as a stooping, tattling, parasitic coxcomb. Even Carlyle had to rename Boswell a "martyr" to the testament of "hero worship" whose self-abasement rose above "Spanielship" to "Discipleship." Boswell himself concluded his opening comments to the *Life* defending himself against those who "think this a degrading task."[36]

Whereas Boswell became the emblem of the obsequious biographer, the Romantics admired Johnson's rebellious disregard for the convention of the deferential biographical narrator and the tradition of submissive panegyric. As Lockhart explained it, "To bestow such an infinity of pains and space upon a single human individual, no matter how distinguished, was a thing below *him*." Johnson's literary biography, even if it entailed the superciliousness of Socrates addressing the rhapsode,[37] gave a critical dignity to biographical prose which Boswell's notorious self-abasement abrogated. Johnson conferred prestige upon the biographer's task by associating it with the establishment of literary canon and the definition of critical standards, just as he awarded artistic status to biography by submitting it to critical assessment.

Literary biographers following Johnson might deplore his critical judgments, but were unwilling to relinquish the voice of authority Johnson bestowed on the biographer.[38] Johnson was the formidable intellectual adversary, whose authority was admired even as his opinions were disputed. Joshua Reynolds's assessment of artistic predecessors in his discourse on inspiration, genius, and imitation, might equally characterize the Romantic response to Johnson's biographies: "Models which you are to imitate, and at the same time . . . rivals with whom you are to contend."[39] Romantic biographical writing may be said to demonstrate anew Harold Bloom's suggestion that great achievement is more likely to arise in rebellion than in imitation,[40] for narrative innovation emerged in Johnsonian antagonisms rather than Boswellian imitations. Boswellian compilations in the Romantic era did not fare well; the two putative successors to the *Life of Johnson,* Thomas Moore's *Byron* and John Gibson Lockhart's *Scott* (Moore's biography used the lavish quarto format of Boswell and Lockhart's seven-volume immensity imitated Boswell's scale), were widely regarded as disappointing.[41] For the Romantics, Johnson was the intellectual precursor to contend with both generically and critically; and their experience of Johnson was foremost as a writer of the collection of literary biographies known as the *Lives of the Poets.*

Ferreting information had come to be incompatible with dignity, authority, and prestige; mere accuracy was of little consequence. Even Boswell sensed compilation brought less admiration than would composition ("Speaking in my own person . . . I might have appeared to have more merit in the execution").[42] The methodological polarity had come to imply an indisputable intellectual hierarchy: the compiler, whose role required no exercise of the understanding, provided a reference quarry of convenient information for the composer who selected anecdotes, critiqued achievements, and only paraphrased the outline of the life. Like Johnson before them, Romantic biographers such as De Quincey and D'Israeli refer condescendingly to their subject's "biographer," the compiler of documents from whom they extract facts. Carlyle reaffirmed the hierarchy in criticizing Lockhart's *Life of Scott,* saying he would have preferred a "well-done composition" instead of the dismembered "well-done compilation."[43] Nearly a century later, Lytton Strachey made the same distinction between his *Eminent Victorians* and "Standard" biographies, "Those two fat volumes . . . who does not know them, with their ill-digested masses of material, their slipshod style, their tone of tedious panegyric, their lamentable lack of selection, of detachment, of design?"[44] Yet André Maurois's suggestion that Johnson's *Lives* might be called "Eminent Jacobeans" and "Eminent Augustans" reminds us not only of the pitfalls of historical relativism, but that by the early twentieth century, generations of generic innovation had been forgotten or misunderstood and remain only now to be rediscovered.[45]

Contemporary biographical historians and critics have tended to favor long biography—Leon Edel describes his own five-volume biography of Henry James as one of the shorter of our time[46]—and in doing so have failed to see that the long Boswellian biography was in many ways uncongenial with Romantic interests. Present critical attitudes, arising from a view of biography primarily as a historicist tool, tend to consider long exhaustive biography as the predominating form against which short anecdotal biography stands in occasional contrast.[47] It has not always been so; long biography did not possess the essential fascination among the Romantics that it does among contemporary biographers and critics. We may usefully speak of the changing shape and emphasis in biography as Erich Auerbach does in speaking of the history of realism: the turn toward anecdotal biography signified a changing sense of what is "worth representing."[48] In a generation that saw the first publication of the diaries of John Evelyn and Samuel Pepys, Walpole's memoirs, Aubrey's fragmented lives, and Spence's *Anecdotes* of Pope,[49] collections of ana, anecdotage, and reminiscences constituted valid and desirable forms of biographical discourse. In the wake of Johnson, composed biography emphasized a selective, anecdotal, admittedly incomplete account, which passed all facts through the screen of interpretive subjectivity; indeed, its permissible inexactness, spontaneity, asymmetry, and narrative fragmentation were privileged attributes in other Romantic genres. The biographies comprising the *Lives of the Poets,* unpredictable and nonuniform in shape, set a precedent of collectivity based not on formal similarities but on a sustained intellectual dialogue. Romantic literary biography came to see itself not as a historicist tool, or an instrument of moral and didactic utility, or a vehicle devoted to exploration of character and personality, but as an agent for theories of criticism, history, genre, genius, and culture.

The new narrative forms that emerged from the precedent of Johnsonian collective biography by and large have eluded conventional generic categorization. Post-Johnsonian collective biography entailed both extensions of received genre and the creation of new narrative strategies. This was partly the Romantic rebellion from the Neoclassical emphasis on conformity to genre; but it is worth remembering Tzvetan Todorov's suggestion that a major work of literature is by definition sui generis, obeying and transgressing previously valid rules of genre.[50] The Romantics were not alone in experimenting with biography, nor were they the first to do so, but the critical library has had difficulty assimilating their radical departures in narrative form, and has largely excluded from definitions of genre, narratives such as those it labels as ana, anecdotage, or character sketch.

The description of biography Edmund Gosse wrote for the eleventh edition of the *Encyclopaedia Britannica,* "Biography is a study sharply defined by two definite events, birth and death," typifies the exclusionary tendencies of existing generic theory.[51] By traditional prescriptive definitions such as Gosse's, biography is the literary form least susceptible to the creation of narrative suspense; even when it is not framed by birth and death, biography is ruled by generic expectations in the manner of opera or ancient drama: readers await treatment of certain anticipated episodes, already acquainted with the salient achievements of the subject. Yet Romantic biography has defied classification because it dismantles conventional expectations. Making use of a term from contemporary historiography, we may say the Romantics transform the emplotment of biography.[52]

Romantic biographies frequently begin in medias res and frequently do not end with death; the exclusion of biographies of the living and sequences of collective biography from generic studies may arise from their absence of closure. A disorienting absence of introductory and concluding statements emphasizes the avoidance of fixed interpretations. Generic disruptions include transgressions of form and social decorum: truncation, iconographic encoding, irresolution, achronology, scandalous revelations based on privileged information, interposition of the biographer's life history, emphasizing narrative authority above mere accuracy. Johnson, like Suetonius and Plutarch before him, frequently organized information thematically; Romantic anecdotal biography allowed symbolic patterning to totally supersede thoroughness and chronological fidelity. A few synecdochic episodes represent the whole of the character and life of the subject. Vladimir Nabokov essentially expressed a Romantic view of biographical narrative when he called his autobiography a "correlated assemblage," and declared that the following of "thematic designs" through the life is the true purpose of autobiography. Such designs in fictional narrative have been called spatial form, rhythm, and leitmotif.[53] Yet as Louis Mink observes, today we find the presence of such patterns or designs in ostensibly factual writing disturbing because it implies an imposition on the truth.[54]

The sense of what is truth and what constitutes an imposition on truth, however, has been by no means stationary. Johnsonian and post-Johnsonian biographical forms are highly self-conscious narratives; the realization and imposition of patterns is what confers truth. Philippe Lejeune, speaking of the currently most visible biographical form, suggests we call the presupposition that nonfiction tells not just truth but a truth contingent on factual verifiability, *"le pacte autobiographique"*; in speaking of Romantic forms of biographical narrative, however, it may be more accurate to think in terms of how Edward Said has described fiction, as reliant on the assumption that truth can only be approached indirectly.[55] From a Johnsonian and post-Johnsonian perspective, all human truth is elusive and subjective; and the designing of biographical verities to capture this truth entails transgressions of conventional factuality.

"Truth Is Not Here As In The Sciences"

Documentation, Subjectivity, and Accuracy

Throughout his writings Johnson called attention to the problems of discourse. Lexicography is at least as much about multiplicity of meaning as fixity;[56] the critical biographies problematize meaning in reading poems and in reading biography. Johnson's investigation of biographical methodologies in the *Lives* illuminates the instability of documentation and the inevitability of subjectivity in biography. Instead of deferring to factuality or accuracy, biographers after Johnson came to invoke the principle of abstract truth, in poetry, in fiction, and in biography. Gérard Genette rightly suggests we speak of narrative license in the same way we speak of poetic license;[57] it may be worth adding the term biographical license to indicate the tentativeness of the biographical verities we call nonfictional truth.

Wordsworth drew attention to the distinction between literal and figurative truth in the 1802 Preface to *Lyrical Ballads*. There he defends poets from the traditional Platonic charge of lying, by upholding the existence of a superior poetic truth: poetry has as its object, "truth, not individual and local, but general, and operative; not standing upon external testimony, but carried alive into the heart by passion; truth which is its own testimony." In his refusal to privilege poetry over prose,[58] he observes it is customary to trace the resemblances between poetry and painting, but not the affinities within verbal discourse. Although he mentions biography only as possessing more factual obligations than poetry ("Obstacles which stand in the way of the fidelity of the Biographer and Historian . . . are incalculably greater than those which are to be encountered by the Poet"), by the time of his essay on Burns (1816), Wordsworth placed biography alongside poetry and prose fiction, as arts licensed for a special truth. Never exclusionary in his definition of art, he says of biographical truth:

> Biography, though differing in some essentials from works of fiction, is nevertheless, like them, an *art*,—an art, the laws of which are determined by the imperfections of our nature, and the constitution of society. Truth is not here, as in the sciences, and in natural philosophy, to be sought without scruple, and promulgated for its own sake, upon the mere chance of its being serviceable; but only for obviously justifying purposes, moral or intellectual.[59]

In declaring "truth is not here, as in the sciences," he may have had in mind the concealment of vice, but the more important scope of his statement locates the distinction between truth and accuracy in biography. Evident in Wordsworth's condemnation of the borrowed pursuit of relentless scientific objectivity, "Plague, then, upon your remorseless hunters after matter of fact" (as in Keats's objection to "reaching after fact and reason"), is the early nineteenth-century tendency to identify science as a growing opponent of literature. But the denunciation of peeping and botanizing in biography was not directed as much to specific Baconian or Boswellian methods as to the illegitimacy of what was perceived as an erroneous scientific spirit in biography: biography could not and should not take measures to attain scientific exactitude or uniformity.[60]

The Romantic innovations in biography that stemmed from Johnson's elevation of biography to a literary form subject to criticism, assumed biography to be an art burdened less by small "local" truth than bound to the "general" larger truth. Although selectivity, abbreviation, and disordering of chronological sequence were some of the many acceptable narrative distortions necessary to achieve biographical truth, they sprang not from an indifference to fact but from a sense that facts did not constitute truth. The Romantics' interest in the boundaries of fiction and nonfiction today has reappeared in the mixed genre of the nonfiction novel and in the debate over the scientific and artistic aspirations of historiography.[61]

Breakdowns of generic boundaries are evident throughout the Romantic era; the presence of "poetic truth" in unexpected places was matched by the presence of fact in unexpected places as well. Fictional designs surface in historiography and biography, and at the same time, factual machinery underlies the autobiographical poetry of Wordsworth and Byron and the historical novels of Scott. Hazlitt says Scott provides a "poetical transcript" of actual events ("truth is presented not *literally,* but *poetically*") and defends historical novels with the assurance that "the charms of a work professing to copy nature cannot be destroyed by the evidence that proves it to be founded upon truth."[62] Writers such as Scott and Wordsworth had to overcome resistance to the presence of overt factuality in genres conventionally fictional, yet while these genres moved toward factuality, biographical narrative appropriated methodologies from fiction.

Johnson, urging the importance of truth, had declared, "The value of every story depends on its being true. A story is a picture either of an individual or of human nature in general: if it be false it is a picture of nothing." But what is truth? Not just the honesty with which, Boswell says, Johnson vowed to write the life of a dunce and "*say* he was a dunce."[63] The *Lives of the Poets* opens with a disapproval of the "mist of panegyrick" (*Cowley*), but the biographies offer constant reminders that truth is not recoverable in mere documentation. The *Life of Addison,* for example, names two temporal obstacles to narrative truth—the inevitable fading of information and the obligatory suppression of "unseasonable detection":

> The necessity of complying with times and of sparing persons is the great impediment of biography. History may be formed from permanent monuments and records; but Lives can only be written from personal knowledge, which is growing every day less, and in a short time is lost for ever. What is known can seldom be immediately told, and when it might be told it is no longer known.[64] . . . As the process of these narratives is now bringing me among my contemporaries I begin to feel myself "walking upon ashes under which the fire is not extinguished," and coming to the time of which it will be proper rather to say "nothing that is false, than all that is true."

Duty and ephemerality were not the only complications. Biographical truth "either of an individual or of human nature in general," was subjective, unschematized, and often ambiguous.

In subverting confidence in documentation as an index of truth, Johnsonian biography implicitly questioned the attainability of accuracy. The

Lives revealed the instability of meaning inherent in every verbal text. Johnson rejected the institutions of biographical verification usually accepted as evidence—reminiscences, letters, conversation, anecdotes. The *Lives* replaced the inherited earlier eighteenth-century issue of propriety—establishing the decorum of what could be told, and with what deference it must be said—with the question of documentary reliability.

Johnson distrusted the very resources of conversation and letters Boswell had turned to in trying to satisfy the mystery of the orange peel. Boswell misleadingly hints that Johnson discussed and sanctioned his own narrative strategies: on the second day of the *Hebrides* tour he quotes Johnson's exclamation, "'I love anecdotes'";[65] in the *Life* he implies Johnson approved the methods of his journal ("he was secretly pleased to find so much of the fruit of his mind preserved") and records Johnson's comment that "'nobody can write the life of a man, but those who have eat and drunk and lived in social intercourse with him.'"[66] Yet Johnson rarely wrote first-generation biography, used personal anecdotes very sparingly, was distrustful of letters, often cited reminiscences to contradict them,[67] and was especially skeptical of conversational records of the sort Boswell made famous.

Even in first-generation biography, Johnson refused to transcribe conversation; writing of his friend Savage he says, "What he asserted in conversation might, though true in general, be heightened by some momentary ardour of imagination, and, as it can be delivered only from memory, may be imperfectly represented; so that the picture at first aggravated and then unskilfully copied may be justly suspected to retain no great resemblance of the original." Conversations, with or about the subject, provide a dubious guide to character, since their unmeditated caprices are compounded by inevitable inaccuracies in transcription.[68] Letters too are misleading evidence of character, not from the momentary passion of conversation, but from the opposite premeditated desire to give "favourable representations" of ourselves: "What we hide from ourselves we do not shew to our friends." The *Life of Pope* contradicts the common belief "that the true characters of men may be found in their letters, and that he who writes to his friend lays his heart open before him":

> There is, indeed, no transaction which offers stronger temptations to fallacy and sophistication than epistolary intercourse. In the eagerness of conversation the first emotions of the mind often burst out before they are considered . . . but a

friendly letter is a calm and deliberate performance in the cool of leisure, in the stillness of solitude, and surely no man sits down to depreciate by design his own character.

Friendship has no tendency to secure veracity.

Pope's manipulation of his correspondence is Johnson's paradigm of epistolary duplicity. Publication was not an uncommon practice—Voltaire arranged printing of his letters, and Mary Wortley Montagu made improvements in hers before publication—but Pope multiplied the innate falsehood of letters by bringing them to press through an elaborate charade of feigned theft. Yet the example of Pope's epistolary stratagems in the *Lives* demonstrates that the disingenuous author involuntarily discloses the duplicity and insincerity he seeks to conceal.[69]

In the context of literary history, Johnson's conspicuous discussion of the untrustworthiness of Pope's letters constitutes an answer to a century-old controversy over the propriety of incorporating letters in biography. Earlier discussions were oblivious to the issue of the equivocal and untrustworthy nature of self-presentation. Thomas Sprat, fellow and historian of the Royal Society, whose putatively scientific use of documents established the first normative critical standards in British biography, said Cowley's familiar letters favorably attested to his moral character. Like Johnson's *Lives* (which opened with a critique of Sprat's methods), Sprat's *Cowley* (1668) was a preface to the works and a statement of biographical theory. Sprat's dictum on letters—"Nothing of this Nature should be publish'd"[70]—defined standards of privacy, protected the honor of the public figure, and dictated the role of biography as a public document.

Not until William Mason's *Life of Gray* (1775), the latest biographical innovation before the *Lives,* was the barrier of public and private life questioned. Mason's *Gray,* also cast as a preface to the poems, completely overturned Sprat's principles; Horace Walpole assured his friend Mason, "You have fixed the method of biography and whoever will write a life must imitate you."[71] So far from excluding letters, Mason does little else than present Gray's letters with minimal orienting commentary. Mason answers Sprat's strictures in a footnote, "I am well aware that I am here going to do a thing which the cautious and courtly Dr. Sprat (were he now alive) would highly censure," initiating an acceptable curiosity into the unpublished dishabille of the literary hero. Mason chooses to be, he says, a "compiler" of letters so that "Mr. Gray will become his own biographer": "I have never related a single circumstance of Mr. Gray's life in my own words, when I could employ his for the purpose." Boswell in turn decided: "I have resolved to adopt and enlarge upon the excellent plan of Mr. Mason, in his Memoirs of Gray. Wherever narrative is necessary to explain, connect, and supply, I furnish it to the best of my abilities; but . . . I produce, wherever it is in my power, his own minutes, letters, or conversation." Whether Boswell essentially imitated Mason or distorted him beyond recognition is questionable, but in assuming Johnson was his own best interpreter, he too followed Mason's acceptance of the reliability of the subject's own words.[72]

The Romantics, however, were inclined to share Johnson's distrust of the subject's own account as a reliable source of biographical information and impressions of character. Isaac D'Israeli wondered at Sprat's motives in suppressing Cowley's letters despite his praise of them: "Would Sprat and Clifford have burned what they have told us they so much admired?" J. L. Adolphus warned biographers against the deceptive "affectation and insincerity" of letters. And Maria Edgeworth declared the uselessness of letters to gauge character: "We shall only see minds like Byron's in prepared undress—and shall never get at the real likeness."[73]

Moreover, the Romantics extended Johnson's distrust of letters and conversation to autobiographies, political memoirs, and diaries, all of which enjoyed great but not necessarily naive popularity. Johnson's *Idler* 84 suggested that autobiography not intended for publication "may be commonly presumed to tell truth,"[74] but as autobiographies increasingly came to be printed (both by their authors and posthumously), they excited a greater skepticism, as might be expected in an era alert to the subjectivity of perception and what the mind might "half-create and what perceive." James Field Stanfield cautioned biographers against trusting the narrative distortion of any autobiographer because "he is the reporter of his own cause . . . however candid and conceding the language and positions may seem to be, the intention will secretly pervert every portion of the work . . . there is an unavoidable suspicion attendant on self-biography."[75] Macaulay warned that Rousseau and Byron are to be "most distrusted when they seem most sincere."[76] Isaac D'Israeli, an admirer of Rousseau long after the tide of favor had turned away in England, praised the passionate honesty of the *Confessions,* but warned, "What in Rousseau was nature, may in others be artifice."[77]

The Romantics did not unhesitatingly embrace autobiographical writings as transparent and guileless effusions of the writer's soul. Many followed Johnson's assessment of Pope's epistolary stratagems in concluding that the revelation of duplicity did not invalidate autobiographical documents, if read correctly. The Advertisement of a thirty-three–volume collection of autobiographies published in 1828 observed, "No man can do so much justice to the springs and motives of his own character and actions as himself; and when even otherwise, by showing what he wishes to appear, he generally discovers what he really is."[78] John Wilson Croker assessed Napoleon's memoirs, saying, "Many of the facts are notoriously false, and most of the commentaries are studiously delusive; but the memoirs are not, on that account, less characteristic of the author, less entertaining to the casual reader, or less important to the critical history of the man." The task of the reader was to puzzle between the lines of the text. The insight of dishonesty surfaced involuntarily in the studiously deceptive text; and, of the unwitting distortions of self-presentation, Leigh Hunt confessed, "I, for one, willingly concede that the reader may know me better than myself."[79]

In recent years, the detection of narrative distortion in autobiography has come to signify literary value, for it is viewed as a testament of the deliberate shaping of facts into narrative.[80] Some autobiographers acknowledge their truth as a psychological truth or a relative truth. Yeats, alluding to the presence of involuntary subjectivity in nonfictional narrative, prefaced his autobiography, "I have changed nothing to my knowledge; and yet it must be that I changed many things without my knowledge"—an essentially Romantic inquiry of what extent the mind is lord and master. The acceptance of figuration and subjectivity is implied in the invocation of fiction and reality, poetry and truth in the title of Goethe's autobiography *Dichtung und Wahrheit*. Ernst Cassirer says the title indicates "truth could only be found by giving to the isolated and dispersed facts of his life a poetical, that is a symbolic, shape."[81]

But as contemporary literary criticism shows, the issues of autobiographical veracity need to be created anew in each generation. Barrett Mandel, for example, believes "most autobiographers are honest" in striving to tell the truth because unreliable narrative is considered a shortcoming in autobiography. William Spengemann and L. R. Lundquist, however, declare autobiography "has nothing to do with factual truth," and Francis R. Hart calls attention to the problem of narrative resemblance—autobiographical passages may be indistinguishable from fictional passages. Georges Gusdorf says of the approximate verity of autobiography that it is a truth not "of things but of persons." Jean Starobinski, mindful of Germaine de Staël's praise of Rousseau's attainment of "verities of feeling," describes autobiographical truth as an "exegesis of the 'heart.'"[82]

Although at present the most far-reaching theoretical contributions to the field of nonfictional prose have arisen in studies of autobiographical writing, the current critical interest in autobiography has eclipsed the larger biographical context, doing a disservice to the study of biography and autobiography alike. The concept of writing one's own life extended back to the ancients, but the term autobiography only began to emerge in the Romantic era; as the then customary term "self-biography" indicates, autobiography was a subgenre of biography. In May 1809, two articles in the *Quarterly Review* (then only a few months old) used the word autobiography. Southey describes a "unique specimen of auto-biography" in Portuguese literature, and D'Israeli (reviewing Percival Stockdale's memoirs) comments on the "rage for auto-biography" by insignificant writers. The term seems to have surfaced in print once before, in 1797, unfavorably, when a critic of D'Israeli's term "self-biography" rejected "autobiography" as a "pedantic" substitute.[83] The title "confessions" seemed to have been used by De Quincey and others partly because of Rousseau, but also because it was one of few available and recognizable terms. What is important here is that the appearance of a new specific term signifies increasing interest in writing about oneself, as well as the growing preeminence of subjectivity as a normative and critical concept.

Compiled biography justified its method as the closest to what the subject would have written, quoting the subject's own words with minimal editorial intervention so, as Mason says, the subject might "become his own biographer." Boswell said he would provide an "accumulation of intelligence" for the reader, letting Johnson speak for himself rather than "melting down my materials into one mass." Lockhart said he would "refrain from obtruding" commentary in order to "let the character develop itself" and allow each "mature reader to arrive at just conclusions"; his biography of Scott would "extract and combine the scattered fragments of an *autobiography*."[84] But in composed biography, the concept of autobiographical biography implied not the subject telling "his own" story, but the biographer telling "his own" story. Romantic biographical composition presumed the inevitable subjectivity of the source documents themselves—whether the prepared undress of the writer of letters, the conversation of Johnson addressing the Boswell whom he knew to be writing a biography, or Byron confiding in friends he hoped would repeat the tales. The biographer's role was equally subjective, whether as a friend appointed custodian of the documents for compilation, or as an unauthorized biographer selecting, abridging, and sequencing. Since no narrative could be presumed unmediated, composed biography accordingly inscribed the perceptual biases of the narrator into the text, to the extent that biographers such as De Quincey and Hunt incorporated their own autobiographical chronologies into the text. Given the subjectivity of all documentation, the only thing remaining that could be documented was subjectivity.

The interest in autobiographical perception paralleled the increasing sense of biography as a narrative construct.[85] The proliferation of multiple biographies of the same subject in the early nineteenth century suggests the widespread acknowledgment of the subjectivity of narrative and the relativity of truth. Boswell saw himself as striving for a definitive biography of Johnson (we shall "'live o'er each scene' with him" and "he will be seen in this work more completely than any man who has ever yet lived"). To this end he volubly resented what he regarded as poaching by Hawkins and Piozzi.[86] Yet nowhere is the critical unwillingness to accept the scientific aspirations of biography more vividly displayed than in the ongoing reception of Boswell's *Life:* the text was promptly revised by the next generation, and new biographies of Johnson rewritten ever since; there is no final word. Despite the increase of authorized biography in the nineteenth century, the Romantics did not welcome the idea of Boswellian finalization. Indeed, the differing accounts by Boswell and Piozzi of several of the same incidents testified to the subjectivity of biographical truth. With their interest in the subjectivity of narrative, the Romantics seem to have little sense of biographical duplication; multiple biographies meant more could be revealed in comparing the perceptions of various biographers. The illimitable subjectivity of meaning permitted infinite, equally privileged readings. The biographical phenomenon of Johnson set a precedent which the Romantics followed by preparing competing biographies of prominent figures such as Burns, Napoleon, and Byron; there was room for Lockhart's seven-volume life and James Hogg's brief conversational memoir of Walter Scott.[87] The Romantics accepted every biography as one of many possible narrative constructs. In a blunt twentieth-century restatement of Romantic priorities, Otto Rank declared that were biography to be objective, it would not fulfill its purpose.[88]

The growing sense of truth as a subjective abstraction placed increasing emphasis on the perceptiveness of the biographer and other readers of the life. Paul Ricoeur's observation that the reliable historian represents the triumph of a good subjectivity over a bad one, may help to reconcile the dissonance between our expectation that biography will be true and the impossibility of absolute biographical truth; like the *histor* who narrates Greek history, the biographer's authority lies not with the sources themselves but with the critical approaches used in consulting them; veracity resides not in documentation but in the biographer who is sufficiently discerning to be entrusted with conflicting accounts, incomplete evidence, deceptive rumors, and the incalculables and unknowns of life.[89] As Keats observed, "very few eyes can see the Mystery" of a life, a view reconfirmed in subsequent generations. André Maurois warned that "critical reasoning alone" is not enough in biography, that "in every psychological truth, there is, and there must be, an element of divination."[90] Like the reciprocal inspiriting of poet and audience described in Wordsworth's *Essay, Supplementary to the Preface,* the perception of biographical truth depends on the sagacity of the biographer and the receptivity of the reader; truth can be approached through factual events, but it is an intuitive truth, as De Quincey called it, to "*'the understanding heart.'*"[91]

The sense of the autonomy of narrative truth is confirmed by standard editorial practices in the eighteenth and nineteenth centuries. Theorizing about the decorum and veracity of various kinds of evidence was accompanied by an unquestioning view of editorial control. Mason combined and changed material in Gray's letters, Johnson abridged and simplified quotations to improve the prose, and Boswell regularly refined and compressed letters and documents.[92] Such alterations seem to have been accepted practice, both to shelter the privacy of the living and because it was the aesthetic prerogative of the biographer to shape the narrative by editing source documents. John Forster, the Victorian biographer of Goldsmith and Dickens, declared he preferred one of Mason's modified letters to Gray's original. Southey omitted Admiral Nelson's liaison with Lady Hamilton lest it interfere with his narrative patterning of events as "a manual for the young sailor."[93] Lockhart altered, rearranged, and deleted portions of Scott's letters—even during his life Scott had told Lockhart to "use the pruning knife, hedgebill, or ax" to edit his works.[94] Romantic biographies indulged in the narration of emblematic scenes, not just dramatic reconstructions but falsifications of events which could not have occurred as biographers such as De Quincey and Lockhart claimed they did.[95] Hazlitt, beginning the account of his conversations with James Northcote under the title "Boswell Redivivus," defied the distinction between fiction and fact, stating, "I have feigned whatever I pleased. I have forgotten, mistaken, mis-stated, altered, transposed."[96] Harold Nicholson, commenting on Mason's editing with an eye to his Bloomsbury colleagues, identifies the modern equivalent in the silent editorializing of selection: "We do not commit such crimes to-day. We do not alter the text: we merely leave out the bits that contradict our own thesis."[97] Although there has yet been no Oscar Wilde to lament the decay of lying in biography, it might more accurately describe biographical truth than the importance of being earnest. Picasso's paradox, "Art is a beautiful lie that tells the truth," perhaps better expresses the objectives of Romantic biography; it is the function of biographical art to create new kinds of truth.

The position of biography within the field of narratology remains problematic, for critics have not viewed biography as a narrative construct, and many remain ambivalent about developing analogous strategies of reading fictional and factual narratives. Tzvetan Todorov observes that "any text can be given a literary reading," and David Lodge suggests reading nonfictional prose "'as if' the criteria of truthfulness did not apply" rather than testing its historical verifiability. At the same time such views have been contradicted by, for example, Paul de Man, who objects to reading fact as if it were fiction and cites autobiography as the example of a genre that responds poorly to elevation in literary status; and John Searle, who dislikes the implication, in contemporary readings which assert the fictionality of all texts, that "'reality' is just more textuality."

A telling critical parapraxis surfaces even in sympathetic requests for new strategies of reading nonfictional prose. Jonathan Culler's declaration that to read a text as literature is to read it as fiction, falls into the critical convention of privileging fictional discourse. Northrop Frye called the impulse to select and pattern "creative, and therefore fictional." Geoffrey Hartman's reproach that the test of close reading has only been applied to "creative writing rather than to criticism or nonfictional prose" similarly excludes all nonfictional prose from the category of creative writing.[98]

In the wake of Johnson, biographical texts are critical texts, inscribing methodologies for reading other works of literature, and reading themselves as works of literature. Studying biography in the Romantic era may be the best place to overcome resistance to considering nonfiction a form of creative writing, for the Romantics disregarded such generic inhibitions. It is the purpose of each of the textual studies in the following chapters to demonstrate ways of reading nonfictional narrative as a literary form.

Chapter II

Samuel Johnson: The *Lives of the Poets* as a Collective Sequence

In his *Life of Pope,* Johnson observed, "It is remarkable that, so near his time, so much should be known of what he has written, and so little of what he has said." It is ironic that the opposite has held true for Johnson himself. The anecdotes and epigrams recorded by Boswell and other contemporaries are largely responsible for shaping the modern impression of Johnson. Boswell's name is so often coupled with Johnson's that his fame as a biographer has popularly superseded that of the master he fancied himself imitating. The study of biography has largely neglected the impact of Johnson. As a result, it has become common to regard Johnson's essays and isolated comments on biography independently from his works, and to see their importance chiefly in terms of their influence on Boswell and his successors. Although Johnson's biographies have received attention individually and have been variously minded for evidence of his doctrines, the *Lives* has remained virtually unexplored as a narrative sequence.[1] This chapter will concentrate on Johnson as a biographer and Johnson's *Lives* as a collective sequence.

As is well known, the project was a commercial venture, rather than Johnson's idea, plan, or order, although as he modestly remarks in the *Life of Watts,* readers may "impute to me whatever pleasure or weariness they may find in the perusal of Blackmore, Watts, Pomfret, and Yalden." In addition to adding these four, it appears from the letter of 3 May 1777, recounted by Boswell, Johnson recommended the inclusion of Thomson as well.[2] These recommendations evidently constitute Johnson's only hand in the choice and sequence of lives. Although schemes for the publication of a canon of the British poets had been contemplated for some time, the immediate commercial incentive was an Edinburgh anthology of poetic works. In response, a consortium of London booksellers invited Johnson to write what he called the "little Lives, and little Prefaces" for a rival London edition. For Johnson, the idea of a biographically outlined canon reached at least as far back as the 1767 interview with

George III recounted by Boswell, during which "His Majesty expressed a desire to have the literary biography of this country ably executed, and proposed to Dr. Johnson to undertake it. Johnson signified his readiness to comply with his Majesty's wishes."[3]

Were we to wish to, it would be hard to determine Johnson's intention for the sequence of the lives. We do know he irritatedly wrote, "It is a great impudence to put *Johnson's Poets* on the back of books which Johnson neither recommended nor revised."[4] Evidently he regarded his task in some measure as separate from the project of selecting and publishing the works, and in print the biographies were physically disconnected. The original title, *Prefaces, Biographical and Critical, to the Works of the English Poets,* reflects the apparent original plan to preface biographies to individual editions of the works; but in 1779 the first four volumes of lives were printed as independent volumes, followed in 1781 by the remaining six volumes of lives. Their physical appearance was from the start a separable set, and it is remarked that prospective buyers were not pleased at having to buy the additional fifty-eight volumes of works—which one might already possess—as well as the lives.[5]

After the *Prefaces* appeared in England they were promptly pirated in Dublin (the first volume in 1779, the remaining two in 1781) as *The Lives of the English Poets; and a Criticism on their Works,* and thus made available without the anthology. In 1781, responding to the visible demand, the original booksellers reprinted the lives in four volumes, this time totally separate from the works, as *The Lives of the Most Eminent English Poets; with Critical Observations on their Works*. It was reprinted again by the London booksellers in a corrected edition in 1783 as simply *The Lives of the Most Eminent English Poets,* the last edition in Johnson's lifetime.[6]

The traditional order of the *Lives,* like the title, is in great measure due to the accidents of publication history rather than to an initial integrity of design. If we look to Johnson's own order of composition for adjudication, we find it largely irrelevant to the experience of the text, although it does bear some sequential resemblances (if we disregard the insertion of the 1743 *Life of Savage* and the 1748 *Life of Roscommon*). He started with *Cowley* and *Waller* in 1777–78, spent six weeks on *Milton* in January 1779, and completed the final two lives of *Swift* and *Pope* in 1780–81.

The original order of the biographies in the *Prefaces* and the Dublin edition was short-lived and was permanently changed in the *Lives* of 1781 (and 1783), which placed the biographies in the approximate sequence of death dates.[7] There is no more than a rough chronological resemblance between the two printed orders. To look for evidence "more carefully at the beginning and at the end," as Petrarch advised Boccaccio on the *Decameron*,[8] we may note that *Cowley* remains the opening life and *Gray* gravitates from the closing to the penultimate position, before *Lyttelton*. Boccaccio's project provides an interesting analogue, for Johnson's *Lives* represent a similar narrative sequence, a hemi-*Decameron* of fifty-two stories of lives: stories stylized by Johnson despite reliance on sources and received tradition, and stories which take on greater importance by being part of a collective narrative than each alone; the narrative whole is greater than the sum of its parts.

Impudence notwithstanding, as "Johnson's Lives" the biographies emerged, and as "Johnson's Lives" they remained. The very act of reading the *Lives* between two covers or in a set of volumes imposed a traditional sequence and an assumption of unity on the experience of the text. Succeeding generations found them available in editions printed nearly every two years for the first quarter of the nineteenth century, editions which biennially codified the form of the 1781 sequence, the form in which they continue to be read to the present day. The 1781 text became the definitive order for subsequent editions by force of repetition, an illustration of the transforming power of print in shaping generic expectations. Just as the lives were physically removed from the selections of poetry, they were removed from their prefatory status. Regardless of its contextual origin, Johnson's *Lives of the Poets* assumed an independent narrative autonomy. Its published form suggested a unified text, and whether Johnson regarded the *Lives* as a sequence (as conceivably might be argued), generations of readers accepted it as a unified statement of genre, canon, and morality.

Reading Cumulatively

Canon, Paratactic Design, and the Biographical Epic

As has often been observed, Johnson was a perfecter rather than an inventor of literary modes.[9] Like the *Rambler*, the *Dictionary*, and the edition of Shakespeare, the *Lives of the Poets* is a testament to Johnson's power of intellectually revitalizing extant forms. In bringing about a generic revival of collective biography, Johnson galvanized the reading and writing of literary biography, set biographical theory into motion, and drew attention to the potential of collective biography as a narrative form.

Like the rise of all genre, the revitalization of collective biography was, to borrow Raymond Williams's term, historically specific.[10] Johnson's experiment in collective biography was itself initiated by the generic expediency of the anthology. Romantic prose writers subsequently found the genre artistically as well as financially congenial, accustomed as they were to serial publication preceding book publication. Lest we be tempted to lament the taint of Grub Street, it is well to remember the example of the Renaissance stage and the rise of the novel, which were to a great extent popular genres fusing the creative imagination and the incentive of the contemporary audience.

The London booksellers provided the financial opportunity for executing the series of authorial lives Johnson had envisioned two decades earlier in *Idler* 102. Having discredited the truism, "It is commonly supposed that the uniformity of a studious life affords no great matter for narration," he suggested that authors write their own lives, "instead of devoting their lives to the honor of those who seldom thank them for their labors."[11] *Rambler* 60 had previously urged biographers to emphasize "the minute details of daily life" rather than celebrated events, and in this respect "there has rarely passed a life of which a judicious and faithful narrative would not be useful," be it scholar, merchant, or minister.[12] *Idler* 102 affirms the usefulness and the need to do justice to the lives of the learned, who share "the common condition of humanity," the universal "hopes and fears, expectations and disappointments, griefs and joys" that give value to biography. As Johnson predicted in *Idler* 102, the vicissitudes of the life of the author—feted when in fashion, neglected when reputation declines, balancing the praise of the age and posterity, negotiating the intrigues of patronage ("from the first glow which flattery raises . . . to the last chill look of final dismission")—are events which "modified and varied by accident and custom would form very amusing scenes of biography." This précis of embryonic scenes, sketched to recommend literary biography in 1760, presaged the detailed exposition in the *Lives of the Poets* in which the varied events of "accident and custom" that form the pageant of human life are illustrated through the sequential lives of authors.

Given the Preface to the *Dictionary* and the Preface to the edition of Shakespeare, we might expect a Preface to the *Lives*. Yet there is no prefatory or concluding statement to the collection. A document like *Idler* 102 might have been an introductory prospectus to the project; instead the absence of editorial intervention at the beginning or end came to be a characteristic trait of the collective sequence, adopted by subsequent biographers. In the architecture of collective biography, less is more; the absence of introductions and conclusions signifies an avoidance of simplification or reductive distillation. Indeed Johnson's writing is more aptly characterized by its irreducible density—as a fellow coach-traveler exclaimed of Johnson's telescopic prose, " 'How he does talk! Every sentence is an essay.' "[13]

Boswell asserted the *Lives* contained "such a collection of biography, and such principles and illustrations of criticism, as, if digested and arranged in one system, by some modern Aristotle or Longinus, might form a code upon that subject, such as no other nation can shew."[14] Nowhere in his works, however, does Johnson provide such a systematic code of critical principles;[15] the *Lives* is no different in avoiding programmatic theories of biography, criticism, and morality.

Nevertheless, Johnson's successors certainly regarded him as leaving a threateningly identifiable Johnsonian body of opinion. Walter Scott called him the "mighty aristarch." Charles Lamb more kindly observed that, "without professing egotism," Johnson's writing is "essentially egotistical": "He deals out opinion which he would have you take for argument; and is perpetually obtruding his own particular views of life for universal truths. This is the charm which binds us to his writings."[16] The *Lives of the Poets* was not merely a collection of literary biography or an outline of literary history; it was a characteristically Johnsonian vehicle for universalizing intellectual speculation: a criticism of literature and, as Matthew Arnold was to urge for all writing, a criticism of life.[17] Practical criticism expanded into pronouncements of canon, theory, and literary history; individual lives together became emblematic of the condition of all lives; the practice of literary biography presumed a commentary on biographical and critical method.

Collectivity in the *Lives,* however, does not arise on the level of explicitly ordered sequence or uniformly shaped biographies. In recent years a tripartite structure, of chronology, character, and critical assessment, has been imputed to Johnson's biographies. Yet the most commonly cited prototype of the tripartite structure is the last written *Life of Pope,* which with its appendix on epitaphs is more accurately described as quadripartite. Were *Pope* to have conformed perfectly to a three-part structure, the wide variety of biographical shapes in the *Lives* would militate against any argument for standard partitioning—from the one-part *Duke* to the four- or five-part *Dryden*. By Johnson's time, the generic convention of separating public and private life by writing a chronology followed by a separate summary character was already breaking down in biographical writing. Moreover, Johnsonian biography further undermined partitioning by emphasizing analogies of action diffused through all aspects of the life.

In identifying the formal dimensions of collectivity, we must look to thematic patterning reverberating within and between the lives, rather than to structural homology. Without introduction or conclusion, the collective unity of the text is visual, implicit, and paratactic. Cumulative narrative is communicated through unstated analogues, juxtaposition of incident, and leitmotifs of discourse. These intertextual connections between separate lives unite the seemingly discontinuous narrative into a sustained dialogue. Like the multiple plot in the novel and drama, collectivity emerges in the recurrent play of resemblances and differences. From the perspective of semiotics, the relation between the individual life and the whole sequence in collective biography is synecdochic. Each life shows a facet of what Johnson called in *Idler* 102 "the common condition of humanity." Individual lives are morally specific, but they are also part of the prospect of human experience; poems are the achievement of one individual, but also part of the chain of human achievement that comprises literary history.

As a study of life, biography held unavoidable elegiac and theological implications; in the largest spiritual sense, the diachronic sequence illustrates the place of individual lives in the supreme cumulative sequence, the ongoing passage of generations. In later editions especially, the sequencing of the biographies based on the year of death underscored the spiritual prospect of human experience, in which each generation gently and irrevocably yields to the next in the chain of human achievement that makes up literary history.

In the course of depicting the literary history of English poetry, the *Lives* presents a literary history of English biography. Beginning with Cowley and ending with Gray, the first edition of the *Lives* began and ended with a critique of their biographers Sprat and Mason, who themselves represented the first biographical theorist and the latest innovator. Alongside the progress of English poetry, generations of biographers also succeed one another, the achievement of each taken up by the next. Implicit in the linear progress of intellectual successors traced by the *Lives* is Johnson's own place at the end, the chronicler of his predecessors.

On its most fundamental level, the *Lives* as a cumulative document constitutes a literary history and, implicitly, a canon of poetry. All surveys of literary history—whether they take the form of collections of literary biography, anthologized selections of poetry, or purportedly objective antiquarian chronologies—participate voluntarily or involuntarily in the process of canon formation. That Johnson appears to have had little choice of authors in the *Lives* was irrelevant to the nineteenth-century experience of the text. The canon of the *Lives* was scrupulously analyzed, and Johnson was held accountable not only for overt critical pronouncements but also for the evaluation implicit in exclusion. Goldsmith had been eliminated because his publisher declined to join the collaborative publishing agreement; others, however, were viewed as less innocently slighted. The length of individual biographies in the *Lives* implies a measure of the poet's achievement, dictated presumably by the importance and size of the oeuvre, but determined in part by the amount of available biographical material and in part, it must be said, by Johnson's bias. Indeed, Johnson, having had the power to suggest four authors, might have chosen others instead: for example, Duck, who appears circumstantially in *Savage;* Behn, who is mentioned in *Dryden;* Colley Cibber, who surfaces in any of a dozen or more lives. Peter Cunningham, the nineteenth-century editor of Johnson, guessed that Gray was shortchanged because he traveled in the rival circle of Mason and Walpole; others have speculated that Johnson omitted Duck because Duck rather than Savage received a royal pension.[18]

The *Lives* was not executed as an ostensibly objective chronicle of literary history. Thomas Warton's contemporaneous *History of English Poetry* (1774–81), also a canonizing document, provides an illuminating methodological contrast.[19] Warton's *History* strives to be impartial, accurate, thorough, and systematic; minimal biographical material, without character analysis, is used to position works within a career. Even had Warton lived to complete it, the chronology was to conclude before the eighteenth century; no one alive would have been acquainted with any of the figures. Johnson, however, knew Savage well, Lyttelton slightly, dealt with Mallet and Collins, and possessed firsthand accounts of several other poets; although he declined to take advantage of personal reminiscences, the extension of the series to poets of nearly the present generation emphasized an unbroken line of filiation. Warton's is an antiquarian and encyclopedic approach to writing literary history. In contrast, the *Lives* critically evaluated an ongoing literary tradition, contemplated the connections between life and works, and explored the community of artists and their position in society.

The diachronic sequence of the *Lives* to some extent assumes an evolutionary model of literary history, in which successive literary generations implicitly evolve to the present state of excellence. The mantle of achievement is passed forward: Cowley's translations surpass his predecessors', and are in turn surpassed by Dryden's and Pope's. Yet it is not purely a linear model of evolution, for Johnson considers the question of historical relativism. In evaluating Dryden, for example, he says, "To judge rightly of an author we must transport ourselves to his time, and examine what were the wants of his contemporaries, and what were his means of supplying them."[20] The achievements of versification are more problematic: Cowley is succeeded by Waller and Denham, then Dryden and Pope, beyond whom "to attempt any further improvement of versification will be dangerous. Art and diligence have now done their best." The evolutionary progress of the arts set forth in *Pope* ("it will be found in the progress of learning that in all nations the first writers are simple, and that every age improves in elegance. One refinement always makes way for another, and what was expedient to Virgil was necessary to Pope") nevertheless possesses the implications of unavoidable decadence and decline, for "repletion generates fastidiousness, a saturated intellect soon becomes luxurious."

On a simple level, intertextuality between lives arises in Plutarchan comparisons that establish rank within the canon. *Denham* and *Waller* are paired in versification, with the verdict, "Praise of strength to Denham, and of sweetness to Waller" (*Waller*). Biographical and critical parallels emerge in *Milton* and *Cowley,* two of "dissimilar genius, of opposite principles." Johnson's observation, "At the same time were produced from the same university the two great Poets, Cowley and Milton," actually conflates the time frame for emphasis (Milton left in 1632, Cowley entered in 1630). Both " 'lisp in numbers,' " plan educational schemes, and write the same kinds of verse. Cowley surpasses Milton in Latin; in elegiac writing each lacks passion; Cowley possesses "the skill to rate his own performances by their just value" that Milton lacks; Milton excels in the epic, Cowley in the "metaphysick style" Milton (and Johnson) "disdained." The *Life of Pope* contains within it the most extensive Plutarchan comparison, that of Dryden and Pope—two of different generations with similar traits. Both have poetic and critical aspirations; neither is vivacious in company; both squabble with contemporary critics; each translates the classics. Dryden is negligent where Pope is meticulous; Pope "never set genius to sale," while Dryden trafficked in flattery to win favor;[21] Dryden "never desired to apply all the judgement that he had," whereas Pope "was not content to satisfy, he desired to excel." The extended comparison of their poetry may be the best known critical assessment of the *Lives:* "Dryden knew more of man in his general nature, and Pope in his local manners," "The style of Dryden is capricious and varied, that of Pope is cautious and uniform," "If the flights of Dryden therefore are higher, Pope continues longer on the wing," "Dryden often surpasses expectation, and Pope never falls below it." Johnson admits to preferring Dryden but the "parallel," he hopes, will "be found just." Johnson once planned to translate Plutarch; and in the background of the Pope-Dryden comparison and other Plutarchan parallels is the antecedent Neoclassical tradition of enumerating and ranking the relative merits of Homer and Virgil—which Johnson's description of Pope's obligation to Dryden's *Aeneid* in translating the *Iliad* acknowledges: "Virgil had borrowed much of his imagery from Homer, and part of the debt was now paid by his translator."[22]

Johnson subverted the diachronic sequence with questions about the evolutionary model; and although he may have begun the *Lives* planning more pairings than ultimately were written, most of the Plutarchan parallels occur among the earlier-written biographies (including the comparison between Dryden and Pope reconstituted from much earlier biographical reflections passed on to his assistant, Robert Shiels).[23] Synchronic collections of lives according to occupation—martyrs, authors, rulers, highwaymen—were not unknown in the eighteenth century, but Johnson's participation in the genre released a flood of lives of statesmen, admirals, children, animals, shoemakers, and, of course, poets. In exploring the common concerns and experience of poets over time—income, popularity, conversation, vanity, versification, use of genre, degree of genius, acquaintance with books, revolutions of fame, friendships, enemies, patronage—the *Lives* functions less as a linear sequence than a cumulative dialogue.

The collection of critical observations that Boswell hoped might form a "code" is the most visible example of the continuous internal dialogue within the *Lives*. Beyond the evaluation of the individual oeuvre in each life is a larger shared critical discourse of poetics: whether there should be an Academy to arbitrate literature and language in England (*Roscommon, Swift*); the nature of devotional poetry (*Waller, Watts*); whether an author is the best judge of his works (*Dryden, Prior, Milton, Cowley, Pope*); how to evaluate juvenilia (*Cowley, Milton, Pope, Stepney*); the value of blank verse (*Milton, Roscommon*); the definition of simile (*Addison, Pope*); the character of poetic diction (*Dryden, Pope*); the confines of the pastoral (*Cowley, A. Philips, Gay, Milton, Pope, Shenstone, Lyttelton*). The discussion of translation (*Denham, Roscommon, Pitt, Broome, Fenton, Dryden, Pope*) is perhaps the most salient critical topic, itself part of the eighteenth-century discourse weighing the ancients and moderns, Homer and Virgil, imitation and genius. Johnson, himself a translator of Juvenal, examined the critical nuances of translation, imitation, paraphrase, metaphrase, and rifacimento, as a way of praising the moderns without disparaging the ancients. In refusing to polarize the issue of ancients and moderns, progress and decline, Johnson problematized the concept of "imitation" in poetics; in dealing with moral matters as well, the question of imitation is multivocal.

Johnson's biographies have been called moral fables; if they are not quite " 'moralities' without the moral," as Henry James described Hawthorne's writings, they are still not morally formulaic. Hazlitt called Johnson "a complete balance-master in the topics of morality. He never encourages hope, but he counteracts it by fear; he never elicits a truth, but he suggests some objection in answer to it."[24] Although Johnson declared the *Lives* a sequence tending "to the promotion of piety," he did not promote piety through hagiographic emulation; the Johnsonian moral balance avoids simple prescriptive didacticism. Johnson's comment on Milton applies to the rest of the lives: "Like other heroes he is to be admired rather than imitated."[25]

The sententiae scattered throughout the *Lives* amplify individual traits into general observations of life, yet they do not form a code or conduct book of models for imitation. Johnson tells us a great deal about the nature of praise, for example, but what are we to conclude about comportment toward it? "One cannot always easily find the reason for which the world has sometimes conspired to squander praise" (*Stepney*); "That praise is worth nothing of which the price is known" (*Dryden*); "Every

man willingly gives value to the praise which he receives" (*Halifax*).[26]
Such aphorisms are common in Johnson, yet they rarely appear as closing
or culminating moral statements. The lives are neither exemplary models
nor Aesopic fables.

As Hester Thrale Piozzi explained, "His first care was for general, not
particular or petty morality."[27] Johnson did not adopt the conventional
propriety of high biography that automatically restricted treatment of
moral dissolution. At the same time he rejected the common exculpatory
practice of justifying any and every text as didactic (of the purported
moral design of the *Dunciad* he said, "I am not convinced"); and he had
little tolerance for what he called "praise merely negative," the custom of
bestowing laudatory euphemisms "arising not from the possession of virtue but the absence of vice" (*Pope*). When it is necessary to indicate the
scope of misbehavior, we hear of the drunken "frolick" of Sir Charles
Sedley, who "stood forth naked, and harangued the populace" (*Dorset*);
and more severely, how the Duke of Buckingham's " 'pimp' " distracted
" 'his Grace' " from providing a pension for Butler. But in the *Life of
Rochester,* where we might anticipate a voyeuristic recitation of scandal,
Johnson only says that Rochester described himself as "for five years
together continually drunk," and that "he played many frolicks, which it is
not for his honour that we should remember, and which are not now distinctly known." The Boswellian dispute over whether biographical depiction deters or sanctions drinking raises more issues about decorum in
theory than in practice, for neither flaw receives more than a sentence in
the *Lives:* that Parnell was "too much a lover of the bottle" Johnson has
heard imputed to grief; Addison "drank too much wine." There are half-
sentence hints that Collins and Somerville drank. Other vices appear
more decadent than drunkenness: Thomson is " 'more fat than bard
beseems,' "[28] and Fenton is so slothful as to " 'lie a-bed, and be fed with a
spoon.' "

Rarely does Johnson directly indicate a subject's fitness for emulation.
Although in *Sheffield* he openly declares, "His character is not to be
proposed as worth of imitation,"[29] more typical is the sympathy for
Savage's excesses as human foibles: "Nor will any wise man presume to
say, 'Had I been in Savage's condition, I should have lived or written
better than Savage.' " Johnson does not require his subjects to recant their
errors in the manner of spiritual autobiography. A life need not be unspot-
ted or consistent for it to be of use; in considering Savage's errors, others

"shall be enabled to fortify their patience." Moreover, the presence of vice need not totally discredit the virtues of a life. Despite his moral flaws, Savage's verse remains free from even "the strictest moral or religious censure." Knowing, as Johnson says in *Rambler* 14, it is "easier to design than to perform," it is easily conceived that "a man writes much better than he lives." Whatever are the vices of Addison, he is vindicated in one of Johnson's few hagiographic borrowings, when Addison summons Lord Warwick, "a young man of very irregular life," to his bedside to say, "'I have sent for you that you may see how a Christian can die.'"

Johnson's rejection of the doctrine of the ruling passion helped remove short anecdotal biography from the pitfall of oversimplification and Theophrastan character writing. Mutability of character is fundamental to Johnson's moral and biographical standards. Rochester, for example, is shown brave when younger and a coward later on, licentious in early manhood and later repentant. Swift's sudden resolution to apply himself to study provides an inspiration and encouragement to those who, "having lost one part of life in idleness, are tempted to throw away the remainder in despair." Johnson explicitly refutes Pope's "favourite theory of the 'Ruling Passion'" as a pernicious determinism likely to promote discouraging notions of "moral predestination." Pope's advice, "To form *Characters*, we can only take the *strongest actions* of a man's life, and try to make them agree," implies it is not the actions that generate insight into character, but the biographer who forces actions into agreement and deliberately considers only the most visible ones.[30] Johnson's rebuttal, "Human characters are by no means constant; men change by change of place, of fortune, of acquaintance," implicitly argued against the convention of writing reductive closing characters in biography, and set a precedent for Romantic interest in the transformation of child into adult. James Field Stanfield's *Essay on the Study and Composition of Biography* (1813), for example, in recommending the integration of characterization throughout the chronology of the life, said the traditional summary character was based on archaic assumptions dating back to Plutarch that character is unchanging and one-dimensional.

More often than not, human action is not amenable to easy moral distillation; the ambiguous and multifarious examples that form the moral canon of the *Lives* demonstrate that moral issues must frequently remain equivocal and judgments ad hoc. In the matter of avarice, what single conclusion can be drawn? Johnson faults the parsimony and profiteering of Swift, Pope, Waller, and Dryden; but he condemns Savage, Smith, and King for their financial profligacy. To conclude that Johnson simply is "varying from himself" undermines the collective value of the *Lives* in illustrating the common condition of humanity, "modified and varied by accident and custom." Addison might drink yet be a good Christian, King might foolishly squander money while Waller might too assiduously pursue it. Individually, the lives demonstrate varying solutions, for good or for bad, to universal problems; cumulatively the *Lives* illustrates the difficulty of prescribing a single infallible path. Johnson may have been resented as the mighty aristarch in literary matters, but his moral fairness was immediately and unflaggingly admired; his harshest criticisms were directed at literary deficiencies rather than human failings. The absence of exemplary codes of behavior, however, did not free humankind, writers, or biographers from moral accountability. It is not surprising that the *Life of Pope,* the last-written of the *Lives,* is the most reflective on the subject of posterity, reputation, and accountability.

Like Johnson's answer to Boswell concerning the orange peels, "You shall know their fate no further," the glimpse of Henry Cromwell in *Pope* is an emblem of the ephemerality of life and the volatile materials of biography. Of Cromwell, a poet and critic who was one of Pope's early correspondents, Johnson reports the solitary relic of posterity: "I have learned nothing particular but that he used to ride a-hunting in a tye-wig." The vanishing of Cromwell provides a cautionary allegory of the situation of Pope, whose vain plan to have his writings posthumously saved was undone by the executors who destroyed his papers. Of Pope's futile attempt to control posterity, Johnson writes: "Let no man dream of influence beyond his life." Witnessing the unreliable accidents of posterity, Johnson resigned posthumous influence over his own documents, telling his biographer, "When I am dead, you may do as you will."[31]

In the *Lives,* regret over now lost and forgotten events promotes respect for the biographer's present-day task of arresting the erosion of memory. "Time has not left us the power of confirming or refuting" the character of Rowe; "the cause cannot now be known" why Milton was alienated from the university; we shall never know to what Addison referred when he told Gay that "he had injured him"; two remaining anecdotes of Dryden alone constitute "all the intelligence" which his survivors have afforded. Even the quarrel between the two greatest rivals of their age, Addison and Pope, cannot be untangled by the biographer, "to whom, as Homer says,

'nothing but rumour has reached, and who has no personal knowledge'"
(*Iliad*, II: 486).

The Homeric reference offers a small allusion to the translations of Pope, but it also suggests analogies between the lives of the ancients as told by Homer, and the new epic of literary heroism, the collected *Lives of the Poets*. The quarrels and disappointments of Addison and Pope replace the battles of the Greeks and the Trojans; the triumphs of the printing press are the victories of war; the yearning is for reputation by the pen rather than the sword. The multiple Iliadic heroes of Johnson's lives tell the story of the modern epic struggle for intellectual glory. The biographer of Pope pursues the biographer of Achilles; writers like Milton are "like other heroes"; *Savage* elevates "the heroes of literary as well as civil history"; "the gradations of a hero's life are from battle to battle, and of an author's from book to book" (*Idler* 102). Boswell extended the epic metaphor of Johnson's *Lives* in his *Life of Johnson* with its sequel hero whose trials may be "assimilated to the ODYSSEY."[32]

In doing justice to literary memory by writing the lives of authors, writers preserve one another from neglect. Johnson completed the *Lives* with a statement about how the act of writing biography, like all forms of writing, is a form of self-perpetuation. At the ending of the last life written, marking the ending of the last of his major projects, Johnson placed his essay on Pope's epitaphs.[33] It stands as a final commentary on the essential themes of mortality implicit in the *Lives* and in all biography. Johnson's critique of Pope's epitaphs addresses the unstated question of the moral accountability of the biographer; and in denoting the elegiac kinship between epitaph-writer and biographer, it places Johnson himself in the literary tradition critically accountable to future generations. His evaluation of the "sepulchral performances" of Pope will in turn eventually be evaluated as the sepulchral performances of Johnson.

In appending the critique, Johnson inscribes the critical standards by which his own biographies are to be judged. Style and meter are only peripheral considerations beside the flaws of illogic, commonplaces, and indiscriminate panegyric: Can a courtier be said to have "sacred ease"? Is to be a "safe companion" any kind of praise? The epitaph of Mrs. Corbet[t] is the most valuable, for memorializing "a character not discriminated by any shining or eminent peculiarities," beyond the tranquillity and felicity of private life; it requires "the genius of Pope" to commemorate such as whom "the dull overlook and the gay despise."

In a closing warning, however, the *Life of Pope* ends not with praise but with an example of verse which "should have been suppressed for the author's sake." The lines Pope has written for another constitute his own legacy; authors in effect prepare their own epitaphs in their printed works, the words by which they will be remembered. The judgments posed in the *Lives* will in turn be tested. Life-writing reveals the moral and intellectual qualities of the biographer as well as the subject. Like Dante meditating on his fellow poet Bertrand de Born, punished for abusing his skill with words in order to misguide (*Inferno,* Canto XXVIII), Johnson implicitly assumes his place in successive generations of biographers; as he holds Pope accountable for his epitaphs, so in turn shall he be.

Johnson's theoretical essays on biography had come twenty to thirty years earlier. More important to the theory and practice of biography than the critical axioms scattered through his works was the implicit methodological precedent of the *Lives.* The *Lives* generated enormous creative momentum in the genre, and its narrative strategies gained greater validity as laws of biographical composition than did his prescriptive criticism. In the *Lives,* life-writing became a commentary on life-writing.

The *Life of Cowley* provides a good springboard for discussing the *Lives* as a metageneric commentary on biographical tradition. It was the first of the biographies to be written for the sequence (excluding the reprinted *Savage, Roscommon,* and *Collins*) and Boswell claims it was the one "he himself considered as the best of the whole."[34] Johnson's comments on metaphysical poetry are well known; but *Cowley,* positioned as the opening life, also contained an extended commentary on biography that established the *Lives* as a treatise on method. "Notwithstanding the penury of English biography," and the penury of biographical criticism, Johnson undertook the task of renovating both genres.

More printed sources were available for *Cowley* than for many of the lives, and Johnson used the opportunity to provide a critique of extant biographical practices. His predecessor Sprat has written "not the life" but the "character" and "panegyrick" of Cowley; he "conceals," he tries to "propagate a wonder," he "could not refrain from amplifying a commodious incident." The conflicting accounts of Cowley's retreat from the court illuminate the subjectivity of biographical interpretation: "So differently are things seen, and so differently are they shown."[35] The information in Johnson's *Cowley* was not new; Sprat's account already had provided the nucleus of facts for other second-generation biographers, and Johnson's material is much the same as in the *Lives of the Poets of Great Britain and Ireland to the time of Dean Swift,* credited to Theophilus Cibber.

Formally, Cibber's *Lives* resembles Johnson's collective biography except that a short selection of verse is directly appended to each life. Johnson's indelible stamp on the genre appears in the critical dimension of the *Lives.* Unlike Johnson's, Cibber's *Lives* includes no rigorous critical assessments beyond admiring a few beauties in the verse; and where Cibber's *Lives* unquestioningly recounts received information, Johnson scrutinizes his biographical sources for fallacy and false reasoning. Cibber's *Cowley* declares he was the son of a grocer; Johnson's *Cowley* explains he was the son of a grocer which Sprat "conceals under the general appellation of a citizen." The Cibber text observes, "It is remarkable of Mr. Cowley, as he himself tells us, that he had this defect in his memory" that he could not retain the rules of grammar; Johnson repeats the identical story as an example of "the natural desire of man to propagate a wonder" and Sprat's inability to "refrain from amplifying a commodious incident."[36]

Like dictionaries and editions of Shakespeare, collections of literary lives preceded Johnson's, although none followed without reference to him thereafter. Even as Johnson was monumentally revising expectations for collective biography, he was himself engaged in a critical dialogue with his generic predecessors. In *Milton,* for example, he alludes to Edward Phillips's *Theatrum Poetarum,* "a small *History of Poetry* . . . of which perhaps none of my readers has ever heard," and in *Dryden* and *Otway* he makes use of Gerard Langbaine's *Account of the English Dramatic Poets.* The most conspicuous text for Johnson, however, was Cibber's *Lives,* which he reminds us in *Hammond* was largely written by Robert Shiels, not by "either of the Cibbers."[37] The bookseller Ralph Griffiths additionally observed, "Many of the best pieces of biography in that collection were not written by Shiels, but by superior hands." Cibber's edition identifies its *Savage* as derived from an account by a "gentleman, who knew him intimately" (Johnson's *Life of Savage*) and Johnson was obliged to reappropriate from Shiels, his amanuensis on the dictionary, some of his early critical meditations.[38] The inclusion of *Savage* is less the sentimental gesture that often has been suggested to account for its disproportionate size, than a reclaiming of property.

In his critical revisionism of the judgments of Cibber's *Lives,* Johnson displays the same anxiety to rewrite literary history we associate with his Romantic successors. Cibber's *Blackmore* opens with some of the jests made about his having been a schoolmaster; Johnson's *Blackmore* omits them and instead observes that "to have been once a school-master is the only reproach . . . ever fixed upon his private life." Watts is not included in the earlier collection, but *Pomfret* and *Yalden,* like *Blackmore,* may well have been added to rebut Cibber's *Lives.* In both biographies Johnson minimizes the scandal, which Cibber's *Lives* willingly repeats, of Pomfret's concupiscence and Yalden's arrest; in correcting such misconceptions Johnson counters the disparagement of the clergy visible in Cibber's *Lives.*[39]

Contradicting the biographical tendency to "propagate a wonder," Johnson propagates the ordinary in the 'great man' or 'genius.' Johnson rejected the overstated anecdote in favor of the overlooked trait: the biographer must know how to write "trifles with dignity." He told Boswell, " 'There is nothing, Sir, too little for so little a creature as man. It is by studying little things that we attain the great art of having as little misery and as much happiness as possible.' "[40] King William teaches Swift "how to cut asparagus in the Dutch way"; Johnson objects to the "wish to find Milton discriminated from other men." Extending the discourse of *Cowley,* he cautions that "the lovers of a wonder" will attempt to see in Milton's alternate bursts of composition and unproductivity the "appearance of deviation from the common train of Nature," when in fact "something of this inequality happens to every man in every mode of exertion, manual or mental." Writers share the common condition of humanity: like Milton, "The mechanick cannot handle his hammer and his file at all times with equal dexterity; there are hours, he knows not why, when 'his hand is out' "; the same frustrations arise for "every man in every mode of exertion." As Johnson says in *Rambler* 60, our "passions" are moved in reading biography by recognizing events "as once our own, or considering them as naturally incident to our state of life." He told Boswell, "I esteem biography, as giving us what comes near to ourselves, what we can turn to use."[41]

Johnson often deflates the most commodious incidents of their spurious prestige or apocryphal traditions. Discounting the legend that Dorset composed a song in a single evening before battle, Johnson declares, "Seldom any splendid story is wholly true."[42] Analyzing false stories, however, has its use in showing how to discern true ones. He discredits the tradition that King read and commented on more than twenty-two thousand books and manuscripts: "The books were certainly not very long, the manuscripts not very difficult, nor the remarks very large; for the calculator will find that he dispatched seven a day, for every day of his eight years, with a remnant that more than satisfies most other students." He "once intended to omit" the "wild story" of Dryden's funeral, but instead proceeds by "supposing the story true" in order to produce his grounds of doubt. He is skeptical of the rumor of Roscommon's clair-voyance, but recounts it in lieu of better evidence: "It must be by preserv-ing such relations that we may at last judge how much they are to be regarded."

As in his discussion of poetics, Johnson builds up an ongoing discourse on biographical principles—how to treat letters, conversation, and per-sonal testimony (*Pope, Cowley, Savage*), how to assess rumor and contradic-tory accounts (*Roscommon, Dryden, Cowley*)—yet as elsewhere, Johnson's advice is chiefly by illustration and indirection rather than construction of any prescriptive code.

Connecting Lives and Works

The Doctrine of Sincerity

The *Lives* was a biographical pronouncement on several levels; it inscribed a commentary on biographical theory, it defined a new form of literary biography by adding valuative criticism of the works to the traditional components of characterization and chronology, and it cleared the way for biographical approaches to reading literary texts. In this, then, we distinguish three phenomena intimately connected with Johnson: the rise of criticism of biography (biographical theory); the invention of critical biography (life writing); and the use of biography as a critical methodol-ogy (biographical criticism), an extrinsic theory of literature which posits the life as connected to the meaning and sometimes the form of the work, and a practical criticism which uses the life to assist in interpretation of the works.

The idea of using biography to inform literature circulated loosely through the eighteenth century, but it had not crystallized into a theory or principle of reading. By the latter half of the eighteenth century, con-templation of the links between life and works was a subject of much

current, if imprecise, interest. Boswell's passion for meeting authors—
Hume, Rousseau, Johnson—attests to the popular curiosity, though his
writing offers no analytical mediation of the links between life and works.
Boswell was not alone in aspiring to meet and to learn about the lives of
Rousseau and other literary figures. Robert Darnton observes that Rousseau's new readership was strangely compelled to correspond with him,
that his writings "inspired his readers with an overwhelming desire to
make contact with the lives behind the printed page"[43]—the lives of the
characters, and what was more important in its novelty, the life of the
author. In his *Essay on the Genius and Writings of Pope,* Joseph Warton
described the conflicting attraction of speculating on the connections
between life and works, a pursuit at once fatuous and legitimate: "What
Addison says in jest, and with his usual humour, is true in fact: 'I have
observed that a reader seldom peruses a book with pleasure, 'till he knows
whether the writer of it be a black or fair man, of a mild or choleric
disposition, married or a bachelor.' "[44] For the popular audience of biography today, reading about a life or way of life remains often more
important than the oeuvre or achievement.

In praise of Bayle's dictionary, Johnson confided his own preference to
Boswell, "the biographical part of literature, which is what I love most."[45]
But what does he mean by the "biographical part of literature"? Reading
biography? Reading for a biographical subtext in works of literature?
Speculating on connections between life and works? Johnson's comment
associates biography with the experience of reading literature, but here, as
in the *Lives,* the precise relationship is a matter for contemplation.

Why did Johnson volunteer Blackmore, Watts, Pomfret, and Yalden?
The consideration of lives seems to have been more important than works,
for his dislike of their poetry did not disqualify their inclusion. Despite its
role as a history and canon of literature, evaluation of poetry is not the
exclusive concern of the *Lives of the Poets.* Sheffield's life as a soldier, the
political negotiations of Prior, the shifting factionalism of Waller, assume
more importance than their poetry. Johnson's interest in how poets lead
their lives and the "common condition of humanity" seems to have been
more important than literary merit.

Johnson often commends a life even as he condemns the poems. The
Lives redefined the responsibilities of literary history and biography by

discouraging the literary hagiography that failed to take up the issue of critical merit. Having replaced the saint's life as the model for literary biography, the *Lives* also avoids extolling literary merits in its practical criticism, eschewing the kind of aesthetic hagiography Pater was to return to in *The Renaissance*. Johnson freed biography not to expect lives and works to morally coincide (although he seems far more tolerant of compromises made in the face of the hardships of life than the hardships of versification). At the same time, the *Lives* often identifies correspondences between lives and works.

Although Johnson usually has not been associated with a valuative criticism based on sincerity, many of his critical judgments are contingent on authorial sincerity. The practice of testing a work of art for its candor, or assuming that powerful emotions in literature spring from the author's personal identification with the subject, is fundamentally a biographical theory of writing. Unlike other uses of biography in reading literature, it is also an explicitly valuative criticism, a standard for assessing the worth of a literary work.

The doctrine of sincerity arose from the longstanding critical inquiry into the connections between author and text. Since the time of the ancients, these connections have been explained by two factions: that expressed by Martial, "*lasciva est nobis pagina, vita proba,*" the view that a life can be moral though the poems be lewd, and the opposite view of Strabo, expressed by Ben Jonson, the "impossibility of any Man's being the good *Poet* without first being a good *Man*."[46] Both, of course, are author-based criticisms, of the kind discountenanced by many twentieth-century critics as part of a preoccupation with validating meaning through authorial intention;[47] indeed, the exploration of whether a good poet need lead a good life has long been replaced with psychoanalytic approaches to the relation between author and text. Although searching for congruence between the text and authorial feeling is now a devalued critical standard, sincerity as a literary criterion was prized among the Romantics. Even then, not all Romantics concurred—theories of the chameleon poet existed alongside theories of the egotistical sublime.[48]

Although it was a standard that ascended to prominence among the Romantics, Johnson himself tinkered with a doctrine of sincerity which evaluated works in terms of their concord with the author's life.[49] The multiple illustrations of the *Lives* suggest the complexities of trying to find any prescriptive formula; a few are good poets and good men; in many the morality of the page and the life do not coincide. In *Thomson* Johnson cautioned against the fallacy of uniformly extrapolating an author's life from the works. The virtues of an author cannot necessarily be assessed from the values expressed in the works:

> The biographer of Thomson has remarked that an author's life is best read in his works: his observation was not well-timed. Savage, who lived much with Thomson, once told me how he heard a lady remarking that she could gather from his works three parts of his character, that he was 'a great lover, a great swimmer, and rigorously abstinent'; but, said Savage, he knows not any love but that of the sex; he was perhaps never in cold water in his life; and he indulges himself in all the luxury that comes within his reach.

As Johnson had observed in *Rambler* 14, we must be prepared to expect "contrariety between the life of an author and his writings." Boswell recounts Johnson's rejection of the assertion that "it appeared from Horace's writings that he was a cheerful contented man"—he declared there was no reason to believe so: " 'Are we to think Pope was happy because he says so in his writings? We see in his writings what he wished the state of his mind to appear. Dr. Young, who pined for preferment, talks with contempt of it in his writings, and affects to despise every thing that he did not despise.' "[50] As with letters and conversation, Johnson distrusted images authors seek to project in published texts.

Although a number of poets in the *Lives,* like Milton and Savage, are charged with writing good poetry and leading bad lives, many more conduct good lives and write bad poetry. As is made clear in the examples of Collins, West, Watts, and Blackmore, a virtuous life does not guarantee excellent versification. That more of Johnson's poets lead better lives than write good poetry seems to suggest it is easier to be moral than a poet; an implication which led in the Romantic era to a sense of the special status and dispensation of the poet, who needs be permitted special liberties in order to produce good verse.

Johnson, however, does not utterly denounce the idea of reading the works as an index to the life and character: as regards Thomson, it is simply "not well-timed." Johnson was happy to declare in praise of Addison, "It is reasonable to believe that Addison's professions and practice were at no great variance." Elsewhere in the *Lives* Johnson does not find it untimely to evaluate authors in terms of the sincerity of their verse. Johnson openly faults Dryden for not writing *"con amore"* (a term Boswell later uses to describe how Johnson wrote the *Life of Pope*).[51] By the early nineteenth century, the idea of writing *con amore* had been absorbed into the Romantic definition of literature, for the Romantic poet had to be authentically inspired, regardless of the sincerity of specific impersonations. Johnson criticizes Prior because "the words did not come till they were called," and complains of *Lycidas,* in some of the best known passages of the *Lives,* "It is not to be considered as the effusion of real passion; for passion runs not after remote allusions and obscure opinions." It is interesting to find the vocabulary associated with the works of Wordsworth and Coleridge—"passion" and "effusion"—evoked by Johnson in a defense of sincerity in literature.

Cowley, the first of the lives, provides the fullest statement of the importance of sincerity in producing good literature. Citing the precedent of Petrarch and Laura, Johnson declares that Cowley merely imitated a convention without possessing any true passion himself, and this must diminish the merit of the work of art he produces. Indeed, Johnson's famous maxim on truth is invoked in the context of evaluating Cowley's sincerity:

> The basis of all excellence is truth: he that professes love ought to feel its power. Petrarch was a real lover, and Laura doubtless deserved his tenderness. Of Cowley we are told by Barnes . . . he in reality was in love but once, and then never had resolution to tell his passion. This consideration cannot but abate in some measure the reader's esteem for the work and the author.

Knowing Cowley's insincerity undermines enjoyment of the work, but even more pernicious, chronic insincerity will impair the quality of any composition:

> The man that sits down to suppose himself charged with treason or peculation, and heats his mind to an elaborate purgation of his character from crimes which he was never within the possibility of committing, differs only by the infrequency of his folly from him who praises beauty which he never saw, complains of jealousy which he never felt.

Curiously, Johnson's assessment rests on the precedent of Petrarch's affection for Laura, itself a biographical fallacy one would think more characteristic of Romantic than Johnsonian sentimentalizing of literature. Yet Johnson measures these lyrics for authentic emotion.

In the *Lives* the issue of truth often appears in conjunction with the question of sincerity. The famous passage in *Waller,* "Poets, indeed, profess fiction, but the legitimate end of fiction is the conveyance of truth," fortifies Johnson's view in *Cowley* that the poet who feigns emotion sacrifices both truth and literary merit. Insincerity is untruth. Had Waller confined his posturing to the "hypocrisy" of transactions such as his feigned adulation of the Duchess of Newcastle's verse, "he might have been forgiven though not praised"; but the flattery and opportunism of Waller taint his political life and corrupt the originality of his verse. The "prostituted mind" of Waller bestowed identical words of praise on the Protector and the Crown,[52] so neither "could value his testimony as the effect of conviction, or receive his praises as effusions of reverence; they could consider them but as the labour of invention and the tribute of dependence." Sincerity is not the only criterion of literary merit in the *Lives,* but the poems of too agile a chameleon forfeit veracity and respect.

The correspondence between Waller's switching of political allegiances and the lack of conviction in his poetry is an example of how Johnson uses analogy of action to explore the connections between lives and works. In *Rambler* 60 he praised Sallust for noticing of Catiline, "'his walk was now quick, and again slow,'" as an indication of a mind revolving something with violent commotion. In the *Lives of the Poets,* the emblematic details of domestic life or political action are often the connecting points between lives and literary works.

The vanity of Pope leads to perpetual disguises and duplicities: "In all his intercourse with mankind, he had a great delight in artifice, and endeavoured to attain all his purposes by indirect and unsuspected methods. 'He hardly drank tea without a stratagem.'" From his genealogy, to misdating his juvenilia, to arranging the piracy of his letters, Pope was more willing to show what he "was not, than what he was." The petty dissimulations of physical vanity—the velvet cap to cover his baldness, three pairs of stockings to shape his legs—provide an emblem of the clandestine disguises of his literary career. The misleading costume of the *Essay on Man* "disguised" its "penury of knowledge and vulgarity of sentiment" through an "array" of imagery and eloquence: when "the doctrine of the *Essay,* disrobed of its ornaments, is left to the powers of its naked excellence, what shall we discover?" The attempt to make himself look better lies at the root of Pope's many literary frauds. The disingenuous Pope "wilfully disguises his own character" in his published letters; the public is "kept ignorant" of the assistants who help him translate Homer; before owning the *Essay on Man* he waits to see how it is received; he ridicules the Dunces and his patron the Duke of Chandos, then must "sneak and shuffle," deny and dissimulate: "He first endeavours to wound, and is then afraid to own that he meant a blow." Even in gardening, vanity and disguise are linked: "Vanity produced a grotto where necessity enforced a passage."

Dryden lived under the pressure of "exigencies"; he shifted his political and religious allegiances in hopes of preferment just as his writings seized the most convenient income and easiest favor: he "snatched in haste what was within his reach; and when he could content others, was himself content." Impelled by the desire to win approbation and social comforts, the "mint of flattery" and "abject adulation" of the social Dryden reappears in the pandering to audience and mass production of his literary works. In consequence, "ten lines are seldom found together without something of which the reader is ashamed," and the cataloging of his plays entails more "tedious and troublesome" labor than they took to write.

Disobedience and rebellion allegorize Milton's life. Milton is descended from partisans in the "times of York and Lancaster" and a father disinherited for becoming a Protestant—a genealogy prefiguring his own active role in the discord of the seventeenth century. For his own first disobedience, he incurs rustication from Cambridge, and his "exile" from the *hortus conclusus* of the university walls is followed by his subsequent rebellions against church and crown. Johnson depicts Milton acting from the desire to disobey rather than any specific ideology: of religion, "He had determined rather what to condemn than what to approve . . . we know rather what he was not, than what he was"; and of politics, "He hated all whom he was required to obey. It is to be suspected that his predominant desire was to destroy rather than establish, and that he felt not so much the love of liberty as repugnance to authority." Like Romantic writers such as Coleridge, Shelley, and Melville, Johnson detects (although he does not approve) a seditious countertext favoring rebellion in *Paradise Lost:* beneath the ostensibly submissive piety of conventional dogma uprears a lionizing disobedience.

As the Romantics were to locate Shakespeare in all his characters, Johnson finds traces of Milton in Adam, Satan, and God. Milton's physical resemblance to "the picture which he has given of Adam" underscores the kinship between his rebellious support of the Commonwealth and the mutinies he chronicles in *Paradise Lost*. The Tory Johnson viewed Milton's own rebellion as less Adamic than Satanic: he refused the "servitude" of "canonical obedience"; his republicanism was "founded in an envious hatred of greatness"; and in the "malignity" of his pamphlets on Smectymnuus, *"hell grows darker at his frown"* (*Paradise Lost,* II: 719). At the same time the rebel Milton crushed insubordination in his own dominion; domestic sinners in the hands of an angry God, his insurgent wife is rebuked for "disobedience" and his daughters' education is suppressed "that they might not break the ranks." Johnson's observation, "He thought woman made only for obedience, and man only for rebellion," syntactically echoes *Paradise Lost* (IV: 299), "He for God only, she for God in him," hinting that Milton's own tyrannical relation between husband and wife was the model for Adam and Eve.

Yet from its collection of examples, the *Lives* sets forth no formulation of the connections between life and works. Concurrences are not accompanied by interpretive assistance; there is no summation, for example, on the tendency of authors to involuntarily or consciously infuse personal experience into their literary works. To what extent does Johnson's discussion of the "design" of *L'Allegro* and *Il Penseroso* as an illustration of the subjective mind, serve as a generalizable biographical theory of composition? Do the objects of the poet's contemplation derive "their colours from the mind," or is it that "every disposition of mind takes hold on those by which it may be gratified"? That Milton resembled "the picture which he has given of Adam" may only suggest authors derive their ideas from the objects and actions with which they are acquainted, or it may indicate a more subliminal autobiographical subtext. No principles are set forth explaining how literature transposes life into art psychologically or sociologically. Dryden's carelessness as a writer is not said to exemplify the plight of literature in a culture of economic determinism. The rebelliousness of Milton and the vanity of Pope are not broadened into any theory of artistic creativity; Johnson supposes Pope's physical infirmity was "in part the effect of his application," but ventures no pathography of art.

Johnson's resistance to univocality made the *Lives* a model for intellectual speculation in subsequent generations. Although the rankings of the early Plutarchan pairings offer some verdicts, most of the issues in poetics, morality, and biography are explorations without resolution; many of these unresolved questions become topoi in collective biography. The Romantics, for example, transformed the issue of translation and imitation into the question of originality and inspiration, took Johnson's comments on nature poetry as an argument for new canons, used the larger context of the subjectivity of perception to examine how objects derive color from the mind, and deduced from the special status of poets a pathology of art. Exploring new contact points between lives and works came to be the fundamental inquiry of Romantic biography and criticism, although equations between author and text remained as unsettled for the Romantics as they had been for Johnson. As Hazlitt observed, "The difficulty of forming almost any inference at all from what men *write* to what they *are,* constitutes the chief value of the problem which the literary biographer undertakes to solve."[53]

The Common Writer

Marginality, Audience, and the Literary Subculture

The relationship between lives and works is now the conventional preoccupation of literary biography. Rivaling the consideration of author and text in the *Lives of the Poets,* however, was the additional component of audience: in the *Lives,* the triangular relation of author, text, and audience represents the three determinants of literary meaning. Within the relation of author and text arose questions of intentionality, sincerity, and autobiographical modes of writing; the relation of text and audience introduced questions of shifting reception, canonical reputation, and abstract literary value; and the relation of audience and author brought forward the everyday toil of earning a literary living and locating a readership, as well as the larger question of the position of the writer in the culture. Through all this writers do partake of "the common condition of humanity" (*Idler* 102), but the *Lives* also suggests they occupy a particular subculture whose common circumstances remain timeless from generation to generation. Linked through its ongoing dialogue of poetics, generic convention, and textual cross-referencing, the community of artists also shares unchanging daily concerns: competitions, misfortunes, successes, struggles with patrons, booksellers, readers, and critics. The *Lives* provides a series of glimpses, like the disjunctive narrative of a Hogarthian sequence, that together comprise a collective portrait of the common experience of writers; and indirectly, through its illumination of the literary subculture, the *Lives of the Poets* sheds light on the common reader as well.

In the cumulative narrative of the *Lives,* writers drift out of their own biographies into the lives of others: Halifax surfaces in *Pope, Dryden, Smith, Stepney, Addison,* and *Congreve;* Sprat figures in *Cowley* and several other lives; Savage provides testimony in *Thomson* and *Pope;* Fenton assists in translations and receives commemorations; the testy friendships of Addison, Swift, Gay, and Pope interknit the lives; Pope's play, *Three Hours after Marriage,* and Prior's parody of Dryden, "Country Mouse and City Mouse," take on lives of their own as literary landmarks bobbing up throughout the *Lives.* Westminster School becomes a kind of nursery for poets: Richard Busby educates Stepney, John Philips, Dryden, Smith, Duke, King, Halifax, Rowe, and Prior; Cowley and Blackmore also attend; so common is the shared education that Sprat is named a significant exception. A program of secondary figures, who like Busby are without their own biographies, circumstantiate the intellectual milieu: Goldsmith is commemorated; Shiels and Collier are abused; Voltaire arrives to visit Pope and Congreve; Bolingbroke advises Pope, sits in the audience of *Cato,* is praised by Savage, and provides a deanery for Swift. The controversial laureateship of Cibber, the antagonism of Dennis, and the patronage under King William arise repeatedly. Wives, children, and parents are rarely detailed, but figures such as Cibber, Wycherley, Warburton, Steele, Tonson, and Arbuthnot enter the narrative so often that their characters materialize in the background. Writers commenting on one another yoke the lives: Gray on Shenstone, Swift on Addison, Prior on Dorset, Addison on Smith, Shenstone on Somerville, Congreve on Dryden, Smith on John Philips, Blackmore on Dryden, Fenton on Roscommon, Savage on Pope and Thomson, Pope on Prior, Tickell, Gay, and Fenton. The interconnections understandably culminate in the *Life of Pope,* the final biography written and the most elaborately cross-referenced.[54] Of the fifty-two authors biographied in the *Lives,* twenty-three figure in the *Life of Pope;* the life and achievements of Pope, in turn, touch nearly every biography and critical issue.[55]

The treatment of the familiar Johnsonian theme, the vanity of human wishes,[56] offers a good illustration of the common condition of humanity and the particular vulnerability of the literary subculture. In the *Lives,* disappointment, disease, mortality, and misfortune blast every achievement, every hoped-for leisure, every short-lived happiness—instead of silver linings, "Human happiness has always its abatements; the brightest sunshine of success is not without a cloud" (*Addison*).[57] The "luxurious indulgence of hope," as Johnson explains in *Rambler* 2, "however necessary to the production of every thing great or excellent," is a temptation to which writers are particularly susceptible. "Perhaps no class of the human species requires more to be cautioned against this anticipation of happiness, than those that aspire to the name of authors," Johnson warns. "Every catalogue of a library will furnish sufficient reason; as he will find it crouded with names of men, who, though now forgotten, were once no less enterprising or confident than himself, equally pleased with their own productions, equally caressed by their patrons, and flattered by their friends." The *Lives* offers an illustration of the forgotten catalogue of vanities, patrons, flattery, and forgotten achievements. Authorship is again the emblem of human futility in *Rambler* 106: "No place affords a more striking conviction of the vanity of human hopes, than a publick library; for who can see the wall crouded on every side by mighty volumes, the works of laborious meditation, and accurate enquiry, now scarcely known but by the catalogue." Indeed, their biographies may survive their works: "The learned often bewail the loss of ancient writers whose characters have survived their works; but, perhaps, if we could now retrieve them, we should find them only the Granvilles, Montagues, Stepneys, and Sheffields of their time, and wonder by what infatuation or caprice they could be raised to notice." What is Johnson's *Lives* some thirty years later but the commemoration of the blasted hopes of Granville, Halifax (Charles Montagu[e]), Stepney, and Sheffield?

The condition of poets illustrates the larger human predicament, the pathos of all human reputation—Henry Cromwell's reputation confined to the tye-wig, Pope's futile attempt to "dream of influence beyond his life"—but for writers in particular, the vanity of human hopes is more emphatically inscribed in the nature of the literary profession. Its preoccupation with the printed text and posterity is the sheer vanity of art in hoping to burst the temporality of human achievement. That Pope should be reduced to delirium near death was, as Pope himself declared, "a sufficient humiliation of the vanity of man," but more emphatically so for an author deprived of that which he took most pride in, the mastery of words. The humbler men of the *Lives,* however, are by no means the greater poets. The *Life of Milton* seems to suggest vanity is an inevitable characteristic (although no index) of literary greatness: Milton possesses the "usual concomitant of great abilities, a lofty and steady confidence in himself, perhaps not without some contempt of others."

Collecting the usual concomitants of great ability is one of the tasks of the *Lives*. Genius is one of its operative terms, and the biographies provide a series of illustrations or case studies that cumulatively posit a definition of genius. In this it is important to distinguish the *Lives* from the systematic post-Lockean philosophical exploration of genius common in the eighteenth century among authors such as Sharpe, Duff, and Gerard. That the discourse on genius was relevant to literary matters is evident in the writings of Joseph Warton, Addison, Young, and Reynolds, whose analyses of genius essentially shifted the moribund ancient-and-modern polemic to the question of what kinds of literary powers can prevail over time. Romantic writers including Coleridge, Hazlitt, Lamb, and D'Israeli were to consider new factors such as spontaneity, inspiration, imagination, and delirium.[58] In this vast dialogue on genius, Johnson's voice is significant because the *Lives of the Poets* introduced biography—in effect, case studies—as a form of methodological inquiry in the field of genius.

Johnson seems to have been more reluctant to bandy the term genius than his contemporaries. If we look at the 112 occurrences of the term genius in the *Lives,* twenty-four occur in the comments of others, leaving some ninety citations by Johnson himself: fourteen occur in *Pope,* fifteen in *Savage,* eight in *Addison,* six in *Milton,* and sixteen in *Dryden,* leaving only some thirty uses of the term distributed among the remaining forty-seven lives. In contrast to Edmund Smith, for example, whose short sketch of John Philips quoted in the *Lives* uses the term genius six times, Johnson uses the word sparingly—every poet does not possess genius.

Johnson's central explorations of the term coincide with the longer lives—five of the six longest lives concern themselves with the subject. Many of the lives do not make any mention of the term,[59] and many others make use of the term only to lament its absence—Gay lacked "the dignity of genius"; of Roscommon's reputation "all the proofs of this genius . . . are not sufficient to form a single book"; of West's writings, "the highest praise, the praise of genius, they cannot claim."

But what is the meaning of this "highest praise"? Johnson wrestled with the definition throughout his works. The *Dictionary* defines genius as "disposition of nature" and "superior faculties," suggesting factors of propensity and intellectual degree, but Johnson's conversation introduced additional factors of diligence and accident. Frances Reynolds recounts Johnson's declaration, " 'People are not born with a particular genius for particular employments or studies, for it would be like saying that a man could see a great way east, but could not west. It is good sense applied with diligence to what was at first a mere accident, and which, by great application, grew to be called, by the generality of mankind, a particular genius.'" Boswell quotes a similar image: "'The man who has vigour, may walk to the east, just as well as to the west, if he happens to turn his head that way,'" with the illustration, "'had Sir Isaac Newton applied to poetry, he would have made a very fine epick poem.'"[60] The eighteenth-century philosophical dialogue on genius was largely concerned with arguing the relative weight of these variables; Johnson's *Lives* provided a practical investigation through its illustrative examples of different lives.

In moving from the assertions of lexicography to the inferential task of the biographer, however, Johnson's writings increasingly question the power of words to encapsulate or explain poetic achievement. In the opening life, Cowley's reading of Spenser makes him irrecoverably a poet: "Such are the accidents, which, sometimes remembered, and perhaps sometimes forgotten, produce that particular designation of mind and propensity for some certain science or employment, which is commonly called Genius. The true Genius is a mind of large general powers, accidentally determined to some particular direction." These first comments on genius in the *Lives* paraphrase his earlier lexicographic constructs, but such definitions, and the possibility of making definitions, are cast into doubt over the course of the *Lives*.

The *Life of Pope,* for example, undercuts the idea of quantifiable categories by which we can assess genius. Pope commands the standard eighteenth-century features of genius ("Pope had, in proportions very nicely adjusted to each other, all the qualities that constitute genius. He had Invention . . . he had Imagination . . . he had Judgement . . . and he had colours of language always before him"), but these are not sufficient to attain, or account for, the highest poetic achievement: "Of genius, that power which constitutes a poet; that quality without which judgement is cold and knowledge is inert; that energy which collects, combines, amplifies, and animates—the superiority must, with some hesitation, be allowed to Dryden."

One might expect Johnson to censure instead of praise Dryden for verse which he says is incautious, "obeys the motions of his own mind," and rises "into inequalities." The qualities of individualism, and the organic metaphors which describe Dryden's genius—an "effusion" (*Dryden*) and a "natural field" (*Pope*)—are terms later spoken by the Romantics in highest praise of poems, as are the animating but undefinable concepts of "power" and "energy" which make the genius of Dryden superior to Pope.

These qualities enjoy cyclical praise; such valuations in some sense revive the seventeenth-century vogue for the Longinian *je ne sais quoi*. Like the rise of genre and critical trends, theories of literature are historically specific and their ascendance at any given time comments on larger cultural tendencies. Johnson's valuations of Dryden counter the dominant mechanistic models of the mind, just as his biographical methodology avoided the systemization of philosophical discourse. When telling Boswell a man might walk to the east or west, a Newton to physics or to poetry, Johnson rejected arguments put forth by Boswell that "'make mind mechanical,'" an anti-mechanism continued by the Romantics.[61]

In the *Lives* genius cannot be appraised by checklists of attributes; if one biography offers evidence in support of the diligence of genius, another attests to its accidents.[62] The definition of genius is inevitably tautologic: Thomson "thinks always as a man of genius"; Milton's poems have "evidence of genius" because the "highest praise of genius is original invention." Genius and original invention might be the "highest praise" in the *Lives,* but the greatest genius is often not reflected in actual accomplishments. The genius of Dryden (in whose biography Johnson most often introduces the term) flares up irregularly in unpredictable bursts of literary excellence; he as often "disgraces" and "abuses" his genius in inferior works. Savage and Collins are likewise examples of genius unfulfilled: without financial support, Savage was hobbled rather for "want of opportunities than genius"; Collins's imperfect critical abilities yielded works that only show the "character rather of his inclination than his genius." Johnson himself became the emblem of the conversationalist as an artist whose talk surpassed his writings—offering a model for Romantics such as De Quincey and Coleridge to fall back upon, and for D'Israeli to observe, "We find great men often greater than the books they write."[63] Genius defies identification not because it so often fails of perfection, but because it is the quality of perpetually searching for an inherently elusive perfection: the mind of genius is one which is "always endeavoring more than it can do" (*Pope*), striving for "ideal perfection which every genius born to excel is condemned always to pursue, and never overtake" (*Blackmore*). It is the error of humankind to "expect from elevated genius a uniformity of greatness." Genius exists independently of its intermittent achievements; the character of genius lies in its loftiest aspirations, and not necessarily its successes. For Johnson, to fathom genius (like the term originality for the Romantic) is to draw the leviathan with a fish-hook: genius must defy codification, it must resist definition, and in so doing, both fulfills and transgresses expectations.

By distinguishing writers as a literary subculture, the *Lives of the Poets* recognized the ambiguous position of artists as luminaries and outsiders. Read as a document in the history of cultural politics, Johnson's *Lives* serves as an indicator of the increasing marginalization of the artist.[64] Before Johnson, the most common and popular forms of collective biography since the early eighteenth century were lives of criminals.[65] Johnson's use of the genre for writers called attention to analogies between poets and criminals, as visionaries and outcasts who roam the margins of society.

The life of the poet Savage, who was tried for murder, appeared in both kinds of collective biographies, and was the most visible bridge between criminal and poetic biography in Johnson's *Lives*. Eighteenth-century fiction popularized the topos of the nobleman's bastard; and the image of the gentleman highwayman and the articulate housebreaker were configurations made common by criminal biography.[66] Savage readily mythologized his own life along these lines: the criminal poet is the mirror image of the gentleman criminal; the man who declared himself the unacknowledged son of the Countess of Macclesfield also titled himself "*Volunteer Laureat,*" to which Colley Cibber pointedly replied, "He might with equal propriety style himself a Volunteer Lord."

In Johnson's account, Savage is acquitted at his murder trial for his tongue rather than his innocence; recounting his eloquent speech in court, Johnson declares, "Applause could not be refused him." The question of Savage's impostures cannot be resolved here, but what Johnson says of Savage is true of all biography: "It was not easy to discover the truth." Johnson appears to have had no doubts of Savage's veracity in believing himself the son of the countess, and gives no clue to factual misgivings current even then. Johnson's details of the murder—"swords were drawn," rival testimony from a "strumpet," the belated mention of the setting in a "house of ill fame"—also favor Savage. The narrative of *Savage* epitomizes the problem of biographical subjectivity and the deceptive rhetoric of objectivity; the reader is the victim of the persuasiveness of the narrator. Applause might well be denied, if shifting perspective, we were shown a drunken altercation in a brothel and a strange man accused of murder who slanders and menaces a woman in her house.

The rhetoric of *Savage* inverts the accusation of crime. Savage is not a murderer, but the target of attempted murder: when his only hope lay in the mercy of the crown, his mother attempted to "take away" his life through calumniations to the queen. In recounting the slaying, the word crime is used only once, to depict Savage a victim rather than a perpetrator: "Both his fame and his life were endangered by an event, of which it is not yet determined whether it ought to be mentioned as a crime or a calamity." Johnson displaces not only the guilt but also the entire notion of criminality. In popular collections, Savage appeared among the criminals, but Johnson's *Savage* is an account of crimes against him and the entire injustice of the artist's position in society. The only crimes Savage is guilty of are literary ("Next to the crime of writing contrary to what he thought, was that of writing without thinking"). The true "crimes" lie in the hands of the society at large, the "crime of his parents" and the larger political crimes of cultural imperialism censured by Savage: "Crimes which have been generally committed by the discoverers of new regions . . . the enormous wickedness of making war upon barbarous nations because they cannot resist, and of invading countries because they are fruitful; of extending navigation only to propagate vice, and of visiting distant lands only to lay them to waste." Cultural imperialism exists in the global suppression of other nations and the domestic suppression of the poetic voice. The poet is an outsider, privileged to comment upon society, but frequently martyrized for it; when Savage indicts the crimes of the nation he is himself jailed.

Johnson's *Savage* chronicles the heroism of authors, not, as he says in *Idler* 84, the heroes of "the stratagems of war" or "fabled heroes, or the revolutions of a fairy region." Savage's life is an emblem for the heroic endurance of every artist: "The heroes of literary as well as civil history have been very often no less remarkable for what they have suffered than for what they have atchieved; and volumes have been written only to enumerate the miseries of the learned, and relate their unhappy lives and untimely deaths." Assailed by "misfortunes" caused by "the crimes of others," Savage heroically perseveres. In a hagiographic inversion, the criminal Savage of popular biography becomes a moral hero, who gives charity to the woman who testified against him at his trial: "This is an action which in some ages would have made a saint, and perhaps in others a hero." As Sartre was to do in *Saint Genet*,[67] Johnson equates criminal and artist; great art is the product of transgression of conventions in literature and in life.

Johnson's *Lives* joins the volumes he says "enumerate the miseries of the learned." Of all the kinds of suffering that describe the life of the artist in the *Lives,* none is more persistent than poverty. The opening line of the *Lives of the Poets* laments "the penury of English biography," a trope anticipating the motif of financial penury in the *Lives*. The poverty of Savage is such that he "suffered fewer hardships in prison than he had been accustomed to undergo in the greatest part of his life";[68] Otway endures "indigence" and lived and died "neglected"; of Butler, "all that can be told with certainty is, that he was poor." The insecure relation between Savage and Lord Tyrconnel (like Otway, Butler, and their patrons) is one of many warnings in the *Lives* against relying upon patronage and its "miseries of dependence." The abasing institution of patronage is imitated by the bookseller, who like a professional thief-taker or procurer encourages vice while profiting from it: "The learned and ingenious are often obliged to submit to very hard conditions, or to avarice, by which the booksellers are frequently incited to oppress that genius by which they are supported."[69] The poet less often writes to support vice than the institutions of patronage and publishing encourage abased writing.

Johnson's own experience of the Grub Street life and the caprice of patronage lies in the background of his prominent depiction of the literary marketplace in the *Lives*—a connection detected by Boswell, who modeled his account of Johnson's letter rejecting Lord Chesterfield's sponsorship of the *Dictionary* on Johnson's account of Pope's letter declining Halifax's patronage.[70] The financial motive of writing is a subject of ambivalence in the *Lives*. Although Johnson told Boswell, "No man but a blockhead ever wrote, except for money," and asserted, "Nothing excites a man to write but necessity" (when asked if he would write *"con amore"* after the *Dictionary*),[71] he recognized that the life of a writer was an ambiguous calling, acknowledging tacitly, as D'Israeli declared explicitly, that the life of literature has "despite its handicaps, still an allure."[72] If the life of a writer is not glamorous, the negotiation between subsistence and posterity still could be conducted with dignity. Savage squanders money, but Dryden, Milton, and Pope are worse in their use of servile flattery to earn it. It is to Dryden's discredit that literature is "his trade rather than his pleasure," and his many paltry works are the result: "Writing merely for money [he] was contented to get it by the nearest way." Johnson allows to Savage what he denies to Dryden, the excuse that poverty "blasted his genius." In analyzing the impact of money on Dryden's poetry, Johnson declines to say that financial rewards will automatically demean or benefit the production of art: "Poverty, like other rigid powers, is sometimes too hastily accused. If the excellence of Dryden's works was lessened by his indigence, their number was increased; and I know not how it will be proved, that if he had written less he would have written better; or that indeed he would have undergone the toil of an author, if he had not been solicited by something more pressing than the love of praise." No deterministic formula governs the production of art.

The condition of the writer in the Johnsonian world is inescapably one of financial insecurity. The obsolete Renaissance courtier poet who disdained a professional writing career had been replaced by the nonaristocratic professional author whose literary life was inextricably bound up with issues of audience, popularity, and the marketplace. Having himself rejected the intellectual parasitism of Lord Chesterfield, Johnson readily detected the ephemeral praise bestowed upon the poet lords of his age. In the *Lives,* the poverty and failed struggles of authors are more ennobling than the dabbling of lords. Three of the four poets whose fading reputations illustrate the vanity of literary hopes in the library catalogue of *Rambler* 106 are titled poets—Granville, Halifax, and Sheffield.[73] If poverty is an impediment, though not an excuse for bad verse, luxury cannot automatically produce a good poet. As Johnson proclaimed he would write the life of a dunce and "*say* he was a dunce," he would as equally write the life of a lord and say he was called a poet through the "servility of adulation" and the "bubbles of artificial fame."

Johnson's contempt of the literary servility of readers toward aristocratic poetasters may be in part a response to works such as Horace Walpole's reverential *Catalogue of the Royal and Noble Authors,* a paean to the hereditary genius of the aristocracy, which Walter Scott dismissed with the remark, "It would be difficult, by any process or principle of subdivision, to select a list of as many plebeian authors, containing so very few whose genius was worthy of a commemoration."[74] Johnson was especially critical of writers who flattered the poetic aspirations of noblemen in hopes of preferment—"Many a blandishment was practised upon Halifax which he would never have known, had he no other attractions than those of his poetry." The case of Pope's breadwinning translations provides several examples of intellectual parasitism among potential patrons: Halifax appears "'a pretender to taste'" who thought Pope's *Iliad* "a lucky opportunity of securing immortality," and Lord Oxford a trifler who "lamented that such a genius should be wasted upon a work not original; but proposed no means by which he might live without it" (the power of the purse in turn brings out the opportunism of Pope, who compiles the notes "with the assistance of his mercenaries" whom he has hired on the basis of those "who would do much work for little money"). Johnson was equally impatient with the critical pretensions of the aristocracy and the readers who admire writers on the basis of their rank. Johnson approvingly quotes Gray's assessment of the widespread fame of Shaftesbury: "'You say you cannot conceive how lord Shaftesbury came to be a philosopher in vogue; I will tell you: first, he was a lord. . . .'"[75] Offering a reminder of the literary catalogue of forgotten poetic lords, Gray concludes, "'An interval of above forty years has pretty well destroyed the charm. A dead lord ranks [but] with commoners.'"

The ambivalent view of audience in the *Lives* reflects the shifting economic base of literature. In an era when the patronage of the individual aristocrat had been replaced by the patronage of multiple subscribers, booksellers, and a growing middle-class audience, the problem of defining audience was matched with the difficulty of addressing one. Is audience a question of "we" as in *Addison,* where Johnson observes, "We love better to be pleased than to be taught"? Is it a question of "they," an alien tribunal, as in *Savage,* where Johnson remarks on the folly of an author ignoring his audience—Savage "paid due deference to the suffrages of mankind when they were given in his favour" but did not find "any thing sacred in the voice of the people when they were inclined to censure him"? Is it a question of the writer bewildered by an intellectually diverse audience (Johnson curtails his discussion of Pope's translations, saying, "I am not writing only to poets and philosophers"), making concessions to uneducated masses (Thomson was reproved by his professor of divinity for "speaking language unintelligible to a popular audience"), or communicating with a trained intellectual elite (Johnson disparages Pope's empty boast, "'I have the town, that is, the mob, on my side'")? Are critics and readers at odds, as Johnson suggests in saying, "Pitt pleases the criticks, and Dryden the people"? Or does the reader look to critics for guidance, as Johnson says of the *Dunciad,* the critics having "declared their approbation of the plan, the common reader began to like it without fear"?

As early as *Rambler* 2, Johnson had discussed the fickleness of the public: he cautions writers that "fame by writing, solicits the regard of a multitude fluctuating in pleasures . . . prepossessed by passions . . . corrupted by prejudices . . . indolent . . . envious . . . unwilling to be taught. . . . The learned are afraid to declare their opinion early, lest they should put their reputation in hazard; the ignorant always imagine themselves giving some proof of delicacy when they refuse to be pleased." The concluding words of the essay, "He that finds his way to reputation, through all these obstructions, must acknowledge that he is indebted to other causes besides his industry, his learning, or his wit," left in abeyance these "other causes," until some thirty years later the inquiry of the *Lives* elaborated the problematic relation between author and audience. The courtship of audience raises troubling questions: Are its opinions antagonistic or ultimately correct? Does the author write for "fit though few" or a mass readership? To what extent does its financial support influence art? As with other controversies, instead of resolving the puzzle of author and audience, the *Lives* multiplied its implications for audience and text, critic and canon, poet and society, high and low culture.

Johnson's most famous comment on the subject of audience is the closing observation of *Gray,* lines that were particularly prominent in the first edition of the *Lives* where they were positioned in the final paragraph of the final life. Speaking in praise of the "Elegy Written in a Country Church-yard," Johnson says,

> I rejoice to concur with the common reader; for by the common sense of readers uncorrupted with literary prejudices, after all the refinements of subtilty and the dogmatism of learning, must be finally decided all claim to poetical honours.

Who is the common reader so blithely attributed to Johnson by Virginia Woolf in the epigraph of her volume of essays *The Common Reader*?[76] Woolf's book did much to promote the fame of the phrase. But the circumscribed portrait of the audience Woolf describes in the Preface is more her own notion than Johnson's. Woolf's common reader—less educated than critic and scholar, "hasty, inaccurate, and superficial," and praised for it—reflects her own patrician audience more than the inquiries of Johnson's *Lives*.

Johnson's portrait of the common reader, like the common writer, is a complicated mosaic. Audience is not a univocal concept in the *Lives,* and the common reader has changing implications: in one sense it is a pejorative leveling, in another it represents the patient test of time, in yet another, it suggests the promulgation of commonsense critical standards. The common reader in Johnson is in part the new audience of commoners, but it is not entirely a question of rank, nor does it necessarily imply mediocrity or mass culture. In saying that Pope resists using the annotations of Anne Dacier's contemporary translation of Homer because "no man loves to be indebted to his contemporaries, and Dacier was accessible to common readers," Johnson is registering a level of erudition short of antiquarianism, but nonetheless still far from accessibility in the sense of popular culture.

In choosing the term common reader, Johnson is reentering his dialogue with Cibber's *Lives,* where the term appears at the beginning of Cibber's *Life of Pomfret:*

> This Gentleman's works are held in very great esteem by the common readers of poetry; it is thought as unfashionable amongst people of inferior life, not to be possessed of the poems of Pomfret, as among persons of taste not to have the works of Pope in their libraries. The subjects upon which Pomfret wrote were popular, his versification is far from being unmusical, and as there is little force of thinking in his writings, they are level to the capacities of those who admired them.

Cibber's term "common readers" is interchangeable with "people of inferior life," a category mutually exclusive with "persons of taste." Where Cibber voices the contempt of Hamlet, "Ay, Madam, it is common," in dismissing the "capacities" of the common reader, Johnson's term has none of the condescension or class implications of Cibber. So close himself to having been "of inferior life," Johnson always presupposes the potential for cultural improvement. Even at his most dismissive, Johnson attributes to the common reader a voluntarily untutored judgment. Thus for Johnson, Pomfret "has been always the favorite of that class of readers, who, without vanity or criticism, seek only their own amusement." The larger deficiencies are finally Pomfret's: "He pleases many, and he who pleases many must have some species of merit." In contrast to the achievement of Shakespeare, whose "just representations of general nature,"

Johnson tells us in the Preface to his edition, "please many, and please long," the achievement of Pomfret is considerably more reserved.

One of the reasons Johnson may have volunteered Pomfret was to include a specimen of a popular author as part of providing a complete spectrum of the condition of literary England. Striving for a popular audience is not necessarily the solution to the financial perils of authorship if it sacrifices merit. That "class of readers" who admire Pomfret is unreliable, since they "seek only their own amusement"; a work appealing only to novelty is "a kind of artifice" and will soon be laid down (*Butler*); works "which owe their reputation to the character of the writer" (*Granville*) and those reliant only on the current popularity of an author "must soon give way, as the succession of things produces new topicks of conversation and other modes of amusement" (*Mallet*). Johnson was skeptical of the transitory judgments of a "publick" whose interest is predicated on amusement, novelty, or celebrity, and he was often exasperated at the inability of readers to judge literary merit; the public is gullible in its praise of lords, willing to bestow praise too carelessly, inclined to a lethargy that ignores new achievement. Savage learns "the folly of expecting that the publick should judge right," and conversely of Stepney we learn, "One cannot always easily find the reason for which the world has sometimes conspired to squander praise."[77]

If Johnson ridicules Dryden for his "servile submission to an injudicious audience," he scorns Pope for superciliously trying to dupe readers through concealed publishing stratagems. Mere submission to the popular judgment is to pursue an abased esteem, and any writer who attempts to please a popular audience must pay the price: "When the end is to please the multitude, no man perhaps has a right . . . to throw the whole blame upon his judges" (*Cowley*).[78] Yet there is a pervasive optimism in the *Lives* that posterity will vindicate literary genius and a critical common sense will triumph—as Johnson says in *Addison*, "About things on which the public thinks long it commonly attains to think right." Thus it is wiser to do as Milton does, await the "impartiality" of time, than as Dryden and Settle do, place their happiness "in the claps of multitudes."

Johnson extends the same warnings to critics who encourage superficial understanding; he objects to the "easy and safe conveyance of meaning" through which Addison made Milton a "universal favourite, with whom readers of every class think it necessary to be pleased." The duty of the critic is to educate, not to level. When he says in *Dryden*, "Minds are not levelled in their powers but when they are first levelled in their desires," Johnson has in mind the critical education of common readers as much as common writers. One of the tasks of the *Lives* is a vindication of criticism as a means of educating judgment: by reversing the penury of biography, advancing the discussion of poetics, and advising the institutions of literature.

Even more than the author, the critic is destined to find an ungrateful audience, and more likely to sink into oblivion. Johnson defends the responsibilities of critics even when their adversaries are poets. Pope's critical attack on the Dunces is valid, despite its malice, for "If bad writers were to pass without reprehension what should restrain them?"; but Johnson censures Pope when he learned to recite "the cant of an author, and began to treat criticks with contempt, though he had yet suffered nothing from them." Held in contempt by authors and taken for granted by common readers, the *Lives* confers dignity upon the unsung critical occupation. Dennis in *Addison,* Collier in *Congreve,* and Milbourne ("styled by Pope 'the fairest of criticks'") in *Dryden* are all credited with importance and given a place in literary history for their endeavors to improve literature. Johnson's sympathy for the thankless task of criticism annuls his individual disputes with his predecessors. Critics have the responsibility of training the literary taste, and having done so, their contributions are carelessly forgotten. He laments of Addison's reputation as a critic, "It is not uncommon for those who have grown wise by the labour of others to add a little of their own, and overlook their masters," and remarks on the ingratitude toward Dryden's critical pioneering, "Learning once made popular is no longer learning: it has the appearance of something which we have bestowed upon ourselves, as the dew appears to rise from the field which it refreshes."

In this Johnson forecasted his own reputation among the Romantics, who in imitating the *Lives,* adopted the genre he revived, appropriated the issues he drew attention to, and sought to usurp his autocracy. Like Johnson overturning the critical judgments of the preceding generations in the canon of the *Lives,* the Romantics share with each new generation what Johnson names Dryden's "favourite pleasure of discrediting his predecessors." Styling theirs the "Age of Criticism,"[79] the Romantics paid Johnson the compliment of imitating him even as they anathematized him.

Chapter III

The Romantic Agenda:
Johnson and the Romantic Canon

In an era when parties of pilgrims were arriving daily at Abbotsford and Rydal Mount, when Byron's reputation derived as much from his person as his poetry, literary biography possessed wider critical and cultural impact than ever before. Yet running counter to the new popular enthusiasm for biographical speculation was a streak of opposition from potential subjects of biography, who viewed the post-Johnsonian trend with uneasiness and dislike. Johnson's prominence, both as a biographer and a subject of biography, had made the lives of artists irretrievably public. Literary biography was no longer the task of occasional authors and a literary sideline for Grub Street denizens, but a mainstream genre for established writers and a standard critical enterprise. Only an authorized biographer or an authorized destruction could hope to deter or preclude the disquieting spectre of posthumous biographical scrutiny. For many Victorian literary figures, rampant Romantic biographical speculation in the wake of Johnson represented an unpleasant prospect; in consequence, Thackeray and Arnold forbade authorized biographies, Dickens burned correspondence, and George Eliot denounced biography as "a disease of English literature." The experience of Jane Welsh Carlyle typifies the new biographical consciousness: Darwin inquired who would write her husband's life, and she herself said of one of her husband's insincere letters, "It will read charmingly in your biography."[1]

A century earlier John Arbuthnot had proclaimed that the prospect of posthumous biography added "new terrors" to death.[2] Johnson himself burned some of his documents; and while he suggested Boswell write a journal, he also assumed Boswell would "surely have a friend who would burn it."[3] Twentieth-century cultural centrism has blamed the nineteenth century for encouraging a retrogressive suppression of information in the name of decorum, but as Robert Folkenflik observes, "All of the Victorian arguments for suppression were adumbrated in the later eighteenth century."[4] At the same time, the Johnson who said "all truth is valuable"

(*Pope*) provided the justification for dismantling conventional restraints of decorum. Although Johnson's critical assessments were often resented in the early nineteenth century, it was Boswell who was held up as the emblem of biographical indecorum. Boswell's name quickly became eponymic for iconoclastic detail in biography, reproached for what the *English Review* called the "voracity of the anecdote-hunter" which debased and injured its subjects ("the veil which human weakness requires has been wantonly drawn aside"). To Boswellize was to pry, quote too often, and reveal too unscrupulously. Yet well before Boswell, Mason had been accused of overstepping decorum in his *Life of Gray* and criticized for "vulgarisms." Piozzi's *Anecdotes* of Johnson also won accusations of prying, including Horace Walpole's disapproving assessment, "Almost every fact that she relates disgraces him." Even Boswell, feeling the ridicule and outrage generated by the *Hebrides* tour, promised greater reserve in the *Life*.[5]

Arguments in favor of biographical plurality, that truth was elusive and any one biography inevitably incomplete, were appropriated by opponents of biography attempting to suppress investigation. The assertion that it was impossible to make a biography accurate often masked the fear that it just might be too accurate. Despite or perhaps because of his biographical research, Freud revealingly wrote an aspiring biographer, "I am alarmed by the threat that you want to become my biographer. . . . Anyone who writes a biography is committed to lies, concealments, hypocrisies, flattery, and even to hiding his own lack of understanding, for biographical truth does not exist, and if it did it could not be used. Truth is unobtainable." Although he follows many predecessors in purporting to denounce panegyric (while revealing his alarm at the "threat" of biographical iconoclasm), Freud may be the only subject to complain that his biography might be too flattering.[6]

The cultural symbolism of biography has never lost its memorial function. The biographer remains the custodian of reputation, whose disinterring of information treads the anthropological boundary of desecration of the dead. The illustrative quotation from Addison in Johnson's *Dictionary* entry on biographer alludes ironically to this generic burden: "'Our Grubstreet *biographers* watch for the death of a great man like so many undertakers, on purpose to make a penny of him.'" In deference to its epitaphic associations, Romantic biography often placed fidelity to reputation above factual fidelity—minimizing, for example, Johnson's tics,

Burns's vice, Scott's dotage.[7] Yet many biographers in the Romantic era rebelled by turning to biographies of the living where, unencumbered by epitaphic obligations (although risking litigation even then), generic conventions of form and decorum could be subverted or dismantled.

The first section of this chapter will explore the lingering ambivalence toward biography amid the rapidly accelerating climate of biographical curiosity, examining writers who tried to subdue post-Johnsonian speculation on the links between life and works, even though many of their literary works encouraged it. The second section will look closely at writers who adopted Johnsonian collective biography as a genre of critical assertion in order to rewrite or refute the canon of Johnson's *Lives*.

Adding a New Terror to Death: The Lives of the Romantic Poets

Scott, Wordsworth, Burns, Coleridge, Byron

Although widespread interest in frank biographies of authors followed Johnson and Boswell's removal of the idealizing veil, many literary figures resisted the new trends. Byron alone among the poets might be said to have unstintingly courted such publicity. Prospective subjects of biography (and in the wake of Johnson and Boswell, literary figures became especially vigilant), along with their relatives and authorized biographers, denounced the avant-garde view of biography as a genre accepting and encouraging violations of domestic privacy. That Johnson emerged unscathed did not lessen the alarm of literary figures that they might be represented as other than invulnerably heroic. The customary safeguard arose of naming as biographer a friend or relative whose dutiful stance and admiration was assured and whose appointment as authorized biographer, if it could not prevent, could at least discredit, any prospective Boswell who might rise up among the acquaintances.

John Gibson Lockhart provides a good example of the nervous critical metamorphosis of literary figures who found their opposition to biographical candor increasing as proximity to such tasks neared. Lockhart initially praised Boswell at the time of reviewing Croker's 1831 edition of the *Life*, but it was yet a year before he would be appointed authorized biographer in the will of his father-in-law, Walter Scott. Although Lockhart's lengthy *Life of Scott* (1837–38) followed the tradition of Mason and

Boswell in "making use, whatever possible, of his own letters and di-aries . . . to let the character develop itself," he announced his refusal to "*Boswellize*" Scott by providing "any detailed record of Scott's familiar talk," and declined all offers of personal reminiscences.[8]

Ironically, despite his denunciation of the Boswellian method, Lock-hart was widely credited with the distinction of having written the sequel to Boswell. The kinship is chiefly length rather than the characteristic Boswellian minutiae and conversational record; and regardless of his disclaimers, Lockhart was criticized for attempting to "dishero Scott" with the same disloyal prying hitherto attributed to Boswell, Piozzi, and Mason.[9]

Henry Nelson Coleridge similarly scorned to Boswellize his uncle and father-in-law in recording his *Table Talk of the late Samuel Taylor Coleridge* (1835), saying, "this volume lays no claim to be ranked with those of Boswell in point of dramatic interest."[10] In contrast to Lockhart's avoid-ance of Boswellian conversation, the popular Romantic genre of "Table Talk" decontextualized conversation altogether from biography, celebrat-ing it as a fragmentary and spontaneous effusion of thought. Unlike Boswell, who boasted that Goldsmith "said I have a method of making people speak,"[11] H. N. Coleridge disparaged the role of active interlocu-tor and refused to undertake the Boswellian choreographing of meetings between Coleridge and visitors: "Although I have been present in mixed company, where Mr. Coleridge has been questioned and opposed, and the scene has been amusing for the moment—I own that it was always much more delightful to me to let the river wander at its own sweet will, unruffled by aught but a certain breeze of emotion which the stream itself produced." For the Romantic transcriber, conversation becomes an aeo-lian harp of the intellect, best allowed to play on its own.

Scott himself provides a convenient example of a prominent Romantic writer who, like Southey and others, met his many expenses by writing conservative second-generation biographies. Although he was willing to fulfill the demand for biography in the post-Johnsonian age, he was reluctant to set any radical narrative precedent for his future biographers. Scott's autobiographical fragment (printed by Lockhart at the beginning of his biography) discourages popular biographical curiosity and guard-edly summarizes his life: "The present age has discovered a desire, or rather a rage, for literary anecdote and private history, that may be well permitted to alarm one who has engaged in a certain degree the attention of the public. . . . I may therefore be permitted, without an extraordinary degree of vanity, to take the precaution of recording a few leading circumstances (they do not merit the name of events) of a very quiet and uniform life—that, should my literary reputation survive my temporal existence, the public may know from good authority all that they are entitled to know of an individual who has contributed to their amusement."[12] Scott's precautionary autobiography uses the modesty topos to delimit what the public is "entitled to know" of literary figures. Yet the biographical scrutiny of literary figures proliferating in the wake of Johnson and Boswell was abetted by regional references in the works of writers such as Scott, Wordsworth, and Byron, which encouraged a new form of biographical tourism to literary sites.

Scott's emphasis on his own "quiet and uniform life" belies an interest in detaching himself from what were becoming increasingly common assumptions about the eccentricities and marginality of the writer: "From the lives of some poets a most important moral lesson may doubtless be derived, and few sermons can be read with so much profit as the Memoirs of Burns, of Chatterton, or of Savage. Were I conscious of anything peculiar in my own moral character which could render such development necessary or useful, I would as readily consent to it as I would bequeath my body to dissection, if the operation could tend to point out the nature and the means of curing any peculiar malady." Omitting mention of his lameness, Scott acknowledges that the proclivity toward "peculiar" tendencies in the "moral character" is associated with great talent. Scott is ready to decline the title of artist to spare himself such biographical investigations: were he to have any "malady" like Burns, Chatterton, or Savage, he would willingly "bequeath" his body to biographical "dissection," but "as I have not been blessed with the[ir] talents . . . I have been happily exempted from the influence of their violent passions."[13]

Behind Scott's medical metaphor resides Wordsworth's "we murder to dissect"; and in the closing pages of *Scott,* Lockhart conspicuously echoes both in reasserting his own refusal to "'peep and botanize'" on Scott's life. Just as the prosopopoeia of the tombstone in "A Poet's Epitaph" denounces posthumous prying into literary works,[14] the epitaphic voice of Scott in the autobiography justified Lockhart's biographical recalcitrance.

Wordsworth's own writings on the theory of biography repeatedly declare the irrelevancy of biographical documentation in understanding works of literature. Yet Wordsworth's conservative biographical theories contradict his reliance on avowedly autobiographical materials in his published poems, his evocation of regional scenery, and his emphasis on the sincerity of first-person narrative voice, all of which effectually encourage the investigation of life and works which he later sought to deter. Indeed, *The Prelude*'s documentation of the relation between life and works indicates much common ground with literary biography on a theoretical level, and Wordsworth's expression "The Child is Father of the Man" is paraphrased in many Romantic texts as a biographical principle for analyzing childhood.[15]

The equation between epitaph and biography that arises throughout Wordsworth's writings is also one that arose in Johnson's *Lives,* but his insistence that "Silence is a privilege of the grave" in his longest statement on biography, *A Letter to a Friend of Robert Burns* (1816), directly countermands Johnson's encouragement of literary biography:

> The general obligation upon which I have insisted, is especially binding upon those who undertake the biography of *authors.* Assuredly, there is no cause why the lives of that class of men should be pried into with the same diligent curiosity, and laid open with the same disregard of reserve, which may sometimes be expedient in composing the history of men who have borne an active part in the world. Such thorough knowledge of the good and bad qualities of these latter, as can only be obtained by a scrutiny of their private lives, conduces to explain not only their own public conduct, but that of those with whom they have acted. Nothing of this applies to authors, considered merely as authors. Our business is with their books,—to understand and to enjoy them. And, of poets more especially, it is true—that, if their works be good, they contain within themselves all that is necessary to their being comprehended and relished.

Wordsworth hints at the merits of a doctrine of suppression, although after Johnson's precedent in the *Lives* and in the *Life,* poets could no longer expect to lead private lives. With the same futility of Scott, Wordsworth denies there should be any particular interest in literary biography, by arguing for the self-sufficiency of literary texts. In Burns's case, since his personal life has already been obtruded upon the texts, Wordsworth recommends a delineation of the extent of the vice ("it is a disgraceful feature of the times that this measure should be necessary") while insisting on the primacy of the poems: "Copy the example which Mason has given in his second edition of Gray's works. . . . the poems are placed first; and the rest takes its place as subsidiary to them."[16]

Paradoxically, Wordsworth's prose strives to deter the biographical speculations encouraged by the personal and regional references of his poetry. Declarations and annotations affixed to his poems attested to the biographical and autobiographical fidelity of his own works—culminating in the extensive notes dictated to Isabella Fenwick in 1843. In naming "poets more especially" in his dictum, "Our business is with their books,—to understand and to enjoy them," Wordsworth not only discourages biographical approaches to his own poetic texts, he posits a valuative scale of literary merit based on exclusion of extrinsic meanings: "If their works be good, they contain within themselves all that is necessary." Many subsequent writers similarly urged the self-sufficiency of texts; Tennyson declared, "What business has the public to want to know all of Byron's wildnesses? He has given them fine work, and they ought to be satisfied." Byron's sensational wildness was to his biographers what Burns had been earlier in the century, and presumably what Savage had been to the generation before.[17]

Although not especially well-known today, the *Letter to a Friend of Robert Burns* drew considerable attention in literary circles, hardly surprising in the "age of personality" when many writers earned money recounting anecdotes of the famous. Hazlitt denounced Wordsworth's essay as "the dullest and most contemptible prose-composition in the language," and later faulted Wordsworth for not taking the opportunity to defend Burns rather than criticize his biography.[18] Lockhart expresses amazement at the narrowness of Wordsworth's position. He quotes the above passage on literary biography and more, exclaiming at Wordsworth's resistance to the biography of "*authors*," and inquiring what statesman's life, given a biography with "Boswellian fidelity," could be of as much interest as that of a writer such as Johnson.[19]

Wordsworth goes beyond Scott in his acknowledgment that the poet has a dispensation from ordinary norms of behavior: "Permit me to remind you that it is the privilege of poetic genius to catch, under certain restrictions of which perhaps at the time of its being exerted it is but dimly conscious, a spirit of pleasure wherever it can be found." Under this special status, the "poet, trusting to primary instincts, luxuriates among the felicities of love and wine." Despite the artistic proclivity toward such indulgence, Wordsworth argues that the illustration of vice in a poet's biography ("this extrinsic knowledge") deducts from "the intrinsic efficacy of his poetry—to please, and to instruct!" Johnson, speaking of Savage, had said that an author after death "ceases to influence mankind in any other character" than through his works. But where Johnson illustrates the "usual concomitant[s] of great ability" in the *Lives,* Wordsworth allows no curiosity about the traits of genius. Were an illustration of vice to add, "which it does not, to our better understanding of human nature and human life," it would only be to confirm ("we needed not those communications to inform us") what we already know: "that genius is not incompatible with vice, and that vice leads to misery—the more acute from the sensibilities which are the elements of genius." Wordsworth assumes the elements of genius imply acute sensibility and certain sensory eccentricities, and in excusing Burns for yielding to certain immoderate "impulses of nature" under which the artist must operate unrestricted, the intemperance of authors is acknowledged in a manner not dissimilar to De Quincey's conclusion that Wordsworth himself was a man of "special infirmity and special strength," Shelley's comment that the poet is "more delicately organized than other men, and sensible to pain and pleasure," and Johnson's view of Savage as "a man equally distinguished by his virtues and vices; and at once remarkable for his weaknesses and abilities." As Ernst Kris was to observe in the twentieth century, the artist is always a target of ambivalence because of the special license that accompanies the creative freedom of the artist.[20]

Wordsworth is unwilling, however, to allow the biographical documentation of this artistic license, a chronicle in which the life may not be in moral concord with the works. Johnson called attention to the frequent "striking contrariety between the life of an author and his writings" wherein "a man writes much better than he lives" (*Rambler* 14); but while the *Lives* explored the continuities and discontinuities between life and works, Wordsworth rejected such biographical explorations as inessential to the text and even detrimental. Yet contradictions boil beneath the surface of the essay. The conduct of the poet seems not to matter when reading classical epic or Shakespearian tragedy (it is unlikely to occur to us "whether the authors of these poems were good or bad men"), whereas other texts depend on equating poet and poem: the works of authors such as Burns rely "upon the familiar knowledge which they convey of the personal feelings of their authors. . . . Neither the subjects of his poems, nor his manner of handling them, allow us long to forget their author." Yet in reading these, Wordsworth prohibits any biographical constructions beyond the favorable simulacra created within the poems. Of the fostering of such illusory poetic myths, Johnson complained to Edmond Malone, "We have had too many honeysuckle lives of Milton."[21]

Yet on the technical practice of writing biography, Wordsworth's insight into the misleading impersonations of the first-person voice concurs with Johnson's verdict on the unreliability of letters to discern character. On interpreting correspondence, he warns,

> Little progress had been made (nor is it likely that, by the mass of mankind, much ever will be made) in determining what portion of these confidential communications escapes the pen in courteous, yet often innocent compliance— to gratify the several tastes of correspondents; and as little toward distinguishing opinions and sentiments uttered for the momentary amusement of the writer's own fancy, from those which his judgment deliberately approves, and his heart faithfully cherishes.

Moreover, Wordsworth's complaint that James Currie's 1800 biography presented masses of "ill-selected" and unanalyzed correspondence ("We have the author's letters discharged upon us in showers; but how few readers will take the trouble of comparing those letters with each other, and with the other documents of the publication, in order to come at a genuine knowledge of the writer's character!") reflects a growing trend against biographical compilations in the manner of Mason and Boswell.

Wordsworth especially objects to Boswell's indecorum, which disrupted "many pre-existing delicacies" only to afford "the British public an opportunity of acquiring experience, which before it had happily wanted."[22] Boswell's record of Johnson's daily manners is inferior to the "tact" of the ancients who wrote few memorials, believing the poems communicate all we need to know of their poets. Wordsworth would not "rejoice" were he to hear that records of Horace and his contemporaries "composed upon the Boswellian plan, had been unearthed among the ruins of Herculaneum": "I should dread to disfigure the beautiful ideal of the memories of those illustrious persons with incongruous features, and to sully the imaginative purity of their classical works with gross and trivial recollections." Wordsworth's opposition to disfiguring "the beautiful ideal" revives the notion of hagiographic idealization; moreover, the strange anomaly of Wordsworth citing classical precedent is additionally bewildering because ancient biography customarily used literary works as emblematic evidence for incidents in the authors' lives (a practice imitated by Romantic biographers and critics such as Campbell and De Quincey, who searched the works of authors such as Shakespeare for plausible biographical evidence and emblematic episodes).

Like Wordsworth's essay, Coleridge's *Biographia Literaria,* published the following year (1817), similarly dispraises extrinsic theories of art that go beyond the literary text to the author: "As soon as the critic betrays, that he knows more of his author, than the author's publications could have told him; as soon as from this more intimate knowledge, elsewhere obtained, he avails himself. . . . He ceases to be a CRITIC, and takes on him the most contemptible character to which a rational creature can be degraded, that of a gossip, backbiter, and pasquillant."[23] Accordingly, Coleridge does not refer to unpublished poems when he assesses Wordsworth.

Yet frequently implicit in the *Biographia* are author-based criteria; Coleridge remarks that works offer a "test of the artist's merit" and he considers "Mr. Southey's works and character" together.[24] Like the contradictions evident between Wordsworth's theory and practice, the very project of writing a book of criticism subtitled *Biographical Sketches of My Literary Life and Opinions* invites autobiographical speculations even as it argues against them. In responding to the earlier inquiries of Wordsworth's Prefaces ("What is poetry? is so nearly the same question with, what is a poet? that the answer to the one is involved in the solution of the other") the *Biographia* offers a new post-Johnsonian redefinition of "poetic genius" based on the individual poet's possession of the "magical power" of imagination.[25]

At several points Coleridge directly engages the existing dialogue on biographical theory. He declares there is "an analogy between genius and virtue,"[26] and turns to "the records of biography" to refute the Horatian convention of the *genus irritabile vatum*. "The men of the greatest genius, as far as we can judge from their own works or from the accounts of their contemporaries, appear to have been of calm and tranquil temper," Coleridge asserts, citing as evidence the temperaments of Chaucer, Shakespeare, Spenser, and Milton, which he infers from their works.[27] His Romantic argument in favor of publishing correspondence ("What literary man has not regretted the prudery of Spratt [*sic*] in refusing to let his friend Cowley appear in his slippers and dressing gown?") legitimizes letters, like other fragmentary and informal texts, as literary artifacts to be read alongside "more finished works."[28]

Coleridge's writings, like Wordsworth's, betray an ambivalence about the biographical dimension of art. An enthusiasm for personal and autobiographical art forms conflicts with the privacy Coleridge urges for "the Closet and the Library" in his essay "A Prefatory Observation on Modern Biography" from *The Friend* (1810), where the biographer is depicted as an idoloclast.[29] Biographical "inquisitiveness" and "worthless curiosity" are one and the same; the biographer abases the "departed Great" with the "crime" of "vulgar scandal" and anecdotes that are misapprehended "by men of weak minds" who relate them "as incorrectly, as they were noticed injudiciously."

Bacon's declaration that the histories of grand public actions are complemented by biographies illustrating the inward springs of life[30] has been misused, according to Coleridge, and "more than once served as an excuse and authority for huge volumes of biographical minutiae, which render the real character almost invisible, like clouds of dust on a Portrait, or the counterfeit frankincense which smoke-blacks the favourite idol of a catholic Village." Coleridge, like Wordsworth, objects not to idolatry but to the false frankincense of trivializing biography that disfigures an idealized portrait: "To scribble Trifles even on the perishable glass of an Inn window, is the mark of an Idler; but to engrave them on the Marble Monument, sacred to the memory of the departed Great, is something worse than Idleness." The epitaphic term "Marble Monument" implies a colossal textual significance in the "great end" and "spirit of genuine Biography," but its actual characteristics are never delineated. Although Coleridge concedes it is "the duty of an honest Biographer, to pourtray the prominent imperfections as well as excellencies of his Hero," like Wordsworth he questions its usefulness: "I am at a loss to conceive, how this can be deemed an excuse for heaping together a multitude of particulars, which can prove nothing of any man that might not have been safely taken for granted of all men." Coleridge's comment purports to place individual idiosyncrasy above general traits, but actually resists the characteristically Romantic use of biography to explore the individual human mind, and only begrudgingly acknowledges the dominant biographical interests of the age: "In the present age (emphatically the age of personality!) there are more than ordinary motives for withholding all encouragement from this mania of busying ourselves with the names of others, which is still more alarming as a symptom, than it is troublesome as a disease." These "more than ordinary motives" for discouraging biography well may be conjectured.

In practical terms, however, Coleridge was a less likely subject than Wordsworth, who was a far more conspicuous literary figure and notoriously reticent about his own life. At first he collaborated with a biography planned by Barron Field by annotating the manuscript, but in 1840 he abruptly refused to permit its publication. Wordsworth's annotations include fierce rebuttals to Field's quotations from Hazlitt and De Quincey.[31] Wordsworth objects to Hazlitt's description of his "narrow forehead"; and of Hazlitt's evaluation of his literary preferences, he declares, "This is monstrous," and "Monstrous again." Wordsworth's counterfeit disinterestedness in *Burns* was in practice a determination to suppress any biographical revelations about himself. In response to Field's footnote explaining that De Quincey's observations from the *Literary Reminiscences* were too sensitive for republication during the Wordsworths' lives, Wordsworth made clear his resistance to allowing them ever to appear: "Not so much as published during their lives as published or intended to be published at all. The man has written under the influence of wounded feelings as he avows, I am told; for I have never read a word of his infamous production, nor ever shall.[32] . . . The particulars shall never by me be recorded." Wordsworth claimed not to have read accounts by his critics and biographers, but he seems to have been well informed; although he said to Henry Crabb Robinson, "I beg that no friend of mine ever tells me a word of their content," his refusal to allow *Tait's* in the house suggests he had heard quite enough. Even Crabb Robinson suggested, to calm Wordsworth over the *Literary Reminiscences*, "A considerable part published thirty years hence would be read with pride and satisfaction by your grandchildren. I dare say the unhappy writer means to be honest."[33]

Although Wordsworth may have resented that Byron's renown derived more from his personality than his poetry, he resisted the kind of biographical speculation which had been commonplace with Byron since the publication of *Childe Harold* in 1812. By 1816, the year of the *Letter to a Friend of Robert Burns,* Byron had become in the wake of his marriage separation "the most talked-of poet in England."[34] Wordsworth did not aspire to emulate the kind of fame based on traffic in sexual and marital rumors (rapidly becoming commonplace with tales of Burns's illegitimate offspring and Byron's incest), and surely could not have relished the prospect of disclosures about his past even beyond those rumors evidently already current. Despite the prominent reputation today of De Quincey's biographies for scandalous disclosures and candor, according to what he told Richard Woodhouse he seems to have considered himself moderate as a biographer in withholding from publication the "unnatural tale current, and which the Opium Eater had heard even in London, of Wordsworth having been intimate with his own sister."[35]

Whether in the wake of Byron such rumors adhered to all poets is less important here than the apprehensiveness of authors toward firsthand accounts. Nevertheless, Wordsworth's interest in transforming the facts of actual lives into art appears to have included veiled reconstructions of his personal life as well as visibly biographical materials. Throughout his works Wordsworth experimented with the relation between biographical fact and fictional representation, ranging from his insistence on the veracity of his biographical materials in *The Excursion* to the peculiar biographical masquerade of "Vaudracour and Julia."[36]

Byron, like other Romantic poets, invited and deterred biographical speculation; even more visibly than Wordsworth's, his poems at once promoted and denied biographical strategies of reading. For example, the Preface to Cantos I–II of *Childe Harold's Pilgrimage* (1812) included the careful disclaimer that the "fictitious character" of Childe Harold is not "some real personage" but "the child of imagination"; yet the Cantos were annotated with first-person reflections on Byron's own Continental travels, glosses that encouraged equations between life and works. Readers readily embraced and embellished such associations; by the time of the publication of the final Canto in 1818, Byron claims to have wearied "of drawing a line which every one seemed determined not to perceive," and declares Harold is only "slightly, if at all, separated from the author speaking in his own person."[37] His private distribution of "Fare Thee Well!" in 1816 at the time of his marriage separation, with the anticipation of subsequent public circulation, suggests the degree to which Byron not only did not discourage such associations but willingly manipulated the institutions of publishing to advance them.

In the matter of overt autobiography, however, while Byron might choose to promiscuously distribute his memoirs, others took custody of his reputation and public morals to suppress them. We cannot know to what extent the memoirs were to be a gloss on his works, but the manuscripts evidently were passed around between the time Byron entrusted them to his friend Thomas Moore in 1819 and their burning five years later.[38] William Gifford asserted that the memoirs dealt with Byron's erotic adventures; Caroline Lamb worriedly sought to ascertain their fate. Evidently, Byron expected them to circulate—at one point he wrote from Italy suggesting Isaac D'Israeli research his book, *The Literary Character,* by taking a look at the manuscripts.[39] Yet he commiserated with Moore at one point, saying, "The biographer has made a botch of your life . . . if that damned fellow was to *write my* life, I would certainly *take his*."[40]

Moore himself seems to have been somewhat divided over whether to be more concerned with upholding an image of moral decorum or reaping the prestige of privileged biographical information. The degree to which he allowed the burning of the memoirs he sold to John Murray is unclear. Three days after London heard of Byron's death in May 1824, the memoirs were put into the fire in Murray's office in the presence of Murray, Moore, and the proxies of Lady Byron and Augusta Leigh. Moore seems then to have been eager to save pieces to reprint in his intended biography; yet he appears to have himself destroyed letters from Byron he later excerpted for it.

The burning seems to have been lamented among disinterested onlookers not as a literary loss of Byron's prose, but as a loss for biographical documentation. The destruction of Byron's autobiography only gave biographers the latitude to invent without fear of verification. The *New Monthly Magazine* declared, "When Mr. Moore consented to the destruction of Lord Byron's Memoirs, he does not seem to have considered, any more than the persons whose vanity and fears were more immediately interested in their suppression, that he was only exciting, in a higher degree, the curiosity of the public . . . done mischief by leaving the ground open for Memoirs of Lord Byron's life, conversation, and habits, less authentic, and at least as objectionable as the noble Poet's own autobiography."[41] The irrepressible flood of Byron memoirists indicates that many opportunists with scant reputation for discretion were glad to rely on the popular belief that "nothing could be more scandalous than the authentic memoirs," as the magazine observed: "It must be taken for granted that the Memoirs were throughout utterly unfit for publication in any shape; and that Mr. Moore and Lord Byron's other friends did not expurgate them, only because they were incapable of expurgation."

Johnson's imperturbable assessment of the destruction of Pope's papers provides an illuminating contrast to the Romantic "age of personality." Pope similarly entrusted his documents to his executors "undoubtedly expecting them to be proud of his trust and eager to extend his fame. But let no man dream of influence beyond his life . . . whatever was the reason the world has been disappointed of what was 'reserved for the next age.'"[42] Johnson cares about neither the content nor the propriety of destroying the papers; significance lies not in the actions of the survivors, but in the vanity of Pope's attempt to influence them: "Let no man dream of influence beyond his life." In his own time, Johnson could safely say, "'Who is the worse for being talked of uncharitably?'"[43] but with the breakdown of standards of decorum in biography, it was a moral assurance no longer possible amid the perilous biographical inquisitiveness of the Romantic era.

Despite his putative concern for propriety, Moore's authorized *Life of Byron* (1830), compiled largely on the Mason method, contains a subtext of eroticism which surfaces despite the studiously moral presentation of biographical documents. What, for example, is the result of the ostensibly modest substitution of asterisks in the following letter?

> They were cousins; Margarita married, the other single. As I doubted still of the circumstances, I took the business in a different light, and made an appointment with them for the next evening.   *   *   *   *   *   *   *
> *   *   *   *   *   In short, in a few evenings we arranged our affairs, and for a long space of time she was the only one who preserved over me an ascendancy which was often disputed, and never impaired.
>   The reasons for this were, firstly, her person;—very dark, tall, the Venetian face, very fine black eyes. She was two-and-twenty years old,   *   *   *
> *   *   *   *   *   *   *   *   *   *   44

Given the practice of silent editing, the narrative decision to show visible deletions through asterisks represent a striking exploitation of textual reception, for at less suggestive moments in the biography (and even within this passage), Moore silently deletes without asterisks. Here the details of the cryptic "circumstances" and "business" engage the reader in participatory speculations limited only by the blush of readerly imagination.[45]

Byron, like Wordsworth and Coleridge, was ambivalent about identifying the precise relation between author and text. But in gestures such as setting unpublished memoirs into private circulation and preparing a program of autobiographical footnotes disclaiming self-referentiality, Byron manipulated an audience first-generation Romantics had already preconditioned; and he demonstrated to even conventional biographers such as Moore how to exploit the tantalus of taboo, by at once presenting and withholding disclosures.

Canon Reformation: Revising the *Lives*

Cunningham, D'Israeli, Wordsworth, Scott, Southey

As Johnson had sought to revise Cibber's *Lives,* so many Romantics sought to revise Johnson's. However loosely Johnson composed the *Lives,* the Romantic prose writers admired and imitated the organic flexibility of the form. The Romantic successors of Johnson often coordinated sequences of collective biography by focusing on a single aspect suggested by Johnson's own thematic threads: D'Israeli was to explore the misfortunes of the poetic life; Hazlitt, the relation of the poet to the age; and De Quincey, the transmission of life into works. The narrative innovations of the great Romantic prose writers, however, surfaced amid a host of epigoni who composed more derivative and predictable sequels to Johnson's lives, and whose chief concern was in revising or enlarging the canon implied by the *Lives of the Poets* rather than in testing the elasticity of the form.

Many critics attempted a revisionism of Johnson, not just because the existence of a status quo cried out for Romantic upheaval, but also because the canon of authors installed by Johnson's *Lives* was found inadequate. Charles Altieri has observed that "Samuel Johnson is the canonical figure most useful for thinking about canon";[46] perhaps this is why Johnson's opinions have ultimately proved so indestructible. Johnson's opinions could not be removed without Johnson himself. Percival Stockdale, one of the Johnsonian revisionists, closed his *Lectures on the Truly Eminent English Poets* (1807) by declaring that Johnson's views were only "recommended by the imperious authority of a name," and would otherwise have been "dismissed with contempt." Stockdale's work is not, properly speaking, a collective biography, for its major concern—its only concern—lies in overturning Johnson's critical judgments and establishing a new canon. But it roughly assumes the form of Johnson's *Lives,* a series of essays on individual poets, as it traces Johnson's critiques virtually line by line and offers counterarguments to Johnson's unfair "tribunal," "sentence," and "animadversions" against poets.[47]

In addition to nonnarrative critical responses to Johnson, there were a great many formal imitators who designed projects as extensions, abridgments, and incorporations of Johnson's *Lives.* Leaving aside post-Johnsonian projects such as the collective biography composed of autobiographies, *A Collection of the Most Instructive and Amusing Lives Ever Published Written by the Parties Themselves* (1826–32), and derivative inspirations such as Godwin's *Lives of the Necromancers* in 1834,[48] let me here consider the Johnsonian model in Romantic literary biography, concentrating on those works that formally imitated and revised Johnson's canon.

Some of the imitators did not even care about redefining Johnson's canon. The 1790 reissue of the original anthology, with "Johnson's Poets" still on the binding, simply added fourteen new biographies (including lives of Johnson and Goldsmith). Alexander Chalmers in 1810 extended Johnson's *Lives* chronologically in both directions in *The Works of the English Poets from Chaucer to Cowper,* prefacing Johnson's and his own biographical essays to volumes of the poets.[49] In a sensible preface, Chalmers concluded that Johnson's *Lives,* "after all the objections have been offered, must ever be the foundation of English poetical biography." None of Johnson's original choices is excluded, and Chalmers rightly perceived the spirit of the original *Lives of the Poets* in choosing additional figures based on both popularity and merit, observing that it is not incumbent on the biographer to represent any as "a prodigy of genius or virtue." He notes that it would be a happy circumstance if both were true, but deplores the tendency to revise lives to produce such uniformity. Such revision, he declares, "violates the principles of truth, destroys public confidence, and defeats every valuable purpose of biography." Chalmers's biographical principles are in accord with Johnson's own, and his short biographies are not entirely graceless. He admits his skill does not lie in Johnsonian critical evaluation; we find that the biographies, while they present his critical opinions, venture nothing so decisive as Johnson's.

In 1819 Thomas Campbell presented his own modification of Johnson, *Specimens of the British Poets,* shortening the lives to only a few pages and freely adding and subtracting from Johnson's list—Duke, Smith, and King are dropped, Behn and Cibber added. The chronology extends back to Chaucer, and forward to the Wartons and Johnson—the same span as Chalmers's, but much more feebly executed. Johnson was seen, as he had implicitly predicted, as part of his own continuum of authors. Henry Francis Cary's *Lives of English Poets from Johnson to Kirke White* (which appeared originally in the *London Magazine,* 1821–24, but was not reprinted until 1846) was designed as a continuation of Johnson's *Lives* and starts where Johnson left off, beginning with Johnson himself. In addition to the poets, Cary seems to take his cue from Johnson's informal history of biography, for his small collection includes Johnson, Goldsmith, Mason, Warton, and Hayley. Meanwhile, Joseph Robertson in 1821–22 printed his *Lives of the Scottish Poets;* and the 100-volume "Chiswick" edition of *The British Poets* in 1822 extended Johnson in uniform binding and scale.[50] These represent but a few of the flood of derivative projects, but they serve to illustrate the typical modifications of Johnson's *Lives* which extended, compressed, and found analogies to Johnson's canon without challenging it and without offering any special innovation in terms of biographical narrative or collective sequence.

Among those texts that do not introduce any narrative innovations, there are some that deserve a little more attention by virtue of their canonical ingenuity and because they especially illustrate the impact of Johnson on the biographical and critical imagination. I shall look first at the half-century revisionist canon proposed by Allan Cunningham in his *Biographical and Critical History* (1833) and at the biographical survey of Isaac D'Israeli's *The Literary Character* (1795–1840), before turning to the projects in Johnsonian canon reformation written by three of the most prolific of the Romantic writers, Wordsworth's *Essay, Supplementary to the Preface* (1815), Scott's *Lives of the Novelists* (1821–24), and Southey's *Lives of the Uneducated Poets* (1831). We might not have expected to find some of these authors in the context of collective biography, but their presence attests to the ubiquity of the genre as an agent of critical prose. All of them perceived deficiencies or limitations in the nature of Johnson's canon, and attempted to revise Johnson's evaluations, broaden the sense of literary genres, or alter his notion of audience and popularity.

Allan Cunningham's *Biographical and Critical History of the Literature of the Last Fifty Years,* printed serially in the *Athenaeum* during the second half of 1833 and reprinted in Paris by Baudry's Foreign Library in 1834, is of interest for several reasons.[51] Cunningham himself appeared as a literary figure in a number of Romantic collective biographies. His son, Peter Cunningham, was responsible for the first soundly annotated posthumous edition of Johnson's *Lives* in 1854. In an introductory tribute, Cunningham explains that the purchase of the four volumes of Johnson's *Lives* became the inspiration for his father's *Lives of the Most Eminent British Painters, Sculptors, and Architects* (1829–33). Although this work is in the tradition of Vasari, Cunningham's collection of lives of British artists derives not from Walpole's brief *Anecdotes of Painting* but from Johnson's fuller *Lives.*[52] In Cunningham's design of providing a "record of the taste and feeling of the times," and following the "vicissitudes of fortune," we can see Johnson's approach to artistic lives as representative human experiences. Whereas Walpole identified with the aristocracy, Cunningham was originally a stonemason before becoming a poet and critic, and often emphasized his identification with the Scottish poor (a trait De Quincey identified as eminently qualifying Cunningham for his task of editing Burns).[53]

Cunningham's collective biography of contemporary writers borrows the Johnsonian tradition, but defines itself in contrast to the Johnsonian canon, common reader, and critical taste. Foremost in the changed literary values is the place of pastoral literature. He opens the *Biographical and Critical History* by identifying himself with rural literature and rural life, a conspicuous rejection of Johnsonian urbanity. Just as Burns published his poems saying "some might like to know how a peasant thought and felt," Cunningham declares of himself as a critic, "I propose to show how another peasant thinks and feels." Rather than the urban Age of Pope, Cunningham's poets center on the rural Age of Cowper, Burns, and Wordsworth. His identification of the characteristic literature of his age as pastoral announces the onset of a new aesthetic, modified from the infusion of the peasantry, as readers, writers, and subjects of literature.

Johnson's view of nature and the pastoral in poetry was troublesome for the Romantics: he declared the pastoral "requires no acquaintance with the living world" (*Cowley*), derided the "cant of shepherds and flocks" (*Lyttelton*), and asserted the "intelligent reader . . . sickens at the mention of the *crook*, the *pipe*, the *sheep*, and the *kids*" (*Shenstone*). His was not simply a dislike of artificial representations of nature found in eighteenth-century pastoral (with which the Romantics concurred) but a total uninterest in nature—he told Piozzi, "'a blade of grass is always a blade of grass.'" Isaac D'Israeli concluded Johnson was "a stately ox in the fields of Parnassus, not the animal of nature";[54] Cunningham regretted that Johnson, "seemed desirous of bringing much of what has since made Cowper and Burns immortal, into discredit: he ridiculed the true pastoral of real life." A new post-Johnsonian canon was required to vindicate the form, and none more qualified to name it than a critic born into the "true pastoral of real life."

Cunningham explained that the new republics attempted in France and America have been paralleled by revolutions in literature: literature has "changed its tone and aspect with the times." Cunningham's egalitarianism, however, was not shared by all of his contemporaries. He complained of those who disavowed their backgrounds, and especially denounced William Gifford as a critic who had no sympathy for those writers who, like Gifford himself, struggled upwards from poverty. If Cunningham was redefining a common readership, the *Athenaeum*'s "Living Authors" series of 1828 had implied a far different literary audience in its declaration that Wordsworth "paints to us the differences of manners and habits between ourselves and the mass of men" and "does much towards making us conceive of weavers and ploughmen, as living and busy beings." The pronouns "us" and "ourselves" do not presume the same post-revolutionary literary audience as Cunningham's view of the "revolution in our literature . . . visible in the chief works of the leading spirits of our times."

The *Biographical and Critical History* was a specific temporal landmark—not just any sequel to Johnson's canon, but a revision of Johnson a half-century since the last edition of Johnson's *Lives* to appear in his lifetime. Cunningham revises Johnson as part of a necessary periodic reassessment of new literary trends. Changes in taste are implicitly generational (though not professedly so), for Cunningham was born in the year Johnson died. The concept of a "biographical and critical" survey is Johnsonian, and Johnson and the *Lives* figure prominently in Cunningham's critical observations. Although the *Lives* was chiefly a canon of poets, it dealt with Addison as an essayist, Congreve as a dramatist, Dryden as a critic, and other diverse achievements; Cunningham's biographies are briefer than Johnson's (and grow briefer as the series progresses) but the literary canon encompasses the entire spectrum of genres, beginning with poetry and followed by "romance" (novel), history, biography, drama, and criticism. Cunningham credits Johnson with the model of collective biography ("we had no connected series of Lives before those of the Poets"), and like Johnson, he draws information from sources close at hand ("I write chiefly from a memory seldom faithless in matters concerning genius"), declares himself deliberately unsystematic, and sees in Johnsonian narrative an opportunity to comment not in a "scientific" way, but in a "fragment."[55]

In identifying a new generation of literary figures and a new canon of poets, novelists, and prose writers, Cunningham does not overturn and denounce the *Lives*. Unlike Stockdale's rampage in the *Truly Eminent English Poets,* Cunningham's objective is not to systematically contradict Johnson's opinions: the manifesto of a new literary age can be announced, but Johnson cannot be stripped of his validity for his own age. In speaking of the *Lives of the Poets,* Cunningham said Johnson "showed a colossal intellect; in those matchless Memoirs he exhibited such knowledge of human life—such skill in the delineation of character—such sagacity in the detection of faults—such insight into the sources of poetic inspiration, as no one mind perhaps ever before displayed—all this, too, was expressed in a style at once masculine and melodious, where every word conveys meaning, and every sentence teems with thought." Cunningham's praise here expresses the dominant respect for Johnson as a commentator on human life. Among the Romantics, Johnson's powers as a critic were not often denied, although the use to which he put those powers was often deplored. Cunningham, however, is content with updating rather than rescinding the *Lives;* when he disagrees with Johnson, he only observes that Johnson's critical values are in places obsolete—but that does not diminish Johnson's powers as a critic or as a biographer.

Isaac D'Israeli widely popularized Johnsonian thought and biographical inquiry by accumulating thousands of biographical anecdotes to illustrate the nature of literary genius. D'Israeli spanned a period of transition, as Benjamin Disraeli's memoir indicates in depicting his father an "Émile" returning from the Continent imbued with Rousseau and Werther, bringing his poems to Bolt Court in 1784 for the adjudication of Johnson (not knowing that Johnson was not to live many more weeks). Two years later in one of his earliest articles, D'Israeli proudly declared Johnson a "Hero" and "THE AUTHOR OF THE CENTURY." Essays on Johnsonian topics punctuated his early works, including his most famous collection of anecdotage, *Curiosities of Literature.* His essay on biographical theory, *A Dissertation on Anecdotes* (1793), provided confirmation of Johnsonian principles in statements such as, "We are more interested in the progress of the human mind, than in that of empires." But his most important extension of Johnson was the project he began publishing in 1795 and would enlarge over the next forty-five years through five revised versions and numerous editions, *An Essay on the Manners and Genius of the Literary Character,* retitled in its many subsequent revisions, *The Literary Character, Illustrated by the History of Men of Genius, Drawn from their own Feelings and Confessions.*[56]

D'Israeli's project was a sequel to the biographical inquiries of the *Lives* not in the sense of imitating the form of Johnsonian narrative, but in assembling illustrative biographical anecdotes to collectively document aspects of the life of genius introduced by the *Lives of the Poets:* "I considered that to form just reflections on Men of Genius, it was proper to collect facts from their biography, and their concatenation produced all my reflections" (1795). In the 1818 preface, he calls himself "the historian of genius," and explains his biographical methodology as a bridge to philosophical speculation, in which theories of genius would be treated not by mere argument but concrete illustration: "It is the fashion of the present day to raise up dazzling theories of genius; to reason *a priori;* to promulgate abstract paradoxes. . . . I have always had in my mind an observation of Lord Bolingbroke—'Abstract or general propositions, though never so true, appear obscure or doubtful to us very often till they are explained by examples. . . . we yield to fact when we resist speculation.'"[57] The abstract propositions D'Israeli explores include eighteenth-century theories of natural and learned genius, the Horatian question of the *genus irritabile vatum,* and most frequently, biographical motifs found in Johnson's *Lives*—the vanity of genius, the economic difficulties of authors, the uncertain relations with audience and critics, and what D'Israeli repeatedly calls the "misfortunes," "maladies," and "miseries of the learned." Each chapter of *The Literary Character* particularizes a topic implicit in the *Lives* (e.g., infirmities, poverty, isolation, youthful indicators, conversation, old age, "habits, and feelings, and disorders") and illuminates it with copious biographical examples drawn from every nation and age.

The misfortunes and travails of genius were especially of interest to D'Israeli. After publishing the first version of *The Literary Character,* he assembled two separate books of biographical evidence documenting the troubles of authors: *The Calamities of Authors* in 1812, and its continuation *The Quarrels of Authors* in 1814 (both eventually published with *The Literary Character* along with a preface describing his own "literary calamity," a disorder of vision which he records "as a warning to my sedentary brothers").[58] In this pair of books, D'Israeli expands thematic concerns derived from the *Lives.* West, Savage, and Collins all had been assailed by what Johnson called "calamities" (*Rambler* 60 opened commenting on the "happiness or calamities" documented by biography), and D'Israeli reminds us that Johnson depicted the quarrels of Dryden and Settle, Dennis and Addison.

Like other Romantic biographers, D'Israeli was interested in furthering Johnson's contemplation of the links between life and works. *The Literary Character* (1795) quotes Johnson's remarks on Thomson and Horace warning of the difficulties of making direct inferences about lives from works, but D'Israeli does go on to venture some connections between formal qualities of texts and domestic life: "Many of the conspicuous blemishes of some of our great compositions may reasonably be attributed to the domestic infelicities of their authors. The desultory life of Camoens [*sic*] probably occasioned the want of connection in his Epic; Milton's distracted family those numerous passages which escaped erasure."

But like other professional writers in a time of a shifting economic basis of literature, D'Israeli took particular interest in the economic tensions implied by Johnson's discussion of the critic, the common reader, and the penury of authors. Many of D'Israeli's topics concern the position of the writer in the culture, and in addressing this issue he always hears the *lasciate ogni speranza, voi ch'entrate* side of Johnson (the warning against the vanity of human wishes in *Rambler* 2, "no class of the human species requires more to be cautioned against this anticipation of happiness, than those that aspire to the name of authors"):

> The title of Author still retains its seduction among our youth, and is consecrated by ages. Yet what affectionate parent would consent to see his son devote himself to his pen as a profession? . . . the most successful Author can obtain no equivalent for the labours of his life. I have endeavoured to ascertain this fact, to develop the causes and to paint the variety of evils that naturally result from the disappointments of genius. Authors themselves never discover this melancholy truth till they have yielded to an impulse, and adopted a profession, too late in life to resist the one, or abandon the other. Whoever labours without hope, a painful state to which Authors are at length reduced, may surely be placed among the most injured class in the community. Most Authors close their lives in apathy or despair.

Alongside this prefatory remark in the *Calamities,* the first misfortune common to all authors he cites is the "perpetual struggle with penury." The public image of the poet is closely connected with these economic travails. D'Israeli's writings reflect a cultural shift increasingly evident to the Romantics, that the collective reputation of art had deteriorated and the presence of the artist no longer conferred honor. The first edition of *The Literary Character* observes, "The Literary Character has, in the present day, singularly degenerated in the public mind. The finest compositions appear without exciting any alarm of admiration"; the second edition complains that it has become the custom "to treat with levity the man of genius, because he is *only* a man of genius." For D'Israeli it is the task of the biographical literary historian to counteract the diminished image of authors; yet as he does so, artists emerge as a group of outsiders, both exalted and plagued.

In this, D'Israeli's writing confirms the view of authors as a unified subculture derived from the *Lives*. *The Literary Character* assembles its biographical evidence to deduce the traits shared by the "family," "community," "kindred alliance," and "brotherhood" of authors. Stretching through time is a "consanguinity" and "genealogy" of genius, a "continuity . . . from age to age," "a singleness and unity in the pursuits of genius which is carried on through all ages, and will for ever connect the nations of the earth."[59] In addressing this issue, D'Israeli transforms Johnson's investigation of the relation between author and audience into the pressing Romantic question of the causal relation between the individual and the age, a subject of increasing concern in an age sensing a growing devaluation of the arts in the face of competing scientific, industrial, and utilitarian claims. Within his study of the commonality of genius and the "genealogical lines of genius," D'Israeli calls attention to the particular connections between a work and its age: "Every work of genius is tinctured by the feelings and often originates in the events, of the times." Yet in D'Israeli's text, the relation between artistic genius and the culture remains an unfixed dialectic: the "man of genius is stamping his own character on the minds of his own people," while at the same time is a product of the culture ("genius is but progressive"; "certain events must precede the man of genius").[60]

D'Israeli traced to Johnson his use of literary biography as a form of literary history, and his sense of collective biography as a cumulative history of the human mind. In the *Quarrels* he called Johnson "our great literary biographer"; Bayle created "the philosophy of literary history," he says, but "Johnson's passion for literary history and his great knowledge of the human heart inspired at once the first and finest model in this class of composition." His own collection of biographical incidents in the *Calamities* is "subservient to a higher purpose—that of our literary history," a form indebted to Johnson's *Lives,* which "laid the foundation of a nobler style of Literary History in our own country."

Yet the locutions of D'Israeli testify to how the *Lives* had been recast for a new era. For D'Israeli, literary history is "the history of the human mind";[61] in the preface to the *Calamities* he described his task as painting the "psychological character" of authors. It is a term, he explains, just entering the language, and useful for "the historian of the human mind."[62] The text begins with a word recently minted to provide a vocabulary for expressing new concerns with the mind; and a one-line paragraph a few pages from the end of the book equally demonstrates how changed attitudes toward reading suffuse the works of even a writer who paid extensive tribute to Johnson. The Johnson of the *Lives* had repeatedly said, "My business is with his poetry" (*Akenside*), "My business is only with his poems" (*Sprat*); the D'Israeli of the Romantics concludes, discussing Prior, "Our business is with his poetical feelings." Indeed, D'Israeli explained Byron's interest in his works using those same words: "The fact is my works being all about the feelings of literary men were exceedingly interesting to him. . . . He told me that he had read my works over and over again."[63]

It is certainly true that some of the Romantics allowed more merit to Johnson than others. Cunningham accepted Johnson's critical sagacity. D'Israeli was willing to draw many of his biographical themes from Johnson. Indeed, Johnson was most congenially assimilated into Romanticism through his biographies. But whereas D'Israeli saw in the *Lives* promising theoretical issues, and looked to Johnson for a model of biographical strength, Wordsworth in contrast saw the *Lives* as an adversarial canon and an unjust tribunal attempting to crush the flexibility of poetic innovation.

In revising Johnson, Wordsworth was chiefly impressed by his points of dissent rather than consonance on critical issues. Wordsworth might have seen in Johnson's *Lives* a curiosity about the life of the poet akin to his own unpublished endeavors; he might well have praised Johnson's interest in the aesthetics of epitaphs as adumbrating his own *Essay upon Epitaphs;* he might have seen his own statements about the importance of the passions in poetry prefigured in Johnson's disapproval of Dryden's failure to exhibit "the genuine operations of the heart" and Cowley's indulgence in meretricious simulation of the passions.[64] Likewise Coleridge might have found Johnson's comments on the "two most engaging powers of an author" in *Pope* ("New things are made familiar, and familiar things are made new") and Johnson's observation that Shakespeare "approximates the remote and familiarizes the wonderful," a herald of his own explanation in the *Biographia Literaria* of the *Lyrical Ballads* division of labor, "the charm of novelty to things of every day" and the "semblance of truth" to the uncanny. That neither Romantic poet chose to perceive these harmonies is a testament to literary intimidation and the rebellion of each generation against its predecessors.

Johnson figures negatively in Wordsworth's thoughts on the *Lyrical Ballads* as well. Perhaps the feature of Johnson that was most incompatible with Romantic interests was his traditional Neoclassical emphasis on the matter of translation. It was in the context of discussing translation that Johnson made his pronouncements in *Dryden* and *Pope* on poetic diction, the language fit for poetry and prose, and the exclusion of subjects unfit for poetry—pronouncements that utterly contradict Wordsworth's own views. Wordsworth's suggestion in the 1802 Preface, for example, that no subject is unfit for poetry ("the remotest discoveries of the Chemist, the Botanist, or Mineralogist" are potential subjects for the poet), contrasts sharply with Johnson's recalcitrance over the topic of Pope's *Essay on Man* ("the subject is perhaps not very proper for poetry"). Wordsworth had no interest in vindicating Pope, of course—his objective was to substitute a new set of poetic values for Johnson's obsolete ones. Whereas Johnson says admiringly that there was "no poetical diction" before Dryden, Wordsworth says there has been too much since.

It would be superfluous here to trace the distinction between Johnson and Wordsworth on poetic diction and the language of prose, beyond observing that Wordsworth felt the legacy of Johnson's *Lives* and used Johnson as his stalking horse. His prose works are crowded with tacit responses, verbal echoes, and explicit rebuttals of Johnson. As early as the 1798 Advertisement to *Lyrical Ballads,* when he observed of querulous readers, "they will look round for poetry, and will be induced to enquire by what species of courtesy these attempts can be permitted to assume that title," we hear rhetorical echoes of Johnson's answer to the same search for a definitive poetry: "It is surely superfluous to answer the question that has once been asked, Whether Pope was a poet? otherwise than by asking in return, If Pope be not a poet, where is poetry to be found?" (*Pope*).

But the 1815 *Essay, Supplementary to the Preface* is of special interest to us in this context, because it is designed as an explicit commentary on Johnson's *Lives*.[65] Like Cunningham, Wordsworth attempts to redefine a new pastoral canon, but he deliberately rebuts the canon formation of Johnson's *Lives*. In rewriting the *Lives* without the lives, Wordsworth casts the *Essay, Supplementary* into the shape of a Johnsonian historical canon. Conspicuously alluding to the "Prefaces biographical and critical," rather than to the *Lives of the Poets,* Wordsworth's counter-canon takes the form of the prefaces divested of biographical commentary. It is a generic rebellion that inadvertently acknowledges the authority of Johnson, yet also foreshadows Wordsworth's argument the following year in the *Letter to a Friend of Robert Burns* against the necessity of knowing any biographical information to interpret poetry. Just as Johnson sought to redress the biographical injustices of Cibber's *Lives,* so Wordsworth's *Essay, Supplementary* sought to redress the critical injustices of Johnson's *Lives.*

In revolving the relation between the poetic genius and readership, Wordsworth was rightly addressing a point vexing to Johnson and unresolved in the *Lives.* Like Cunningham, and characteristic of the Romantic emphasis on the individual, Wordsworth uses a prominent first-person narrator throughout. Wordsworth establishes himself as one qualified to speak: even those critics who treat him most harshly, he confidently observes, "genius none of them seem to deny me." Again, both rebelling and inadvertently conforming, Wordsworth borrows authority from the term genius, a term closely associated with Johnson's discussion of the poets. The closing pages of the *Essay* respond to the Johnsonian issue of pinning down the elusive nature of genius:

> Of genius the only proof is, the act of doing well what is worthy to be done, and what was never done before: Of genius, in the fine arts, the only infallible sign is the widening sphere of human sensibility, for the delight, honour, and benefit of human nature. Genius is the introduction of a new element into the intellectual universe: or, if that be not allowed, it is the application of powers to objects on which they had not before been exercised, or the employment of them in such a manner as to produce effects hitherto unknown. What is all this but an advance, or a conquest, made by the soul of the Poet?

Wordsworth's definition is no more conclusive than any other voice in the dialogue on genius. Johnson found the mere dictionary definition of genius reductive and turned instead to a group portrait; so Wordsworth offers a series of proofs that drift into the realm of rhetorical questions and unverifiable assertions.

Wordsworth's antipathy to the canon of Johnson's *Lives* misses Johnson's point, for Johnson too saw himself as vindicating past critical injustices for posterity. Wordsworth seems to mistake Johnson's view of the audience, though in a different way from Virginia Woolf. For Johnson, the voice of the masses is not infallible, and needs the mediation of the critic to distinguish between the purblind "publick" who acclaim Pomfret and Granville, and the discerning audience who rightly, if belatedly, find

Addison's *Cato* unstageable and read *Paradise Lost* despite its incompatibility with court fashions.

Wordsworth faults Johnson for rising to the bait and attempting to "prove, by the sale of the work" Milton's recognition; yet in this again he misreads Johnson to his own purposes. The issue of whether Milton's work can be said to have sold well remains as uncertain in Johnson as it is today, although Wordsworth sought to prove the sales low. Johnson's ambiguous observation, "the sale, if it be considered, will justify the publick," represents an attempt to assess the situation of the audience and writer in Milton's time, a theme sustained throughout the *Lives*. Johnson's discussion of the sales record of *Paradise Lost* attempts to take into account historical relativism in publishing conditions, just as he had called attention in *Cowley, Dryden,* and *Pope* to the changing context of literary taste and the necessity of considering different "habits of thought" over the ages.[66] *Milton* provides a study of the early stages of the development of a reading public: the circumstances of Restoration publishing, the fear of incurring court disfavor, the absence of advertising, and the distinction between a reading public and a buying public. Johnson uses this historical context to illustrate that sales are no measure of a work's general esteem. Johnson certainly did not believe a popular audience was the measure of artistic merit when he warned that one must trust to the "impartiality of a future generation" rather than to "the claps of multitudes." Wordsworth misreads Johnson, but the depiction of Johnson apologizing for low sales provides a foil for Wordsworth's own praise of low sales as an indication of merit. Whereas Wordsworth implies his own disappointing sales offer a badge of distinction, he belittles Johnson as one who offers critical pronouncements "mid the little senate to which he gave laws."

Wordsworth's motives for bringing forth this reading of Johnson are commensurate with the unpopularity of his own 1807 *Poems in Two Volumes*.[67] The second edition of the *Poems,* for which he prepared the *Essay,* could not have been expected to fare much better. Moreover, Wordsworth well knew the nature of publishing expedients—he had turned to various economic projects such as the lake guide to generate income—and he does not spare Johnson's *Lives*. As Wordsworth observes, Johnson was solicited

to furnish Prefaces biographical and critical for some of the most eminent English Poets. The Booksellers took upon themselves to make the collection; they referred probably to the most popular miscellanies, and, unquestionably, to their Books of accounts; and decided upon the claim of Authors to be admitted into a body of the most Eminent, from the familiarity of their names with the readers of that day, and by the profits, which, from the sale of his works, each had brought and was bringing to the Trade.

Wordsworth does not credit any nationalist zeal to the project; though his consciousness of the *Lives* as an economic rather than a poetic project might have given him insight into why Johnson's narrative so incessantly returns to the financial context of the lives of authors. Wordsworth is shrewd in his perception of the economic genesis of the *Lives* and the booksellers' self-interest in constructing a canon based on best-selling poets. But he fails to recognize in Johnson's accounts of the misery and poverty of authors' lives a sadly ironic response to the booksellers' lucrative aims.

Wordsworth, however, does not exculpate Johnson from the booksellers' scheme, and Wordsworth faults him for the authors he recommended within the limited discretion he was allowed—authors "scarcely to be mentioned without a smile." Wordsworth's counter-canon ("a hasty retrospect of the poetical literature of this Country for the greater part of the last two centuries") follows the dominant post-Johnsonian trend of extending the *Lives* backward in time. Wordsworth does not touch on all the poets of Johnson's *Lives,* but concentrates on Spenser, Shakespeare, Milton, Thomson, and Collins, with some attention to Dryden, Pope, and the metaphysical poets. Johnson receives little praise even when he unmistakably concurs with Wordsworth—when Wordsworth decries the "extravagant admiration" bestowed on the metaphysical poets, he gives Johnson no credit for the same views. When Wordsworth uses the Johnsonian term wonder, in warning that "we must distinguish between wonder and legitimate admiration," he does not acknowledge the background presence of Johnson's constant caution against novelty being mistaken for poetic merit. Throughout the *Lives,* Johnson spurned misplaced critical and biographical gullibility, from his opening denunciation in *Cowley* of Sprat's propagation of "wonder," to his impatience in the last-written *Life of Pope,* that "wonders are willingly told and willingly heard."

Likewise Wordsworth's governing criterion, the issue of whether an author eschews a mass audience, is derived from the prominent Johnsonian theme of the dangers of pandering to "the claps of multitudes." Johnson had himself criticized Dryden for his "servile submission to an injudicious audience" and his willingness "to enjoy fame on the easiest terms." For Wordsworth, the mass public is even more uniformly wrong in its judgments than Johnson. Wordsworth's praise of the new rural voice is far from the egalitarian peasantry of Cunningham. Wordsworth begins by codifying the kinds of poetic audience, the "Classes" of readers for poetry: the passion of the young, the occasional recreation of the adult, the solace of the old, and the study of a few. Purported critics abound in all, but are only valid in the last category, among whom there may be collected opinions of "absolute value, and worthy to be depended upon." In defining an ideal audience standing between the scornful professional critic and the untutored popular reader, Wordsworth might be seen as identifying the uncommon reader Johnson is too generous to pinpoint.

The writers comprising Wordsworth's canon are examined in terms of their refusal to heed a popular audience, and whether their works were received with discerning unpopularity. Spenser was honorably neglected. Shakespeare, like all stage writers, was obliged to adapt himself to an audience who flocked as undiscerningly to his plays as to those by inferior writers. Gay's pastorals were ludicrous but were widely accepted as just representations of rural life (even to Johnson's astonishment, Wordsworth concedes). Thomson deserves skepticism precisely because *The Seasons* won "unanimous" praise from the "prepared sympathies" of the "undiscerning." The very approbation of the public calls into question the traits of the work in the very commonplace "wonder" they excite; it is not that *The Seasons* won attention because it was especially original or accurate as a poem of nature, but that preceding works were so exceedingly inaccurate. Next to such unwarranted astonishment, the true merits of "Thomson's genius" lay unperceived.[68]

A dozen other poets within and without the *Lives* are briefly named and dismissed, included by Wordsworth only to demonstrate a popularity "worthless and useless" except "as evidence what a small quantity of brain is necessary to procure a considerable stock of admiration, provided the aspirant will accommodate himself to the liking and fashions of his day." Wordsworth tells us Milton deserves praise for the noble unpopularity of his work, his refusal to accommodate himself to any but the fit though few, and his indifference to the popularity of *Paradise Lost*. Wordsworth does not comment on Addison's attempt to popularize *Paradise Lost* through his critical essays, which Johnson found superficial; it is difficult to know whether Wordsworth would find the attempt to popularize a distinguished author abasing.

Wordsworth addresses Johnson's history of poetry through the issues

Johnson himself takes up: the nature of genius, the financial context of literature, the nature of the common reader. Moreover, he addresses Johnson's essays as a coherent sequence with specific cumulative objectives. It is true that Wordsworth's canon is, after all, more in concert with current tastes than is Johnson's. But Wordsworth's response to the financial aspect of writing and the economics of book dealing is far more reductive than Johnson's, for Johnson recognizes a vast system of possibilities: contemporary popular opinion may or may not correspond with later assessments or some ultimate canonical judgment; it may or may not reflect the true merits of a work of literature; it may or may not evolve to an appreciation. The cumulative discussion of the *Lives* better illustrates the variety of text-to-reader ties and the complexities of reputation than does Wordsworth's resolute reliance on his self-appointed canon.

Wordsworth's depiction of the artist's position in society is closely tied to the question of originality. Rather than being borne forward by mass approval, the author must expect to be an isolated leader conducting a reader willing to be "invigorated and inspirited by his Leader." The few capable of perceiving true poetic merit recognize the poet as a forerunner of the culture: "to create taste," the task of the true poet, "is to call forth and bestow power." Such cultural leadership will be invisible to the passive reader, "stretched on his Palanquin, and borne by his Slaves." Wordsworth and Coleridge reconcile the problem of imitation and originality with the solution that the author must create the taste "by which he is to be enjoyed," scant consolation for the frustrating isolation of the poet suffering the neglect of contemporaries. Wordsworth's response to the longstanding dialogue on the ancients and moderns is much indebted to Johnson and Reynolds in its mediation of innovation and tradition: "The predecessors of an original Genius of a high order will have smoothed the way for all that he has in common with them;—and much he will have in common; but, for what is peculiarly his own, he will be called upon to clear and often to shape his own road."[69] It is the nature of the true poet to both conform to and transgress received rules in unanticipatable ways.

Hazlitt (who regarded the Johnsonian canon as a lesser enemy than did most of his contemporaries) observed in "My First Acquaintance with Poets" (1823) that being thought original was far more important to Wordsworth than he professed. In the *Essay, Supplementary,* Wordsworth is very generous about indebtedness to the received tradition, but Hazlitt's anecdote suggests otherwise:

> I once hinted to Wordsworth, as we were sailing in his boat on Grasmere lake, that I thought he had borrowed the idea of his *Poems on the Naming of Places* from the local inscriptions of the same kind in Paul and Virginia. He did not own the obligation, and stated some distinction without a difference, in defence of his claim to originality. Any the slightest variation would be sufficient for this purpose in his mind; for whatever *he* added or omitted would inevitably be worth all that any one else had done, and contain the marrow of the senti-ment.[70]

One wonders whether Hazlitt's accusation of Wordsworth's intellectual ungenerousness is borne out in Wordsworth's conclusion to the *Essay*. Wordsworth ends with an ingratiation more apt to solace the poet than educate the reader. He differentiates the faithful "Vox Populi"—the "Peo-ple," fit audience for the poet though few—and the contemptible, low-minded, and unthinking "Public."[71] The distinction is perhaps intended to circumvent offense by allowing readers to winnow themselves. Al-though it does not diminish the merit of Wordsworth's reading of the poet and received tradition, Wordsworth's vision of a finite audience is ultimately a less generous and less optimistic prospect than Johnson's implicit infinitely educable audience.

Not all variants of Johnson's *Lives* were disputes over the link between text and audience and the poetical canon. Piozzi records Johnson's re-sponse after completing the *Lives of the Poets*, when sequels were proposed:

> Many of our friends were earnest that he should write the lives of our famous prose authors; but he never made any answer that I can recollect to the proposal, excepting when Sir Richard Musgrave once was singularly warm about it getting up and intreating him to set about the work immediately; he coldly replied, "*Sit down, Sir!*"[72]

No equivalent lives of the nonfictional prose writers has ever been assem-bled—such is the confusing literary status of that genre—but in the years 1821 to 1824, Walter Scott undertook to write the lives of the novelists in the form of prefaces to *Ballantyne's Novelist's Library*. It was a selective reprinting of mostly English novels accompanied by biographical intro-ductions, following the original format of Johnson's *Lives*.

The project appears to have arisen in collaboration with John Ballan-tyne, Scott's publishing agent, in the years before Scott's financial col-lapse. According to existing accounts of the genesis of the project, Scott appears to have had some role in the selection of authors. Like Johnson's scheme, the lives first appeared as prefaces and were only incidentally, and by afterthought, reprinted as an independent sequence. A pirated edition in Paris in 1825 prompted its republication in Britain. Following the hint of reviewers of the Paris volume, the *Lives of the Novelists* was included in *The Miscellaneous Prose Works of Sir Walter Scott* issued in 1827.[73] The *Quarterly Review*'s favorable account of the Parisian collective biography provides an interesting observation on the status of the genre at the time:

> These essays are among the most agreeable specimens of biographical composition we are acquainted with: they contain a large assemblage of manly and sagacious remarks on human life and manners—and much ingenious criticism besides; and, thus presented in a compact form, must be considered as throwing a new and strong light upon a department of English literature, perhaps the most peculiar, certainly the most popular, and yet, we cannot help thinking, among the least studied of all that we possess.[74]

The declaration that collective biography is "the least studied" but "certainly the most popular" and "perhaps the most peculiar" genre attests to the significant and anomalous stature of collective biography in the Romantic era.

Among the Romantics, no fitter person than Scott could have been found to write the lives of the novelists. His critical authority was unquestioned because he was the paramount novelist of the age (although he refused to admit his authorship until 1827, it was known in literary circles well before then). Scott's statements on theory and his evaluation of relative merits of novels were at least as momentous as the presence of a history of the novel. For many of Scott's contemporaries, the inclusion of novelists in the dispute over poetical canon and the discussion of text and audience might be regarded as an audacious commentary on the issues raised by Johnson's *Lives*, for novels were clearly perceived as a popular form. Wordsworth, for example, notoriously disdained novels as a genre for degraded tastes.[75] Nevertheless, the inclusion of novelists in the critical dialogue on canon following Johnson's *Lives*, vindicated by Scott's analysis of the history and formal qualities of prose fiction, constituted an important step in justifying the ambitions of the novel as a literary form.

The generic dialogue signified by the *Lives of the Novelists* surpasses the value of its biographies and practical criticism. The work introduced the concept of novelistic canons on equal footing with poetic canons. The presence of Johnson in the background of the *Novelists*—and in the background of Scott's *Life of Dryden* as well[76]—lent authority to the project as an extension of Johnson's *Lives*. Johnson is present as the "mighty aristarch"; as the subject of one of the lives; as the writer of "nervous language"; as the author of Goldsmith's epitaph. We hear Johnson's critical and social opinions of Richardson and Sterne. We are invited to concur with Johnson that Macheath's acquittal will not induce people to become highwaymen. Cumberland possesses the distinction of being the last of the "constellation of genius" surrounding Johnson. Johnson appears as a critic, a novelist, and a biographer, and Scott is conscious of analyzing—and honoring—the novel as a genre that was evolving its social role and formal qualities in Johnson's own time.

Like Johnson's *Lives* and most post-Johnsonian anecdotal biographers, Scott's lives were written from general wisdom and the privilege of experience and authority, rather than from research and the journeyman's date reckoning. As he says in the Advertisement to the 1827 edition, "the Lives do not lay claim to the merit of much research, being taken from the most accessible materials," and modestly adds, "the Critical Opinions are such as have occurred without much profound study." Nonetheless, like Johnson's *Lives,* Scott's *Novelists* provided biographies where before there had been none. Today the text deserves attention not for the new material it provides, but for the record of Scott's critical opinions and the historical place it assumes conferring dignity on the novel as a literary form. Placing the novel in the formal context of Johnson's *Lives of the Poets* asserted that the novel was more than a popular genre and deserved critical attention, a history of its filiation, and a classification of its types. Clara Reeve's *The Progress of Romance* (1795), which explored the distinctions between novel and romance, is often described as the first book in England devoted to the study of narrative,[77] but Scott's *Novelists* may be said to have legitimized the critical dialogue on narrative theory by using the format of Johnsonian prose.

If we are tempted to regard Scott's endeavors with a jaundiced eye—as Carlyle observed, Scott made a career "of writing impromptu novels to buy farms with"[78]—let it be said that these lives are not as lackluster as one might fear. The 1827 reissue was probably a stopgap to counteract the financial downfall of the previous year, but that circumstance does not detract from Scott's canny observations. Like Johnson, Scott's interests in the economics of publishing arose from personal experience. Scott examines the publishing strategies of Fielding's bookseller, and discusses in

"Smollett" the "difference in opinion which sometimes occurs betwixt the author and the reader" regarding the merits of a work. Scott, himself a wearer of many hats, takes a particular interest in the "writer of all work," as he calls it in the chapter on Johnson. The *Novelists* records the many shifts an author is put to in order to make a living by the pen; writers are always trying new publishing schemes, or at odds with readers, or trying to win them over.

Scott's narrative often borrows Johnsonian tone as well as subject. He was capable of imitating Johnson's wry ingenuousness in pretending not to comment on a biographical fact, while indirectly controlling the narrative response. For example, he tells the story of Fielding's worthless squandering of his funds: "He established an equipage, with showy liveries; and his biographers lay some stress on the circumstance, that the color, being a bright yellow, required to be frequently renewed,—an important particular, which, in humble imitation of our accurate predecessors, we deem it unpardonable to suppress." The story is, in fact, apocryphal, though it aptly illustrates Scott's use of biographical detail. The closing of "Smollett" also indicates Scott's indebtedness to the "vanity of human wishes" theme of Johnson's *Lives:* "But criticism, whether candid or unjust, was soon to be of little consequence to the author." Anecdotes, conversation, and extracts from letters are even less important for Scott than for Johnson. Scott chiefly relies on his authority to speak generically on the subject of the history of the novel and to offer criticism on individual works.

The *Novelists* does speculate on links between lives and works, although it was a practice Scott's autobiographical fragment attempted to dissuade. In discussing the popular assumption that Smollett placed "his own early adventures under the veil of fiction," Scott concludes, "the public carried the spirit of applying the characters of a work of fiction to living personages much further perhaps than the author intended." Yet in "Richardson," Scott declares, "Who loves not to know the slightest particulars concerning a man of his genius?" He connects Richardson's "circumstantial" style and his early affinity for letter writing; and although he warns that the conduct of the author might not always be inferred from the text, "the author of *Clarissa* was, in private life, the mild good man which we wish to suppose him." Similarly, Scott views Fielding's style as a reflection of his life as an improvident man-about-town who learned to delineate Squire Western from his brief sojourn in rural life.

Scott had previously written longer biographies of Dryden (1808) and Swift (1814) to preface collections of their works, and the short biographies of the *Lives of the Novelists* bear the mark of that experience. Scott used his *Life of Dryden* to illuminate part of the history of English literature, and the accounts of the novelists are dedicated to the same cumulative purpose. The chronological, personal, and critical materials tend to be smoothly integrated throughout each life with very few narrative segmentations. Even more than Johnson, Scott defines biographies by the subjects' literary achievements. Scott's chief concerns are the evaluation of character as it influences the works; the analysis of specific novels; and the codification of subgeneric types of fiction. Like Johnson, Scott was very interested in the nuances of genre, and the *Novelists* surveys the available forms of the novel.

Although the sequence of lives in the original series appears to have been somewhat accidental—like Johnson's *Lives,* it was dictated by the arrangement of the volumes of the anthology—the sequence of the 1827 collected edition in Scott's *Miscellaneous Prose Works* deserves attention as a more definitive sequence. Scott himself collected and prefaced the order of the text in his own lifetime. The 1827 sequence of lives uses the organizational motif of grouping kinds of fiction writers, rather than a chronology, to examine the historical diversity of the novel. Scott begins with Richardson, whose writings he places in the context of romance; and then contrasts him to Fielding, foregrounding the narrative difference between the two authors through the dispute over *Joseph Andrews.*

The *Novelists* makes use of this form of progressive juxtaposition to connect adjacent lives, as well as even more explicit Plutarchan pairings. Fielding is compared with Smollett, much as Johnson assesses Dryden and Pope, although Scott confesses such Plutarchan comparisons "are not in general the best mode of estimating individual merit" (*Smollett*). Their narratives and lives are compared: both wrote plays and travelogues and sought political preferment. Scott next turns to a discussion of the writings of Johnson's circle, including Cumberland, Goldsmith, and Johnson himself. He then progresses to the sentimental and formally mosaic narratives of Sterne and Mackenzie; then groups the gothic romances of Walpole, Reeve, and Radcliffe (although he is at some pains to distinguish the various kinds of gothic romances); and finally treats the picaresque and morally inconsequential novels of Le Sage, Johnstone, and Bage. The series does not rise to a splendid conclusion—the final grouping is evidently somewhat residuary—but it must be remembered that the original series ended unfinished. After Ballantyne died, it trailed on somewhat listlessly for a few years. The reprints of the novels were largely unsuccessful, but Scott's republication of the essays indicated he recognized the value of his study of the generic subdivisions of fictional narrative.

The title of Southey's 1831 collective biography, *Lives of the Uneducated Poets,* misleadingly sounds like the *Shepherd's Week* or *Shamela* of post-Johnsonian biography. It is certain Southey did not mean it as such. Approached by John Jones, "an old servant," he arranged to print Jones's verses, and wrote a segmented "essay" on what Southey styled the uneducated poets to accompany the *Attempts in Verse.* By the second edition, Southey's publishers inverted the evolution of the project—much as an earlier booksellers' project became "Johnson's Lives"—by placing Southey's contribution before Jones's and retitling the work Southey's *Lives of the Uneducated Poets.*[79] Southey's dismay over the change seems to have been motivated less by the fear of slighting Jones than of publicizing the laureate as a poetry editor. In anticipation of the risk, throughout the text he vowed his refusal to ever read any more manuscripts submitted to him—lest any other working-class authors take up the idea of approaching him in hopes of social elevation.

Southey, like Scott, was engaged in a wide variety of projects by which he "'*made the pot boil,*'" as De Quincey quoted him in the *Literary Reminiscences.* As a result, he was inevitably involved in many biographical projects, including a life of Henry Kirke White on the Mason model (1807–8); the *Life of Wesley* (1820), admired by Coleridge as a "favourite among favourite books";[80] the *Life of Cowper* (1835), which prefaced an edition of the works; and the *Life of Nelson* (1813), held by many of his contemporaries to be the finest biography of the age (Cunningham's *Biographical and Critical History* called it "the most perfect piece of biography in the language"). The *Life of Nelson* was intended in part as a "manual for the young sailor," a kind of conduct book in moral courage for shipboard. In the same vein, he was later to compose the *Lives of the British Admirals* (1833),[81] a type of collective biography that became a major subgenre in the heyday of the empire, perhaps more popular and abundant than lives of ecclesiastics or statesmen. Having experimented with various forms of biography, it was reasonable Southey should try his hand at the Johnsonian mode of literary biography. The result was the *Lives of the Uneducated Poets*, a work that resembled *Nelson* (which was and remains his most famous biography) in its tone of moral exhortation, and, perhaps less fortunately, in its class consciousness.

In part, Southey seems to have been motivated by an innocent social curiosity. Southey sentimentally laments that with the widespread advance of education Jones might be "the last versifier of his class," although the *Quarterly Review* offered the dubious reassurance that this was not likely to be the case for quite some time.[82] In part, as well, Southey's project responded to Johnson, who was equally contemptuous of the unearned patronage of working-class poets as of the servile flattery paid to the dilettante poet lord. Boswell reports Johnson's unfavorable meeting with James Woodhouse, the shoemaker poet: " 'They had better (said he,) furnish the man with good implements for his trade, than raise subscriptions for his poems. He may make an excellent shoemaker, but can never make a good poet.' "[83] Johnson excluded upstarts in gender and class from his canon. Southey's *Uneducated Poets,* in contrast, includes John Taylor "the water-poet," Stephen Duck "the thresher poet," James Woodhouse "the poetical shoemaker," John Bennet "the cobbler of Woodstock," Ann Yearsley "the milkwoman of Bristol," and John Frederick Bryant "the tobacco-pipe-maker," in addition to the short autobiography and poems of John Jones, whose own self-appointed epithet was "an old servant."

Southey's counterargument to Johnson was well-intentioned, but his charitable notions remain unwittingly class-conscious. He praises the writing of poems by the working-class authors, but he establishes a separate and inferior canon to contain them. The chief benefit of the writing of verse by the working classes is its contribution to moral rectitude. "Exercise of the mind" and "intellectual enjoyment" attained in "humble life" are beneficial to moral and social restraint. Of the socially reassuring effect of literature, Southey writes: "Instead of rendering the individual discontented with his station, [writing verse] had conduced greatly to his happiness, and if it had not made him a good man, had contributed to keep him so." The questionable political liberalism of Southey's declaration that the writing of poetry by the working classes "can do no harm" is accompanied by the intended critical rigor of his reassurance that bad poetry can do no harm unless it passes for good, and "vitiate[s]" taste.

Southey imagines himself generous in suggesting that working-class poets are entitled to patronage, an essentially harmless act; even if it cannot improve the verse it will not vitiate taste because booksellers will be unwilling to speculate in such wares. Literature runs little risk of excellent working-class verse as long as the intellectual elite keeps a close rein on critical standards. D'Israeli had declared that although patronage "cannot convert dull men into men of genius, it may preserve men of genius from becoming dull men."[84] Southey reassures us that the writing of poetry, even abetted by patronage, will not make the working classes discontented, and perhaps even more important to Southey, will not endanger poetic standards: as the *Uneducated Poets* illustrates, working-class poets need not be considered by the same standards of reference at all.

Southey purports to champion a literary egalitarianism. Condemning the aristocratic poets, Southey writes, "'Persons of quality' require no defence when they appear as authors in these days: and, indeed, as mean a spirit may be shown in traducing a book because it is written by a lord, as in extolling it beyond its deserts for the same reason." But even as he cautions against blind enthusiasm for the poetry of lords—an indignation shared by Johnson, although Southey may well have had one particular lord, Byron, in mind—Southey's "defence" of working-class poetry does not move to the conclusion we might expect, a praise of critical standards independent of class. At his most outspoken, he expresses only a benevolent and patronizing outrage "when we are told that the thresher, the milkwoman, and the tobacco-pipe-maker did not deserve the patronage they found,—when it is laid down as a maxim of philosophical criticism that poetry ought never to be encouraged unless it is excellent in its kind,—that it is an art in which inferior execution is not to be tolerated,— a luxury, and must therefore be rejected unless it is of the very best."[85]

Southey, in his concern over vitiating taste, does not seem to see how his approach vitiates literature. He sees that lack of education undermines intellect, but it does not occur to him to draw any reformist conclusions in terms of improving education or redefining genre. Southey unequivocally states that Jones's verse contains "abundant proof of a talent for poetry, which, if it had been cultivated, might have produced good fruit," but he does not suggest the advantages of widespread cultivation. Poverty is lamentably accompanied by "low breeding and defective education," but Southey's support of working-class poetry does not go beyond bestowing his "favorable opinion" on the verse Jones submits to him, and relegating it to a canon of uneducated poets. The unexamined premise behind Southey's observations is that working-class poets will inevitably be of a lesser order: that the status quo of literary merit demands an intertextuality acquired through an education denied to all but the intellectual and social aristocracy. In some sense Southey is accurate that poetic genres depend on access to an inherited intellectual tradition, but he makes no effort to redefine genre. Instead, Southey provides a canon of lower forms for the working-class poet and audience.

Southey's *Uneducated Poets* scales itself down to accommodate working-class achievement: it concerns itself with a different level of biographical detail and poetic ability. The publication of John Jones's poetry—and that of the water poet, the milkwoman of Bristol, and the rest—affords a moral lesson about contentment in one's place. It is equally interesting to examine which poets he includes and which he omits. The *Quarterly Review* observed that although others—Charles Crocker, "the cobbler of Chichester," and John Wright, "the cotton miller of Glasgow"—had recently published verses, Southey's caretaking "will float John Jones to posterity." John Jones has not exactly floated to posterity, and it is unfair to suggest that the achievement is Southey's rather than Jones's; but it is certain that the laureate's patronage won him more attention that he would have otherwise obtained. Notably, the most prominent working-class poets of the age—Burns, Hogg, and Cunningham, the ploughman, the Ettrick Shepherd, and the stonemason—go unmentioned by Southey. He explains that the "respectable name of [Robert] Dodsley" (known as the "muse in livery") is omitted along with the shoemaker Robert Bloomfield because their "poems are worthy of preservation separately, and in general collections." Those self-taught poets who successfully cross class lines to create poems in step with high literary convention are critically honored, presumably, by being removed from the context of social class. The *Uneducated Poets* is a collection of secondary achievements of authors too remote from the social and intellectual hierarchy to influence or revise taste.

Perhaps the most mystifying element of Southey's *Uneducated Poets* is the difficulty of determining to what audience Southey directed his remarks. The text shifts between providing canon for a working-class audience of alien tastes, and looking over the heads of that audience to discuss the phenomenon of the working-class literacy. Southey declares that the literature written by the uneducated poets will afford some gratification to those "readers there still are, who, having escaped the epidemic disease of criticism, are willing to be pleased, and grateful to those from whose writings they derive amusement or instruction." On one level the comment succumbs to a temptation to idealize a golden age of listeners—"Leaving great verse unto a little clan," as Keats says in the fragmentary "Ode to Maia." At the same time the implication of primitive and rudimentary taste undercuts the merit of having escaped the "epidemic disease of criticism" without immunization. Those who are willing and grateful to be uncritically amused are satisfied with poets who might have achieved more under other circumstances.

Southey's text magnifies the received dilemma over classes of readers which derives from Johnson. There is no equivocation over the commonness of Southey's common reader. Johnson is at once optimistic about the eventual accuracy of public taste and despairing of it; but he is uniformly skeptical of an audience seeking mere amusement, such as the audience of Pomfret ("the favourite of that class of readers, who, without vanity or criticism, seek only their own amusement"). Southey paradoxically attempts to cultivate an inferior audience, while acknowledging his superiority to it: for he cultivates that audience not for his own writing, but for an inferior canon of poets. Yet what aristocratic reader would be pleased to choose poetry proclaimed as not worth the reading? And what working-class reader would be pleased to choose poetry proclaimed as only worth reading by an undiscerning audience obliged to be content with seeking moral improvement by reading and writing mediocre verse? Fredric Jameson has described genres as social contracts between writer and public, specifying the use of a particular cultural artifact—in the *Uneducated Poets,* we have a failed social contract.[86]

The pastoral counter-canon of Cunningham's *Biographical and Critical History* two years later ultimately serves a more useful political end, by providing a mainstream canon without differentiating a separate one for "peasant" taste, peasant authors, and peasant audience. Despite Cunningham's defiant statement of his antithetical critical perspective, his canon makes no effort to isolate a special class of readers. There is, of course, a tradition of counter-canons in collective biography: Suetonius reportedly wrote a lost *Lives of the Courtesans* as well as the *Lives of the Caesars;* and collections of the lives of highwaymen abounded in the eighteenth century alongside collections of ecclesiastics and poets. In grouping working-class poets it was not Southey's strategy to posit a negative canon, a canon of bad poetry or failed poets, but a separate stratum of literature; yet the effect was the same.

Like other genres, collective biography contains many repetitive and formless works, as well as many brilliant and innovative transgressions of genre. But regardless of achievement, the idea of anecdotal biography is tied closely to the financial facts of literary life; and perhaps more than other genres, anecdotal biography is tied to issues of audience because of its easiness to read and its ready absorption into the periodical press. The late eighteenth and early nineteenth centuries were a time of upheaval in the literary life, of movement from the patronage of wealthy, educated individuals to the necessary appeal to an expanded bourgeois populace. Johnson's own life is symbolic of this shift: he first desired patronage from Lord Chesterfield, and then, after being thrown on independent resources, found himself not needing patronage and spurning it. Throughout the Romantic era there is an intensified sense of the economics of the publishing world, evident in ubiquitous complaints and observations about the life of authors, education of readers, role of booksellers, nature of reviews, and conditions of literary popularity.

The finances of literature inevitably influenced all kinds of writing. Collective biography, like all biography, became an enormously popular form in this era. If biographers were lamenting the neglect of poets and other literary figures, they were at the same time enjoying the widespread interest in biographical narrative. The study of nonfictional prose in the nineteenth century offers us unusual access to the economics of the literary publishing world. Wordsworth, Scott, and De Quincey all turn unequivocally to nonfictional prose to make money. Nevertheless, it must not be thought that such projects—the guides to the lakes, the literary biographies, the autobiographies of the opium-eater—emerged without any literary integrity. Whether economic competition betters the product is as dubious, as Johnson says, as assuming had Dryden written less he would have written better. Examination of such works, however, demonstrates not only generic continuities but literary excellences; in the biographies of Johnson and his Romantic successors, the social and economic context of literature is enacted in the self-conscious investigation in which the biographer writing for money foregrounds the lives of those who wrote for money.

We have examined how Johnson and his more literal imitators used collective biography as a vehicle for sustained critical statements, and for exploration of aspects of the life of the writer and the nature of the audience and canon. In the following chapters we will examine collective biographies that also derive from Johnsonian themes, but whose central importance is in narrative innovation. It is not surprising to find the authors who experiment with genre are also the most astute in their long-term forecasts of canon. Romantic writers, in the wake of Johnson, came to treat biography as an infinitely malleable narrative, unconstrained by standards of either formal or ethical decorum. The biographer is not a submissive hagiographer, but a "mighty aristarch"; not bound by generic convention, but valiantly obliged to reveal truth through the infinite possibilities of narrative experimentation.

Chapter IV

William Hazlitt:
Narrative Hieroglyphics

In recent years, William Hazlitt has received the most critical attention of all the Romantic essayists. Most of the attention has centered on Hazlitt's philosophy and aesthetics, while the narrative form of Hazlitt's writings has gone virtually unconsidered. It is the aim of this study, however, to redirect attention to Hazlitt's essay sequences as collective narratives.[1] Hazlitt used the formal properties of discontinuous narrative as a way of spatializing his critical investigations of the *Zeitgeist* and the progress of the arts. Moreover, his sequences encouraged the use of collective biography as a mode of historical and epistemological inquiry; and his observations on the creative mind promoted new inquiries into the pathogenesis of art.

Perhaps even more than Johnson, Hazlitt was not an originator of forms but an innovator and stylist within existing genres. He experimented with virtually every nonfictional form. He first aspired to be known as a philosopher, but following the unpopularity of his early writings and lectures,[2] he turned to make his reputation first as a parliamentary reporter and then as a writer of familiar, political, and critical essays, and as an art and drama reviewer. By 1814, he had established himself as a critic, and he made his way by lecturing, writing biographies, reporting on art and drama, and publishing books of essay collections. In short, Hazlitt's career was that of a typical prose writer of the age. He earned a living through all the popular genres of periodical writing; wrote as much as possible; lectured when he could; procrastinated; negotiated with magazines; relied on those materials closest at hand; wrote about his contemporaries for profit; compromised his prose when necessary. Lamb accused Hazlitt of drawing "too entirely on his own resources. He never refers to the opinions of other authors (ancient or modern) or to the common opinions afloat on any subject, or if he does, it is to treat them with summary or elaborate contempt." De Quincey complained of Hazlitt's "habit of trite quotation," a practice "which places the reader at the

mercy of a man's tritest remembrances from his most school-boy reading."
And Henry Crabb Robinson said, "I was indignant at certain articles I had
read, and at the breach of private confidence in the detail of conversation,"
to which Hazlitt replied, "'You know I am not in the habit of defending
what I do. I do not say that all I have done is right. . . . It may be
indelicate, but I am forced to write an article every week, and I have not
time to make one with so much delicacy as I otherwise should.'"[3]

In the course of all this, Hazlitt experimented with virtually every
biographical form—long, short, collective, living, posthumous, character
sketch, autobiography. Two full-length biographies flank his career as a
journalist. Under pressure from Godwin, Hazlitt wrote the *Memoirs of the
late Thomas Holcroft* (written 1809–10, printed 1816), using the Mason
method of connecting long passages of autobiography, diary, and letters
with minimal narrative. His largely derivative *Life of Napoleon Buonaparte*
(1828–30) relied on translations, paraphrases, and quotes from existing
sources.[4] In addition, the *Conversations of James Northcote* (serialized between 1826 and 1829, and finally collected in book form in 1830) was a
Boswell-inspired chronicle of another member of the Johnson circle, the
painter and biographer of Reynolds. Its opening essay, under the title
"Boswell Redivivus," chided the accuracy of such conversational records:
"I differ from my great original and predecessor (James Boswell, Esq., of
Auchinleck), in this, that whereas he is supposed to have invented nothing, I have feigned whatever I pleased. I have forgotten, mistaken, mis-
stated, altered, transposed"; but when the essays were revised as a book he
emphasized its veracity and dropped the comment.[5] His autobiographical
Liber Amoris (1823) also purported to record a series of conversations,[6] and
throughout his career he wrote character sketches of his contemporaries.

Amid all these biographical experiments, the form Hazlitt returned to
most often was collective biography. Each of his three major lecture series,
Lectures on the English Poets (delivered twice, 1818), *Lectures on the English
Comic Writers* (delivered 1818–19), and *Lectures chiefly on the Dramatic
Literature of the Age of Elizabeth* (delivered 1819), as well as his best-known
work, *The Spirit of the Age: or, Contemporary Portraits* (1825), assembled
critical and character sketches. The genre of collective biography was
especially amenable to serialization in the periodical press and to the
lecture circuit (as Emerson and Carlyle were later to discover). Biography

had always been a Grub Street staple; for writers who earned a living as literary journalists, the popularity of biographical anecdotes of living authors in the Romantic era meant articles could be produced easily under the rubric of informal, firsthand glimpses.

Hazlitt's affinity for the collective sequence was to a great extent financial. But like other nineteenth-century prose writers, Hazlitt made an aesthetic virtue of the necessities imposed by the periodical press. The fragmentation prompted by serial publication, procrastination, deadlines, or financial need became an ethos of spontaneity, discontinuous narrative, and inconclusivity. Perhaps the most successfully enterprising of the Romantic Grub Street writers, he brought an astonishing efficiency to the uncertain life of the freelance writer through his aptitude for the familiar essay, his facility for popularizing as well as meeting public cravings, and his publishing savoir faire in recycling his ideas and reprinting many of his miscellaneous essays as books.[7]

Like the work of other writers under the pressure of weekly journalism and popular taste, much of Hazlitt's writing is derivative and relies on standard belletristic topics. Hazlitt was himself what he said Coleridge called James Mackintosh: "a master of the topics . . . the ready warehouse-man of letters, who knew exactly where to lay his hand on what he wanted."[8] Discussions of conversation, fame, taste, imagination, pulpit oratory and character writing were journalistic staples. Hazlitt often refreshed the same topic from new directions—"On Reading Old Books" (1821) and "On Reading New Books" (1827); "On the Love of Life" (1813), "On the Fear of Death" (1825) and "On the Feeling of Immortality in Youth" (1827); "On Pedantry" (1816) and "On the Ignorance of the Learned" (1818). He essentially described his own frequent strategy when he explained that Romantic poets imitated the method "which Rousseau did in his prose paradoxes—of exciting attention by reversing the established standards of opinion and estimation in the world."[9]

Many thought Hazlitt merited the same charge of "balance-master" he brought against Johnson, whom he said converted "general topics" into "perpetual paradox," and enslaved himself to "the periodical revolution of his style . . . keeping up a perpetual alternation of perfections and absurdities. . . . more bent on maintaining the equilibrium of his style than the consistency or truth of his opinions."[10] Leigh Hunt called Hazlitt "a connoisseur in the spirit of contradiction," and Allan Cunningham described Hazlitt as "a singular mixture of sagacity of remark and oddity of opinion. . . . His passion for singularity was injurious to his fame. . . . Hazlitt was underrated, and considered by many as a lover of paradox, and a man who could only utter odd and remarkable things." Speaking of his own writings, Hazlitt acknowledged "a fondness for paradox" and defended it as a way of popularizing abstract thoughts and bringing "out some obscure distinction."[11]

His criticisms of Johnson frequently illuminated the very traits for which he was censured. Indeed, he read Johnson as he said others read Boccaccio: Hazlitt's criticisms "only seized on those things in his works which were suited to their own taste, and . . . reflected their own grossness back upon the writer."[12] While he scorned Johnson for "making criticism a kind of Procrustes' bed of genius where he might cut down imagination," Hazlitt was regularly accused of the same traits of moroseness, cutting ill temper, and neglecting to say the good that he knew. Like other Romantics, Hazlitt held a great ambivalence toward Johnson. He borrowed from Johnson but was reluctant to acknowledge the debt. The *Lectures on the English Poets* calls Johnson "a lazy learned man" and "churlish," yet his views are cited in nearly every chapter. Indeed, in some measure Hazlitt styled himself a Johnson of his age: he adopted the post-Boswellian affectation of addressing everyone with the Johnsonian idiolect "Sir," cultivated a reputation for intimidation and censoriousness, and, like Johnson, declined to systematize his thoughts on taste, genius, and imagination.[13]

Many of Hazlitt's works were post-Johnsonian exercises in canon formation. In his first such endeavor, *The Eloquence of the British Senate; or, Select Specimens from the Speeches of the Most Distinguished Parliamentary Speakers* (1807), Hazlitt wrote condensed biographical sketches to preface oratorical selections. Each of his three major lecture series was published afterward as an essay sequence, and like Johnson's *Lives of the Poets,* each posits a literary canon. The *Lectures on the English Poets* (1818) is a history of English literature from Chaucer to "The Living Poets"; the *Lectures on the English Comic Writers* (1819) is a history of comedy across conventional boundaries, from Shakespeare, through Johnson and the essayists, the novelists, and Hogarth; the *Lectures chiefly on the Dramatic Literature of the Age of Elizabeth* (1820) is a history of the drama, poetry, and prose surrounding Shakespeare. All emphasize characterization without biographical chronologies, and like Johnson's *Lives* (after its first edition), they quote passages but do not append anthologies.

If in the present we tend to read Hazlitt primarily for his critical assessments rather than his biographical characterizations, it is a sign of recently changed tastes. Hazlitt was prized as a character writer by his contemporaries; in the twentieth century, Roy Park has said his profiles are "of poets rather than poetry," and R. L. Brett called him "a biographical critic who believed ideas are best seen as an expression of personality." *Tait's Magazine* (1836) declared his strength was in a "justness, sagacity, and a delicate discrimination of the finer shades of characters," and in praising Hazlitt's record of "characters, habits, and *idiosyncrasies,*" even regretted that he diluted the biographical characterizations with poetry criticism: "He has often mixed up criticism . . . with personal and intellectual portraiture; but the latter is then the first in importance.[14]

As the subtitle *Contemporary Portraits* of his best-known work *The Spirit of the Age* indicates, Hazlitt's biographical method was a prose portrait, rather than an overview of the life. Throughout his works Hazlitt used biographical details to signify the whole of character: Bentham "turns wooden utensils in a lathe for exercise, and fancies he can turn men in the same manner"; Coleridge's "nose, the rudder of the face, the index of the will, was small, feeble, nothing—like what he has done."[15] Although he wrote no systematic biographical theory, his reviews of new biographies confirm his practice. Of Spence's *Anecdotes* of Pope, he observed, "There is no species of composition, perhaps, so delightful as that which presents us with personal anecdotes of eminent men . . . an apparently insignificant anecdote often throws an entirely new light on the history of the most admired works." A few years later he affirmed, "There are few works more engaging than those which reveal to us the private history of eminent individuals," and explained that the strength of biography must lie in anecdotal details, "the immediate appeal to facts instead of theories."[16]

Hazlitt's characterizations heavily rely on the physical descriptions that one might expect of a painter-turned-writer. Charles Fox has a "brilliant, elastic forehead"; William Pitt, "a nose expressing pride and aspiring self-opinion"; Lamb, "a fine Titian head" (indeed, Hazlitt's most famous painting is, in the style of Titian, Lamb dressed as a Venetian senator).[17] He frequently considered the analogy between painting and writing. In his art criticism he declared, "Portrait-painting is the biography of the pencil, and he who gives most of the peculiarities and details, with most of the general character . . . is the best biographer, and the best portrait-painter." What a loss to biography, he exclaimed repeatedly, if Boswell had not shown Goldsmith "strutting about in his peach-colored coat" or Reynolds had not painted Johnson "as 'blinking Sam' "—a portrait Hazlitt not surprisingly admired, since it corresponded with Hazlitt's own allegorization of Johnson's impaired vision as a metaphor for his critical distortion (as "doubtful of the faculties of his mind, as of his organs of vision").[18]

Yet Johnson himself had called upon emblematic anecdotes in, for example, the *Life of Pope*. Despite Hazlitt's many disavowals, he kept returning to Johnson. The influence of Johnson's criticism and biography pervaded Hazlitt's prose, especially the model of the *Lives of the Poets* as a biographical approach to criticism and as a narrative cycle. Hazlitt's interest in epistemology and the iconic properties of collective narrative transformed Johnsonian collective biography. His biographical writings brought new ideological perspectives to issues implicit in the *Lives*: he repositioned literary history and canon within the question of the progress of the arts; transformed the question of the artist and audience into a discussion of the relation between individual achievement and the spirit of the age; and reconsidered the question of the unique troubles of genius as a pathology of the artist.

The Progress of the Arts and the Spirit of the Age

Writing Cultural History: Hume, Shelley, and Hazlitt

Toward the end of his life, in discussing his movement away from philosophical discourse to a new literary style, Hazlitt said of his writings: "They are not, then, so properly the works of an author by profession, as the thoughts of a metaphysician expressed by a painter. They are subtle and difficult problems translated into hieroglyphics." He says he rejected the "void of abstraction" and "severe train of reasoning" of philosophical discourse in favor of hieroglyphs—"tropes," "ornaments," "objects," "circumstances," "allusions," "picturesque imagery," "illustrations"—the figures of literary discourse through which meaning is deciphered.[19]

It is in this semiotic or iconic sense that we must understand Hazlitt's narrative cycles. Just as in individual biography the synecdochic anecdote indicates the whole of character, in Hazlitt's collective biography the individual portrait is a clue to the entire group. His interest in pictorialism resurfaces in the question of how a text communicates visually or spatially.

More than any of his contemporaries, Hazlitt was concerned with how form contributes meaning in collective narrative, and he came to use the iconic properties of discontinuous sequential narrative to frame epistemological questions. He said of Hogarth, "Other pictures we see, Hogarth's we read"; in reading Hazlitt's collective sequences we might well say, other narratives we read, his we see.[20] In spatializing two companion models of historicist inquiry, the diachronic progress of the arts and the synchronic spirit of the age, Hazlitt's narrative cycles translate the abstract concepts of unavoidable decline and the *Zeitgeist* current in philosophical discourse into the hieroglyphics of literary discourse.

Here, as elsewhere, Hazlitt was more overtly sympathetic with the eighteenth century than many of his contemporaries. In the *Lectures on the English Poets,* he continued Johnson's own dialogue with Warton, saying, "The question, whether Pope was a poet, has hardly yet been settled, and is hardly worth settling; for if he was not a great poet, he must have been a great prose-writer, that is, he was a great writer of some sort." Hazlitt often vindicated the Neoclassical poets. His own ranking of Pope and Dryden is unmistakably an echo of Johnson, and indeed, each chapter of the *English Poets* implies a Plutarchan pairing: Chaucer and Spenser, Shakespeare and Milton, Dryden and Pope, Thomson and Cowper.[21] The Plutarchan process of arriving at judgments by comparison is a critical methodology analogous to trends in eighteenth-century philosophy. Jean Hagstrum notes that Johnson's opening comment in the *Preface to Shakespeare,* that literary merit is determined by comparing examples, resembles Hume's assertion in "The Standard of Taste" that universals arise from consideration and comparison.[22] Conversely, Hume borrowed from literary biography in closing his history of the Stuarts with the neglect of the poets; he also began a translation of Plutarch's *Lives.*[23] In the eighteenth century, an era when the empirical study of the mind was the paramount concern of philosophy, as Anthony J. Tillinghast observes, it was inevitable that there would be some correspondences between biography and philosophy.[24]

In his own time, Hazlitt's bridge of the philosophical and the literary was typical of the writer of nonfictional prose.[25] The writings of Coleridge (philosopher, political writer, critic, theologian) and those of other Romantics—including Wordsworth's contemplation of the great philosophical poem—situated themselves between philosophical and literary discourse. In the longstanding tradition, the term literature (like "man of letters") assumed all forms of writing were part of an ongoing dialogue of letters. Certainly the Romantics deemphasized generic separations, which they associated with the normative rule making of the Neoclassical era.[26] Hazlitt, for one, retained the broad definition of literature; *The Spirit of the Age* encompasses all forms of the written or spoken word, by poets, preachers, essayists, philosophers, and political commentators.

Yet Hazlitt's narrative affiliations were fundamentally with the dialogue of belles lettres. Despite his early philosophical aspirations, Hazlitt chose, as Johnson had, a deliberately nonphilosophical mode of discourse.[27] Like the process of comparison, the concept of primitivism and progressivism in the arts and the concept of the character of an age appeared in the *Lives*, and there too possessed silent correspondences with contemporaneous philosophical inquiries. In Hazlitt, however, these are amplified as narrative motifs, using a vocabulary of concepts acquired from eighteenth-century philosophical discourse, in particular from Hume's literary essays.

Hazlitt's interest in Hume has often been noted.[28] He repeatedly praised Hume; and in moving from philosophical discourse to familiar essays and a more literary style, Hazlitt in some measure followed Hume's precedent.[29] In "On People with one Idea" (1825) he asserted that since Hume "there has been no metaphysician in this country worth the name. Yet his Treatise on Human Nature, he tells us, 'fell still-born from the press.'"[30] In "On the Causes of Popular Opinion" (1828) Hazlitt explicitly echoed Hume's autobiography in his statement that his own first book of philosophy, the *Essay on the Principles of Human Action*, "fell still-born from the press," though it was "nearly as subtle and original as anything in Hume or Berkeley." The identification of affiliations with Hume is not to suggest Hazlitt had any widespread effect of calling attention to Hume; Hume's work was well-known. Rather, in the manner of Coleridge or Emerson, he introduced certain concepts affiliated with the philosophical tradition into the literary dialogue; and of even more significance, he found innovative narrative expressions of them.

Hazlitt's view that the arts, once reaching a peak, inevitably decline is an idea explored by many writers in the eighteenth and nineteenth centuries. Johnson himself had set a kind of terminus with Pope—"to attempt any further improvement" will be "dangerous" and trivial: "what shall be added will be the effort of tedious toil and needless curiosity."[31] The idea of inevitable decline extends back to the heroic and Edenic motifs in ancient and Christian thought, and had literary antecedents at least as far back as the seventeenth century in the form of the quarrel between the ancients and the moderns. The reverse idea of cumulative improvement implicit in Godwinian perfectibility, the rise of Whig history, and the optimistic championing of modern creativity by poets such as Young, Wordsworth, and Shelley, drew attention to the issue of progress and decline. John Scheffer, in his history of the idea in the eighteenth century, believes Hume's essay gave currency to the argument of unavoidable decline.[32] Hume, therefore, stands as one of a number of presences behind Hazlitt's interest in the idea. But Hume particularly drew the attention of Hazlitt and other literary figures because he illustrated his argument with the art of writing; moreover, his concern for the discouragement of the "young poets" arose from his own early publishing efforts, and he placed the responsibility for failed literary endeavors on an unsympathetic audience rather than on deficient creativity.

After discussing how the arts arise in various favorable situations, Hume states in the fourth and final part of the "Rise and Progress of the Arts and Sciences" (1742), "When the arts and sciences come to perfection in any state, from that moment they naturally, or rather necessarily decline, and seldom or never revive in that nation." In Hume's view, "natural genius" is the same in all ages and nations. Each nation starts anew in "fresh soil" but is alike destined to the same process of decay. In early times writers are animated with aspirations that are later extinguished by the sophistication of the culture. Facing the intimidating abundance of excellent models, tyros are discouraged by inevitable critical comparisons between new productions and old masterpieces. Against the works of seasoned artists, juvenile works are regarded with "indifference and disdain," and first efforts are "coldly received" by an audience whose taste and criticism have been refined by acquaintance with excellence. Once immature productions are suppressed, a new generation of mature masterpieces can never arise:

> When the posts of honour are all occupied, [an artist's] first attempts are but coldly received by the public; being compared to productions, which are both in themselves more excellent, and have already the advantage of an established reputation. Were MOLIERE and CORNEILLE to bring upon the stage at present their early productions, which were formerly so well received, it would discourage the young poets to see the indifference and disdain of the public. The ignorance of the age alone could have given admission to the *Prince of* TYRE; but it is to that we owe *the Moor:* Had *Every man in his humour* been rejected, we had never seen VOLPONE.

For Hume, the cause of decline is not a failure of creativity, but a creativity repressed by literary intimidation and an audience coldly regarding new artworks; such a view of artistic decline that blames the culture at large rather than the individual artist is obviously one more welcome to writers. Johnson too had questioned an indifferent public (as he says of learning in *Dryden,* once made popular "it has the appearance of something which we have bestowed upon ourselves, as the dew appears to rise from the field which it refreshes") although his concern was less with cultural decline than the life of poverty and discouragement caused by a thoughtless audience.

Hazlitt was not the only Romantic to posit a theory of cultural decline, but others did not center the blame on the audience. Notably, the view of irremediable poetic decline was more prevalent among the Romantic critics than poets. Peacock ironically discussed the progressive subversion of literary values in "The Four Ages of Poetry" (1820), and Macaulay (reviewing the new edition of Dryden in 1828) observed that improved critical reasoning signifies the decline of the poetical faculty. Even those who were not part of the "anti-poetical faction," as D'Israeli called it in the *Calamities of Authors* (1812), questioned the literary achievements of the day, and many Romantics considered theirs a fallen age, although it was by no means a universal view. Thomas Noon Talfourd's "An Attempt to Estimate the Poetical Talent of the Present Age" (1815) specifically argued against the age's tendency to "underrate its poetical genius," and vowed to "counteract" the idea that the progress of poetry is finite and in a state of inevitable decay. Many critics propounded models of literary decline that simultaneously pointed out the progress and improvement of critical discourse; the growing tendency to separate the critical faculty from the poetical faculty in the late eighteenth and early nineteenth centuries permitted critics to praise the evolution of literary theory while lamenting the decline of its practice. The age's most characteristic self-image is expressed by Allan Cunningham, who declared, "This is the century of criticism." D'Israeli remarked, "We have become . . . a critical nation," and Hazlitt concurred: "'We are nothing, if not critical.' . . . let us be critical, or we shall be nothing."[33] Hazlitt, like other critics and prose writers, was conspicuously unwilling to blame professional critics for the literary decline.

Hazlitt often discussed the failure of the arts to inevitably progress. In the series of articles "Fine Arts: Whether they are Promoted by Academies and Public Institutions" (1814), Hazlitt warned that constant reference to the best models enervates the mind (a fear of excessive contact with

predecessors consistent with the Romantic preoccupation with originality over imitation). Echoing Hume's "posts of honour," Hazlitt discussed
finite demand in "The Periodical Press" (1823): "While the niches are
empty" artists and audiences are avid, but "when they are full" demand
subsides leaving no room for new art and "little or nothing to do, but to
think and talk about" the works of the past.[34]

His most sustained discussion of audience and cultural decline occurs in
"Why the Arts are not Progressive," an 1814 essay he repeatedly enlarged
and reprinted: "Those arts, which depend on individual genius and in-
communicable power, have always leaped at once from infancy to manhood" and declined thereafter. In "after-ages, and more refined periods"
there is a move toward artificiality and a decline of public taste. When the
"man of true genius" had "the privilege of being tried by his peers," before
"connoisseurship" had "become a fashion," only those with "natural
genius" pursued the arts and only those with "natural taste" would judge
them; poets did not have to contend with "pretenders to taste" and
"factitious patronage." Like Hume, Hazlitt places responsibility for failed
literary endeavors on the audience; in Hume, a sophistication of taste
crushes the juvenile poet; in Hazlitt, a corrupted taste assaults art.[35]
Hazlitt observes that this process of decline runs counter to prevalent
hopes; the fallacy of believing that "what has been once well done constantly leads to something better" leads to the frequent expressions of
"complaint and surprise" that present artistic genius does not equal past
excellence. Hume also noted this common error, and observed that the
notion of inevitable decline "may at first sight be esteemed contrary to
reason." Rewriting the essay for the *Lectures on the English Poets,* Hazlitt
even more cynically emphasizes the argument as one of necessary decline:
"In looking back to the great works of genius in former times, we are
sometimes disposed to wonder at the little progress which has since been
made in poetry." But in the arts, progress will always be checked: "What is
mechanical, reducible to rule, or capable of demonstration, is progressive,
and admits of gradual improvement: what is not mechanical, or definite,
but depends on feeling, taste, and genius, very soon becomes stationary,
or retrograde, and loses more than it gains by transfusion."[36]

The issue of progress and decline is the central concern of Hazlitt's
three lecture series on the arts. Inevitable decline is the organizing princi-

ple underlying the essay sequences of the *English Poets,* the *Comic Writers,* and the *Age of Elizabeth* (delivered within a few months of each other in 1818–19). A number of the constituent essays had been published earlier as freestanding essays, but gained new significance contextualized as part of a narrative sequence. As collective biographies, these three narrative cycles on the progress of the arts analyze history, genre, and genius as aspects of inevitable cyclic decline.

Lectures on the English Poets represents Hazlitt's first attempt to illustrate the theory of the progress of the arts. Its movement from Chaucer, Spenser, Shakespeare, and Milton, the "natural" poets, through the "artificial" poets of the eighteenth century, to the living poets, can be said to represent a descent from a literary golden age.[37] But the structure may be even more precisely understood when recognized as a narrative elaboration of its embedded earlier essay, "Why the Arts are not Progressive." The series of illustrative chapters implicitly traces the progress of English poetry from its early excellence through its inevitable decline into artificiality into a decadent present. He ends with the apology, "I have felt my subject gradually sinking from under me as I advanced, and have been afraid of ending in nothing. The interest has unavoidably decreased at almost every successive step of the progress, like a play that has its catastrophe in the first or second act. This, however, I could not help. I have done as well as I could."

On a global scale decline is inevitable, but there are second chances to excel. As Hume indicates, there is a history of the rise and progress of the arts in the course of the world, beginning with the ancients, and a separate history of the rise and progress of the arts within the fresh soil of each nation. To this Hazlitt contributes a third factor, the rise and progress of each genre. A nation may renew itself through excellence in the birth of a new form. The closing chapter of the *Lectures on the English Comic Writers* poses the question "*Why there are comparatively so few good modern Comedies?*" and answers it with the theory of generic decline: "It is because so many excellent comedies have been written." The intellectual depletion of genre is illustrated through the devolution of comic art from its peak in Shakespeare and Jonson, through the metaphysical poets, the Restoration dramatists, the eighteenth-century periodical essayists, to the modern novelists and Hogarth's visual narratives. There are individual excellences in each comic mode, but the larger narrative structure of decline indicates that the later forms are nevertheless inevitably degenerative forms. Thus, as Hazlitt succinctly states in "The Periodical Press," England saw its first excellences in tragedy, which inevitably declined; but comedy in the drama rose as tragedy fell; and as comedy in the drama inevitably declined, wit in the essay supplanted it; which in turn was succeeded by achievements of the novelists. Each of the "classes of excellence" has its own "rise and progress . . . maturity and decay."

The *Lectures chiefly on the Dramatic Literature of the Age of Elizabeth* introduces a synchronic dimension into Hazlitt's narrative cycles on the progress of the arts, a strategy that was to culminate in *The Spirit of the Age*. The collectivism here profiles a specific epoch, what might be called the spirit of the age of Elizabeth. The organizing principle is not merely to survey the dominant genre of the Renaissance, part of an antiquarian revival Lamb and others participated in (culminating in Pater's *The Renaissance*), but also to explore the relation between the individual and the age and show how mistaken evolutionary notions of progress impede our understanding of the nature of genius. The sequence begins by refuting the idea that Shakespeare was an anomaly springing forth amid rudeness and barbarism; Shakespeare was not "a sort of monster of poetical genius" but rather "one of a race of giants" of which he was the tallest. Of the relations between genius and epoch, Hazlitt observes, "His age was necessary to him; nor could he have been wrenched from his place in the edifice of which he was so conspicuous a part, without equal injury to himself and it." Hazlitt's discussion suggests a collaboration, or mutuality, between the individual and the age. In his later essay "The Periodical Press," Hazlitt declines to answer the question "'*Whether Shakespeare could have written as he did, had he lived in the present day?*'" yet his assessment of Rembrandt is tantamount to an answer: "Had he lived in our time, or in a state of manners like ours, he would have been a hundred other things, but not Rembrandt—a polite scholar, an imitator probably of the antique, a pleasing versifier, 'a chemist, statesman, fiddler, and buffoon,'—every thing but what he was, the great master of light and shade!" The decline of the world is so complete, Hazlitt does not even allow Rembrandt would have been a genius of any sort (a cynical contrast to Johnson, who declared, "I am persuaded that, had Sir Isaac Newton applied to poetry, he would have made a very fine epick poem").[38] The sole remaining excellence is critical refinement: "We complain that this is a Critical age," but instead should be grateful one thing remains to be done well. Amid the Sisyphean struggle to excel, all the genres have risen and declined, leaving only the residual excellence of taste—and criticism, his own genre.

The relation between the salient individual and the general culture raised in the Renaissance synchronic study, the *Age of Elizabeth,* is questioned in greater detail in Hazlitt's synchronic study of the present age. *The Spirit of the Age: or, Contemporary Portraits* presents the cynical culmination of the motif of decline, its series of individual profiles together forming a composite image of the present fallen age.

"The Spirits of the Age" was the running title for the original series of five essays written by Hazlitt for the *New Monthly Magazine* in 1824. In publishing it as a collective sequence, Hazlitt significantly changed the title to *The Spirit of the Age,* emphasizing the project's collective unity and its fundamental inquiry into whether there can be a univocal character to an age.[39] In this period of the genesis of the English *Zeitgeist,* three influential names stand out in connection with the term: Hume, Shelley, and Hazlitt.

The *Oxford English Dictionary* records Shelley as the first to use the expression "the spirit of the age," in an 1820 letter to Thomas Medwin, where he accepts the morbid effects of a poem with resignation: "It is the spirit of the age, and we are all infected with it." The term reappears the next year in the exuberant closing paragraph of the unpublished *Defence of Poetry:*[40]

> The most unfailing herald, companion, and follower of the awakening of a great people to work a beneficial change in opinion or institution, is Poetry. . . . It is impossible to read the compositions of the most celebrated writers of the present day without being startled with the electric life which burns within their words. They measure the circumference and sound the depths of human nature with a comprehensive and all-penetrating spirit, and they are themselves perhaps the most sincerely astonished at its manifestations; *for it is less their spirit than the spirit of the age.* Poets are the hierophants of an unapprehended inspiration; the mirrors of the gigantic shadows which futurity casts upon the present; the words which express what they understand not; the trumpets which sing to battle, and feel not what they inspire; the influence which is moved not, but moves. (emphasis added)

Poets are oracular witnesses, uttering "words which express what they understand not," embodying "a comprehensive and all-penetrating spirit."

Compelled to serve, uncomprehending, but nevertheless inspired and inspiring, poets utter words which are "less their spirit than the spirit of the age." Shelley does not concern himself, however, with defining the precise link between the artist and the larger society—we do not learn how the poet can be at once the "herald, companion, and follower."

Shelley's *Defence* contains the best-known citation of "the spirit of the age," but the earliest usage seems to have occurred some seventy years earlier in Hume's "Of Refinement in the Arts" (1752),[41] a citation that appears to have gone unrecognized bibliographically. In an extension of his interest in primitivism and progressivism, Hume uses the term "the spirit of the age" to analyze the relation between the individual artist and the larger culture in the process of political and artistic sophistication. Refinements in the mechanical arts, Hume asserts, are always accompanied by simultaneous refinements in the liberal arts:

> The same age, which produces great philosophers and politicians, renowned generals and poets, usually abounds with skilful weavers, and ship-carpenters. We cannot reasonably expect, that a piece of woollen cloth will be [w]rought to perfection in a nation, which is ignorant of astronomy, or where ethics are neglected. *The spirit of the age affects all the arts*; and the minds of men, being once roused from their lethargy, and put into a fermentation, turn themselves on all sides, and carry improvements into every art and science. Profound ignorance is totally banished, and men enjoy the privilege of rational creatures, to think as well as to act, to cultivate the pleasures of the mind as well as those of the body. (emphasis added)

An age is characterized by the analogous achievement of poets, philosophers, generals, politicians, astronomers, weavers, carpenters: "The spirit of the age affects all the arts." Any one advancement stimulates others; and refinement, rather than encouraging sloth, banishes ignorance, poverty, and vassalage, and permits cultivation of the mind: "Can we expect, that a government will be well modelled by a people, who know not how to make a spinning-wheel, or to employ a loom to advantage?"

Hume does not explain whether the agency of transmission is through diffusion of knowledge, rivalry, or mere contiguity. In examining the cyclic nature of refinement and the question of why one culture or nation or age excels, "Of the Rise and Progress of the Arts and Sciences" had already touched on the process of diffusion of refinement and the sequence of cultural refinements. There Hume observed that only a few in any nation or age can cultivate the arts and sciences "with such astonishing success, as to attract the admiration of posterity," but the multitude alike are "seized by the common affection"—the spirit of the age. These prominent figures characterize the entire age precisely because the refinement of the arts concerns not just the "taste, genius, and spirit of a few," but the entire nation: "It is impossible but a share of the same spirit and genius must be antecedently diffused throughout the people among whom they arise, in order to produce, form, and cultivate, from their earliest infancy, the taste and judgment of those eminent writers. The mass cannot be altogether insipid, from which such refined spirits are extracted." Certain achievements may be more likely to arise first—advances may be made in poetry before refinements of municipal laws, and the legal arts must first produce the security that will foster growth and refinement of other skills—but none is an isolated, unindebted act of genius. Hume's is not a vision of poetic genius and individuality, however; poets may claim the contrary, but the fire of poetic inspiration "is not kindled from heaven. It only runs along the earth; is caught from one breast to another; and burns brightest, where the materials are best prepared, and most happily disposed."[42]

Although the local source for Hazlitt's use of the term "spirit of the age," along with the sense of epoch and the progress of the arts through refinement and decay, seems to have come from Hume, we can only say local source because as is often observed, the late eighteenth and early nineteenth centuries witnessed the global rise of interest in the concept: *Zeitgeist* in Germany, *esprit du temps* in France, *spirit of the age* in England. Among the English Romantics, Percival Stockdale uttered the commonplace belief in saying that "the mind of the greatest genius will be more or less tinctured with the complexion of the times in which he lives." Most took the individual as an allusive index of the age, leaving the specifics of prophet, representative, and agent unaddressed; but once the concept had been tamed somewhat through familiarity, European and American thinkers anatomized the relation between the artist and culture and the dialectic implications of the individual and the age. Carlyle's statement of the heroic leader in history followed a longstanding eighteenth-century dialogue on the relation between the individual and history: Gibbon examined figures who embodied rather than servilely illustrated an age; Hume looked at the accretion of less conspicuous achievements rather than individual breakthroughs; Emerson saw each American as a potential hero, and the prominent figure as both representative of the age and a role for emulation; Arnold and Pater endorsed the idea of an epoch of artists—an age of Elizabeth, an age of Pericles, an age of Renaissance; Strachey saw in salient individuals the emblematic flaws of the culture. On the Continent, Voltaire's interest in *le siècle* cannot be disconnected from the rise of interest in the *Geist der Zeiten* emerging from Herder's view of cultural decline, and Hegel's concern with the *Volksgeist, Weltgeist,* and the inevitable force of time. Hazlitt himself placed an irrevocable stamp on the issues of epoch and progress through his use of the term the "spirit of the age" to discuss the direction and degree of genius, much as the term "great man" came to bear the mark of Carlyle. The writings of Sainte-Beuve (who borrowed Hazlitt's subtitle for his *Portraits contemporains*) and Taine on *milieu* derive directly from the English tradition of Hazlitt; and the German tradition led eventually to Dilthey's exposition of the individual as a crossing point for cultural systems and Marx's analysis of social determinism.[43]

Hume's sense of the diffusion of arts in a given age and nation, however, especially deserves our attention with regard to Hazlitt because of its implications for the synecdochic relation between the individual and the group. The year of *The Spirit of the Age,* 1825, invited a sense of epoch, marking the first quarter of the nineteenth century.[44] In Hazlitt's collective biography, individual achievement is reverberation of the spirit of the age; the prominent figures who seize the attention of posterity are part of the larger spirit, as Hume says, "antecedently diffused throughout the people among whom they arise." In Hazlitt's narrative, the individual portrait is a hieroglyphic emblem of the culture; a mosaic of biographical illustrations yields a composite historical portrait encoding the spirit of the age.

Many collections of contemporary figures preceded and followed Hazlitt, but Hazlitt's inquiry goes beyond Hume and other contemporary sequences in skeptically exploring the relation between the part and the whole, and the epistemology of the *Zeitgeist*. The *Monthly Magazine* ran an occasional *Contemporary Authors* series beginning in 1817. In 1828 the *Athenaeum* ran its series of *Sketches of Contemporary Authors* covering nearly the same figures as Hazlitt had; Richard Hengist Horne's *A New Spirit of the Age* (1844) explicitly updated Hazlitt's series with a new generation of names, as did George Gilfillian's *Gallery of Literary Portraits* (1845) and its two sequels.[45] In 1821 Hazlitt himself had been asked to continue the *Living Authors* series John Scott had begun for the *London*

Magazine, but he added only one article (an essay on Crabbe he subsequently used in *The Spirit of the Age*). Leigh Hunt's *Sketches of the Living Poets,* begun later the same year for the *Examiner,* seems to have demonstrated to Hazlitt the potential of collective biography.[46] Hazlitt's "Contemporary Portraits" enlarged a variety of cues in Hunt's series. As Hazlitt was to do, Hunt appropriated Coleridge's phrase ("This is said to be 'an age of personalities'") to underscore the way in which character sketches are inherently appropriate illustrations of the age; he used a pictorial metaphor to describe his task ("to give sketches of the principal features of the living poets, as an artist might sketch those of their faces"); and he relied on portraiture and the distillation of character to connect lives and works. Hazlitt's series, however, gave currency to synchronic collective biography in the nineteenth century. The very idea of a "life and times" biography reflects assumptions arising in the wake of Hazlitt, as evident in Philip Guedella's twentieth-century assertion that the subject of a biography should be "a person whose career summarizes in a convenient form the tone and temper of his age."[47]

Hazlitt did not merely collect biographies; he used *The Spirit of the Age* to examine the character of the age and the possibility of characterizing the age. Twice before Hazlitt had used the term. In an 1820 article "The Drama: No. IV," Hazlitt analyzed the impact of the French Revolution on dramatic writing, saying, "A bias to abstraction is evidently, then, the reigning spirit of the age." Abstraction and political partisanship are incompatible with the dramatist's need to leave behind "poetical egotism" and identify with the differing views of each character (the need to become, as Keats had said, a chameleon poet). But, he concludes, no artist can escape the age: "The poet (let his genius be what it will) can only act by sympathy with the public mind and manners of his age."

The term reappears in "On the Pleasure of Hating" (1826), an essay Hazlitt wrote in November–December of 1823, just before he started the series of profiles "The Spirits of the Age" for the *New Monthly Magazine* in January. Using Hume's same conjunction of terms, "refinement" and "the spirit of the age," Hazlitt observes, "Even when the spirit of the age (that is, the progress of intellectual refinement, warring with our natural infirmities) no longer allows us to carry our vindictive and headstrong humours into effect, we try to revive them in description . . . in imagination." Refinement warring with natural infirmity is manifested in the burning of Guy Fawkes in effigy, or loathing an insect even though we refrain from crushing it: "The spirit of malevolence survives the practical exertion of it." We give up the demonstration of hostility, but not the feeling of it. Literary preferences "at this time of day" confirm the character of the age; Scott's historical novels are popular because people can recognize in "the havoc, the dismay, the wrongs, and the revenge of a barbarous age" a climate similar to their own. In the act of reading we identify with lawlessness and "throw away the trammels of civilisation," a sublimation preventing us from enacting our lawless impulses. The presence of chaos in the present accounts for the popularity of romances evoking the chaos of the past: they make the disorder of the present age seem by comparison civilized, orderly, manageable.

Hazlitt saw the spirit of his own age as possessing the worst forms of cultural anarchy, far before Arnold saw the danger of doing as one likes.[48] The character of the age is uniform in its predation and confusion, a time of "wild beast[s]" and "hunting-animals," each rushing its own way under "lawless, unrestrained impulses." No "Jeremy Bentham Panopticons" can solve the lawlessness of his age, for it is a lawlessness not of legality, but of the spirit—a spirit of disunity and animosity for which there is no solution. In a society where foolish reformers stand alongside contemptible partisans, there is no cure for the havoc, dismay, and injustice: "I see folly join with knavery, and together make up public spirit and public opinions. I see the insolent Tory, the blind Reformer, the coward Whig." Reader and narrator join in, the "whole town runs to be present at a fire," in order to watch its own disaster and contribute to the decline: "We grow tired of everything but turning others into ridicule, and congratulating ourselves on their defects." Politicians vie; preachers damn those who do not concur; friends who are some of "the choice-spirits of the age" betray other friends. The spirit of the age is a climate of barely suppressed mutual contempt and repressed barbarism. Refinement is a matter of the cynical observance of forms; the propriety of sparing a victim continues to war with the impulse to loathe it.

He closes the essay wishing he had learned to hate his age sooner to preclude the disappointment of seeing "custom prevail over all excellence, itself giving way to infamy—mistaken as I have been in my public and private hopes." The best that can be hoped for is to elicit constructive hating that denounces the wrongs of the age.

"On the Pleasure of Hating" is sometimes called a precursor to *The Spirit of the Age* because of the coincidence of figures who reappear, but the crucial similarity lies in the shared tone of cynicism and despair.[49] Literary critics like to find in *The Spirit of the Age* an unstated subtext of optimism about the creative potential of the arts. But Hazlitt's correlation of poet and legislator bears no trace of Shelley's ecstatic view of the poet's oracular spirit; and the rubric "the spirit of the age" points to a sinister similarity between poet and legislator. None of the representative figures emerges unscathed; each biographical portrait is suffused with the pleasure of hating. If the spirit of the age is unclear, it is not because, like Shelley, it fills and inspires through vatic pronouncement; it is because the words written and spoken by politicians, poets, and preachers of the age are divisive, adversarial, and contradictory. The spirit of the age encompasses everyone; dissidents and adherents alike are joined by posterity through their opposition. The epigraph paraphrasing *Hamlet* (V.ii.142), "To know a man well, were to know himself," implicates narrator and reader also: everyone participates in the decline, running to be present at the fire.

Yet we must be wary of trying to overspecify a connection between "On the Pleasure of Hating" and *The Spirit of the Age,* for the essay was never attached in any fashion. Moreover, as in Johnson, no guiding editorial intrusion, no preface or conclusion, situates us at the beginning or the end of the sequence.[50] Unlike the embedded "Why the Arts are not Progressive" in the *Lectures on the English Poets,* for example, no organizing concept is made explicit in *The Spirit of the Age,* no unifying theoretical statement, no headnote of explanation, no steering definitions; we have nothing to guide us beyond juxtaposition of the fragments that comprise the essay sequence.

Hazlitt worked consistently in a collective manner, and of all the Romantic texts examined in this book, critics seem most inclined to respect the collective form of Hazlitt's *The Spirit of the Age*; yet because it has not been seen as part of an existing genre, it has posed greater confusion than need be. In the final form published by Hazlitt, the essays follow a fairly straightforward sequence:[51] the three philosophers, Bentham, Godwin, Coleridge; overlapping the three preachers and talkers, Coleridge, Irving, Tooke; the four most prominent poets, the two titled poets Scott and Byron, and the two lake poets Southey and Wordsworth; the two philosopher-historians, Mackintosh, Malthus; the rival political editors, Gifford, Jeffrey; the political speakers and writers, Brougham, Burdett, Eldon, Wilberforce, Cobbett; the minor poets, Campbell, Crabbe, Moore, Hunt;

the anachronistic essayists, Lamb and Washington Irving. The sequence implies some analogies by juxtaposition,[52] but does not remove the problem posed by the absence of introduction or conclusion, and does not put to rest the central question of the text: the dispute over what actually is the spirit of the age.

We need not rehearse every citation of the term in the book to recognize it is scattered and inconclusive—that exercise has been performed by other critics already.[53] Considerable critical energy has been devoted to determining a univocal meaning of *The Spirit of the Age*, under the assumption that artists impose a distinctive and personal design on cultural history. But what is that design in Hazlitt? David Levin claims the term "the spirit of the age" is usually invoked to describe the most progressive aspects of an era, but Hazlitt juxtaposes liberals and Tories, reactionaries and revolutionaries. M. H. Abrams believes Hazlitt designed an exploration of the impact of the French Revolution. Roy Park says the text thematically demonstrates how the crushing force of the age suppressed the imaginative spirit. Patrick Story believes the series shows how the effeminacy of the arts lost out in the war between mechanistic logic and creative originality. Conversely, Ralph M. Wardle, René Wellek, and George Levine argue that Hazlitt failed to produce any coherent unification, from either laziness or inability. Wardle concludes Hazlitt never provides a recurring pattern in his use of the term "the spirit of the age." Wellek sees Hazlitt's use of the term as merely a stock phrase, with hardly any continuity in the text. Levine excludes Hazlitt from an anthology of the same name because *The Spirit of the Age* "makes no generalized statements sufficient to give a sense of what Hazlitt is up to."[54]

Current critical opinion, then, divides between the idea that Hazlitt thematically unified the collection of portraits into a sequence and the idea that he failed to unify them; one argues for a competent unity, the other for an incompetent disunity. Yet there is a third possibility, to view the narrative as a competent disunity, a narrative of fragmentation. This is not to claim that the author imposed upon the genre a disunified sequence, but rather that in *The Spirit of the Age* meaning arises from the iconic properties of Johnsonian collective biography. Its discontinuous narrative symbolically echoes the age's confusion, contention, hypocrisy, feuding, and contradiction.

The absence of preface, conclusion, overriding order, or guiding editorial force takes on added significance when we remember Hazlitt's fundamental interest in paradox and contradiction. The only uniformity of the age is paradoxically in its disunity: there can be no crystallizing introduction or conclusion in a splintered and partisan era. The time is out of joint: neither Hazlitt nor the Hamlet of the epigraph can set it right. The composite fragments of the text provide an iconic emblem of the cultural fragmentation of the times: the chaos of individuality is the spirit of the age. No single case study can typify the age for there is no representative type, only innumerable pursuits of singularity, scattering in all directions.

The Spirit of the Age uses multiple, contradictory examples to depict the first quarter of the century as an age of volatility, paradox, and caprice. Scott can be a splendid prose writer and a despicable political entity; an Eldon can advance the machinery of slavery and retard reform, alongside a Brougham who urges the opposite; a poet like Southey can capitulate to the government as a laureate, while another like Coleridge can refuse to enter the gates of the city; a single writer can be as inconsistent as Cobbett within his own works; a writer like Lamb can wander as ingenuously ignorant of the prevailing trends as a preacher like Irving can exploit them or a poet like Byron can pander to them. Philosophers are recognized outside their own nation, but not within it; others are the passing fancy of an era, and still others are unable to complete an unflawed project. Poets, though their poetry be good, abase themselves in obsequiousness; others lead contemptible lives alongside admirable verse. Politicians are abetted in folly, or are hypocrites aided by the partisanship of editors. A few writers, standing in the periphery, maintain their integrity, and they are ineffectual because they foolishly keep themselves outside the mainstream.

The narrative of fragmentation reflects the anarchy of an age in which the parts cannot be added into a whole. Categories are deconstructed as soon as they are set up; an age can be characterized only by its disunities. Accordingly, the text can provide no culminating final statement. The refusal to generalize a univocal voice of anarchy is itself an extension of the Romantic emphasis on the individual that devalued uniformity and yielded a havoc of individualism. It would be possible to end discussion of *The Spirit of the Age* with this note of resolution and closure, reading the narrative discontinuity as an iconic emblem of Romantic individualism. But the narrative goes beyond a captious unity of defiance, and its importance lies not in propounding a theory of the age but in the epistemological implications of the narrative of fragmentation.

The very allegiance to individuality that led Hazlitt to resist cultural generalities led him to doubt the nature of synchronism and question the possibility of making any kind of design. The impossibility of a paradigm for the age casts doubt on epistemological groupings such as a dominant spirit of the age, or a characterizing *Zeitgeist,* concepts that essentially try to force a ruling univocal voice from multiplicity of meaning.

Hazlitt's approach to cultural analysis is not far removed from Michel Foucault's distrust in *The Archaeology of Knowledge* of "the notion of 'spirit' "and "unities of discourse." Like Foucault, he rejects the notion of a "particular spirit of an age" which establishes a uniformity.[55] In breaking up categories and continuities instead of forming them, in studying divisions, interruption, and dispersion instead of uniformities, Hazlitt anticipates Foucault's call for the formulation of a theory of discontinuity. Indeed, Hazlitt's *Spirit of the Age* implicitly deconstructs the possibilities of synchronism suggested in his earlier work, the *Age of Elizabeth.* Similarly, Foucault's work in *The Archaeology of Knowledge* rejects the essentially structuralist unities implied by the concept of episteme in *The Order of Things,*[56] which replaced diachronism and evolutionary continuities with a synchronic typology of analogous discourse in grammar, natural history, and economics.

Hazlitt's skepticism offers a bridge between Hume and Foucault, but *The Spirit of the Age* goes beyond either in questioning the validity of successive synchronic units as epistemological categorizations. To doubt the nature of synchronism is, in turn, to question the essentially structuralist endeavor to periodize history and literature. Foucault rejects the perception of false continuities between eras but Hazlitt goes further in rejecting the establishment of analogies within a given age; Foucault's deconstruction of conventional evolutionary diachronism is in turn deconstructed by Hazlitt, who suggests the artificiality of making synchronic categories. *The Spirit of the Age* undercuts the stabilities posited by Foucault's synchronic concept of a simultaneous intellectual transformation at the end of the eighteenth century. Its rejection of narrative continuities offers a warning against Foucauldian synthesizing gestures; we can speak of the position of the salient individual in the culture but we must be as wary of synchronic analogies as of diachronic evolutionary models. For Hazlitt, the closest we may come to unity in speaking of the Romantic spirit of the age, or episteme, is in its disunity. On a larger scale, in dismissing the notion of synchronism, *The Spirit of the Age* questions the entire notion of periodization, which in its smallest reverberation concerns the issue of whether we should speak of *romanticism* or *Romanticism,* and which in its largest form calls into question the possibility of the term altogether; and ultimately questions whether any literary-historical period is no more than a reification of an age, a futile attempt to reconcile irreconcilables through false analogies. In the grand perspective, cultural fragmentation is not just a characteristic of Hazlitt's own age, but of any age; the narrative of fragmentation suggests the powerlessness of synchronic analogy beyond discovering the irreconcilable anarchy of an era. *The Spirit of the Age* dramatizes the inaccuracy of labeling and grouping individuals, and the fundamental impossibility of imposing an order on things.

Contemporary Lives: "Yarrow Unvisited"

Hunt, Byron, and the Pathology of Genius

The morose skepticism that underlies Hazlitt's greatest intellectual innovations was also the trait that made him critically unpopular (he made editorial adversaries of *Blackwood's* and the *Quarterly Review*) and a social pariah (De Quincey, Wordsworth, Coleridge, and Byron all found reasons for avoiding his company). It was not merely a fear that a negative critical appraisal or some ruthless biographical detail might surface in the pursuit of journalism: like his epistemological deconstructions, Hazlitt's thoughts on the pathology of the artist called into question fundamental myths about the special image of literature and the poet.

Biographers commonly invoked the reverentiality of Shakespeare to justify potentially revealing anecdotes. Boswell apologized for his portrait of Johnson, saying, "How delighted should we have been if thus introduced into the company of Shakspeare, and of Dryden, of whom we know scarcely any thing but their admirable writings!" and De Quincey excused his descriptions of Wordsworth declaring, "How invaluable should we all feel any record to be, which should raise the curtain upon Shakspeare's daily life." Hazlitt also argued on behalf of Spence's *Anecdotes,* "What would we not give to any modern Cornelius who would enable us to catch a glimpse of Pope through a glass door. . . . Cicero's villa, the tomb of Virgil, the house in which Shakespear was brought up, are objects of romantic interest, and of refined curiosity to the lover of genius; and a poet's lock of hair, a *fac-simile* of his handwriting, an ink-stand, or a fragment of an old chair belonging to him, are treasured up as relics of literary devotion." Although he helped supply some of the reliquary anecdotes which allowed readers to make their own comparisons of the lives and works of contemporary writers, for Hazlitt the central ambition of literary biography was not mere nostalgia or factual validation but scrutinizing lives and works: "The difficulty of forming almost any inference at all from what men *write* to what they *are,* constitutes the chief value of the problem which the literary biographer undertakes to solve."[57]

Like other Romantic critics, Hazlitt often conjectured the character of the poet directly from the character of the works: there is "an obvious similarity between the practical turn of Chaucer's mind and restless impatience of his character, and the tone of his writings"; Byron makes characters "after his own image . . . he gives us the misanthrope and the voluptuary by turns; and with these two characters . . . he makes out everlasting centos of himself."[58] All germane information, however, is not necessarily evident in the works; and ultimately we must be equally prepared for demystifications or reliquiae. Hazlitt's observation, "We have no means to discover whether the moral Addison was the same scrupulous character in his writings and in his daily habits, but in the anecdotes recorded of him. . . . there is nothing to show that the writer of the Eloise to Abelard was a little, deformed person, or a Papist," also presumes we might have some reason for wanting to know whether 'a good poet is a good man,' a convoluted one, or subjective in some other way. Wordsworth's *Letter to a Friend of Robert Burns* had argued that biographical reflections should be confined to the rosy inferences made from the works alone; to which Hazlitt replied, Burns could not have described the "indulgence" of Tam o'Shanter "if he himself had not 'drunk full ofter of the ton than of the well.'"[59]

Wordsworth, like other Romantic poets, upheld the traditional lofty vision of the poet as an influential and oracular leader. The *Essay, Supplementary* depicts the reader "invigorated and inspirited by his Leader." Coleridge's *Biographia Literaria* declares "an analogy between genius and virtue." Shelley's *Defence of Poetry* contains perhaps the most emphatic vision of the high calling in which the greatest poets are the greatest men:

> A poet, as he is the author to others of the highest wisdom, pleasure, virtue and glory, so he ought personally to be the happiest, the best, the wisest, and the most illustrious of men. . . . the greatest Poets have been men of the most spotless virtue, of the most consummate prudence, and if we could look into the

interior of their lives, the most fortunate of men: and the exceptions, as they regard those who possessed the imaginative faculty in a high yet inferior degree, will be found on consideration to confirm rather than destroy the rule.

Hazlitt threatens different conclusions at the end of the *Lectures on the English Poets,* where he comments forebodingly on the dangers of biographical knowledge—"I happen to have had a personal acquaintance with some of these jealous votaries of the Muses." Invoking the discourse of Wordsworth, he cynically observes:

> Poets are not ideal beings; but have their prose-sides, like the commonest of the people. We often hear persons say, What they would have given to have seen Shakspeare! For my part, I would give a great deal not to have seen him. . . . It is always fortunate for ourselves and others, when we are prevented from exchanging admiration for knowledge. The splendid vision that in youth haunts our idea of the poetical character, fades, upon acquaintance, into the light of common day; as the azure tints that deck the mountain's brow are lost on a nearer approach to them. It is well, according to the moral of one of the Lyrical Ballads,—"To leave Yarrow unvisited."

Biographical knowledge compels us to exchange admiration for knowledge; but unlike the Wordsworth of "Yarrow Unvisited" ("We have a vision of our own; / Ah! why should we undo it?"), Hazlitt confronts the inevitability of disillusionment in visiting Yarrow ("And is this—Yarrow? —*This* the Stream"?). To visit with the poets, as Hazlitt and De Quincey did, inevitably leads to demystification, but in doing so brings the new insights of biographical investigation to the revisited text ("Beheld what I had feared to see").[60]

"My First Acquaintance with Poets" depicts the demystified Yarrow of living poets in which "the poetical character, fades, upon acquaintance, into the light of common day." The vision of a Christ-like Coleridge Hazlitt saw in his youth (when "the splendid vision" of the "poetical character" is still plausible) is canceled by the reality he now perceives with unidealizing eyes. A countertext of portraiture is at work throughout: Coleridge's incidental actions reveal his carelessness about literary achievement (he decides to accept the Wedgwoods' offer of an annuity "in the act of tying on one of his shoes") and his wavering commitment to the ministry ("I observed that he continually crossed me on the way by shifting from one side of the foot-path to the other. This struck me as an odd movement; but I did not at that time connect it with any instability of purpose or involuntary change of principle, as I have done since"). Coleridge rushes out into the chaos of precipices and waves in a thunderstorm, "running out bare-headed to enjoy the commotion of the elements in the Valley of Rocks, but as if in spite, the clouds only muttered a few angry sounds, and let fall a few refreshing drops"—like Coleridge's own productivity, much sound and fury yielding only "a few refreshing drops." The essay ends with Godwin, Holcroft, Coleridge, and Lamb debating "which was the best— *Man as he was, or man as he is to be*," with Lamb's closing observation providing a commentary on the idealized image of the poet: " 'Give me,' says Lamb, 'man as he is *not* to be.' "

The tradition of celebrating genius, and the expectation that biography would confirm it, conflicted with new post-Johnsonian insights into the relation between lives and works. Johnson's *Lives* had called attention to the subculture of artists and its special concerns, which D'Israeli later chronicled in more detail—the life of poverty, desolation, and unrecognition. As with the theory of decline, there is a critical dissonance between the poets' idealization of the poetic calling and what was increasingly becoming evident in Romantic biography and criticism, the dark side of the alienage and marginality of the artistic community, which poets were reluctant to see explored. Just as Johnson's *Lives* had identified the analogous ostracism of the poet and criminal, the archetype of the sick artist that emerged in the critical dialogue of Hazlitt and Leigh Hunt illuminated the poet as a cultural outsider. The intellectual reciprocation of Hazlitt and Hunt not only resulted in the collaboration of *The Round Table*; Hunt's *Living Poets* series drew Hazlitt's attention to the potential of the genre he was to bring into vogue with *The Spirit of the Age*; and Hazlitt's essay on the pathology of genius provided a theoretical basis for ideas developed by Hunt in his collective biographies.[61] Hazlitt and Hunt's exploration of the pathology of genius adumbrated twentieth-century psychoanalytic approaches to the creative mind, and investigated how the image of the marginal poet has corresponding social implications for art.

Although Freud said of his own age, "Readers to-day find all pathography unpalatable"[62] ("Be Yarrow stream unseen, unknown! / It must, or we shall rue it"), Hazlitt's theory of the pathology of genius awakened considerable interest in its own time. His 1815 essay "On the Causes of Methodism" (reprinted in *The Round Table* in 1817), although little known today, was a contemporary landmark in the study of creativity, locating artistic predisposition in constitutional infirmity and articulating perhaps the first general theory of the pathology of artistic genius. Where Edmund Wilson was to use the image of Philoctetean "wound and the bow" as a parable of the artist,[63] Hazlitt uses the image of the convert to Methodism. Methodists are, he says, "a collection of religious invalids" attached to a doctrine of the elect, who turn to faith because they are incapable of reason. Methodism attracts those who are morally unsteady, intellectually insubstantial, and physically unsound: "You may almost always tell, from physiognomical signs," who will walk into a Methodist chapel—"melancholy . . . consumptive. . . . half-starved." They are, he says, "unsound in body and mind." In the key analogy of the essay, these symptomatic maladies, these "Causes" of Methodism, are the same that draw people to become poets: "The same reason makes a man a religious enthusiast that makes a man an enthusiast in any other way, an uncomfortable mind in an uncomfortable body." Hazlitt does not idealize the poetic calling. Art springs not from Helicon but from "original poverty of spirit," physical sickliness, and isolation from society:

> Poets, authors, and artists in general, have been ridiculed for a pining, puritanical, poverty-struck appearance, which has been attributed to their real poverty. But it would perhaps be nearer the truth to say, that their being poets, artists, etc. has been owing to their original poverty of spirit and weakness of constitution. As a general rule, those who are dissatisfied with themselves, will seek to go out of themselves into an ideal world. Persons in strong health and spirits, who take plenty of air and exercise, who are 'in favour with their stars,' and have a thorough relish of the good things of this life, seldom devote themselves in despair to religion or the Muses. Sedentary, nervous, hypochondriacal people, on the contrary, are forced, for want of an appetite for the real and substantial, to look out for a more airy food and speculative comforts.

Hazlitt reversed the eighteenth-century tradition that the intellectual rigors of the poetic or scholarly life bring about constitutional weaknesses;[64] the poetic life is pursued from inherent physical and intellectual inadequacies. Here, poetry is a symptom of illness, the muses the resort of despair, a view implicitly questioning the general cultural validity of poetic utterances. The religion of Methodism is able to offer its invalids only a "forlorn hope" at best. What then of the religion of art, and the "airy" and "speculative comforts" offered by poets?

Hazlitt's later description of Shelley points out the same traits: "As is often observable in the case of religious enthusiasts, there is a slenderness of constitutional *stamina*."[65] In place of Shelley's image of the poet as the "happiest," the "best," the "most fortunate," Hazlitt uncovers the sickly and near hysterical enthusiasm of the "philosophic fanatic," a "fire in his eye . . . fever in his blood . . . hectic flutter in his speech." The idealized images of poetry are not the product of prophetic inspiration but of a diseased fanaticism.

Lionel Trilling, justly regarding Freud's work as a culmination of Romantic thought ("The poets and philosophers before me discovered the unconscious"),[66] argued that the "myth of the sick artist," the notion of the artist as aberrant, mad or weak, arose from the poets themselves. Yet the idea of analyzing connections between the generation of works of art and the pathology of the artist arose, in England at least, not just from mere poetic curiosity about the subjectivity of perception, but from the post-Johnsonian biographical investigation of links between lives and works. Hazlitt does not explain why some persons become Methodists and others poets; and why some become good poets and others not. Trilling, addressing Wilson's comments on the wound and the bow, points to the unanswered question of how genius and disease are bound together: Is the wound the price of the bow? Does effectiveness in the arts depend on sickness? Is artistic ability traded for or gained by suffering? His explanation is that the artist is not "unique in neurosis," but rather, unique in "his successful objectification of his neurosis."

Johnson's assertion that artistry is only the manifestation of a particular direction taken by genius had implicitly raised the same fundamental questions: May a person walk to the east as well as west, to creativity, to neurosis, or to Methodism? In his biography of Leonardo da Vinci, Freud himself only says that the artist channeled repression into art, and cautions that "health and illness, normal and neurotic" are not sharply distinguished. Ultimately "artistic talent and capacity . . . the nature of the artistic function . . . the fact of Leonardo's artistic power" are only partially and finitely accessible along psychoanalytic lines. The psychoanalytic method cannot account for genius itself (neither "the artistic gift" nor "artistic technique") but it can make "its manifestations and limitations intelligible" by explaining certain aspects of the imagination, the choice of subjects, and the "impulses at work" behind the work of art. These are, in fact, precisely the concerns of Hunt, who, like Freud, declined the traditional biographical task of "idealization" in favor of a psychological portraiture popularly supposed to " 'blacken the radiant and drag the sublime into the dust.' "[67]

More than any other figure after Johnson, Byron elicited memoirs and biographical speculation, so it is not surprising to find Romantic psychobiographical theories of creativity surrounding the figure of Byron. Hunt ended his biographical essay on Byron in *Lord Byron and Some of his Contemporaries* (1828) with the letter Byron wrote him in response to "On the Causes of Methodism." Byron agreed with the "paper on the Methodists," rather than with Hunt's rebuttal printed the next month,[68] and offered a series of biographical illustrations:

> The paper on the Methodists was sure to raise the bristles of the godly. I *redde* it, and agree with the writer on one point in which you and he perhaps differ; that an addiction to poetry is very generally the result of "an uneasy mind in an uneasy body;" disease or deformity have been the attendants of many of our best. Collins mad—Chatterton, *I* think, mad—Cowper mad—Pope crooked— Milton blind—Gray—(I have heard the last was afflicted by an incurable and very grievous distemper, though not generally known) and others—. I have somewhere redde, however, that poets *rarely* go mad. I suppose the writer means that their insanity effervesces and evaporates in verse—may be so.

Byron makes no mention of his own lameness, although his assertion that "disease or deformity have been the attendants of many of our best" offers a reminder that his own career might well have been described as afflicted with " 'an uneasy mind in an uneasy body.' "[69]

Byron was extremely interested in checking his credentials against contemporary discussions of genius. He repeats this same formulation in letters to several other correspondents.[70] The idea of listing biographical examples as evidence seems to be inspired by Isaac D'Israeli's best-selling studies of artistic genius, which Byron repeatedly admired, and which (from the evidence of their frequent reprinting) provide a helpful index of popular Romantic thought. Byron told Murray, "I have a great respect for *Israeli* and his talents, and have read his works over and over and over. . . . I don't know a living man's books I take up so often, or lay down more reluctantly"; and echoing Johnson's earlier admiration, he named D'Israeli, "the Bayle of literary speculation."[71] He seems to have had a particular interest in *The Literary Character*; D'Israeli reprinted Byron's marginalia from the 1795 and 1818 editions (and sent him a copy of the 1822 edition), including the remark that he had read D'Israeli's works "oftener than perhaps those of any English author whatever."[72] More tellingly, Byron revealed his eagerness to be included in the work, subtitled *The History of Men of Genius, Drawn from their own Feelings and Confessions,* by inviting D'Israeli to consult his unpublished autobiographical writings as evidence: "Mr. Murray is in possession of a MS. memoir of mine (not to be published till I am in my grave). . . . I do not know whether you have seen those MSS.; but, as you are curious in such things as relate to the human mind, I should feel gratified if you had."[73]

The Romantic interest in the imitability of genius and the individual pathology of the artist was essentially a repositioning of traditional eighteenth-century concerns: valuative studies weighing ancients and moderns, mechanistic studies of the mind, critical and biographical studies of genius such as Johnson's and the Wartons'. The increasingly common Romantic notion of the suffering, antisocial, or tainted artist represents a sharp contrast with, for example, Joseph Warton's assumption that "many of our English poets have been in their persons remarkably handsome."[74] The Romantic "disease or deformity of many of our best" in some measure rejuvenates the ancient Tiresian or Homeric image of the seer whose strange (privileged) power of speech is accompanied by special punishments.

Byron's brief remark that the madness of poets "effervesces" in verse was a topic often considered by other writers. Lamb's well-known argument against the insanity "of true genius" attests to the prevalent view of artists as alien or injured beings. Scott was anxious to detach himself from common assumptions about the "malady" and eccentricities associated with great talent ("violent passions" and "peculiar . . . moral character"). Byron's image of the "addiction of poetry" reappears in De Quincey's description of creativity as a "convulsion" akin to opium derangement.[75] Coleridge, Keats, and Hazlitt all addressed the question of the Horatian *genus irritabile vatum,* revived by D'Israeli's biographical case studies.[76] Although the *Biographia* rejected the notion of the fanatical poet and distinguished between those who embody "the shaping spirit of Ruin" and those "of the greatest genius" who possess a "calm and tranquil temper,"[77] the visionary delirium at the end of "Kubla Khan" ("Beware! His flashing eyes") suggests links between derangement and creativity; as did its preface implying Byron's approval of the poem's merits as a "psychological curiosity" illustrating the action of the creative mind.[78] Like Philoctetes, whose bow of Hercules had sacred overtones, the Ancient Mariner (1798) possesses a cross-bow, and likewise initiates action only to be punished with heroic suffering and exile for an inexplicable transgression. Like Philoctetes (vanquisher of Troy) he is at once an

outcast and a redeemer; only those few who listen to him (like Neop-
tolemus) share the poet/Mariner's special stature. The same archetypes of
physical and spiritual exile appear in the biographies of the poets—
although interestingly none of the above writers acknowledges any personal physical disability (lameness, consumption, addiction) when discussing the question of a pathology of genius.[79] Like the theory of
decline, the theory of artistic pathology was more willingly probed by
critics and biographers than by poets.

Hunt's earliest writing on the subject, the 1815 essay which Byron
opposed (revised as "On the Poetical Character" in *The Round Table* in
1817), had refuted Hazlitt's "On Methodism" with the antiquated view
that poets sometimes weaken their constitutions by study, but on the
whole have an unusual healthiness of mind and body. He identifies the five
sole poets in European history who had nervous disorders.[80]

But later Hunt's collective biographies took up where Hazlitt left off. In
writing the *Sketches of the Living Poets* (1821), Hunt began to venture a
pathology of art. Campbell has "the usual sickness of the sedentary and
industrious." The lameness shared by Byron and Scott is connected with
mutual qualities in their writing: "It is remarkable that the two eminent
living writers, whose portraits of humanity are upon the whole mixed up
with a greater degree of scorn than those of any of their contemporaries,
are both of them lame." While Hunt does not suggest how deformity and
ill health predispose the life of writing, he does consider how the psychological position of the writer influences the literary text. Those who have
"thought to worry his Lordship's feelings" by maligning Byron's lameness have risked the pernicious consequences of an art in which Byron
turns even more malevolently against humanity: "they might yet awake in
him thoughts about human nature, for which a defect of this sort does not
help to sweeten the kindest." The effect of sickness on verse in turn holds
malevolent consequences for the poet's depiction of society.

In *Lord Byron and Some of his Contemporaries* (1828),[81] Byron is the
central figure of Hunt's collective biography of the expatriate literati of
the age: the first third profiles Byron; the second third sketches literary
figures including Moore, Shelley, Keats, Lamb, and Coleridge; the final
third is his own autobiography. The depiction of Byron drew considerable attention on the basis of its indiscretions, which had the ostensible
credibility of having been revealed by a longtime intimate of Byron.
Byron is fat; jealous of Wordsworth; unaristocratically gossipy ("fond as a

footman of communicating unpleasant intelligence"); pretends each visitor is receiving privileged confessions; has a poor library; behaves vulgarly; knows nothing of the fine arts; has little regard for liberty; demands deference as a "man of letters" and a lord; has the "remnant of his hair oiled and trimmed with all the anxiety of a Sardanapalus"; is so parsimonious he intended to regain the money he loaned to Greece. Of all the collective biographies examined in this study, Hunt's is the most explicitly directed at demythologizing the poet.[82]

The genesis of Hunt's book held questionable financial motives. Some saw Hunt as an opportunist, but the *New Monthly Magazine*'s review (1828), for example, exempted Hunt from the low gossip characteristic of Byron memoirs, singling him out as one who "shows himself ready to be devoted as a martyr to truth."[83] Byron was the greatest biographical phenomenon of his age; from the publication of *Childe Harold* (in 1812) onward, people assumed autobiographical referencing in Byron's poetry, a situation encouraged and abetted by Byron himself. Although in the wake of Johnson and Boswell, poets were inescapably conscious of being public figures, Byron was a perfecter of public image. Maria Edgeworth said Byron appeared in "prepared undress";[84] others thought Byron confided personal anecdotes hoping they would be repeated; the *London Magazine* (1821) said Byron "studiously calculated" the conflation of the personal and poetic, and predicted that Byron would purchase posterity not through poetic merit but by appealing to the "idle and most unpoetic curiosity of the public."

The insights of Hunt's book do deserve some distinction from the industry of gossip and moral assessment that emerged at Byron's death. The parapraxis of the book's title in Hunt's statement that he presents "a portrait of Lord Byron and his infirmities" draws attention to the centrality of Hunt's examination of the pathology of genius. Hunt distinguishes ordinary peccadilloes ("Faults which arise from an exuberant sociality, like those of Burns, may safely be left to themselves") from larger cultural symptoms: poets overcast with "scorn and alienation, it is as well to see traced to their sources. In comparing notes, humanity gets wise." In an era when the term psychology was just beginning to rise into English use,[85] Hunt's book probed the realm of compensation, the role of childhood, and the ubiquity of problems stemming from parental influence.

Hunt, of course, was not alone in connecting childhood and adulthood. Wordsworth's phrase "The Child is Father of the Man" was appropriated by De Quincey to show how adulthood is blighted by "the deep deep tragedies of infancy," and by Hazlitt to underscore his view of the inexorable repetitions of life: "No one ever changes his character from the time he is two years old . . . two hours old."[86] But of his contemporaries Hunt explicitly locates the source of negative adult behavior in childhood events and parental relationships. Byron was the offspring of quarrelsome parents who "embitter[ed] his nature" and "embittered his memory of them." Traits such as his adult scornfulness arise from torment at school and unhappiness at home. The pain and ridicule of lameness "put sarcasm and misanthropy in his life"; his physical "defect" taught him to be "impatient with deficiency." Parental relations prefigure the child's subsequent view of gender roles: "His father was a rake of the wildest description; his mother a violent woman" who reproached him with the threat that "he would be as great a reprobate as his father."

Byron's stylized public image was problematic for biography. Responding to Byron's affectations of madness and excess, Hunt concluded Byron "did not take a hawk for a handsaw," although like Hamlet, he raised questions about a posturing not wholly volitional: his "real pretensions were mixed up with imaginary ones."[87] Hunt's text is concerned with the problem of establishing normative definitions of sanity; his suggestion that the "causes" of Byron's "faults" are "common to us all" implies the fundamental tenet of Freud, "we are all ill."[88] Hunt situates Byron's case within the ubiquity of such distorting childhoods and the limitations of explaining genius solely through pathology:

> I would as little deny that his Lordship had a spice of madness in him, as I deny that he had not every excuse for what was unpleasant in his composition; which was none of his own making. . . . a great part of the world . . . although they are rational enough to perform the common offices of life . . . are in reality but half rational beings, contradicted in the very outset of existence, and dimly struggling through life with the perplexity sown within them. . . . I look upon Lord Byron as an excessive instance of what we see in hundreds of cases every day; namely, of the unhappy consequences of a parentage that ought never to have existed,—of the perverse and discordant humours of those who were the authors of his being.

In Hunt's image, parents author the texts of their offsprings' childhood, the events of which reach print in the texts authored by their children. Yet the volatile combination "born handsome, wilful, and lame" might not have resulted in either ill temper or creativity:

A happy childhood might have corrected his evil tendencies; but he had it not; and the upshot was, that he spent an uneasy over-excited life, and that society have got an amusing book or two by his misfortunes. The books may even help to counteract the spreading of such a misfortune; and so far it may be better for society that he lived. But this is a rare case. Thousands of such mistakes are round about us, with nothing to show for them but complaint and unhappiness.

Are we to conclude that a less tormented life would have produced more or better books; or perhaps conclude, in the manner of Otto Rank, that a well-balanced life would have obviated the need to write books?[89] What Hunt makes clear is that an unhappy childhood alone does not make for genius; nor can we say why Byron turns to art, why he has something "to show" beyond "complaint and unhappiness." The text posits no universal or predictive system of compensation or successful objectification of neurosis. The world has got a "book or two by [Byron's] misfortunes," but Hunt does not try to explain the nature of artistic gifts or why some are moved to write; he is compelled to halt, as Freud was to do in discussing Leonardo, with making the "manifestations and limitations" of artistic power legible.

The modern era has been more ambitious than the Romantics in the direction of systematizing pathography. In an age lionizing the individual inspiration of genius, any potentially mechanistic theories of intellectual or cultural determinism were suspect; yet Romantic biographical theorists more willingly accepted a pathology of genius because it did not altogether undermine existing notions of a special poetic dispensation. Romantic writers defended the artist's singular weakness and privileges: D'Israeli said the artist was an "anomalous being among his fellow creatures"; Wordsworth excused Burns for yielding to the immoderate "impulses of nature" under which the artist must operate unrestricted; Shelley declared the artist "more delicately organized than other men"; De Quincey concluded that Wordsworth was a man of "special infirmity and special strength."[90]

Yet what are the ramifications of a pathology of genius for art itself and for the position of the poet in the culture? In the twentieth century, Georg Lukács condemns a valorization of the poet as an abnormal outsider. In his essay "Healthy or Sick Art," he opposes the view of sickness as the condition of literature, and dispraises poets who affect to despise society. Freud suggests the poet attempts to impose "[his] same mental constellation" on readers.[91] Most Romantics hesitated to pursue the possible implications of a pathology of genius for art and its audience, yet to some degree Byron's own writing introduces the paradox of social aberrancy and questions the distortions and representativeness of art that arises from an isolated and marginalized visionary.

The last Canto of *Childe Harold* (written 1817, printed 1818) is of particular interest in this context. The iconic setting at the beginning of the Canto, "A palace and a prison on each hand," is an emblem of the mind of the artist (caught between special gifts and special torments) and an emblem of the artist's place in the culture (both exalted and outcast). Byron identifies the creative mind as intrinsically unhealthy: art is produced by "the mind diseased"; the mind "fevers into false creation" (IV:122). Wordsworth had called poetic genius "the faculty divine" in *The Excursion* (I: 79); in Byron, the same artistic gift is linked with punishment not the "abundant recompense" of "Tintern Abbey": "From our birth the faculty divine / Is chain'd and tortured—cabin'd, cribb'd, confined, / And bred in darkness" (IV: 127).[92] Yet there is no call to minister to the "mind diseased," for it is the source of creativity: the "Paradise of our despair . . . o'er-informs the pencil and the pen." The state of the artist is a fortunate fall; the disease of genius is the faculty divine, both the source of suffering and the source of art. Although the poet suffers from a consuming wound—"My mind may lose its force, my blood its fire, / And my frame perish even in conquering pain" (IV: 137)—the bow, the product of art, remains to avenge his injuries if it cannot remedy them: "In this page a record will I seek" (IV: 134).[93]

In this relationship between wound and page, the poem implicitly addresses the Romantic paradox of individualism and the public role of poetry. When art springs from the artist's inconsolable torment, how representative is its vision? In saying, "Our life is a false nature—'tis not in / The harmony of things" (IV: 126), Byron situates the poet as a cultural outsider; the poet in society is irreconcilably "amid the alien corn."[94] Wordsworth finessed unpopularity as a mark of greatness; in Byron, the misanthropic outcast is redeemed for his heroic defiance—the very role that Lukács condemns, the figure of marginality and taboo, the poet who "send[s] us prying into the abyss" (IV: 166). Amid the scenery of ancient ruins, Byron invokes a variety of tormented and heroically defiant Philoctetean images: Prometheus punished for his transgression of trying to help humankind (IV: 163); the fallen gladiator wounded in battle (IV:

140); Laocoön punished in excess for his foresight (IV: 160); adding himself to the transgressing "heroes" who "have trod this spot" (IV: 144). The "shaping spirit of Ruin," rejected by Coleridge as a legitimate source of art, becomes the Canto's governing autobiographical image of the poet: "despoiled yet perfect" (IV: 147), "a ruin amidst ruins" (IV: 25). Hazlitt's Methodist, Wilson's Philoctetes, Coleridge's Mariner, and Byron's narrator of *Childe Harold* are finally the same image of the isolated poet, a tormented yet visionary outsider.[95]

In a curious closing equation of Byron, pathology, and Methodism, Hunt reported of *Don Juan* that Byron "had a great mind to make him die a Methodist—a catastrophe which he sometimes anticipated for himself."[96] Can poetic genius only express an abnormal or alien vision of life? It is a question unwittingly raised by John Stuart Mill's comment on Byron's depiction of marginality, zealotry, and the burden of the poet. He said he could not read Byron during his own mental crisis, when his mind resembled the state "in which converts to Methodism usually are. . . . The poet's state of mind was too like my own. . . . His Harold and Manfred had the same burthen on them which I had."[97] The poetry of illness can present no restorative vision.

In *Lord Byron and Some of his Contemporaries,* Hunt nullifies the reverential mystifications of the artistic subculture. Byron is at the center of a generation of valetudinary and exile poets—the disease and deformity of "many of our best." Physical disorder and malaise pervade the portraits. Shelley and Keats look consumptive, Lamb fragile ("He has seen strange faces of calamity"), Moore slight, Coleridge sluggish; Hunt says of himself, "I live too much out of this world." The geographic remoteness of the poetic community (Moore is seen in Paris, Keats on his way to Rome, the Pisan junta in exile) is a physical exile emblematic of its intellectual exile from the culture. Hunt alone journeys into exile and returns to testify.

In his demythologized portrait of Byron, Hunt examined the subjectivity of the self-image Byron styled for the public. By extension, Hunt's book, based almost completely on conversation and personal reminiscence, makes no pretense of objectivity. Indeed, he acknowledged the subjectivity of all narrative by inscribing his own autobiography as the closing portrait, thus encoding within the collective biography an explanation of his own subjectivity: the difficult sea voyage, the shock of the death of Shelley, the financial straits of family life, and the intellectual struggle with Byron. Autobiographical biography, in which the subjective background of the biographer is inscribed within the biography, became a key Romantic strategy in navigating interpretive bias. As in the preliminary *Prelude* of Wordsworth's projected *Recluse,* explaining the subjectivity of perception was at least as interesting to the Romantics as the narrative itself.

De Quincey's *Literary Reminiscences* is in some measure a "Wordsworth and Some of his Contemporaries." Like Hunt's collective biography, De Quincey's series revealed indiscretions, studied a regional intellectual community, and inscribed an autobiographical substructure. Responding not necessarily to Hunt's memoirs of Byron, but to the widespread attention given to Byron at the expense of the lake poets, De Quincey vindicated the canon of the lakes. While the exile poet was flattered with attention (he and other outsiders "blunder" in assuming Wordsworth, Southey, Scott, and others mixed "only with little adoring coteries") De Quincey declares of Wordsworth, "Never had poet or prophet less honor in his own country."[98] Hunt profiled the urban expatriate poets crystallizing around Byron, as he witnessed them; in the *Literary Reminiscences,* De Quincey refocused critical attention on the rural community of poets crystallizing around Wordsworth, and brought new insights into the relation of biographer and subject.

Chapter V

Thomas De Quincey:
The Allegory of Everyday Life

De Quincey's accounts of Wordsworth and Coleridge are easily the most famous biographies of the Romantic era, yet critical attention has always centered on De Quincey's iconoclastic disclosures—Coleridge's plagiarisms, the Lamb family madness, Wordsworth's vanity—rather than his innovations in narrative form. The well-known recollections of the lake poets are actually part of a now little-known larger series of biographical sketches of contemporary rural and urban literary figures, a sequence cumulatively known as the *Literary Reminiscences*. Although these biographical essays customarily have been treated as detachable sketches and valued chiefly as historicist records, they benefit from being returned to their collective context. Viewed as a narrative sequence, De Quincey's *Literary Reminiscences* assumes its rightful position as a pivotal text in the dialogue between Romantic poetry and prose, and a central document in understanding Romantic nonfictional narrative. Moreover, De Quincey's critical observations on biographical theory and practice elucidate the transmission of high Romantic poetics into prose by demonstrating Romantic theories of poetic interpretation and the Romantic use of biography as a critical methodology.

The early biographical historian James Johnston called De Quincey a biographer, and this perspective still may remain the most useful way of considering his works. In the wake of recent critical enthusiasm for autobiographical narrative, De Quincey has most frequently been called an autobiographer; Gertrude Stein's observation "anything is an autobiography" may well be taken as a motto for the contemporary critical enthusiasm for autobiography; indeed, Stein's collective portraits of her literary generation offer a reminder of the endurance of the Romantic notion of biography as a dual portrait of author and subject.[1] The core of De Quincey's writing is the description of all the people he knew, met, or thought about: the account of his experiences is the account of his acquaintances, and his sustained narratives almost always resolve into biographical sketches, often, as in the case of the *Literary Reminiscences* and the *Sketches of Life and Manners,* placed in the narrative context of his own life. As in Leigh Hunt's *Lord Byron and Some of his Contemporaries,* the Romantic interest in the subjectivity of perception contributes to the formal qualities of the text. De Quincey's autobiographic biography shares the perceptual and narrative concerns of Romantic poetry and criticism, but like other Romantic collective biographies, De Quincey's fragmented, digressive, ahistorical biographies have largely eluded categorization.

De Quincey's contemporary, Henry Crabb Robinson, said of him, "As a writer he is indisputably one of our best."[2] Yet the modern tendency to see poetry as the main expression of British Romanticism has eclipsed De Quincey's reputation, and the absence of a reliable modern edition has generally limited critical study of De Quincey to the relatively few sound available texts. E. M. Thron's observation that critics gravitate to works that provide a "secure reading" within existing assumptions about literature is evident in the reluctance to view Romantic prose as sharing the aesthetic values of Romantic poetry. The common belief expressed by critics such as V. A. De Luca in saying "his imagination is revealed clearly in but a few wholly satisfying works, such as the *Confessions of an English Opium-Eater, The English Mail-Coach,* and *Suspiria de Profundis,*" and Thron himself in saying that De Quincey's fame rests on works "that were never completed to his or our satisfaction," reflects the textual obstacles surrounding De Quincey's prose. Furthermore, it suggests that the aesthetic of fragmentation in Romantic poetry (unhesitatingly accepted in texts such as "Kubla Khan" and evident anew in the recent valorization of early drafts of *The Prelude*) has not been extended to the critical reading of Romantic prose.[3]

The difficulty of finding a conventional generic classification for De Quincey's writings has contributed to the undeserved obscurity of the *Literary Reminiscences* and most of De Quincey's works, with their strange and eclectic amalgam of scholarship, journalism, translation, philosophical meditation, and reminiscence. He himself foresaw the problem of narrative innovation when he lamented, "The advantage lies in doing anything which has a name, an assignable name." Despite the prominence of De Quincey in his own lifetime, we now have difficulty in giving De Quincey's works—like most Romantic prose, and nonfictional narrative in general—assignable names. Unlike prose writers such as

Hazlitt, his works resisted the easy formal categorizations of mass culture and left him in a state of incessant financial difficulties; as Henry Crabb Robinson was to observe, "his talents are not marketable."[4] Indeed, De Quincey never expected to have to market his talents. He had sufficient patrimony to manage social climbing by traveling with Lord Westport and attending Oxford. Even before the oft-invoked "pecuniary embarrassments" which he tells us drove him to writing, De Quincey held a strong intellectual reputation. R. P. Gillies, speaking of the winter of 1815–16, says of De Quincey's stature: "Up to that time, De Quincey though he had spent long years in assiduous study, and by his friends was regarded as a powerful author, had not, so far as I know, published a single line. He seemed, indeed, to live for the sake of the labour alone, and to fling overboard all considerations of the *palma* or *pecunia*."[5]

By 1818 all that had changed. The years of prosperity and aristocratic mingling of his youth[6] had given way to poetic aspirations and hobnobbing among writers,[7] and that, in turn, to the financial pressure of an enlarging family and a diminishing patrimony; at various points he contemplated the possibility of a law career or professorship,[8] but found himself dependent on his pen for the rest of his life. More than any other Romantic prose writer, De Quincey embodied the frustrations of the scholar-writer: ghostwriting John Wilson's lectures at the Edinburgh University but never himself standing for a chair; planning scholarly projects he had no time to complete; generously donating his youthful patrimony only to find himself struggling to write enough to survive; producing in the spurts of creativity that alternated with lassitude more articles in advance than a magazine could absorb in several years from one contributor. Like the Johnson who called his works "the dreams of a poet doomed at last to wake a lexicographer," De Quincey dreamed of being a poet and awoke into the intellectual compromises of Grub Street.[9]

Having exhausted his capital, De Quincey plunged into the editorship of the *Westmorland Gazette* in 1818–19, and with the hindsight of his later projects, it is not surprising to discover that one of the first schemes he planned in the opening months was a series of English poets in imitation of Johnson's *Lives*.[10] Amid the waning friendship with the Wordsworths,[11] he found himself increasingly self-confident as a writer. With the meteoric success of the *Confessions of an English Opium-Eater, Being an Extract from the Life of a Scholar* in the *London Magazine* in 1821,[12] De Quincey found his opinions and writings in demand. He alternated scholarly and sensationalistic projects under the nom de plume of the Opium-Eater, producing among other things a series of review biographies (as early as 1823 De Quincey was learning the standard journalistic practice of taking a book under review as an "orange to squeeze for the public use") as well as biographical sketches of contemporary intellectual figures.[13] In 1832–34, *Blackwood's* serialized his first collective biography, a classical reassemblage he called *The Caesars*.

The *Confessions*, of course, had inscribed the stories of Ann and the parsimonious lawyer, but as De Quincey increasingly came to objectify his reminiscences, he used an autobiographical chronology as a trellis for his biographical sketches. His next series of biographical essays, *Sketches of Life and Manners; from the Autobiography of an English Opium Eater* (*Tait's*, 1834–36),[14] chronicled the aristocratic vagabonding of his youth ending with his Oxford years (1803–8), before he quit school to join the Wordsworths and exchanged the cachet of aristocratic associations for the cachet of poets (as De Quincey described it, "originally as a boy, moving amongst the circles of the nobility, and now courting only those of intellectual people").[15] The death of Coleridge inspired the first of the contemporary literary biographies (1834–35) which became the "nest-egg" (as he described the relation of Johnson's *Savage* to the later-developed series of *Lives*)[16] for the long series of *Literary Reminiscences* (*Tait's*, 1837–41) in which the London literary reminiscences frame his retreat to the lakes, the central and best-known of the lives.

His profiles of contemporary literary figures led him to write essays in the 1830s and 1840s on literature and biographical essays and reviews in which he developed the theories of reading and writing implicit in his earlier works.[17] In the 1840s and 1850s he returned to autobiographical reminiscences of his contemporaries and his own past, including the visionary writings of *Suspiria de Profundis* (*Blackwood's*, 1845).[18] Throughout his life he prepared so many other writings—prose romances, discussions of politics, religion, German and classical philology—that he was unable to remember them, and he relied on his daughters and the initiative of the Boston publishing house Ticknor and Fields to assemble his fugitive oeuvre for a collected edition (1850–59). There is reason to believe many of his writings went unpublished, lost in piles of paper at his many addresses, or cut and discarded by editors oversupplied with his contributions. It is a testament to his fame that despite the opium addiction, procrastination, and large family which kept him continually in poverty, De Quincey was the only Romantic prose writer honored in his lifetime by two collected editions of his work, in Britain and America. The reclusive writer was evidently a subject of considerable attention on the few occasions he went out in public; he saw few visitors and dreaded autographs. Having supervised the successful American edition, he decided to redistill a number of the writings for a British collective edition with the assistance of the Edinburgh publisher James Hogg (1853–60), using the American edition as a copy text. He devoted the last few years of his life to rewriting his works from the new perspective of old age—recombining the autobiographical sketches with *Suspiria* (1853), radically abridging the lake and London biographies (1854), and extending the *Confessions* (1856)—palimpsestic revisions which demonstrate anew the Romantic interest in the perceptual and temporal constructs of biographical narration.

But De Quincey's many revisions, as well as the dispersal inherent to periodical publication, present considerable bibliographical problems that have impeded the study of virtually all of his works. Accustomed to the practice of serial publication, De Quincey usually cast his writings into multipart essay sequences, most of which are not available in modern editions. Early and late drafts of *Confessions* and *Suspiria* can be ferreted out, but the absence of accurate current editions of two of his most significant series, the *Literary Reminiscences* and the *Sketches of Life and Manners,* have resulted in his critical undervaluation and neglect in favor of contemporary prose writers whose works are more tidily available.[19] Meditating in 1834 on the fate of his and Coleridge's writings in the periodical press, he lamented, "Worlds of fine thinking lie buried in that vast abyss, never to be disentombed or restored to human admiration."[20]

In looking at the *Literary Reminiscences,* it is worthwhile to begin by establishing the correct text.[21] As usual with De Quincey, the actual composition of the text offers some, but limited, assistance in discussing narrative unity. Internal evidence and his own testimony indicate the essays were written in a short burst around 1837–38, and printed serially in *Tait's* magazine from 1837–41. In line with the common practice of Romantic serial publication, when he presented his editors with a lengthy narrative, the complete series often awaited publication over the course of several years (a publishing practice which still bedevils freelance writers in the present day) as the editors gradually doled out the text in installments for fear of overexposure or letting one author dominate a publication.[22] Publication of the series appears to have been suspended for a year under the shadow of libel (a fate similar to Hazlitt's "Boswell Redivivus" in 1827), following complaints about the first installment from one of the Liverpool "literary coterie" described by De Quincey; it afterward ran virtually uninterrupted on a monthly basis.[23]

Although poetry has been the central concern of British Romantic studies, it is important to recover the place of the *Literary Reminiscences* and biography in general for an understanding of the Romantic era. De Quincey's writings on biographical theory provide a valuable context for understanding the importance of biography and the position of the *Literary Reminiscences,* not only in the canon of De Quincey's achievements, but in the mainstream of Romantic literature and the genre of collective biography.

Let us first examine how De Quincey's writings share the intellectual and formal concerns of high Romantic poetry and criticism by breaking down and synthesizing generic conventions, indistinguishing poetry and prose, endorsing the poetics of spontaneity and the aesthetics of fragmentation, and studying the action of subjectivity, childhood, and creativity; we shall then examine De Quincey's use of the exegetical tradition to analyze art and the hidden actions of the mind. From this perspective, we shall finally be able to look closely at how the *Literary Reminiscences* has certain alliances with the tradition of travel writing and the prose picturesque but, on a narrative and critical level, its paramount affiliations lie with the poetic tradition and the poetic use of the pastoral to allegorize nature, art, temporal change, and the passage of human life.

De Quincey and Wordsworthian Narrative

The Burden of the Present: Wordsworth, Keats, and Coleridge

Accustomed to the practice of serial publication, De Quincey cast almost all his works into multipart essay sequences. Yet the discontinuous narrative of collective biography was both amenable to serialization and devalued by it, for today the collectivism of the *Literary Reminiscences,* like that of the *Lives of the Poets,* has been forgotten in the usual critical practice of studying the individual essays separately. The dismemberment and interruptions of serialization, a format that once accustomed audiences to discontinuous narrative, now hinder De Quincey's biographies from being read as a specific linear sequence. Moreover, understanding the formal qualities of the *Literary Reminiscences,* and Romantic biographical narrative in general, requires the acceptance of now unfamiliar aesthetic values; narrative continuity in Romantic nonfictional prose cannot be judged by, say, the serialized Victorian novel or even Johnsonian collective biography. De Quincey in particular compels us to override present-day assumptions about biographical responsibility and protocol, for in his theoretical writings on biography he posits Shakespearian drama and Wordsworthian poetry as his narrative antecedents, and lavishly appropriates strategies from the entire history of Western literature.

De Quincey placed the aesthetic of the short fragment in a longstanding literary tradition: "Plato, for instance, has but one of his many works large enough to fill a small *octavo.* Aristotle, as to bulk, is a mere pamphleteer. . . . Neither Shakspeare nor Milton has written any long work. . . . All poets of any length are read by snatches and fragments when once they have ascended to great popularity." He praised the brief works of his fellow essayist John Wilson as a block of coal ready-hewn for fuel: "They lie now in short and detached papers—that is, in the very state fitted for reading" rather than "conglutinated into one vast block, needing a quarryman's or a miner's skill to make them tractable."[24]

The discontinuous narrative of Plutarch's *Lives* had always been the most prominent classical antecedent for biographers, but it is indicative of the age (accustomed to taboos broken by Byron and the marginal taste of *Blackwood's* itself) that De Quincey eschewed the moral collective biographies of Plutarch in favor of Suetonius and the Augustan historian(s), whose racy anecdotage and rumor he revived in a paraphrased and reconstructed form in his sequence *The Caesars.*[25] Indeed, he calls Suetonius the first "collector of *anecdotage*" and the predecessor of Plutarch in using anecdotal biography as a "mode of History." De Quincey's writings typically combine recondite information with material inclined to capture the popular eye (John Stuart Mill said De Quincey took "a strange delight in drawing illustrations from subjects ten times more abstruse than what they are designed to illustrate").[26] *The Caesars,* by recounting the "sketches and biographical portraits" of "these obscure but most interesting memorialists," allowed him to bring to light his classical erudition as well as to reveal the "private and personal memoirs" behind the well-known incidents of "public life."[27]

De Quincey's belief in the importance of personal details and his denunciation of mere chronology ultimately derive from Johnson (as does his interest in seemingly insignificant lives), although like other Romantics, he entertained considerable ambivalence toward his predecessor. In "Some Thoughts on Biography"[28] he praised the *Lives* as "the best in point of composition" and "the most highly finished amongst all masterpieces of the biographic art," Johnson's "best work"; he dares anyone to find "a collection of lives, or even one life (though it were the 'Agricola' of Tacitus), which as a work of refined art and execution can be thought equal to the best of Dr. Johnson's." While he had misgivings about Johnson's judgment, he praised him for writing "*con amore*" and "*con odio*"[29]—either way testified to Johnson's sincerity: "As to the critical part of his *Lives*, if no thoughtful reader can be expected to abide by his haughty decisions, yet, on the other hand, every man reads his opinions with pleasure, from the intellectual activity and the separate justice of the thoughts which they display." De Quincey repeatedly complained of the injustice of Johnson's ridicule of Milton, yet he declared the best biographies abided by Johnsonian principles.[30] "The great effort for a biographer," he wrote, is "to weld the disconnected facts into one substance, and by interfusing natural reflections to create for the motions of his narrative a higher impulse than one merely chronologic. In this respect, the best of Dr. Johnson's 'Lives' are undoubtedly the very best which exist."

Indeed, De Quincey goes beyond Johnson in declaring that chronology is disruptive to the objectives of biography. His comments on biographical composition printed at the time of the *Literary Reminiscences* in the essay on his brother Pink ("My Brother," 1838) pointedly shun chronology in favor of selectivity, subjectivity, and the shaping role of the narrator who draws "philosophical inference" and invests material with emblematic value: "It is, by the *setting,* and not by the jewels *set,* that the whole course of a life is woven into one texture."[31] Praising Johnson's "admirable" *Lives,* De Quincey rejects mere "vulgar" chronology and the plodding of a stenographic biographer ("in this year he did this"), to endorse what he calls a Shakespearian selecting and sequencing of events: "The connexions of a life . . . must resolve themselves into intellectual abstractions . . . meditative reflections upon the whirling motions of life . . . like a perpetual spray or atmosphere, such as is thrown off from a cataract, and which invests all surrounding objects." A good biography must edit and compress factual chronology into narrative significance instead of an "auctioneer's catalogue."

Under the shaping hand of the biographer, the depiction of emblematic incidents resembles the Shakespearian creation of character (indeed, in *The Caesars* he places Shakespeare's assessment of Marc Antony alongside regular historical records), and in some sense the narrative of collective biography functions like a Renaissance multiple plot. "In the hands of a great poet like Shakspeare," De Quincey observes, events and reflections invisibly "*are* made, to anticipate and mould the course of what is to follow. . . . They seem to be mere passive results or products from the narration; but, properly managed, they assume the very opposite relation, and predetermine the course of that narration." Instead of tracing lives year by year, De Quincey's biographies are similarly "fused into unity" through a perpetual spray of unifying "anticipations," "ambidexter[s]," and "reverberations"; they are not historical tools, but interpretive narratives.

The Coleridge reminiscences, prompted by Coleridge's death in 1834,[32] probably gave De Quincey the impulse for writing a full set of contemporary literary biographies. The four-part sequence contains one of De Quincey's clearest statements of his narrative strategy—like other Romantic writers, he inscribes within his text "the taste by which he is to be enjoyed."[33] His biography of Coleridge, he explains, seeks after "graces" which belong to "modes of composition professedly careless," graces that include a "desultory" first-person narration, "conversational tone," "indulgent construction," and the overall format of the "personal memoir" and biographical "sketch," instead of "preconceived biography." This "desultory" style, De Quincey explains, evolved from the "sudden but profound impulse communicated to the writer's feelings" at the time of Coleridge's death, and the need to meet "the public feeling": "Both purposes required that it should be written almost *extempore:* the greater part of was really and unaffectedly written in that way." But after the urgency subsided, he found he wanted to continue in the same impulsive "unpremeditated" state of feeling he had stumbled upon; having started, "it seemed proper to sustain it, even after delays and interruption had allowed time for throwing the narrative into a more orderly movement."[34]

The same digressive graces are at work throughout the *Literary Reminiscences* (and De Quincey's works as a whole). He is forever reminding us that he "has no books at hand" and is working from memorials of books "unrefreshed for twenty years"—he casually remarks he does not even know Coleridge's age at death although it might be gathered from "the public newspapers."[35] The epistolary form, one of the "professedly careless" models he cites, had been evident five years earlier in the "Sketch of Professor Wilson: in a Letter to an American Gentleman" (1829), which established many of the traits apparent in all his biographical reminiscences: an emblematic account of the first meeting; details of appearance, dwelling, and associates; a very brief tabulation of some events of the life; and the presence of De Quincey's autobiographical chronology, personal associations, and erudition suffused throughout.

De Quincey's style has often been described as a wandering prose, a term he himself used to describe his indulgent construction. Explaining his antichronology in "My Brother," he declares, "I have wandered backwards and forwards, obeying any momentary impulse, as accident or sometimes even as purely verbal suggestions might arise to guide me"; he refers to his own essay on Coleridge as a "wandering narrative." Coleridge's conversation becomes an emblem of Romantic narrative form, as he defends Coleridge against those who charged that he "seemed to wander." Coleridge's transitions were always "just," De Quincey argues, but the larger plan remained imperceptible to those who saw only "the separate beauty of the thoughts" but failed to detect the "dominant theme": "The compass, and huge circuit, by which his illustrations moved, travelled farthest into remote regions, before they began to revolve. Long before this coming-round commenced, most people had lost him, and naturally enough supposed that he had lost himself."[36] In analyzing Coleridge, De Quincey analyzed some of the obscurities of his own prose.

De Quincey declared in defense of his own writing and Coleridge's, "A digression is often the cream of an article."[37] In one of De Quincey's most famous images in *Suspiria de Profundis,* he characterizes the course of his narrative as "a *caduceus* wreathed about with meandering ornaments," and justifies subjective meandering with the image of the traveler in a coach, who must choose a thoughtful and desultory route, rather than a merely efficient one, in order to survey the terrain: " 'Might it not be as well to ask after the most beautiful road, rather than the shortest?' " The same concepts of digression and subjectivity are embodied in the *Literary Reminiscences,* wherein the first-person narrative, the trellis of autobiographical chronology, is wreathed about with the flowers and tendrils of biographical sketches. The collective portrait of acquaintances, places, and associations blooms and twines with as much interest for De Quincey as the "sullen cylinder" of his own chronology; the sequence can have no digressiveness but in the flowers and tendrils which define it as much as they adorn it.

The question of digression has posed the most troubling aesthetic problem for modern readers of De Quincey. Rather than thinking in the pejorative terms of false memory and randomness, we must judge Romantic digression in terms of subjective association ("the writer's feelings"), inspired spontaneity, and, to borrow an expression from Wordsworth, "the mind's *excursive* power" (*Excursion,* IV: 1263). De Quincey himself developed a vocabulary for thinking about nonfictional narrative from the Romantic poets—inspired not by their prose styles, but by their theories of poetry.

In this context it is easier to understand why De Quincey dismissed factual verification as a suppression of the spontaneous impulse of the creative mind—an aesthetic akin to Coleridge's own disclaimer in the prefatory note to "Kubla Khan." The biographer relies on the power of the mind's "archives" to draw connections, instead of turning to the archives of documentation. De Quincey's often-quoted remark in *Suspiria* on the "deep memorial palimpsest of the brain"[38] applies to biographical reflections as well as autobiographical: there are no "incoherencies" in life, he says, for in inspired recollection (the moment before drowning, the logic of opium, the action of the creative imagination) the mind can see through the seeming randomness or discontinuity of existence to those "organizing principles which fuse into harmony, and gather about fixed predetermined centres, whatever heterogeneous elements life may have accumulated." Like the biographer in whose hands the incidents of a life are "fused into unity" ("My Brother"), in autobiography the same principles are at work to detect and "fuse into harmony" the seemingly unconnected events of human life.[39] To assume that the relation or reminiscence of twenty years past is incongruous with accuracy is to misunderstand; for De Quincey, accuracy comes in recognizing patterns of the life from the process of reflection, an action akin to Wordsworthian emotion recollected in tranquillity. Insight, not fact, constitutes narrative objectivity for the Romantic biographer. Accuracy may be sacrificed to the more important veracity, what De Quincey calls, truth to "'*the understanding heart.*'"[40]

Wordsworth is, of course, the central figure behind De Quincey's idea of a poetic prose. The visionary "passages of life" that Wordsworth names "spots of time" (1805 *Prelude,* XI: 257–78) reappear in the emblematic anecdotes of biography which suddenly and unexpectedly throw human character into brilliant illumination (upon meeting Coleridge, De Quincey recognizes that Coleridge chases "abstract truths" as an "escape out of his own personal wretchedness"). De Quincey's embrace of a discursive, fragmentary, and "extempore" style adopted the Wordsworthian aesthetic of recreating the spontaneous overflow of powerful feeling; and in naming the highest category of prose "impassioned prose,"[41] De Quincey devised a critical vocabulary indebted to Wordsworth's call for a literature recreating "the essential passions of the heart." Fundamentally, De Quincey's theoretical writings make explicit the prose aesthetic implied in Wordsworth's comments on poetic diction and Wordsworth's insistence on the similarity of subject and language in prose and metrical composition in the Preface to *Lyrical Ballads.*[42] For Wordsworth, the poet's function was independent of verse, and his own practice suggested a justification of prose as an artistic endeavor equal to poetry: in his works he habitually joined nonmetrical prefaces and appendices to his poetry, and he regretted not having written more prose.[43] De Quincey's boyhood aspiration to write poetry disappeared, but in its place he found himself translating Wordsworthian poetics into prose and creating an "impassioned," a poetic, prose.

The very idea of a palimpsest is in some sense a development of Wordsworthian concerns. *The Prelude,* like other poems by Wordsworth, validated subjective perception and provided a model of adult reflection on the past, upon which De Quincey based his own story of the growth of a prose writer's mind. Although the *Literary Reminiscences* is likewise a commentary on temporality, De Quincey went even beyond Wordsworth in analyzing the changing subjectivity of the mind. The versions of Wordsworth's autobiography, like De Quincey's variants, incidentally freeze the ephemeral states of mind that would otherwise be lost or only dimly recoverable in the layers of human memory; but De Quincey went on to redefine the essential nature of literary composition as a reflection of the "natural and mighty palimpsest" of the brain.

Like the poet of "Tintern Abbey" comparing "what then I was" to the present day, De Quincey's *Literary Reminiscences* is largely about the passage of time and the way his perceptions have changed. De Quincey's authority is based on his subjectivity: "In sketching the state of the literary society gathered or gathering about the English lakes, at the time of my settling amongst them, I have, of course authorized the reader to suppose that I personally mixed freely amongst the whole." But that subjectivity is an inherently mutable one; De Quincey explains that although he has described the district "at the time, (viz. the winter of 1808–9) when I became a personal resident in that district," since then, all has changed: "The case is now altered."[44] The *Literary Reminiscences* is a narrative palimpsest chronicling these cultural changes, both personal and national. Once a friend, De Quincey is now estranged from Wordsworth; formerly unknown, Wordsworth is now renowned; having lost his boyhood idolatry of Wordsworth, De Quincey's abundant recompense is his own literary celebrity. Finally, as will become clear later in this study, not only did De Quincey annex the geography and *locus amoenus* of Wordsworth's poetry in originally moving to Grasmere in his youth; but from the distance of adulthood he took *The Excursion*'s tour of the lakes as an antecedent for the story of his own intellectual travel to and from the lakes.

Two kinds of intellectual intimidation are inevitably at work in literary biography, one arising from the biographical tradition and the other from the relationship of biographer and subject. Johnson posed a formidable prose tradition that every Romantic prose writer, and particularly biographer, was forced to answer. But De Quincey's *Literary Reminiscences* was less concerned with the burden of the past than the burden of the present. De Quincey's description of his relationship with Wordsworth provides a conscious narrative inversion and a commentary on Boswell's depiction of his relationship with Johnson; the innate involuntary tendency of the biographer to identify with the subject surfaces as an explicit narrative strategy. Instead of trying to assert a spurious objectivity, De Quincey acknowledges the inherent self-referentiality of literary biography and explores the role of the acolyte imposed on the biographer.[45]

The prototype of the relation between biographer and subject has always been Boswell's identification with Johnson. He struggles to obey his own injunction to "be Johnson." Many critics have observed there might have been no *Life of Johnson* if Boswell had been on better terms with his father.[46] But though he could not live up to his father's ambitions, he fancied himself an heir of Johnson, and his narrative decisions mirror these closer psychological themes. Boswell adopts the dramatic voice of the autobiographer, structuring the biography largely along autobiographical chronology. He pursues Johnson's attention, joins Johnson's circle of friends, basks in the reflected glory of Johnson's prestige, steers the dialogue to his own favorite subjects, and daydreams in his journal of purchasing Johnson's garret.[47] He seeks out Johnson's literary approval for writing the journal, and his biographical narrative assumes the structure of a public diary edited from those journals. He officiously assists Johnson in his publishing tasks; and he deceptively maximizes the limited number of days of friendship into a glorified and prolonged intimacy. We note Boswell uses his own writings to associate himself with Johnson's corpus, but at the same time he passes judgment on Johnson. He corrects Johnson's Latin and establishes himself as a revisor of Johnson's achievements—offering the *Tour to the Hebrides* (1785) as a kind of corrected and improved commentary or gloss on Johnson's *Journey to the Western Islands* (1775).

Indeed, implicit in the first meeting of Boswell and Johnson in Tom Davies's book shop, when Boswell imagines himself Hamlet encountering the ghost of his father ("'Look, my Lord, it comes'"), is the paradigm of biographer and subject. Boswell's well-known fear of ghosts calls even more attention to his threatening image of literary paternity in casting Johnson as the terrifying ghost of Hamlet senior commanding his son to perform deeds equal to previous generations.[48] Figuratively speaking, the biographer is often haunted by the achievements of the subject, a literary intimidation doubled in the biography of a biographer. Boswell's anxiety about equaling his literary predecessor is evident in his citation of Johnson's biographical theories to justify his methodology—injunctions which he professes to follow but at the same time usurps.

Johnson, of course, haunted all subsequent biographers, but for De Quincey, Wordsworth is the paternal ghost hovering in the text on a narrative and psychological level. Although De Quincey perceived continuities between his life and Coleridge's—the addiction, the procrastination, the presentation of "psychological curiosities," the journalistic life— it was Wordsworth whose approval he sought and whom he longed to imitate. The essays on Wordsworth open with De Quincey visiting the lakes twice without the courage to introduce himself, curiously casting himself retreating "like a guilty thing" (*Hamlet* filtered through Wordsworth's "Immortality" ode), as he moved about in a world not yet realized, with a "sense of mysterious pre-existence" of his future residence.[49]

Like Boswell, De Quincey in the *Literary Reminiscences* pursues Wordsworth's attention, adopts the Wordsworthian community as his own, uses
his friendship with the lake poets to draw prestige to himself, and slants
events to coincide with his own interests. Staying in the room of Wordsworth's son on his first visit, De Quincey imagines himself Wordsworth's
intellectual heir. Like Boswell, he seeks out Wordsworth's literary approval, assists Wordsworth in his publishing projects, and structures the
biography along the somewhat limited intersection of their lives, a sleight
of hand expanding the illusion of prolonged familiarity. Like many Romantic biographers, he eschews the stenographic function of recording
conversation, but instead substitutes a network of quotations drawn from
Wordsworth's poetry. And like Boswell, who uses Johnson's critical methodologies as endorsements of his own biographical projects, De Quincey's
use of autobiographical narrative in biography permitted him to share the
Romantic preoccupation with the individuality of perception and the
subjectivity of knowledge. Like Boswell, De Quincey seeks to associate
himself with Wordsworth's canon by correcting Wordsworth's political
errors, and by making use of the community of minor figures who appear
in Wordsworth's poetry in his own *Literary Reminiscences*.

Even more assiduously than Boswell, De Quincey searches for similarities between Wordsworth's life and his own, on the grounds that
accuracy of his critical and biographical insights is affirmed by the resemblances. He and Wordsworth emerge from the same inarticulate boyhood; he too knows the lake district, competes with Wordsworth for
friends, and outgrieves Wordsworth over the death of little Kate—indeed,
as Keats's friend Richard Woodhouse would have it, he was not displeased
to insinuate himself into Wordsworth's place in the paternity of Kate,
repeating rumors that "he was himself the father of Mrs. Wordsworth's
child that died."[50] De Quincey adopts Wordsworth's friends, activities,
and acquaintances, and sees in Wordsworth's works adumbrations of his
own interests. Thus De Quincey makes much of Wordsworth's mystic
dream in Book V of *The Prelude,* an implicit connection to De Quincey's
own reputation for opium dreaming. Moreover, he achieves Boswell's
cherished aspiration by moving into the very cottage inhabited by Wordsworth. By settling into the vacated Town End cottage, furnished and
arranged under the guidance of Dorothy Wordsworth, De Quincey imagined himself following Wordsworth's footsteps.

The plot of Boswell's narratives has been identified as that of the young man come from the country to the city.[51] De Quincey inverts the scene into a Romantic context: the young man sets out from the confines of the city to the countryside to make his literary way. Yet there is in De Quincey at the same time another structural inversion of the Boswellian biographical prototype: for De Quincey's narrative is indisputably the account of what occurs when a Johnson rejects his Boswell. Johnson's embrace of his disciple Boswell is matched by Wordsworth's rejection of De Quincey. We can only speculate how Johnson's attitude and conversation must have altered in 1772–73 when Boswell revealed his intention to write a biography and his decade of note taking: but we can explicitly read, in De Quincey's *Literary Reminiscences,* what the inverse impact of rejection would have been.[52] The narrative recounts a failed Boswellian endeavor to seek out and venerate a literary hero, and chronicles the impact of ostracism on the would-be Boswell ("I witnessed a case where a kind of idol had, after all, rejected an idolater that did not offer a splendid triumph to his pride").[53] The dramatic thread of the *Literary Reminiscences,* then, is the retreat of the literary worshipper to the lake district to venerate Wordsworth; at the price of disillusionment and rejection, he is forced to flee the lakes, yet recovers as a writer famous in his own right, in his forced return to the public world.

The innate tendency of the writer to identify with the subject has been documented by Freud, Kris, and Erikson, but it was already evident to the Romantics in Boswell.[54] In 1796 Isaac D'Israeli, anticipating Keats's image, said that in a successful biography the chameleon biographer must identify with the subject: "It has now become the labour of criticism, to compose the life of an author; and no writer can now successfully accomplish his Biographic attempts, unless he comes with a portion of that genius, the history of whose mind he records; he must possess a flexibility of taste, which, like the cameleon, takes the colour of that object on which it rests."[55]

In literary biography, identification of the biographer and subject takes on direct competitive footing. Literary biography invites an involuntary ranking of the journeyman and the master, the successful writer who merits the biography, and the aspiring writer, the satellite to literary greatness whose identity will be vicariously established through biographical service. The literary biographer is in a constant struggle to change the relation between self and subject: thus we often find in biography the paradox of admiration and derogation.

The self-referentiality of literary biography is closely linked to the ideological concepts of influence, anxiety, and intimidation called up by W. J. Bate and Harold Bloom[56] to describe the impact of the literary canon on the individual. The *Literary Reminiscences* provides a commentary on this self-referentiality of literary biography. The biographer's desire to become a writer is allegorized in De Quincey's own evolution from what he calls an aspiring literary "novitiate" to a successful literary "lion."[57] De Quincey's narrative strategy provides a commentary on the twofold mechanism of literary intimidation from intellectual forebears present in biography: the burden of the past (the eighteenth-century legacy of Johnson and Boswell) and the burden of the present (the inescapable identification of biographer and subject).

De Quincey styles himself the first to recognize the lake poets' genius, champion their reputations, and interpret their works to the world. The narrative oscillation between past and present is intended to imply as well the intellectually privileged status of De Quincey as the present literary biographer who interprets the poets. That biographical criticism is an important component of Romantic criticism has long been understood; theories of autobiographical writing, influence, and personal history as a literary determinant are crucial to the poetic mainstream. For the Romantics, biography offered a strategy for reading, a critical methodology: both an extrinsic theory of literature which posited the life as connected to the meaning and sometimes the form of the work, and a practical criticism which used the life to assist in interpretation of the works. Anecdotes did not just enhance the vicarious pleasure of the text—much of Byron's appeal—but provided the key for decoding its meaning.

De Quincey, then, was not alone in assuming that character analysis of the author was the chief activity in reading a work of literature, or in assuming every work of art was directly or indirectly autobiographical. The literary biography could be used to illuminate the work of art—and conversely, the work of art could illuminate the life of its author. Following earlier Romantic readings, De Quincey unveiled Shakespeare embodied in Prospero, Anne Hathaway in *Twelfth Night*.[58] His review of John Forster's life of Goldsmith (1848) affirmed the reciprocal interest of lives and works: "Both unfold together: and each borrows a secondary interest from the other: the life from the recollection of the works—the works from the joy and sorrow of the life." The same year, reviewing Thomas Noon Talfourd's biography of Lamb, De Quincey said that an understanding of Lamb's "character and temperament" was essential to appreciating his writing:

> A capital defect it would be if these could not be gathered silently from Lamb's works themselves. It would be a fatal mode of dependency upon an alien and separable accident if they needed an external commentary. But they do *not*. The syllables lurk up and down the writings of Lamb which decipher his eccentric nature. His character lies there dispersed in anagram; and to any attentive reader the regathering and restoration of the total word from its scattered parts is inevitable without an effort. Still it is always a satisfaction in knowing a result, to know also its *why* and *how*.

Essential biographical information is present, if hidden, in the literary text; it is the duty of the literary critic to perform the task of deciphering the character "dispersed in anagram."

De Quincey's use of literary quotation in the biography of Wordsworth, for example, illustrates the wide range of Romantic interpretive possibilities. He assumes correctly that *The Prelude* is autobiographical, and quotes "Tintern Abbey" to describe Dorothy Wordsworth. Additionally, he infers "Lines on the Castle of Indolence" and "She was a Phantom of Delight" allude to Coleridge and Mary Hutchinson Wordsworth ("From these verses, I say, it may be inferred what were the qualities which won Wordsworth's admiration in a wife"). But he moves a step further, assuming all poetic episodes contain identifiable seeds of life incidents. Hence he uses the lyrics of Wordsworth to gloss unverifiable observations of his own, under the assumption they must correspond to some buried autobiographical inspiration. He quotes the "Beggars" to describe Dorothy's face as "Egyptian brown," the "Matron of Jedborough" to describe madness in the eye of Mary Lamb, "a remnant of uneasy light," and twice paraphrases lines from "Resolution and Independence" to describe both Wordsworth and Coleridge in the throes of unhealthy lassitude, "who for himself will take no thought at all." Both the Pedlar and the Solitary are at times described as modeled on Wordsworth himself. De Quincey assumes other readers engage in the same strategies of reading; when Wordsworth quotes a description by Tasso one evening for another purpose, De Quincey surmises Wordsworth actually "had his sister in his thoughts."[59]

In the Romantic critical context, the literary text stood empty, if not indecipherable, without a biographical commentary understood as a sub-text or critical appendage. Application of biography was not a matter of verification of the text, but giving meaning to a text which was independently meaningless or unintelligible. Such theories pertained not just to purportedly veiled autobiography, such as Byron's work, or to the general subjectivity of narration; all kinds of writing benefited from biographical commentary. Wordsworth's poem, "Written after the Death of Charles Lamb," forms the core of De Quincey's discussion of the Lambs. De Quincey assumes that the poem cannot be comprehended without knowledge of incipient strains of madness in Lamb himself: a fissure in the poem camouflages its meaning, and Wordsworth himself, De Quincey intimates, is perhaps not fully aware of what his poem responds to in Lamb.[60] Thus De Quincey's role as a literary biographer was to interpret the texts not only to the uninitiated but to the poets themselves.

Not content to infer the poet from the poem, De Quincey records his own curiosity to meet writers and confirm his inferences. Although he was uninterested in Boswellian conversational records, De Quincey was far more sensitive than Wordsworth to the value of firsthand accounts to posterity. Tacitly replying to Wordsworth's *Letter to a Friend of Robert Burns* (biography is particularly unnecessary as regards "authors" and "poets more especially"), he exclaims that "Commensurate with the interest in the poetry, will be a secondary interest in the poet. . . . how invaluable should we all feel any record to be, which should raise the curtain upon Shakspeare's daily life—his habits, personal and social, his intellectual tastes, and his opinions. . . . I cannot, therefore, think it necessary to apologize for the most circumstantial notices, past or to come, of Wordsworth's person and habits of life."[61] He adds, tacitly answering Coleridge's charge against biographical gossip ("the cravings of worthless curiosity") in *The Friend*, "It is under no such gossiping taste that volumes have been written upon the mere portraits and upon the possible portraits of Shakspeare." Sketching his friend John Wilson in 1829, he emphasized readers' curiosity about an author's appearance, "that precise section . . . which it is most impossible for them to supply for themselves by any acquaintance with his printed works." Yet De Quincey was always aware of his privileged access to information, and warned, "Let me hope that you have not so far miscalculated my purpose as to have been looking out for anecdotes (*i.e.* scandal)." He denied taking advantage of "opportunities thrown in one's way by the confiding negligence of affectionate friendship," although he was not oblivious to the voyeuristic side of his biographies, observing, "Writers and readers must often act and react for reciprocal degradation."[62]

Although De Quincey declared in the *Literary Reminiscences,* "I see no reason why I should mystify the account of Coleridge's life or habits, by dissembling" and "What man does *not* scruple who values, above all things, the reputation for veracity?,"[63] some readers wondered about the relation of fiction and fact. The *North American Review* wrote in 1824 of the *Confessions,* "We are sometimes in doubt whether what is stated apparently as narrative is not meant for brilliant fiction, or at least for 'fiction founded on fact.'" A. H. Japp refuted contemporary questions over the fictionality of the *Confessions* by quoting De Quincey's explanation in *Suspiria* that he disguised the address of the Oxford Street house not only to prevent its identification and protect the innocent, but to preclude rival subjectivities: what if the lawyer were to "publish *his* Confessions? Or, which would be worse, a supplement to mine—printed so as exactly to match. . . . Besides, he would have cross-examined me before the public in Old Bailey style; no story, the most straightforward that ever was told, could be sure to stand *that.*" For De Quincey, the question of verification was a fundamental misapprehension of narrative truth; no story could withstand cross-examination precisely because every account has a different and unimpeachable subjectivity. Nevertheless, De Quincey was concerned not to appear an exaggerator or poseur, and he was protective of his reputation as a writer of nonfiction. He told the *London Magazine* publisher James Hessey in 1822 that he considered composing the "imaginary confessions of a murderer," but hesitated: "Yet do not mention this, if you please, to anybody: for if I begin to write imaginary Confessions, I shall seem to many as no better than a pseudo-confessor in my own too real Confessions."[64]

Johnson himself contemplated the problem of dealing with unverified accounts in *Roscommon:* "'Do not wholly slight them, because they may be true; but do not easily trust them, because they may be false.'" But though Johnson might say "seldom any splendid story is wholly true" (*Dorset*), in the Romantic and post-Romantic inversion, seldom is any story wholly false. Writing of Coleridge's patrons, the Wedgwoods, De Quincey includes a story discredited by one of the brothers as "pure fable": he retains it "simply as a version." Revising his autobiography, De Quincey denounces mis-statement in biography, then explains, "I once began a very elaborate life myself, and in these words:—'Jeremy Taylor . . . was the son of a barber, and the son-in-law of a king'— alluding to the tradition (imperfectly verified, I believe)."[65] Johnson's biographical theory had emphasized insignificant details; Boswell's narrative implied that the occasions he happened to witness were Johnson's most revealing; De Quincey's took the next step by suggesting the least noticed and even least credited events are the most illuminating.

Contemporary psychoanalytic biography has been equally curious about rumor. W. J. Bate prefaces Johnsonian apocrypha saying, "People have been reluctant to surrender the story." Erikson and Sartre assume some core of truth in recurrent rumors: recounting an incident in the childhood of Jean Genet, Sartre declares, "That was how it happened, in that or some other way," exactly how is "unimportant"; Erikson, discussing the persistent "fascination" of "alleged" events in Martin Luther's life, says conflicting accounts do not matter because we can assume "that something like this episode happened."[66] De Quincey's use of apocrypha and epitomizing rumor, then, stands within the larger matrix of tentative solutions in the genre.

A frequent misconception of present-day biographical criticism is that biography showed no psychological analysis before the psychoanalytic codifications of the twentieth century.[67] In truth, Romantic literary biography was deeply concerned with probing the veiled actions of life. The Romantic analysis of the symbolic basis of human action was modeled on the tradition of scriptural exegesis, borrowing fundamentally textual methodologies to decipher the workings of the mind. De Quincey amalgamated a modern vocabulary in declaring that the behavior of the woman he calls the "Saracen's head" was "as Mr. Coleridge expresses it, a psychological curiosity," and that his passion of grief at Kate Wordsworth's death has "a permanent interest in the psychological history of human nature."[68] But Romantic biographical analysis of character essentially transferred a vocabulary used for reading textual allegories to reading allegories of human life. Keats's famous letter on the subject illuminates the relationship between Romantic psychological insights and techniques of literary analysis. Discussing the Reynolds family's susceptibility to Benjamin Bailey's philandering, Keats observes that motives are often unintelligible to those who read literally actions that must be read allegorically:

this may teach them that the man who redicules [*sic*] romance is the most romantic of Men—that he who abuses women and slights them—loves them the most—that he who talks of roasting a Man alive would not do it when it came to the push—and above all that they are very shallow people who take every thing literal. A Man's life of any worth is a continual allegory—and a very few eyes can see the Mystery of his life—a life like the scriptures, figurative— which such people can no more make out than they can the hebrew Bible.[69]

In the allegory of everyday life, the mysteries or motives of human be- havior are decoded, or read, as if the life were a literary text.[70] The seemingly literal events of life require probing just as the incidents of scripture.

Nineteenth-century literary biographers welcomed the analogy be- tween interpretations of daily actions and literary actions. Keats's analysis of literal and allegorical levels of interpretation resurfaces in De Quincey's own theories of biographical writing. Keats's statement that few eyes can read the living text corresponds with the Romantic ideal of the fit though few capable of understanding the written text. For De Quincey, the good biographer is one skilled at reading and writing the allegories of life: "Of the many memorials dedicated to the life of Milton, how few are entitled to take their station in the literature!"[71]

Literary biography, by positing a connection between the life and works, offered itself as a strategy for reading, and by the time of De Quincey it was the dominant critical approach to literature. In particu- lar, De Quincey's use of dreams as indicators of the mind, and his view of life as a pattern developing from childhood, are allied with later psychoan- alytic theories. There is considerable methodological overlap between the conjectures of the Romantic literary biographer, who sees autobiographi- cal implications in the writings of the subject, and the psychoanalytic biographer of today, who attempts a reconstruction of motivations from autobiographical writing. Yet Romanticism in English biography is pri- marily a literary impulse, a vocabulary derived from literary interpretation and arising in the practice of literary biography—it is in this context we must place Keats's comments on the "allegory" of life and the secular exegesis of interpreting "life like the scriptures."

Wordsworth's Preludic typology identified in childhood the seeds of the adult; De Quincey expressed a similar view in *Suspiria,* explaining, "What- soever in a man's mind blossoms and expands to his own consciousness in mature life, must have pre-existed in germ during his infancy." The task of the biographer is to read the life as a text in order to decipher the mysterious "handwriting" of biographical evidence and, in depicting the events of childhood, to utter what the child cannot verbalize: "*I* decipher what the child only felt in cipher. . . . In the child lay the handwriting mysterious to *him;* in me the interpretation and the comment." Revising this and other autobiographical writings in 1853, De Quincey borrowed the "Immortality" ode to underscore the relation between childhood and adulthood: " '*The child,*' says Wordsworth, '*is father of the man.*' . . . all that is now broadly emblazoned in the man, once was latent—seen or not seen—as a vernal bud in the child. But not, therefore, is it true inversely— that all which pre-exists in the child finds its development in the man." Under auspicious circumstances (the *Literary Reminiscences* describes the case of Wordsworth), the child flourishes; but as often, the "frost of counterforces" blights the childhood promise.[72]

The posthumously published "Conversation and S. T. Coleridge" provides a striking example of De Quincey putting these theories into practice. In 1847 H. N. Coleridge reissued the *Biographia Literaria,*[73] with a biographical supplement containing the five autobiographical letters Coleridge wrote to Thomas Poole in 1797 and 1798. In these records of early childhood grief and turmoil, De Quincey finds clues to Coleridge's ruined erudition and the "waywardness" of his conversation, thought, and actions. Recounting the tyranny of Coleridge's older brother in the cheese-mincing episode, De Quincey emphasizes its connections to his later writings: "The 'Ancient Mariner,' then about seven years old, could not stand this. 'With *his* cross-bow'—no, stop! what are we saying? Nothing better than a kitchen knife was at hand—and 'this,' says Samuel, 'I seized. . . .'" De Quincey connects Coleridge's subsequent running away and near-death of exposure to his painful ague twenty years hence— and by implication, to the opium nostrum of his adulthood. The Ancient Mariner is the avatar of this early episode, taunted, punished, unjustly persecuted anew after his sufferings ("Whip the Ancient Mariner, indeed! . . . a virtuous boy matched in duel with adversity"), and condemned in his adult life and his works to retell the story of his childhood persecution. Using the same bud imagery, De Quincey traces Coleridge's adult frailties and failed achievement to the psychological consequences of a blighted youth; this domestic "drama substantially so fearful" and "sufferings so durable in their effects" reveal the consequences "of early experience combining to thwart all the morning promise of greatness and splendour; the flower unfolding its silken leaves only to suffer canker and blight; and to hang withering on the stalk, with only enough of grace and colour left to tell pathetically to all that looked upon it what might have been." The sufferings were durable, but the blossom of promise was not; the lingering consequences of a stormy childhood were flawed achievements and unrealized genius in adulthood.

On an unstated level, just as Coleridge tells the story of his own life in the "Ancient Mariner," the biographer silently retells the story of his own life in recounting the tale of Coleridge. Doubtlessly De Quincey recognized and rued similar patterns in his own life, contrasting the literary productivity he traced to Wordsworth's happy childhood with the turbulent childhood he shared with Coleridge. Although De Quincey does not identify the correspondences with Coleridge's life, the early death of his father, running away, his overbearing brother William, his banishment to an unhappy urban school life, and a persistent sickliness relieved by opium, are all chronicled in De Quincey's own autobiographical writings. By all accounts he was considered a conversationalist in his own right; he flattered himself a metaphysician and political theorist; and he inescapably recognized his own blighted ambitions, procrastination, and unrealized powers. It is not surprising that in the published *Literary Reminiscences* De Quincey preferred to look at his resemblances to Wordsworth.

The Romantics essentially secularized the traditional forms of exegetical reading. Just as Dante identified the polysemy or multiple allegory of nonscriptural texts,[74] we can identify multiple levels of allegory in De Quincey's narrative. The exegetical task of the biographer in reading the life is, in turn, the reader's task of understanding these layers of significance. Behind the literal narrative of events in the *Literary Reminiscences,* De Quincey allegorizes the passage of time, the aspirations of the literary biographer, and the conventions of pastoral retreat. To create this program, De Quincey borrows the poetic topos of the movement from city to country to city, playing on the Arcadian expectations created by literary biography, the prose tradition in lake literature, and the pastoral poetic tradition.

Readers often comment on the close texture of Romantic prose, but as De Quincey said of Coleridge's listeners, they often fail to discern the "compass" of the narrative; in De Quincey's essay sequences, we must not forget to look beyond local texture to allegorical design. Of the many critics who have remarked De Quincey's digressions, only Elizabeth

Bruss has called attention to their allegorical dimension in observing of the early autobiographical sketches that "his life has mirrored the historical process" and the seemingly digressive discussion of the Irish revolution is an analogue for De Quincey's own rebelliousness and "restless transition."[75] To put the case even more strongly, the *Sketches of Life and Manners* can be seen as an array of tyrants and rebels—the private rebellions of De Quincey and his brothers intermixed with reflections on the Irish insurgency, the French Revolution, and Napoleon. In the same way, a few years later, the *Literary Reminiscences* allegorizes the condition of literature and the experience of the literary life through De Quincey's own attempt to become a writer. On a further level, the *Reminiscences* multiplies the reverberations of polysemic design: beyond his personal retreat to the lakes is the "pensive allegoric memorial of . . . our human pilgrimage" and the anagogy of nature decipherable in the "mysterious tendencies . . . written hieroglyphically in the vicissitudes of day and night, of winter and summer, and throughout the great alphabet of Nature."[76]

Et in Arcadia Ego: The *Literary Reminiscences*

Guides to the Lakes

In discussing the structure of the *Literary Reminiscences* it is necessary to keep in mind that De Quincey's famous lake recollections are set within a matrix of the literary society of the first two decades of the nineteenth century. It is, as De Quincey tells us repeatedly, a portrait of the literary society in England, in which the jewel of the lake district is placed in a setting by contrast to the urban world; and moreover, a setting of place and time which has passed and yielded to an inexorably fallen world. Let us look first, then, at this urban frame: the youthful acquaintance with Liverpool literary society and London literary society, including figures such as Charles Lamb. Structurally, this life of the "literary novitiate" fills the opening quarter of the book; the large central section of the book is the group portrait of the lake district—Wordsworth, Coleridge, Southey, and the many lesser literati, gentry, and peasantry. The final quarter of the book is his return from the lake district to the urban literary life, beset by financial need, opium, and despair, yet paradoxically no longer a literary observer but himself a writer.

The opening essays depict a world of urban literary corruption. De Quincey is sent out from school into the world with a talismanic copy of the *Odyssey*. Embarking upon the world, he encounters a literary society in Liverpool characterized by every possible compositional evil: affectation, coarseness, low buffoonery, intellectual larceny, conventional usages, and blind servility. Worse yet are the London Grub Street practices of piracy, literary hoax, rushed deadlines, and scant salary. It is a world of mediocrity and literary dishonesty, in which the "false Florimel" of literature and taste prevails—in which the "conversational manipulation" of Humphry Davy is preferred to the genius of Coleridge; in which the literary forgeries of Scott are first palmed off in Germany, and then deceptively foisted upon the public anew in England; in which geniuses are given "*'leave to toil,'*" and a fickle public is deluded by "momentary attractions."[77]

De Quincey pictures himself forced unwillingly into this meretricious literary world. Indeed, as we come to see, only Wordsworth is magically immune, nurtured in the literary paradise of the lake district, preserved and fostered by bequests and sinecures in a benevolent Arcadia of poetic productivity. In contrast, even Coleridge is tangled in ineffectual journalistic schemes, and Southey is seen making "*'the pot boil.'*"[78]

De Quincey depicts himself, even in his boyhood, as straddling the two worlds. He is part of the corrupted urban world, but he also possesses the privileged status of the literary commentator. The fraudulence and mediocrity of the Liverpool circle are transparent "to me, who, in that year, 1801, already knew of a grand renovation of poetic power—of a new birth in poetry, interesting not so much to England as to the human mind." De Quincey is one empowered to see beyond the limitations of his contemporaries—even Lamb is guilty of undermining the lake "philosophers in the caves," Lamb who is himself, according to De Quincey, only a "second[ary]" talent. Again, and again, De Quincey exclaims at the oblivion of Wordsworth and Coleridge in the public eye, and contrasts the sanctity of the *Lyrical Ballads* on his own shelf. They are known to "no man, beyond one or two in each ten thousand"—and when not unknown, "abject in public estimation" and known "only to scorn."[79]

Yet perforating the early section of the *Reminiscences* are harbingers of the anticipated visit to the lakes (the pilgrimage to his venerated "idol" and "Elijah" Wordsworth) as well as the ultimate reversal of the scorn and oblivion, "a position which thirty and odd years have altered, by a revolution more astonishing and total than ever before happened in literature or in life."[80] By the return of De Quincey to the urban present at the end of the *Reminiscences,* the reputation of Wordsworth has been publicly vindicated. Yet as is hinted even in the early chapters, the critical revolution De Quincey longed to bring about was a mixed blessing; for it brought about the concomitant disillusionment of De Quincey, as well as the physical decay of the purity of the lakes, and, it is hinted, the purity of Wordsworth's poetry.

Notably, De Quincey uses the opening installment of the *Literary Reminiscences* as a commentary on biographical writing. Like Boswell, misappropriating Johnson's methodology to justify his own quite different project, De Quincey manages to praise Wordsworth's perspicuity in the *Letter to a Friend of Robert Burns,* regarding "the delicate task of following a man of original genius though his personal infirmities or his constitutional aberrations." But unlike Wordsworth, De Quincey urges that such aberrations be explored. Moreover, at the center of the Liverpool literary circle are William Roscoe, William Shepherd, and James Currie; contemptible poets manqué according to De Quincey, but in fact publicly prominent as biographers.[81] De Quincey particularly ridicules Currie's well-known 1800 biography of Burns, and asserts Allan Cunningham's life of Burns is far preferable, for Cunningham is "far more capable of understanding Burns's situation" from the similarity of his own struggle. This necessity for the biographer to identify with the subject is of great critical importance to De Quincey; and Wordsworth is the target of De Quincey's own most passionate identification.

Wordsworth is the most prominent figure in the *Literary Reminiscences,* and his biography assumes the largest position in the series. About half of the central lake recollections, however, is a collective portrait of subordinate lives associated with Wordsworth and the lakes. While De Quincey saw in Coleridge's life unfortunate similarities to his own—the struggling journalist, the world of rushed Grub Street deadlines, the pains of opium—he saw in Wordsworth's life the fulfillment of what he wished to be. De Quincey clearly was someone who expected to do more with his life, yet his plans never came to fruition—possibly due to opium, possibly to poverty, possibly to the corruption of journalistic writing (he himself suggested all three), and very possibly due to the psychological impediment associated with his Wordsworth years. As his youthful diary attests, De Quincey planned many literary projects, but foremost he asserted, "I have . . . always intended of course that poems should form the cornerstones of my fame."[82] Although he maintained the gentleman's disdain of publication for the press (he told Emerson *Tait's* had "vulgarized" his work)[83] at the same time his achievement was completely defined by his journalism. De Quincey repeatedly laments he came to write out of financial necessity; yet the question remains whether without the financial impetus he would have written at all.

Everywhere throughout the lives we see the mark of Wordsworth's influence. We have already spoken of the parallels De Quincey drew between his own life and Wordsworth's in the identification of subject and biographer. Wordsworth dominates the *Reminiscences,* however, on a narrative level as well. In pausing here to consider Wordsworth's actual writing during their friendship, it must be remembered that the period of De Quincey's intimacy with Wordsworth was short-lived. He introduced himself by letter in 1803; the first meeting with Coleridge, then Wordsworth, took place in 1807; he revisited the lakes the following year. Between 1809, when he moved into Dove Cottage, and 1813, when opium addiction, the affair with Margaret Simpson, and general social attrition estranged him from the Wordsworth circle, De Quincey was enjoying what were to be his closest observations of the Wordsworths.

Significantly, during this time Wordsworth was preoccupied with writing two books on the lakes. By the 1790s, the lake district was securely established as a popular tourist area, partly as a result of travelogues touting Cumberland and Westmorland as the embodiment of the picturesque aesthetic in England—Gilpin, Gray, West, Budworth, and Radcliffe had all written them, and many in the Wordsworth set turned to the genre to make money. William and Dorothy were working on accounts; and Coleridge's detailed journal entries of August 1802 suggest he may have been planning a lake account as well. In 1824 Wordsworth's friend, the Quaker Thomas Wilkinson, published a lake tour written some time earlier. John Wilson periodically published sentimental and scenic lake district sketches including three pseudonymous "Letters from the Lakes" (*Blackwood's,* 1819), which pretended to recount a tourist's first visit, including meetings with Southey and Wordsworth. William Combe's *The Tour of Doctor Syntax in Search of the Picturesque* parodied the fad and coincidentally appeared the very year Wordsworth decided a guide would earn him money.[84]

The project of the prose lake guide to introduce Joseph Wilkinson's *Select Views* arose in the summer of 1809, and was written in serial form through 1810. Before it was finished, Wordsworth began to revise material for his own expanded lake guide, although it was temporarily laid aside in 1813. Meanwhile, having moved to Allan Bank, Wordsworth was also renewing work on what had been known as *The Pedlar,* and revising it for publication as *The Excursion,* a task completed in 1813 except for final revisions. At the end of February 1810, all three parts of the *Essay upon Epitaphs* had been completed, at about the same time Books V, VI, and VII of *The Excursion* were being written. The first part of the *Essay upon Epitaphs* was to be incorporated at the end of Book V, right before the important two-book necrology, "The Churchyard Among the Mountains." The years, then, between the publication of the first guide to the lakes and *The Excursion,* 1809 to 1814, were the source of almost all De Quincey's written memorials of Wordsworth (even though he continued to maintain the cottage until 1835). Wordsworth's prose and poetry excursions in the lakes were being written at exactly the same time; they were the last works De Quincey was to witness the daily progress of; and it should not surprise us to find De Quincey subsequently writing his own book on the lakes.

Needless to say, the poem which was to become *The Prelude* was also an integral and familiar part of the Wordsworth oeuvre for De Quincey. In 1804 Wordsworth wrote to him, "I am now writing a Poem on my own earlier life," and explained it would not be printed "till I have finished a larger and more important work to which it is tributary." The next year De Quincey described himself as looking for "Some great intellectual project, to which all intellectual pursuits may be made tributary;"[85] as early as 1818 he alludes to "my life which I have partly written and design to publish before my death." In 1822 in the successful wake of the *Confessions,* he was contemplating an eclectic project of wider scope, "a sort of Ana" intended to contain "Criticism—Human Life—Love—Marriage—Courtship—Political Economy—Mathematics—Morals—Coleridge—Wordsworth—Myself in childhood . . . in short the flower of all my reading, thinking and scheming for twenty odd years."[86]

By 1810, De Quincey had read Wordsworth's poem in manuscript—in 1848 he told Ralph Waldo Emerson he had once possessed a copy of the poem. *The Prelude* was the source for most of the facts on the early life of Wordsworth: a poem important enough for De Quincey to quote at length from published and unpublished segments, and important enough for De Quincey to assume its autobiographical principles for his own growth of a prose writer's mind.[87]

But looming larger for De Quincey than even the "tributary" *Prelude* was the "more important work" in what portion was complete, *The Excursion*. In the atmosphere of *The Excursion*'s current disfavor, we must make a particular effort to understand the ideological importance of the projected *Recluse* for Wordsworth's adherents. Like Wordsworth, De Quincey saw his career as a series of projects hinging on Romantic subjectivity. Wordsworth had declared in the 1814 Preface to *The Excursion* that his oeuvre resembled a gothic church, with *The Prelude* spoken in his own person as the "ante-chapel" to the "dramatic form" of *The Excursion,* and all the minor lyrics serving as "cells, oratories, and sepulchral recesses." Just as Wordsworth began with an autobiographical narrative and moved onward to reclothe his autobiographical experience in a more objective form in *The Excursion,* so De Quincey moved from the explicitly autobiographical *Confessions* to the more objectified narrative strategy of the biographical *Reminiscences.*[88]

In making the pilgrimage to Grasmere, planning to be a poet, and later quitting the university to join Wordsworth, De Quincey was not just affecting an imitation of Wordsworth's life; nor was he a Boswell exulting in acquaintances for acquaintance's sake.[89] By insinuating himself into Wordsworth's orbit, De Quincey hoped to be accepted into the Wordsworth intellectual circle. As Thomas McFarland and F. A. Pottle[90] have shown, there existed among Wordsworth, Coleridge, and Dorothy Wordsworth an exchange of creative ideas and intellectual projects, an exchange De Quincey idealized, and to which he tried to annex himself. In 1809, for example, he eagerly took on some of Wordsworth's mechanical literary tasks as the factotum in the troubled venture of seeing the *Convention of Cintra* to press. He would willingly have done more, but by 1812 relations had already begun to cool, and Wordsworth turned down De Quincey's offer to write a Danish dialect appendix for the guide to the lakes.[91]

The appropriation of Wordsworthian elements is most obvious in De Quincey's reliance on Wordsworth's own language. The *Literary Reminiscences* includes identifiable direct quotation from at least forty different Wordsworth poems—adding paraphrases, echoes, and indirect allusions, the number would rise still more. Notably, there are at least fourteen extended references to *The Excursion,* far more than to any other poem, particularly to Books VI and VII. Wordsworth's better-known poems are of course present, but poems such as "Glen Almain" and the "Vernal Ode" are quoted as equitably as "Resolution and Independence" and the "Immortality" ode.

Like Wordsworth, De Quincey draws attention to Westmorland dialect—often glossing the same words Wordsworth does in "An Evening Walk." Furthermore, De Quincey derives his sense of the scenic picturesque from the lake guide, even though Wordsworth declined his assistance. Wordsworth's own poems contained a measure of sentimental associationism from landmarks already familiar to readers of travel books. His repeatedly issued lake guide was replete with the usual references to Gilpin, scenic viewing stations, landscape architecture, and painterly commentary on the visual merits of the area. When Wordsworth commends a "sublime combination of mountain forms" or lands a spot "rich in picturesque beauty" or critically observes that "the chief defect in the colouring of the country . . . is an over-prevalence of a bluish tint," he is clearly participating in the picturesque manner of evaluating landscape as though it were painting.[92] In aesthetically assessing the shape of cottage chimneys, depicting lake scenery, and discussing the hazards of mountain climbing, De Quincey likewise calls to mind the valuative and descriptive writing of picturesque travelogue.

Wordsworth's assessments of the aesthetics of nature are frequently the source of De Quincey's observations. He cites Wordsworth's opinion on the superiority of English valleys over the "glaring imperfection" of the Welsh; commends Wordsworth's eye for landscape; and agrees with Wordsworth's antipathy to the planting of larches. Even the aesthetics of literary quotation are derived from Wordsworth's use of illustrative quotes from classical and contemporary landscape poetry, a precedent common in picturesque writing. Wordsworth himself quotes from his *Excursion* in revised editions, reminding us that his decision to write a poetic excursion was a project deliberately drawing on the motifs of traditional travel literature; for at the same time Wordsworth was writing the lake guide, he was working on the less conventional tour of the lakes.[93]

Just as "Tintern Abbey" derives from the form of topographic poetry, so *The Excursion* is cast into the mold of a lake tour.[94] But at this point, such connections cease; for *The Excursion* is less a tour of scenery than a portrait of humanity.[95] In contrast, Joseph Budworth's scenic placement of the Maid of Buttermere, Mary Robinson, in the landscape of his 1792

Fortnight's Ramble to the Lakes led to her status as a tourist attraction alongside the vale of Buttermere and the steps her father cut for tourists seeking the view from Scale Force. William Gilpin's 1776 *Observations . . . of Cumberland and Westmoreland* was only interested in the "picturesque inhabitants of the landscape" insofar as their "loitering" enhanced the panorama; and Robert Heron's 1793 *Observations made in a Journey through the Western Counties of Scotland* (cited by Wordsworth in the notes to *The Excursion*) presents the inverse scenery of edifying peasant industriousness.[96] Unlike most topographical poetry of the countryside, Wordsworth's poems left behind the abstract pastoral swain, vicar, and damsel in favor of detailed and individualized biographies, and invited the reader to equate the condition of rural life with the human condition. Indeed, Coleridge suggested in the *Biographia* that some of Wordsworth's *Lyrical Ballads* "would have been more delightful to me in prose, told and managed, as by Mr. Wordsworth they would have been, in a moral essay, or pedestrian tour."[97]

The growing genre of the biographical picturesque in literary travel writing had been generally unconcerned with identifying the figures in the pastoral landscape. John Gibson Lockhart's epistolary *Peter's Letters to His Kinsfolk* (1819) pretended to give a traveler's first impressions of Edinburgh intellectual society. William Howitt entrenched the touring of literary landmarks with his *Visits to Remarkable Places* (concurrent with the *Literary Reminiscences* in 1839 in *Tait's*) and later the well-known *Homes and Haunts of the Most Eminent British Poets* (1847), which provided biographical sketches for sites chosen for having "the picturesque" about them. H. D. Rawnsley, best known for his interviews with Westmorland Dalesmen about Wordsworth, continued the genre of literary travel biography in his *Literary Associations of the English Lakes* (1894), which recounted picturesque literary anecdotes of every tourist spot in the lakes.[98]

But the people of *The Excursion* and the *Literary Reminiscences* are pointedly not figure groupings of the picturesque, or anthropological curiosities, or Rousseauvian primitives. Rural verisimilitude and individualized biographical detail, especially in "The Churchyard Among the Mountains," particularized these lives in a way that tourist manuals, Virgilian paternalism, and Cowper's eighteenth-century gentleman of leisure could not, through their mere substitution of ink and quill for shepherd's crook. Wordsworth mixes living and dead, great and small, honorable and prodigal in a collective portrait of the lake district.

In an 1823 *London Magazine* squib, De Quincey said he had a collaborative guide to the lakes in the works, but when Lockhart suggested in 1830 that he write a book on the lakes, he demurred on the grounds that Wordsworth had done the scenic descriptions in his guide and Wilson was working "on the rest"; besides, he confided, he was not very interested in fish and birds.[99] He was, however, interested in people. When De Quincey did come to write a lake tour, it was a book on the lakes in the same sense *The Excursion* was a book on the lakes. De Quincey's lake tour, the *Literary Reminiscences,* was far more indebted to the biographical profiles of *The Excursion* than to the scenic conventions of Wordsworth's lake guide and prose travelogues. Following the three chapters summarizing Wordsworth's life (largely from *The Prelude*) come the series of lake district stories—first the stories of Coleridge and Southey and their families, then the "Saracen's Head," "Recollections of Grasmere," and the four "Society of the Lakes" episodes filled with short anecdotal biographies of lake dwellers of every rank—lesser literati, gentry, Dalesmen. In the *Literary Reminiscences,* it is just as Johnson said: "There has rarely passed a life of which a judicious and faithful narrative would not be useful" (*Rambler* 60).

Yet they are not figures chosen at random; they are all linked by their proximity to Wordsworth. Each biographical sketch originates in some connection with the Wordsworths—knowledge of which, De Quincey assumes, will enrich the reading of the poetry. Visits made with William or Dorothy, for example, initiate the sketches of John Wilson, Charles Lloyd, Mr. King and the Saracen's head. Even more conspicuously, De Quincey retells, interrupts, and updates Wordsworthian stories. Wordsworth writes about the corruption of the Maid of Buttermere in Book VII of *The Prelude,* the death of Charles Gough in "Fidelity," and the disaster of the Greens in "George and Sarah Green"; De Quincey expands the stories of the Maid of Buttermere, Gough, and the Greens. In "To the Spade" Wordsworth writes about Thomas Wilkinson, who at one point praised the literary endeavors of Elizabeth Smith; De Quincey incorporates details on Wilkinson and tells at length the life of Smith. Wordsworth tells the story of the tragic deaths of the Sympsons in "The Churchyard Among the Mountains"; De Quincey adopts the story from *The Excursion* wholesale. Wordsworth writes "Characteristics of a Child Three Years Old" about his daughter Kate; De Quincey ties it to the story of the Greens, and his own superior affection. De Quincey expands, contradicts, and intertwines them into a group portrait of Wordsworth's lake society, in the attempt to make his writing a part of the canon of the lakes.

Following the Wordsworthian precedent of poetically adopting the lake district and his personal history, De Quincey casts his lake acquaintances into the dramatis personae of literary biography. The *Literary Reminiscences* may be read in the way *The Excursion* was to be read, as actual events, places, and individuals transposed for philosophical purposes (the meditations "on Man, on Nature, and on Human Life" declared by *The Excursion*'s Prospectus). Both texts seek to intersect biographical responsibility with poetic vision. The lives of all the characters in *The Excursion* are taken from life models, as Wordsworth affirms in the Fenwick note wherein he apologetically punctuates the retold biography of each character with verifications: "my old schoolfellow," a tale "told to Mrs. Wordsworth and my sister," "an exact picture of what fell under my own observation," "nothing introduced but what is taken from nature and real life." But Wordsworth, unlike De Quincey, labored under what Edmund Gosse called "the anxiety to be truthful."[100] He is obliged to repeatedly assure the poem's autobiographical fidelity—its truth to life—despite the small geographic deviances of poetic license. Yet paradoxically, De Quincey, with his more questionable compositional liberties—of placing interpretation above strict attention to fact—was actually freer than Wordsworth to invent and exaggerate with impunity. Given the authorial contract between nonfictional narrator and reader, De Quincey's lives pass as accurate without specific disclaimer; prose biography possesses an inherent verisimilitude which Wordsworth's poetic biographies could only aspire to achieve by appending prose affidavits in the form of prefaces and notes assuring us that the literary license taken had not been too great.

The sketches of the *Literary Reminiscences* are particularly related to the life stories told by Wordsworth in "The Churchyard Among the Mountains," Books VI and VII of *The Excursion*.[101] Like the lives Wordsworth's pastor recounts in the graveyard of St. Oswald, nearly all of the minor lives De Quincey tells are at chapter end consigned to the tomb—Southey's son, the Greens, Gough, Lloyd, Smith, and Sympsons: all conclude with De Quincey meditating upon their graves. In this chronicle of the lives of the lakes, we see the "record of human passion" which defined for De Quincey the highest form of prose, that of the poetic "impassioned prose." De Quincey was certainly attracted to those works of Wordsworth that coincided with the morbidity dominant in his own life. Thus he found the necrology of "The Churchyard Among the Mountains" a congenial form of biography. Death there is an unresisted and almost pleasurable end, as Wordsworth says in Book VI, "Pleased though sad, / More pleased than sad" (VI: 1063–64). Indeed, in Part I of the *Essay upon Epitaphs* appended to *The Excursion,* Wordsworth stresses the analogy between the writer of epitaphs and the biographer by making use of the vocabulary of biographical criticism, and his additional comments on epitaph-writing identify the writer of epitaphs as a "funereal Biographer" and, conversely, biography as a form of expanded epitaph.[102]

As Wordsworth nostalgically observed of the unmarked mounds in Grasmere's churchyard before tombstones were introduced, the oral record of the dead is invested in the pastor, the village "historian." The biographer continues this link with oral poetic tradition. Like the pastor who preserves and recites life stories in "The Churchyard Among the Mountains," the poetic privilege of walking between great and small is conferred upon the biographer. Surely Wordsworth had in mind the "mute inglorious Miltons" of Gray's "Elegy" in writing "The Churchyard Among the Mountains," and exclaiming in the opening of Book I, "many are the Poets that are sown / By Nature; men endowed with highest gifts, / The vision and the faculty divine; / Yet wanting the accomplishment of verse" (I: 77–80).[103] De Quincey alludes to this passage often, and like Wordsworth, he recounts the lives of these mute inglorious Miltons. Much of De Quincey's writing was epitaphic, and he recalls in the revised *Confessions* that he first was drawn to Wordsworth in the years 1799–1801 when he came across "Ruth" and "We Are Seven" (the poem Wordsworth characterized in the 1800 Preface to *Lyrical Ballads* as showing "the perplexity and obscurity which in childhood attend our notion of death").

In answering Johnson's *Life of Pope,* the *Essay upon Epitaphs* (which De Quincey praised as a "valuable paper")[104] posits epitaph writing as a critical litmus test. Wordsworth declares the literary faults of an age can be gauged in its epitaphs ("the Reader need only look into any collection of Epitaphs to be convinced that the faults predominant in the literature of every age will be as strongly reflected in the sepulchral inscriptions as any where; nay perhaps more so, from the anxiety of the Author to do justice to the occasion," Part III)—and in its critical writings on epitaphs. As R. H. Tawney has observed, "As archaeologists know, there are worse clues to the convictions of a period than the tombs prepared by it for its dead."[105] Epitaphs and biographies can both be studied as reflections of culture, but the naive properties of epitaphs mirror the literary practices of their age perhaps even more than biography. Like Johnson, Wordsworth censures Pope; but whereas death in Wordsworth stirs emotion toward nature and the criterion of literary sincerity, in Johnson it illuminates the issues of theological and technical proficiency.

Johnson was impatient with what he perceived as a superficial Arcadia of rustic life in pastoral literature.[106] Wordsworth sought to counteract the Johnsonian view of the pastoral as a shallow genre—as well as to stem the tide of modern pastoral which encouraged only sentimental meditation on rural utopias—by distinguishing the realities of rural life from a Spenserian faeryland, Shakespearian Arden, or Arcadian golden age "sequestered" in felicity (1805 *Prelude,* VIII: 183–91) and dismissing "all Arcadian dreams / All golden fancies of the golden Age" ("Home at Grasmere," ll. 625–26).

Wordsworth is also careful to deny the impression that all inhabitants of churchyards lived exemplary lives, as might mistakenly appear from scanning tombstones. The *Essay upon Epitaphs* notes that a graveyard, like a town, affords a profile of humanity ("A Village Church-yard, lying as it does in the lap of Nature, may indeed be most favourably contrasted with that of a Town of crowded Population," Part I). But Wordsworth warns, quoting Gray's "Elegy," that epitaphs " 'teach the rustic moralist to die' ": the prettiness of the rural graveyard must not lead us to imagine "in a Village Church-yard the eye or central point of a rural Arcadia" (Part II). Rather than a picturesque mosaic of virtue, "The Churchyard Among the Mountains" shows how the biographies of the cemetery offer a record of the span of human passions: "The universal forms / Of human nature, in a spot like this, / Present themselves at once to all men's view" (VIII: 14–16). The pastor warns midway through his recitation, lest we think all rural lives Arcadian, "We should not leave / Wholly untraced a more forbidding way" (VI: 661–62).

As we have observed, the *Literary Reminiscences* tells the story of the rise of Wordsworth from rural anonymity to poetic fame. Indeed, most of the quotations from Wordsworth in the *Reminiscences* pass unidentified in the text, unstated allusions to the Wordsworth corpus, recognizable only to the cognoscenti who belong to, as Wordsworth himself says in the Prospectus to *The Excursion,* that " 'fit audience let me find though few.' " This intertextual anonymity represents a small reverberation of De Quincey's larger narrative objective: anonymity and lack of recognition is very much a theme of the entire sequence of biographies.

The perplexing final quarter of the *Literary Reminiscences* can be seen as a culmination of this theme. As the hoped-for public recognition of Wordsworth finally is achieved, De Quincey's own friendship with him wanes. De Quincey, once venerating Wordsworth, comes to see Wordsworth as "a *mixed* creature, made up of special infirmity and special strength." What was described in the opening chapter as a longed-for "revolution" in public taste becomes in the end of the *Reminiscences* a "revolution in my feelings" as well.[107] As Wordsworth's fame increases, the district itself physically decays; as recognition comes to the lake district, it brings about a decline in what it had embodied. The popularity of the lakes and lake poets results in a corruptive plague of tourists, widened roads, decadent architecture, and the destruction of old trees for the planting of the despicable new larches. Wordsworth in Book VIII of *The Excursion* likewise followed the bucolic "Churchyard Among the Mountains" with a description of the encroachment of industrialization and the manufacturing spirit, and the attendant deterioration of landscape, education, and life in the countryside.

As the narrative ends, De Quincey is driven back to the urban literary realm. It is still filled with the same frauds and desperation—but De Quincey's status is altered. He returns, he tells us, no less than a "literary lion." On the *London Magazine,* he finds himself one of an urban prose constellation, a "*Pleiad*" including Hazlitt, Lamb, Clare, Cunningham and others.[108] His fame is nevertheless a mixed blessing. He only finds literary recognition at the price of having lost the lake district poets; his writings are the consequence of financial despair; his literary reputation is inextricably linked to his bodily destruction as an opium addict. This paradox is evident in all of De Quincey's writings (as he says in the *Sketches of Life and Manners,* "No man needs to *search* for paradox in this world of ours"). His losses are also his literary inspiration: opium in the *Confessions,* Wordsworthian disillusionment in the *Reminiscences,* death in the *Suspiria.* De Quincey emerges at the end, not the initiator of libels (as in the opening section) but the recipient of them, struggling to discover why and who attacked the privacy of his family.[109] Attendant on all fame is the potential of violation of privacy, the other side of literary mythmaking. De Quincey was always aware of walking the narrow line between the two in his own biographical sketches. Accordingly, the situations used to close the *Literary Reminiscences*—discussions of libel, Junius, and casuistry—allegorize the compromised state of the Romantic prose writer.

De Quincey's meditation on the Junius case is linked to the authorship of a book on Junius by John Taylor, editor of the *London Magazine*,[110] and it illuminates De Quincey's dilemma of writing for the press. Junius's forever hidden identity appears to have particular significance for the early nineteenth-century writer, who, desiring literary recognition, is nevertheless condemned to what De Quincey calls the "self-mortification" of the enforced anonymity of the press. Through the sobriquet Opium-Eater, like Elia and Junius, De Quincey was able to give his writing some stamp of identity and continuity in a publishing world dominated by anonymous articles. Yet in Junius, De Quincey may also be thinking of his own equivocal situation in another way: one who enjoys a reputation through the violation of taboos. He describes how Junius, having won private political confidences, "betrayed secrets" afterward by "treachery" and by "larceny"—as De Quincey says, "having obtained power like a thief, he had sold it like a traitor." Was he himself anxious about the way in which he may have, as Wordsworth charged, breached "the law of hospitality" when trusted as an "inmate of his house"?[111]

Yet De Quincey may offer an answer in the condemnation of auricular confession he uses to imply a dissociation with the Augustinian tradition of autobiography, and indeed, with any biographical method governed by convention and rules. The natural reverie and public self-revelation of opium confessions liberate autobiography from the structured review of discreditable secrets demanded by auricular confessions.[112] Regardless of genre, De Quincey identifies the best narrative as one based not according to preset laws of "artificial review and interpretation" but according to the action of the flickering imagination. Using the image of the mind so common in De Quincey, he describes the creative literary narrative as one "by which the mind, like the lamps of a mail-coach, moving rapidly through the midnight woods, illuminate, for one instant, the foliage or sleeping umbrage of the thickets; and, in the next instant, have quitted them, to carry their radiance forward upon endless successions of objects." In *The English Mail-Coach* (1849) as well as in *Suspiria,* the movement of the coach becomes an image of the imagination and the action of the interpretive mind. And throughout the *Literary Reminiscences,* beyond the familiar model of the passage of time and the journey of life implicit in the image of the traveler on a dark road, the motion of the mail-coach additionally becomes the symbol of narrative exploration.[113]

Just as De Quincey renounces the false casuistry of the confessional tradition in autobiography, he replaces the spiritual movement toward God[114] with a geographical movement. The structure of the *Literary Reminiscences* moves from city to country to city, taking on the conventional shape of the pastoral form, although, like Wordsworth's pastoral, De Quincey's pastoral is not one of shepherds and pipes. De Quincey shows how his own Arcadian expectations were undermined. He arrives at the lakes, finding at first beauty, serenity, and intellectual community. As a worshipper, the literary novitiate who enters Grasmere uses Edenic and paradisal language to depict his retreat of poets into the countryside, this setting so benevolent to genius.

In place of these expectations, the narrative comes to recount how his belief in the possibility of a scenic and intellectual golden age is corrected by disillusionment. Just as De Quincey sees the harshness of winter storms in the lake district, he strips away his own Arcadia of literary expectations—discovering flaws in his admired poets, death and disappointment in his own aspirations, and the *memento mori* everywhere in the landscape. Madness, disease, and the elements bring about the constant presence of death, as De Quincey returns again and again to stand by the graveyard— Southey becomes hopelessly disconsolate after the death of his son; the writer Charles Lloyd goes mad; Elizabeth Smith dies of tuberculosis; the Greens perish in a storm; little Kate Wordsworth dies by the carelessness of the Greens' daughter, whom the Wordsworths themselves have befriended; "intrusive gentry" deform the landscape; even Wordsworth, once a deity, has become a prideful "Lucifer."[115] The decay of friendships, the corruption of morals, and the encroachment of financial hardships are everywhere. The presence of individual human death and tragedy is underscored by the gradual incursion of cities into the sequestered beauty of the lakes. The mutability of life is matched in the temporality of nature.

This fragility of the Edenic lake community is mirrored in the transitoriness of De Quincey's stay there. The lake district is a temporary retreat into nature, flanked by the urban life from which he fled as a boy and was forced to return to as a man. It is an ephemeral paradise[116]— sheltering Wordsworth only through his miraculous ability to attract fortuitous bequests in a kind of charmed prelapsarian "inability to toil." De Quincey's retreat into nature was, as for all mortals, a temporary one.

When he proposes small protective shelters, "sanctuaries," be built for mountain storms, they form "a pensive allegoric memorial of that spiritual asylum . . . to the poor erring roamer in our human pilgrimage, whose steps are beset with other snares, and whose heart is made anxious by another darkness or . . . the storm of affliction."[117] Such temporary sanctuaries are offered by the perishable Arcadian delusions and visionary glimpses of escape, admiration, longing, and success, moments to be treasured before death and disappointment inevitably curb them. The art that sought to immortalize the lake district involuntarily helps to demolish it; like the Maid of Buttermere, ruined by the suitor who read about her, the landscape is inexorably altered by the narrative that seeks to preserve it.[118] The innovations of the Wordsworthian pastoral are echoed in the unidealized landscape and lives of De Quincey's *Literary Reminiscences;* but De Quincey additionally was doubtful of Wordsworth's uncritical idealization of an intellectual Arcadia and an untroubled childhood. There is no untroubled age, no lucky oblivion in De Quincey—neither a golden age in the remote past, nor honeysuckle recollections of childhood, nature, or poetic inspiration. De Quincey's writings dispel the Arcadian vestiges in Wordsworth's notions of the unconscious child and the inspired poet. From Wordsworth's writings, he expected in the lakes a green world which contained a golden age of poets ("that enchanting community of your's [*sic*]"),[119] but found there contention, madness, disease, and unproductivity; it is even poetic genius that makes Wordsworth incapable of friendship.

Yet the lake sojourn has for De Quincey its restorative properties. De Quincey emerges as the literary lion he aspired to be, invested with creative abilities; and as he says in the end of the *Literary Reminiscences,* he found other kinds of happiness. In this sense De Quincey makes use of the conventional literary curative of the pastoral retreat into nature—a convention evident in eighteenth-century poets such as Cowper, as well as in the retreat of Rosalind into Arden, and Calidore into the realm of Pastorella—whence all return metamorphosed and ameliorated. The narrative topos of city to country to city is historically more often than not beset by an imperfectly idyllic retreat;[120] the restorative and metamorphic properties of the green world possess elements of tragic potential not only in the presence of the death's head (*et in Arcadia ego,* as Erwin Panofsky has shown)[121] but in the temporality of any possible sojourn, and in the transitoriness of its own Edenic state.

De Quincey allegorizes his own life within the traditional literary conceits of the pastoral green world narrative, embedding his own bildungsroman as a narrative thread. Thus his own experience of temporal mutability exchanges his boyhood illusions of a pastoral world—an imagined golden age of poets and landscape—for a sojourn in the lakes, during which he is both scathed and inspired to emerge as a writer. The narrative traces a parallel between his own subjective experience and the objective perception of nature, art, and human life.

This allegorization of personal life, as M. H. Abrams reminds us, is part of the tradition of secular polysemism, multiple allegory, which for Romantic authors meant at once objectifying and individualizing one's own experience.[122] We can see likewise the narrative unity of the *Literary Reminiscences* functioning on multiple levels—the interleaving of the portrait of urban and rural life, the polarity between morbidity and pastorality, the growth of the writer's mind. All are topoi from the literary tradition placed within biographical narrative. As we do with other literary genres, we must accustom ourselves to thinking of biographical narrative as a symbolic structure. De Quincey himself gained access to this poetic tradition by reconsidering Wordsworthian poetic narrative in prose; it was an interest not only in the geography of Wordsworth, but in the terrain of the mind and the forms of narrative thought.

Notes

CHAPTER I

1. There are three reliable studies on Romantic biography, but all concern themselves with long biography and the Boswellian influence: Francis R. Hart, "Boswell and the Romantics: A Chapter in the History of Biographical Theory," *English Literary History* 27 (1960): 44–65; Joseph W. Reed, *English Biography in the Early Nineteenth Century* (New Haven: Yale Univ. Press, 1966); and Francis R. Hart, *Lockhart as Romantic Biographer* (Edinburgh: Edinburgh Univ. Press, 1971).

2. John A. Garraty's *The Nature of Biography* (New York: Random House, 1964), p. 97, is otherwise the most thorough survey of biographical history.

3. René Wellek, *The Rise of English Literary History* (Chapel Hill: Univ. of North Carolina Press, 1941), p. 134.

4. William C. Spengemann, *The Forms of Autobiography* (New Haven: Yale Univ. Press, 1980), p. 77.

5. Coleridge refers to "this AGE OF PERSONALITY, this age of literary and political *Gossiping*" in *The Friend* No. 10 (19 October 1809), a passage quoted in a footnote to chapter two of the *Biographia Literaria*. He refers again to "the present age (emphatically the age of personality!)" in *The Friend* No. 21 (25 January 1810), both collected and revised in the 1818 edition. *The Friend*, ed. Barbara E. Rooke (Princeton: Princeton Univ. Press, 1969), I: 210, 358, II: 138, 286. *Biographia Literaria*, ed. James Engell and Walter Jackson Bate (Princeton: Princeton Univ. Press, 1983), I: 41. All citations are from these editions.

6. Wilbur L. Cross, *An Outline of Biography from Plutarch to Strachey* (New York: Holt, 1924), p. 8. Cornelius Nepos appears to have written the earliest collective biography, *De Viris Illustribus,* a collection of military, political, and literary figures, extant only in fragments. Plutarch's *Bioi Paralleloi* is the most famous classical antecedent; of the many collective biographies attributed to his contemporary, Suetonius, only *De Vita Caesarum* survives, and some fragments of his literary collection, *De Viris Illustribus*. The unknown author or authors of the *Historia Augusta* offered an undependable sequel to Suetonius's Caesars.

7. Edward Phillips, *Theatrum Poetarum* (London: Smith, 1675); William Winstanley, *The Lives of the Most Famous English Poets* (London: Clark, 1687); Gerard Langbaine, *An Account of the English Dramatic Poets* (Oxford: West and Clements, 1691); Theophilus Cibber, *The Lives of the Poets of Great Britain and Ireland to the Time of Dean Swift,* 5 vols. (London: Griffiths, 1753); Horace Walpole, *A Catalogue of the Royal and Noble Authors of England,* 2 vols. (Strawberry Hill, 1758).

8. *Biographia Britannica,* ed. William Oldys, 6 vols. (London: Innys, 1747–66); 2nd edition, ed. Andrew Kippis, 5 vols. (London: Bathurst, etc., 1778–93). Pierre

Bayle, *Dictionnaire historique et critique*, 1697, rev. ed. 1702. The preface says Bayle chose "articles only as he knew were either in themselves, or could be made by him entertaining to every reader."

9. Boswell, *The Life of Samuel Johnson*, ed. George Birkbeck Hill and L. F. Powell (Oxford: Clarendon, 1934), I: 425. All citations of the *Life* and the *Tour to the Hebrides* are from this edition.

10. In this regard I disagree with Donald C. Yelton, *Brief American Lives: Four Studies in Collective Biography* (Metuchen, NJ: Scarecrow, 1978), and Paul Sturges, "Collective Biography in the 1980s," *Biography* 6 (1983): 316–29, who include texts such as encyclopedias. Literary collective biography is also to be distinguished from quantitative collective biography, or prosopography, used by modern historical statisticians. See Richard Beringer, *Historical Analysis* (New York: Wiley, 1978), pp. 204–20, and Lawrence Stone, "Prosopography" (orig. 1971), in *Historical Studies Today*, ed. Felix Gilbert and Stephen Graubard (New York: Norton, 1972), pp. 107–40. Carlyle observed, "History is the essence of innumerable Biographies" ("On History," *Fraser's*, 1830; and 2nd review of Croker's edition of Boswell, *Fraser's*, 1832); echoed by Wilhelm Dilthey, "Biography is the basic form of historiography," quoted in Georg Misch, *A History of Autobiography in Antiquity* (London: Routledge and Kegan Paul, 1950), I: 339. In this study, however, we will exclude such historians as Leopold von Ranke who contributed to notions such as the *Zeitgeist* independent of biography.

11. Walton's lives *Donne* (1640), *Wotton* (1651), *Hooker* (1665), and *Herbert* (1670) were published collectively in 1670, *Sanderson* in 1678; Fuller's *Worthies of England* (1662) was revived by the publisher John Nichols's edition in 1811; Wood's *Athenae Oxonienses* was published in 1691–92; his assistant John Aubrey's own collection of lives was published in 1813 as part of the same Romantic revival. Roger North's lives of his brothers, *Francis* (1742), *Dudley*, and *John* (1744), began to be printed with his autobiography in 1887.

12. Ira Bruce Nadel's discussion of Victorian biography mentions the many Plutarchan series of statesmen published earlier in the century, but repeats the common error of saying that other than Johnson's *Lives* no series of literary lives were written until the 1877 *English Men of Letters* series. *Biography: Fiction, Fact and Form* (New York: St. Martin's, 1984), p. 31.

13. Johnson's chief essays on biographical theory are *Rambler* 60 (1750) and *Idler* 84 (1759); on literary reputation, see also *Rambler* 2 (1750), *Rambler* 14 (1750), *Rambler* 106 (1751), and *Idler* 102 (1760). All citations are from *The Idler and The Adventurer*, ed. W. J. Bate, John M. Bullitt, and L. F. Powell (New Haven: Yale Univ. Press, 1963); *The Rambler*, ed. W. J. Bate and Albrecht B. Strauss, 3 vols. (New Haven: Yale Univ. Press, 1969); and *The Lives of the English Poets*, ed. George Birkbeck Hill, 3 vols. (Oxford: Clarendon, 1905). The brevity of Johnson's lives (unlike Boswell's *Life*) and the availability of sound reprints make it unnecessary to cite page references to Hill. I shall adopt the common practice of referring to this text by its short title, the *Lives of the Poets*, as well as using short titles to refer to Johnson's individual lives (e.g., *Life of Pope*) and the other biographical texts under consideration in this study.

14. The now standard English translation and sequence is Arthur Hugh Clough's 1859 revision, *The Lives of the Noble Grecians and Romans* (New York: Modern Library), of Dryden's 1683 edition. The first English translation of Plutarch was Thomas North's in 1579.

15. James D. Averill, "The Shape of Lyrical Ballads (1798)," *Philological Quarterly* 60 (1981): 387–407.

16. See, Thomas McFarland, *Romanticism and the Forms of Ruin* (Princeton: Princeton Univ. Press, 1981); Marjorie Levinson, *The Romantic Fragment Poem* (Chapel Hill: Univ. of North Carolina Press, 1986).

17. Geoffrey Hartman, *Criticism in the Wilderness* (New Haven: Yale Univ. Press, 1980), pp. 189, 201.

18. Jacques Derrida, *Margins of Philosophy* (Chicago: Univ. of Chicago Press, 1982), p. 225.

19. Boswell, II: 330–31.

20. Boswell, IV: 204–5.

21. Johnson's letter to Hill Boothby, 31 December 1755, was the 358th letter, misnumbered by Boswell. *The Letters of Samuel Johnson,* ed. R. W. Chapman (Oxford: Clarendon, 1952), I: 80–81.

22. In the opening pages of the *Life,* for example, Boswell implies his methodology was sanctioned by Johnson. He alludes to *Idler* 84 on writing one's own life; quotes Johnson's approval of intimate detail in *Rambler* 60, "'The business of the biographer is . . . to lead the thoughts into domestic privacies, and display the minute details of daily life'"; and in echo of Johnson's *Cowley,* distinguishes his biography from "panegyrick"—"I do what he himself recommended, both by his precept and his example." Boswell, I: 25, 32–33, 30.

23. R. G. Collingwood, *The Idea of History* (Oxford: Clarendon, 1956), p. 19.

24. Boswell, I: 7.

25. Cross, pp. 39–40.

26. Boswell, III: 344.

27. As in the mystery of the oranges, Boswell fretted over what he perceived as Johnson's carelessness about facts. After assisting Johnson in researching Thomson's family name, Boswell complained, "Dr. Johnson was by no means attentive to minute accuracy in his 'Lives of the Poets'; for notwithstanding my having detected this mistake, he has continued it." He later complained that Johnson "omitted to correct the erroneous statement" about Lord Marchmont being the executor of Pope's papers, pointed out to him by Boswell and Edmond Malone, and then explained in a footnote that Johnson's actions arose "from inattention; just as he neglected to correct his statement concerning the family of Thomson the poet, after it had been shewn to be erroneous." Boswell, III: 359, IV: 51. Later editors have sought various explanations. Peter Cunningham enumerates Johnson's errors in the first annotated edition of the *Lives of the Most Eminent English Poets, with Critical Observations on their Works,* 3 vols. (London: Murray, 1854), pp. xii–xv, observing that although Johnson does not cite authorities for accessible material, he is scrupulous in attributing new information. Hill, editing the twentieth-century *Life of Johnson,* explains Johnson's inexact quotations of poems

saying Johnson simply did not think himself bound to look anything up (Boswell, IV: 36n). Paul Fussell simply says Johnson was uninterested in the "mere biographical fact," *Samuel Johnson and the Life of Writing* (New York: Harcourt, 1971), p. 267. Paul J. Korshin explains that Johnson was not defined as a scholar in his own time, "Johnson and the Scholars," in *Samuel Johnson: New Critical Essays,* ed. Isobel Grundy (Totowa, NJ: Barnes and Noble, 1984), pp. 51–64. In contrast, Isaac D'Israeli, writing a Romantic sequel to the *Lives,* the *Calamities of Authors* (1812), admiringly said Johnson came to write the *Lives* prepared only "with the maturity of his genius."

Boswell's own emphasis on accuracy must be filtered through his equivocal declaration, "What I admire is nature improved by art" (3 February 1763), *London Journal,* ed. Frederick A. Pottle (New York: McGraw-Hill, 1950), p. 177. On Boswell's literary figuration and distortion, see, for example, Paul Alkon, "Boswell's Control of Aesthetic Distance," *Univ. of Toronto Quarterly* 38 (1969): 174–79, and "Boswellian Time," *Studies in Burke and His Time* 14 (1973): 239–42; Paul Fussell, "The Force of Literary Memory in Boswell's London Journal," *Studies in English Literature* 2 (1962): 351–57; Richard B. Schwartz, *Boswell's Johnson: A Preface to the Life* (Madison: Univ. of Wisconsin Press, 1978), pp. 98–104.

28. Boswell, I: 29.

29. The public seems to have been equally unconcerned with antiquarianism. When the corrected edition of the *Lives* was published in 1783, the additions were printed for distribution to buyers of the first edition, but few went to get the free pamphlet. Hill's note, *Lives,* IV: 36. In the *Lives,* Johnson does not hesitate to judge Congreve's plays even though he says he speaks from memory—"since I inspected them many years have passed."

30. See Leo Braudy, *Narrative Form in History and Fiction* (Princeton: Princeton Univ. Press, 1970), pp. 25, 47–48, 218. Bolingbroke, *Letters on the Study and Use of History* (London: Millar, 1752), pp. 14–16, 48.

31. Boswell, IV: 34; see Johnson's use of the phrase "promotion of piety" in *Pope.*

32. Boswell, III: 155, IV: 53. Boswell observes that at one point Johnson declared of Addison's drinking "'more ill may be done by the example, than good by telling the whole truth,'" but at another time, "'If a man is to write *A Panegyrick,* he may keep vices out of sight; but if he professes to write *A Life,* he must represent it really as it was.'" An account by Edmond Malone in the *Life* again testified that Johnson rejected the need to repress Addison's vice: "'If nothing but the bright side of characters should be shewn, we should sit down in despondency, and think it utterly impossible to imitate them in *any thing.*'" Yet in *Rambler* 164 (1751) he had proclaimed, "It is particularly the duty of those who consign illustrious names to posterity, to take care lest their readers be misled by ambiguous examples," since "the greater part of humankind speak and act wholly by imitation." In the *Hebrides* Boswell had simply quoted Johnson's opinion with reference to Swift that the revelation of vice is justifiable "after the man is dead; for then it is done historically." Boswell, V: 238. The issue continued to be a problem in criticism. In the nineteenth century, see Peter Cunningham, pp. xiff.; and early in this century, Bergen Evans, "Dr. Johnson's Theory of Biography," *Review of English Studies* 10

(1934): 308–9; and for a modern recapitulation, Robert Folkenflik, *Samuel Johnson, Biographer* (Ithaca: Cornell Univ. Press, 1978), pp. 79–85.

33. Lawrence Lipking, *The Ordering of the Arts in Eighteenth-Century England* (Princeton: Princeton Univ. Press, 1970), pp. 103, 408. Anthony J. Tillinghast points out resemblances between observations by Johnson and Boswell and passages in Hume, Kames, Smith, Reid, and Locke; but beyond the general currency of ideas, he refuses to conclude explicit connections between eighteenth-century biographical theory and philosophy, "a philosophy almost wholly concerned with the empirical study of man." "The Moral and Philosophical Basis of Johnson's and Boswell's Idea of Biography," in *Johnsonian Studies,* ed. Magdi Wahba (Cairo: dist. Oxford Univ. Press, 1962), pp. 115–31. James Noxon argues that eighteenth-century biographical practice showed very little methodological or interpretive exchange with philosophic theories of the human character, and concludes that the unsystematic biographies Hume embedded in his histories "bear no trace whatever of the psychological theories upon which he had based his science of human nature." "Human Nature: General Theory and Individual Lives," in *Biography in the 18th Century,* ed. J. D. Browning (New York: Garland, 1980), pp. 8–27.

34. Roland Barthes, "From Work to Text" (orig. 1971), *Image-Music-Text* (New York: Hill and Wang, 1977), pp. 155–64; Hartman, *Criticism,* p. 269.

35. A half-century after the publication of Johnson's *Lives,* John Wilson Croker's edition of *The Life of Samuel Johnson, LL.D., including A Journal of a Tour to the Hebrides,* 5 vols. (London: Murray, 1831) generated considerable discussion and was reviewed by Macaulay (*Edinburgh Review,* September 1831), Lockhart (*Quarterly Review,* November 1831), and Carlyle (*Fraser's,* April and May 1832).

36. Boswell, I: 34.

37. Johnson was not unwilling to align himself with Socrates. On the subject of what constitutes knowledge, he says, "Let me not be censured for this digression as pedantick or paradoxical, for if I have Milton against me I have Socrates on my side. It was his labour to turn philosophy from the study of nature to speculations upon life" (*Milton*). Since Boswell's own time, Xenophon's *Memorabilia* of Socrates has been proposed as Boswell's narrative model for the *Life of Johnson.*

38. Johnson in some sense exploits the conspiratorial strategy he described in *Rambler* 2, "Censure is willingly indulged, because it always implies some superiority." If some of the poets needed vindication from Johnson, his successors were reluctant to relinquish the authority his prose conferred on the critic and biographer.

39. Reynolds, *Discourse* 6, 10 December 1774; collected as *Discourses on Art,* 1797. Modern edition, ed. Robert R. Wark (San Marino, CA: Huntington Library, 1959).

40. Harold Bloom, *The Anxiety of Influence* (Oxford: Oxford Univ. Press, 1973).

41. Thomas Moore, *Letters and Journals of Lord Byron: with Notices of His Life,* 2 vols. (London: Murray, 1830); there is no accurate modern edition. John Gibson Lockhart, *Memoirs of the Life of Sir Walter Scott,* 7 vols. (Edinburgh: Cadell, 1837–38); all citations are from the modern edition, *Memoirs of Sir Walter Scott,* 5 vols. (London: Macmillan, 1900). Carlyle's declaration that England has "simply one

good Biography" to imitate (first review of Croker's Boswell) is offset by judgments such as James Stephen's that Boswell has "well nigh ruined the art of biography" and Leon Edel's that "modern Boswells have ended in disaster." Waldo Dunn, *English Biography* (New York: Dutton, 1916), p. 154; Edel, "The Figure Under the Carpet," in *Telling Lives: The Biographer's Art,* ed. Marc Pachter (Washington, DC: New Republic Books, 1979), p. 22.

42. Boswell, I: 29. William Mason, on whose *Poems of Mr. Gray: to which are prefixed Memoirs of his Life and Writings* (York: Dodsley, 1775) Boswell based his narrative, said the same: had he chosen composition over compilation it would have been "perhaps with more reputation to myself." Each says he chooses the accuracy of the compilation over the vainglory of composition, which Mason downgrades as the "common form" and Boswell calls a "melting down."

43. According to Carlyle, compilations are merely reference works awaiting composition: "The scattered members of Scott's Life do lie here, and could be disentangled." At present the life stands "uncomposed," but with the documentary evidence "printed and indestructible . . . in the elementary state" it "can at any time be composed." Carlyle endorses one-volume biographies, saying, "There is a great discovery still to be made in Literature, that of paying literary men by the quantity they *do not* write." Review of Lockhart's *Scott* (*London and Westminster Review,* 1838).

44. Strachey, *Eminent Victorians* (London: Chatto and Windus, 1918). His statement of his intentions, "to illustrate rather than to explain," and "to examine and elucidate certain fragments of the truth which took my fancy," might describe Romantic biographical sketches as well. His rebellion against "the Age which has just passed" resembles the Romantic rebellion against Neoclassical values. And when Strachey says, "It is perhaps as difficult to write a good life as to live one," he is directly echoing Carlyle's comment, "A well-written Life is almost as rare as a well-spent one." Review of Heinrich Döring's biography of Richter (*Edinburgh Review,* 1827).

45. André Maurois, *Aspects of Biography* (Cambridge: Cambridge Univ. Press, 1929), p. 62, participates in the common twentieth-century misconception of regarding composed biography as a modern innovation. Leon Edel, *Writing Lives: Principia Biographia* (London: Norton, 1984), p. 82, overstates Strachey's role in overthrowing the Boswellian model with his "becoming brevity." Hesketh Pearson recalls having heard Strachey say that in Johnson's *Lives* might be found "a foretaste of Stracheyan artistry"—forgetting that Strachey's model is Johnson. Mark Longaker, *Contemporary Biography* (Philadelphia: Univ. of Pennsylvania Press, 1934), p. 31. Reflecting contemporary historical centrism, Jeffrey Meyers opens his edition, *The Craft of Literary Biography* (New York: Macmillan, 1985), p. 1, saying, "Biography has become one of the major literary genres of the twentieth century."

46. Edel, "Figure Under the Carpet," p. 23, argues that the significance of the subject is the controlling factor in the length of a biography. Frank E. Vandiver, "Biography as an Agent of Humanism," in *The Biographer's Gift,* ed. James F. Veninga (College Station: Texas A&M Press, 1983), pp. 4–5, reveals

similar preconceptions in saying "evocation of personality, of character is the highest biographical art. . . . evidence is, of course, the main ingredient in life writing."

47. Hart, *Lockhart,* p. 42, says, "The Romantic biographer would not work without voluminous original materials"; Nadel, p. 6, says eighteenth- and nineteenth-century biography placed research and investigation over interpretation and narrative. Both impose the current esteem for long Boswellian biography on biographical history, without recognizing the emergence of two strains of biography.

48. Erich Auerbach, *Mimesis: The Representation of Reality in Western Literature* (Princeton: Princeton Univ. Press, 1974), pp. 85, 87.

49. New publication of old documents included: John Evelyn, *Memoirs,* ed. William Bray, 2 vols. (London: Colburn, 1818); Samuel Pepys, *Memoirs,* ed. Richard Braybrooke, 2 vols. (London: Colburn, 1825); John Aubrey, *Letters, Written by Eminent Persons in the Seventeenth and Eighteenth Centuries . . . and Lives of Eminent Men,* ed. John Walker (London: Longman, etc., 1813); two editions of Joseph Spence in the same year, *Anecdotes, Observations, and Characters of Books and Men,* ed. Samuel Weller Singer (London: Carpenter, etc., 1820) and *Observations, Anecdotes, and Characters of Books and Men* (London: Murray, 1820); Horace Walpole, *Memoires of the Last Ten Years of the Reign of George the Second,* 2 vols. (London: Murray, 1822); not to mention reissues such as Thomas Fuller, *The History of the Worthies of England,* ed. John Nichols (London: Rivington, etc., 1811), and new assemblages such as *Literary Anecdotes of the Eighteenth Century,* ed. John Nichols, 9 vols. (London: Nichols, 1812–16).

50. Tzvetan Todorov, *The Poetics of Prose* (Ithaca: Cornell Univ. Press, 1977), pp. 42–43.

51. Edmund Gosse, "Biography," *Encyclopaedia Britannica,* 11th edition (Cambridge: Cambridge Univ. Press, 1910), III: 953. Similarly, Sidney Lee, *The Perspective of Biography* (London: English Association, 1918), p. 19, declared, "No man is fit subject for biography till he be dead." And in the present day, Ira Grushow says biography possesses an "unashamedly primitive notion of story. Between the fixed points of birth and death the plot moves with inexorable chronologicality." "Biography as Literature," *Southern Humanities Review* 14 (1980): 156.

52. See Hayden White, *Metahistory: The Historical Imagination in Nineteenth-Century Europe* (Baltimore: Johns Hopkins Univ. Press, 1973), pp. 5ff.

53. Vladimir Nabokov, *Speak, Memory* (New York: Putnam, 1979), pp. 9, 27. On novelistic patterning, for example, see David Lodge, *Modes of Modern Writing* (London: Arnold, 1977), p. 45; and Joseph Frank, "Spatial Form in Modern Literature," *Sewanee Review* 53 (1945): 221–40, 432–56, 643–53.

Otto Rank discusses recurrent folkloric patterning in the birth and early life of artists and heroes in *The Myth of the Birth of the Hero* (New York: Brunner, 1952, orig. 1914); Ernst Kris discusses typical biographical formulae apparent in biographies of artists (abandoned infant, child prodigy, childhood as a prehistory of the life) in "The Image of the Artist," *Psychoanalytic Explorations in Art* (New York: International Universities Press, 1952), pp. 65–67.

Counterarguments to biographical patterning have been made by A. O. J. Cockshut, who says autobiography tends to be formless, *Art of Autobiography in 19th and 20th Century England* (New Haven: Yale Univ. Press, 1984), p. 82; and Jean Starobinski, who discusses autobiography as inherently picaresque, "The Style of Autobiography," in *Autobiography: Essays Theoretical and Critical*, ed. James Olney (Princeton: Princeton Univ. Press, 1980), pp. 82–83.

54. Louis O. Mink, "Narrative Form as a Cognitive Instrument," in *The Writing of History*, ed. Robert H. Canary and Henry Kozicki (Madison: Univ. of Wisconsin Press, 1978), p. 147. Donald Greene, for example, remarks that when discovery of the journals revealed Boswell had modified his account of Johnson's conversations for the published life, apologists felt obliged to argue that Boswell, decades later, made the changes because he remembered more clearly what had happened. "Samuel Johnson," in *Literary Biography*, ed. Meyers, p. 24.

For specific studies of historiographic patterning, see: Collingwood, pp. 48–50, on the Christian plot of medieval historiography; Kieran Egan on the Aristotelian tragic model, "Thucydides, Tragedian," in *The Writing of History*, ed. Canary and Kozicki, pp. 63–72; Braudy, p. 267, on the epic sweep of Gibbon's *Decline and Fall*; White, pp. 7–9, on comic, satiric, tragic, and romance models of history.

55. Philippe Lejeune, *Le pacte autobiographique* (Paris: Seuil, 1975), pp. 13–46; Edward Said, *Beginnings* (New York: Basic Books, 1975), p. 90.

56. In the Preface to the *Dictionary* (1755), Johnson rejects the idea that a dictionary "should fix our language," and remarks the futile hope to "embalm" the language by stopping the alterations of "time and chance." The opening essay of the *Rambler* (1750) also introduces the problems of language arising from "the difficulty of the first address on any new occasion."

57. Gérard Genette, *Narrative Discourse* (Ithaca: Cornell Univ. Press, 1980), p. 121.

58. Wordsworth's 1802 Preface adds this discussion on truth, although the assertion, "There neither is, nor can be, any essential difference between the language of prose and metrical composition," appears in a slightly different form in the 1800 Preface.

59. Wordsworth, *A Letter to a Friend of Robert Burns* (London: Longman, 1816).

60. The concept of scientific biography has been more bruited than identified. There have always been a few theorists who believe an identifiable scientific method is possible in biography (though even some of these do not find it desirable). Bacon's observations have been periodically invoked, although more to justify the importance of biography than to provide a prescriptive methodology. In the early nineteenth century, James Field Stanfield's obscurely published and little-circulated *Essay on the Study and Composition of Biography* (Sunderland: Garbutt, 1813) proposed systematizing biography using eighteenth-century psychological theory to produce a biographical science of human nature. In the early twentieth century, Harold Nicholson depicted an irreconcilable dichotomy between scientific and literary biography in *The Development of English Biography* (London: Hogarth, 1927). Freud's case studies implied the possibility of uniform biographical analysis and form. Yet Stanfield had no disciples, Nicholson's discus-

sion is useless for identifying examples of the polarity, and the host of contemporary psychobiographies have not been modeled on the formal attributes of Freud's biographies. On early twentieth-century endeavors to systematize a biographical science, see John A. Garraty, "Gordon Allport's Rules for the Preparation of Life Histories and Case Studies," *Biography* 4 (1981): 283–92, and Allport's *The Use of Personal Documents in Psychological Science* (New York: Social Science Research Council, 1942).

61. On the "literary" traits of historiographic composition, see for example: Marc Bloch, *The Historian's Craft* (New York: Knopf, 1953); David Levin, *History as a Romantic Art* (Stanford: Stanford Univ. Press, 1959); Hayden White, *Metahistory* (1973); Peter Gay, *Style in History* (New York: Basic Books, 1974); Louis O. Mink, "History and Fiction as Modes of Comprehension," in *New Directions in Literary History*, ed. Ralph Cohen (Baltimore: Johns Hopkins Univ. Press, 1974), pp. 107–24; and *The Writing of History: Literary Form and Historical Understanding*, ed. Canary and Kozicki (1978).

62. Hazlitt, "The Waverly Notes" (1829).

63. Boswell, II: 433, II: 137. In *Waller* Johnson says, "The legitimate end of fiction is the conveyance of truth"; and Boswell, IV: 396, records his declaration, "'There is something noble in publishing truth, though it condemns one's self.'"

64. "The delicate features of the mind, the nice discriminations of character, and the minute peculiarities of conduct are soon obliterated; and it is surely better that caprice, obstinacy, frolick, and folly, however they might delight in the description, should be silently forgotten than that by wanton merriment and unseasonable detection, a pang should be given to a widow, a daughter, a brother, or a friend."

65. "'I fancy mankind may come, in time, to write all aphoristically, except in narrative; grow weary of preparation, and connection, and illustration, and all those arts by which a big book is made.—If a man is to wait till he weaves anecdotes into a system, we might be long in getting them, and get but few, in comparison of what we might get.'" Boswell, V: 39. Johnson's approbation seemed to sanction Boswell's collection and subsequent assemblages of unwoven anecdotes and ana popular in the early nineteenth century. Much has been said of the relative merits of Johnson's and Boswell's use of anecdotes. It has been suggested that Boswell imitates what Johnson would have done had he possessed more firsthand accounts, that Boswell excels Johnson in the narrative of anecdotes, that Johnson is deficient in selecting anecdotes, that both are guilty of numbering the streaks of the tulip. See, for example, C. R. Tracey, "Johnson and the Art of Anecdote," *Univ. of Toronto Quarterly* 15 (1945): 86–93; Paul J. Korshin, "Ana Books and Intellectual Biography in the Eighteenth-Century," pp. 191–204, and Robert Folkenflik, "Johnson's Art of Anecdote," pp. 171–81, in *Studies in Eighteenth-Century Culture*, ed. Harold E. Pagliaro (Cleveland: Case Western Reserve Univ. Press, 1973).

66. Boswell, I: 433, II: 166, III: 260. In a footnote to a passage on the conversations he has recorded in the *Hebrides,* Boswell says, "It is no small satisfaction to me to reflect, that Dr. Johnson read this, and, after being apprized of my intention,

communicated to me, at subsequent periods, many particulars of his life, which probably could not otherwise have been preserved." Boswell, V: 312. In the *Life* Boswell boasts that he has preserved anecdotes of Johnson's life through Johnson's recommendation that he keep a journal: "He counselled me to keep in private, and said I might surely have a friend who would burn it in case of my death. From this habit I have been enabled to give the world so many anecdotes, which would otherwise have been lost to posterity." Yet the event as Boswell tells it seems to suggest Johnson recommended he keep a journal full of anecdotes ("'There is nothing, Sir, too little for so little a creature as man'") and then burn it—not edit and publish it. Boswell, I: 433. Such representations cast a new light on Boswell's assertions that Johnson sanctioned his methodology. In the same spirit we may take Boswell's implication at the beginning of the *Life*, I: 25, 30, that he is compiling the autobiography Johnson himself did not do, using methods paraphrased from *Rambler* 60 and *Idler* 84.

67. Answering the exaggerated praise of Fenton's character of Roscommon, Johnson remarks how surprising it is to discover that Roscommon's works do not fill a single book: "But thus it is that characters are written: we know somewhat, and we imagine the rest."

68. Nor is conversational skill a reliable index of literary abilities in the *Lives:* neither Pope nor Dryden excelled in conversation, and from Cowley's conversation "no man could draw from it any suspicion of his excellence in poetry." Of Savage, Johnson observed the "inconsistency of his writings with his conversation," and in *Rambler* 14 he had called attention to the frequent "contrariety between the life of an author and his writings," and specifically, "the graces of writing and conversation are of different kinds."

69. Johnson parodied the gullibility of the epistolary reader in a jesting letter to Hester Thrale, 27 October 1777, in which he boasts of candor and reveals nothing but pretense: "In a Man's Letters . . . his soul lies naked, his letters are only the mirrour of his breast, whatever passes within him is shown undisguised in its natural process. Nothing is inverted, nothing distorted, you see systems in their elements, you discover actions in their motives." *Letters,* II: 559.

70. Sprat argues that letters are intended for an intimate audience: "Letters that pass between particular Friends, if they are written as they ought to be, can scarce ever be fit to see the light. . . . In such Letters the Souls of Men should appear undress'd: And in that negligent habit they may be fit to be seen by one or two in a Chamber, but not to go abroad into the Streets." "An Account of the Life and Writings of Mr. Abraham Cowley, Written to Mr. M. Clifford," in *The Works of Mr. Abraham Cowley* (London: Herringman, 1668).

71. John W. Draper, *William Mason, A Study in Eighteenth-Century Culture* (New York: New York Univ. Press, 1924), pp. 273, 276. Relatives, friends, and appointed biographers were among those who remained loyal to the neutrality of the Mason method, or even more innocuous forms of panegyric.

72. Boswell, I: 29–30.

73. D'Israeli, *Calamities of Authors* (1812); as a matter of principle, both D'Israeli and Johnson print the isolated letters they have found. John L. Adolphus, *Biography: A Prize Essay* (Oxford: Collingwood, 1818), pp. 21–22, says Sprat's restraint at

least cautions against indiscriminate publication of correspondence. For Maria Edgeworth's letter to John Gibson Lockhart, 7 November 1832, see Hart, "Boswell and the Romantics," p. 55. Hart, *Lockhart,* pp. 30–36, gives examples of Romantics who trusted letters.

74. "The writer of his own life has at least the first qualification of an historian, the knowledge of the truth; and though it may be plausibly objected that his temptations to disguise it are equal to his opportunities of knowing it, yet I cannot but think that impartiality may be expected with equal confidence from him that relates the passages of his own life, as from him that delivers the transactions of another" (*Idler* 84). Boswell opens the *Life of Johnson* alluding to "the opinion which he has given, that every man's life may be best written by himself." Boswell, I: 25.

75. Stanfield's *Essay on the Study and Composition of Biography* (1813) is sometimes erroneously cited as the earliest full-length treatise on biography; probably that distinction belongs to Isaac D'Israeli's *A Dissertation on Anecdotes* (London: Kearsley and Murray, 1793).

76. Macaulay, review of Croker's edition of Boswell (*Edinburgh Review,* 1831).

77. Moreover, D'Israeli criticized the superfluity of contemporary autobiography: "If the populace of writers become this querulous after fame (to which they have not pretensions) we shall expect to see an epidemical rage for auto-biography break out." "Some Observations on Diaries, Self-Biography, and Self-Characters" (1796); review of the *Memoirs* of Percival Stockdale (*Quarterly Review,* 1809). John Gibson Lockhart echoed the sentiment, complaining, "Modern primer-makers must need leave *confessions* behind them, as if they were so many Rousseaus . . . we are already rich in the autobiography of pickpockets. . . . The mania for this garbage of Confessions, and Recollections, and Reminiscences, and Aniliana, 'is indeed a vile symptom'" (*Quarterly Review,* 1826); Hart, *Lockhart,* p. 4.

78. Anon., *A Collection of the Most Instructive and Amusing Lives Ever Published Written by the Parties Themselves,* 33 vols. (London: Hunt and Clark, 1826–32). Herder had earlier begun to collect autobiographies from different countries and Goethe called for a "collation of the so-called Confessions of all ages," Misch, I: 2.

79. Croker (*Quarterly Review,* 1832); Hunt, Preface to *Lord Byron and Some of his Contemporaries* (1828); Hart, *Lockhart,* pp. 27–28, says Pepys's diaries were admired by the Romantics because "they lacked dignity, proportion and form."

80. James Johnston, *Biography: The Literature of Personality* (New York: Century, 1927), p. 164, interestingly observes that critical values shift depending on whether an autobiography is published during the lifetime of the subject or posthumously. He suggests De Quincey's *Confessions,* for example, entered the canon early as literature because it was published by him in his lifetime, indicating a consciousness of audience—and thus the text was willingly considered foremost for its literary merits, and only incidentally regarded as a life.

It is provocative to consider how our perception of a biographical work changes depending on its publishing history. Are we more inclined to test the biographies and autobiographies of the dead for concealments? Or are we freer from historicist verification in treating the biographies and autobiographies of the living?

81. Stephen Shapiro, "The Dark Continent of Literature: Autobiography,"

Comparative Literature Studies 5 (1968): 427, 447; Ernst Cassirer, *An Essay on Man* (New Haven: Yale Univ. Press, 1979), p. 52. In contrast, Freud wrote in a 1929 letter, "What makes all autobiographies worthless is, after all, their mendacity." Patricia Meyer Spacks, *Imagining a Self: Autobiography and Novel in Eighteenth-Century England* (Cambridge: Harvard Univ. Press, 1976).

82. Barrett Mandel, "Full of Life Now," in *Autobiography,* ed. Olney, p. 66; William C. Spengemann and L. R. Lundquist, "Autobiography and the American Myth," *American Quarterly* 17 (1965): 54; Francis R. Hart, "Notes for an Anatomy of Modern Autobiography," *New Literary History* 1 (1970): 488; Georges Gusdorf, "Conditions and Limits of Autobiography," in *Autobiography,* ed. Olney, p. 44; Jean Starobinski, "The Authority and Feeling and the Origins of Psychological Criticism," in *Literary Criticism and Psychology,* ed. Joseph P. Strelka (University Park: Pennsylvania State Univ. Press, 1976), pp. 79, 87.

83. *Quarterly Review* (May 1809), pp. 282, 386. That the term should not be found in print and then should occur twice, pages apart in the same publication, may indicate less an innovation by either article than by the editorial board of the *Quarterly;* perhaps the codification of the term should be credited to William Gifford. D'Israeli in later works used "autobiography" interchangeably with "self-biography." On the *Monthly Review* critique of D'Israeli's *Literary Miscellanies,* see James Ogden, "A Note on 'Autobiography,'" *Notes and Queries,* n.s. 8 (1961): 461–62, who observes that the omission of the word autobiography from dictionaries in 1818 indicates it still had not entered common usage. Jerome Buckley, *The Turning Key: Autobiography and the Subjective Impulse Since 1800* (Cambridge: Harvard Univ. Press, 1984), p. 38, suggests that even by 1866 the French considered the term and practice of autobiography rare in France but common in England.

84. Boswell, I: 30; Lockhart, *Scott,* IV: 19, V: 433.

85. Also increasing was the sense of the integrity of the biographical document, evident in Wordsworth's annoyance at De Quincey's excerpting and paraphrasing *The Prelude,* and in Macaulay and Carlyle's objections to the tumbling together of narrative accounts from Boswell, Hawkins, and Piozzi in Croker's *Life of Johnson.*

86. Boswell's assertions about his biography, I: 30, appear to parallel Rousseau's opening declarations of the thoroughness of his self-portrait in the *Confessions.* But Boswell wanted his text unrivaled by competition. See for example, his complaints of Hawkins, "a man, whom, during my long intimacy with Dr. Johnson, I never saw in his company, I think but once, and I am sure not above twice . . . nor had Sir John Hawkins that nice perception which was necessary to mark the finer and less obvious parts of Johnson's character"; and Piozzi, "I have had occasion several times, in the course of this work, to point out the incorrectness of Mrs. Thrale." Boswell, I: 27, IV: 343. Boswell does not mention that he spent relatively few days in Johnson's company, and those were limited to the last twenty-two years of Johnson's life. In the *Hebrides* he announces his trove of conversation, and adds, "By assiduous inquiry, I can make up for not knowing him sooner." Boswell, V: 312. Donald Greene makes the generous estimate that Boswell spent 425 days of companionship with Johnson. "'Tis a Pretty Book, Mr. Boswell, But—," in

Boswell's Life of Johnson: New Questions, New Answers, ed. John A. Vance (Athens: Univ. of Georgia Press, 1985), pp. 118, 132–42. On the presentation of similar scenes in Boswell, Piozzi, and Hawkins, see: Ralph W. Rader, "Literary Form in Factual Narrative," in *Essays in Eighteenth-Century Biography,* ed. Philip B. Daghlian (Bloomington: Indiana Univ. Press, 1968), pp. 10–13; and William R. Siebenschuh, *Form and Purpose in Boswell's Biographical Works* (Berkeley: Univ. of California Press, 1972), pp. 51–54.

87. James Hogg's *Familiar Anecdotes of Sir Walter Scott* (New York: Harper, 1834) first appeared in New York; because of Lockhart's disapproval, Hogg did not intend it to be published in Great Britain, but an evidently pirated edition appeared later that year as *The Domestic Manners and Private Life of Sir Walter Scott* (Glasgow: Reid, 1834). On textual history, see Douglas S. Mack's editions of *Memoir of the Author's Life and Familiar Anecdotes of Sir Walter Scott* (Edinburgh: Scottish Academic Press, 1972) and *Anecdotes of Sir W. Scott* (Edinburgh: Scottish Academic Press, 1983).

88. Otto Rank, *Art and Artist: Creative Urge and Personality Development* (New York: Agathon, 1968, orig. 1932), p. 383. Hart, "Boswell and the Romantics," p. 58, describes a shift in the Romantic era "from the objective biographical fact to the biographer's experience."

89. Paul Ricoeur, "Objectivity and Subjectivity in History," *History and Truth* (Evanston: Northwestern Univ. Press, 1965), pp. 21, 30; on the *histor,* see Robert Scholes and Robert Kellogg, *The Nature of Narrative* (Oxford: Oxford Univ. Press, 1966), p. 242.

90. Maurois, p. 118.

91. De Quincey's review of William Roscoe's edition of Pope (1848), best known for its distinction between the literature of knowledge and the literature of power, here alludes to Solomon's request in 1 Kings 3:7, "Give therefore thy servant an understanding heart to judge thy people, that I may discern between good and bad."

92. On Johnson's abridgment of Steele in *Savage,* see Folkenflik, *Johnson,* p. 181; on Boswell's compression, see Marshall Waingrow's introduction to *The Correspondence and Other Papers of James Boswell Relating to the Making of the Life of Johnson,* Yale Edition of the Private Papers of James Boswell (New York: McGraw-Hill, 1969), II: xxxi. John W. Draper, pp. 271–74, agrees that Mason's alterations were unremarkable in his time.

93. Preface of Southey's *Life of Nelson,* 2 vols. (London: Murray, 1813).

94. See Davidson Cook, "Lockhart's Treatment of Scott's Letters," *The Nineteenth Century and After* 102 (1927): 382–98; Robert Rait, "Boswell and Lockhart," in *Essays by Divers Hands,* ed. R. W. Macan, Transactions of the Royal Society of Literature, n.s. 12 (1933): 105–27; and Hart, *Lockhart,* pp. 199ff.

95. Both include scenes that could not logically have occurred—for example, Coleridge's unlikely confession to De Quincey, upon meeting him, of his marital troubles, addiction, and compulsive procrastination ("Coleridge," I, *Literary Reminiscences,* 1834). On Lockhart's unlikely scenes of Scott's lucid last words and nighttime ride to reassure himself of his financial affairs, see Ian Jack, "Two

Biographers: Lockhart and Boswell," in *Johnson, Boswell and Their Circle,* ed. James Clifford, et al. (Oxford: Clarendon, 1965), pp. 283–84. The manufacture of death-bed scenes and last words was inherited from the common practice in hagiography.

96. Hazlitt, introductory footnote to "Boswell Redivivus, No. 1" (*New Monthly Magazine,* 1826).

97. Nicholson, p. 77.

98. Tzvetan Todorov, "The Notion of Literature," *New Literary History* 5 (1973): 1; Lodge, pp. 6–9; Paul de Man, "Autobiography as De-Facement," *The Rhetoric of Romanticism* (New York: Columbia Univ. Press, 1984), pp. 67–70; John Searle, "The World Turned Upside Down," *New York Review of Books,* 27 October 1983, pp. 74ff., in response to Jonathan Culler's assertion, "truths are fictions whose fictionality has been forgotten"; Culler, *On Deconstruction* (Ithaca: Cornell Univ. Press, 1982), pp. 181–82; Northrop Frye, *Anatomy of Criticism* (Princeton: Princeton Univ. Press, 1973, orig. 1957), p. 307; Hartman, *Criticism,* p. 1.

CHAPTER II

1. The inattention to the *Lives* as a whole unit has been observed by Fussell, *Johnson,* pp. 245–48, 255; and Lipking, p. 408.

2. Boswell, III: 109.

3. Boswell, II: 40, III: 109ff.

4. Hill's note, Boswell, IV: 35.

5. Hill's note, *Lives,* I: xxvi, quotes Mrs. Boscawen's complaint, "They are not to be bought unless you buy a perfect litter of poets in fillagree [*sic*] (that is very small print, whereas one already possesses said poets in large letter)."

6. Johnson, 1st ed., *Prefaces, Biographical and Critical, to the Works of the English Poets,* 68 vols. (10 vols. of prefaces, 58 vols. of works and index) (London: Nichols, for Bathurst, etc., 1779–81); pirated, *The Lives of the English Poets; and a Criticism on their Works,* 3 vols. (Dublin: Whitestone, etc., 1779–81); 2nd ed., resequenced, *The Lives of the Most Eminent English Poets; with Critical Observations on their Works,* 4 vols. (London: Bathurst, etc., 1781); 3rd ed., corrected, *The Lives of the Most Eminent English Poets,* 4 vols. (London: Bathurst, etc., 1783). On subsequent editions see William Prideaux Courtney and David Nichol Smith, *A Bibliography of Samuel Johnson* (Oxford: Clarendon, 1915), pp. 129–52.

7. The following chart shows the original sequence of the 1779–81 *Prefaces* (Vols. I–IV printed 1779, Vols. V–X printed 1781) alongside the reordered sequence of the four-volume 1781 (and 1783) reissue of the *Lives,* which has become the standard twentieth-century format. The three-volume Dublin edition pirated the 1779–81 London sequence as it came out: Cowley-Hughes, Vol. I (1779); Addison-Swift, Vol. II (1781); Gay-Gray, Vol. III (1781).

1779–1781	1781 (1783)
Vol. I: Cowley	*Vol. I:* Cowley
Waller	Denham

	1779–1781		1781 (1783)
Vol. II:	Milton		Milton
	Butler		Butler
Vol. III:	Dryden		Rochester
Vol. IV:	Denham		Roscommon
	Sprat		Otway
	Roscommon		Waller
	Rochester		Pomfret
	Yalden		Dorset
	Otway		Stepney
	Duke		J. Philips
	Dorset		Walsh
	Halifax	*Vol. II:*	Dryden
	Stepney		Smith
	Walsh		Duke
	Garth		King
	King		Sprat
	J. Philips		Halifax
	Smith		Parnell
	Pomfret		Garth
	Hughes		Rowe
Vol. V:	Addison		Addison
	Blackmore		Hughes
	Sheffield		Sheffield
Vol. VI:	Granville	*Vol. III:*	Prior
	Rowe		Congreve
	Tickell		Blackmore
	Congreve		Fenton
	Fenton		Gay
	Prior		Granville
Vol. VII:	Pope		Yalden
Vol. VIII:	Swift		Tickell
	Gay		Hammond
	Broome		Somerville
	Pitt		Savage
	Parnell		Swift
	A. Philips		Broome
	Watts	*Vol. IV:*	Pope
Vol. IX:	Savage		Pitt
	Somerville		Thomson
	Thomson		Watts
	Hammond		A. Philips
	Collins		West
Vol. X:	Young		Collins
	Dyer		Dyer

1779–1781	1781 (1783)
Mallet	Shenstone
Shenstone	Young
Akenside	Mallet
Lyttelton	Akenside
West	Gray
Gray	Lyttelton

8. Petrarch, *Epistolae de rebus senilibus,* 17: 3.

9. See for example, Lipking, pp. 408–9; Joseph Wood Krutch, *Samuel Johnson* (New York: Holt, 1945), p. 484.

10. On genre as a formulation of culture, see Raymond Williams, *Marxism and Literature* (Oxford: Oxford Univ. Press, 1977), pp. 145–50, 180–85.

11. Johnson's complaint of the thankless task of the biographer may reflect his feelings about the scientific and political biographies he produced for the *Gentleman's Magazine,* some of his earliest professional writings: Hermann Boerhaave (1739), Admiral Robert Blake (1740), Sir Francis Drake (1740–41), Jean-Philippe Barretier (1740–41).

12. In *Rambler* 60 Johnson answered the complaint that "it is frequently objected to relations of particular lives that they are not distinguished by any striking or wonderful vicissitudes," and called for the writing of inconspicuous biographies such as "the scholar who passed his life among his books." Mason's *Life of Gray* similarly opened with the apology "The lives of men of letters seldom abound with incidents."

13. Identified as "Miss Beresford," Boswell, IV: 284.

14. Boswell, IV: 35–36.

15. Lipking, p. 408, says those who assemble books on Johnson's systems "reduce to order what Johnson himself chose not to do."

16. Scott, "Samuel Richardson" (*Lives of the Novelists,* 1821–24); Lamb's unpublished review of Hazlitt's *Table Talk* (1821), reprinted by Robert Ready, *Hazlitt at Table* (East Brunswick, NJ: Associated Universities Press, 1981), and Roy Park, *Lamb as Critic* (London: Routledge and Kegan Paul, 1980). For many readers the most distinctive feature of Johnson's prose is the presence of the autocratic "I." The short-title "Johnson's Poets," the misnomer Johnson objected to (which remained on the binding of the reissued and expanded 75-volume anthology of 1790), implies the same narrator-dominated discourse we can hear in the authorial "I" of *Pope:* "The man who threatens the world is always ridiculous; for the world can easily go on without him, and in a short time will cease to miss him. I have heard of an idiot who used to revenge his vexations by lying all night upon the bridge." Narrative intervention can again be heard in *Milton,* when the poet returns from the Continent to support the rebellion and hires lodgings to start a school for boys: "Let not our veneration for Milton forbid us to look with some degree of merriment on great promises and small performance, on the man who hastens home because his countrymen are contending for their liberty, and, when he reaches the scene of action, vapours away his patriotism in a private boarding-

school." But in *Sprat,* however, the text allows favorable moral conclusions to be drawn, all the more convincing for being unstated, like the modesty expressed by Sprat himself: "When the preacher touched any favourite topick in a manner that delighted his audience their approbation was expressed by a loud *hum,* continued in proportion to their zeal or pleasure. When Burnet preached, part of his congregation *hummed* so loudly and so long that he sat down to enjoy it, and rubbed his face with his handkerchief. When Sprat preached, he likewise was honoured with the like animating *hum;* but he stretched out his hand to the congregation, and cried, 'Peace, peace, I pray you, peace.'"

17. Matthew Arnold, "The Study of Poetry," *Essays in Criticism: Second Series* (London: Macmillan, 1888; written, 1880); Arnold prepared an edition of Johnson, *The Six Chief Lives* (London: Macmillan, 1878).

18. See Arthur Tillotson, "Dr. Johnson and the *Life of Goldsmith,*" *Modern Language Review* 28 (1933): 439–43; Peter Cunningham's introduction, p. xxii; J. S. Childers, editor of Southey's *Lives and Works of the Uneducated Poets* (London: Humphrey Milford, 1925), p. 184.

19. Thomas Warton, *The History of English Poetry from the Close of the Eleventh to the Commencement of the Eighteenth Century,* 4 vols. (London: Tegg, 1824, orig. London: Dodsley, 1774–81). Some critics wondered who should succeed Warton, evidently not a coveted task since discussions seem to have outnumbered contenders. The prominent literary workmen Isaac D'Israeli and Robert Southey were suggested to complete Warton's task by the critic Allan Cunningham in his *Biographical and Critical History* (1833). D'Israeli's *Amenities of Literature,* published in fragmentary form in 1841, might have been a project like Warton's had his health lasted to complete the task. Southey mentions that his *Lives of the Uneducated Poets* (1831) is not intended as a complete history of the subject, though he willingly alluded to "my predecessor Warton," predecessor as literary historian and laureate. Although neither rushed to produce a sequel to Warton's literary history, both completed more than one collection of Johnsonian "Lives," including D'Israeli's *Calamities of Authors* (1812) and *Quarrels of Authors* (1814), and Southey's *Specimens of the Later English Poets with Preliminary Notices* (1807) and *Select Works of the British Poets from Chaucer to Johnson with Biographical Sketches* (1831), before and after the laureateship.

20. Ironically for Johnson, the evolutionary model became an ideology that was to become associated in the nineteenth century with the term Whig history. On the matter of historical relativism, Wellek, *English Literary History,* pp. 139–40, also calls attention to *Cowley,* "Wit . . . has its changes and fashions, and at different times takes different forms." In evaluating Pope's Homer, Johnson considers "the change which two thousand years have made in the modes of life and the habits of thought," and that Pope wrote "for his own age and his own nation." On the other hand, in *Milton* Johnson speaks of awaiting "the impartiality of a future generation." See Braudy, p. 221, on the growing tendency (encouraged by Warton, Hurd, and Percy) to study earlier literature for its uniqueness and differences rather than for its similarities or for its superiority.

21. In *Dryden,* Johnson disdains the "strain of flattery which disgraces genius,

and which it was wonderful that any man that knew the meaning of his own words could use without self-destestation."

22. Boswell, IV: 382. Writing paired lives was a standard biographical format in the eighteenth century—Johnson was later coupled with Chesterfield in William Hayley's *Two Dialogues: Containing a Comparative View of the Lives, Characters, and Writings of Philip, the Late Earl of Chesterfield, and Dr. Samuel Johnson* (1787), which omits their quarrel and compares the two as moralists in their lives and works.

23. Benjamin Boyce, "Samuel Johnson's Criticism of Pope in the Life of Pope," *Review of English Studies,* n.s. 5 (1954): 37–46, discusses Johnson's reappropriation of the Dryden-Pope comparison from Shiels.

24. Fussell, *Johnson,* p. 257; Henry James, "Nathaniel Hawthorne" (*Library of the World's Best Literature,* 1896); Hazlitt, "On the Periodical Essayists" (*Lectures on the English Comic Writers,* 1819).

25. Johnson's attitude toward heroes, and the subsequent demythologizing impulse of Romantic biography, expose the reactionary conservatism of Carlyle's later veneration of heroes and his literal use of the ironic eighteenth-century term "great man." In *The Life of Mr. Jonathan Wild the Great* (1743), Henry Fielding had parodied the hagiographic depiction of unequivocal good and evil, and declared the occasional benevolence and clemency of "great men" should be omitted in biography lest it destroy "the great perfection called uniformity of character." Boswell jests, "Being *the Great Man* has been quite our cant word for some time" (9 July 1763), *London Journal,* p. 298.

26. Lipking, p. 460, views the *Lives* as a conduct book.

27. Hester Thrale Piozzi, *Anecdotes of the Late Samuel Johnson,* ed. Arthur Sherbo (London: Oxford Univ. Press, 1974, orig. 1786), p. 97. Wordsworth declares the object of poetry "is truth, not individual and local, but general, and operative" (1802 Preface to *Lyrical Ballads*), and the task of the poet should be "studious more to see / Great truths, than touch and handle little ones" (1805 *Prelude,* XII: 58–59).

28. Johnson's quotation here of Thomson's *Castle of Indolence* prefigures the practice, favored among Romantic biographers, of glossing the life with lines from the works.

29. Johnson's impatience with Waller is evident in his sarcasm, "Of his behavior in this part of his life it is not necessary to direct the reader's opinion," and ultimately, "More than sixty years had not been able to teach him morality."

30. Pope's Argument to "The Characters of Men" (1734) continues: "To find (if we can) his RULING PASSION: That will certainly influence all the rest, and can reconcile the seeming or real inconsistency of all his actions." Hill's note, *Lives,* III: 173–74, remarks that the concept of ruling passion, shared by others besides Pope, derived from earlier theories of the humours. David L. Passler, *Time, Form, and Style in Boswell's Life of Johnson* (New Haven: Yale Univ. Press, 1971), pp. 33, 127–32, relates the lack of character development evident in Boswell's *Life of Johnson* to contemporary historiographic trends that assumed human nature was constant in all countries and times. On traditional character-writing see Benjamin Boyce, *The Theophrastan Character in England to 1642* (Cambridge: Harvard Univ. Press, 1947); John Butt, *Biography in the Hands of Walton, Johnson, and Boswell* (Berkeley:

Univ. of California Press, 1966), pp. 11–16; and Martine Watson Brownley, "Johnson's *Lives of the English Poets* and Earlier Traditions of the Character Sketch in England," in *Johnson and His Age,* ed. James Engell (Cambridge: Harvard Univ. Press, 1984), p. 32.

31. Boswell, II: 60. On Cromwell, see Hill's note, *Lives,* III: 92. Different accidents of biography might have left us knowing no more of Johnson than Cromwell hunting in a tye-wig: "Mr. Hamilton called out one day upon Brightelmstone Downs, Why Johnson rides as well, for aught I see, as the most illiterate fellow in England"—although Piozzi, p. 129, declared, "I think no praise ever went so close to his heart." On the caprice of critical reputation, one might cite Aretino's threat to disparage his patrons to posterity; and Thomas Nashe's slanderous comments on Gabriel Harvey in *Have With You to Saffron Walden* (1596) which have been left by the attrition of history as the chief source of Harvey's life. Johnson, knowing well the power of biography, investigated the rumor that among Pope's papers was found "a defamatory *Life of Swift,* which he had prepared as an instrument of vengeance to be used, if any provocations should be ever given" (*Pope*).

32. 1793 Advertisement to the second edition, Boswell, I: 12. Carlyle called Boswell's *Life* a "*Johnsoniad*" (2nd review of Croker's Boswell, *Fraser's,* 1832).

33. Many editors, attempting to impose closure on Johnson's narratives, omit this section and the preceding letter Johnson quotes. The essay is his earlier-written "A Dissertation on the Epitaphs written by Pope" (*The Universal Visiter* [*sic*], 1756); he had previously written "An Essay on Epitaphs" (*Gentleman's Magazine,* 1740). See Hill's note, *Lives,* III: 254.

34. Boswell, IV: 38, says Johnson favored the *Life of Cowley,* "on account of the dissertation which it contains on the *Metaphysical Poets.*" *Savage* was originally published in 1744, additional editions in 1748 and 1767; *Roscommon* originally appeared in 1748 in *The Gentleman's Magazine; Collins* originally appeared in 1763 in *The Poetical Calendar,* reprinted 1764. All were rewritten in varying degrees for the *Lives.* See J. D. Fleeman, ed., *Early Biographical Writings of Dr. Johnson* (Westmead, England: Gregg International, 1973).

35. Whereas "the morose" Anthony Wood says Cowley retired to the country for lack of preferment, "the courtly" Thomas Sprat says Cowley was "'weary of the vexations and fatigues of an active condition'" and so retreated to "'the true delights of solitary studies, of temperate pleasures, and [of] a moderate revenue'" (*Cowley*). Johnson concludes in compromise, "actions are visible, though motives are secret . . . [he] wisely went only so far from the bustle of life as that he might easily find his way back."

36. Although he accuses Sprat of propagating a wonder for relating that Cowley could not "retain the ordinary rules of grammar," the early biographer Johnson opens *Roscommon* saying that "he was never able to retain the rules of grammar."

37. The publishers were evidently willing to encourage the misconception about the book's genesis by evasively identifying the author in the first volume as "Mr. Cibber," and in subsequent volumes as "Mr. Cibber and others."

38. For comparisons of specific lives in Johnson and Shiels, see the following

works: Boyce, "Samuel Johnson's Criticism of Pope," pp. 37–46, discusses Shiels's use of Johnson's comparison of Dryden and Pope; Walter Raleigh, *Six Essays on Johnson* (New York: Russell and Russell, 1965), pp. 119–25, elucidates Cibber's role of adding anecdotes and striking out Jacobite and Tory sentiments; William R. Keast, "Johnson and 'Cibber's' Lives of the Poets, 1753," *Restoration and Eighteenth-Century Literature,* ed. Carroll Camden (Chicago: Univ. of Chicago Press, 1963), pp. 89–101, discusses Shiels's use of Johnson's *Savage,* and Johnson's use of Shiels in *Hammond, Rowe, Fenton, Smith, A. Philips,* and *Thomson;* James L. Battersby, "Johnson and Shiels: Biographers of Addison," *Studies in English Literature* 9 (1969): 521–37, examines Johnson's reappropriation of material from Shiels; Albert H. Campbell, "Shiels and Johnson: Biographers of Thomson," *Studies in English Literature* 12 (1971): 535–49, discusses elements of Shiels's originality independent of Johnson.

39. Johnson's views are made clear in *Dryden:* "Malevolence to the clergy is seldom at a great distance from irreverence of religion."

40. Hill's note, Boswell, IV: 34; Boswell, I: 433.

41. Boswell, V: 79.

42. Martin Maner, *The Philosophical Biographer: Doubt and Dialectic in Johnson's Lives of the Poets* (Athens: Univ. of Georgia Press, 1988), p. 19, says Johnson has a "doubting cast of mind." De Quincey parodies the biographical aggrandizement of incidents, in his posthumously published essay "Conversation and S.T. Coleridge": "The story is current under a thousand forms of the man who piqued himself on an interview which he had once enjoyed with royalty; and being asked what he could repeat to the company of his gracious Majesty's remarks . . . he confessed candidly that the King, happening to be pressed for time, had confined himself to saying, 'Dog, stand out of my horse's way.'"

43. Robert Darnton discusses the eagerness of a merchant, Jean Ranson, to hear about Rousseau from friends who knew the author, "Readers Respond to Rousseau, The Fabrication of Romantic Sensibility," *The Great Cat Massacre and Other Episodes in French Cultural History* (New York: Basic Books, 1984), pp. 248, 251.

44. Joseph Warton, *An Essay on the Genius and Writings of Pope,* rev. ed. (London: Dodsley, 1782), II: 227–28.

45. Boswell, I: 425.

46. Martial, *Epigrams,* I.4. Jonson, Dedicatory Epistle of *Volpone,* 1607, derived from Strabo, *Geography,* I.ii.5.

47. For example, author-based criticisms are denounced by Roland Barthes, "The Death of the Author," *Image-Music-Text,* pp. 142–48; and Michel Foucault, "What Is an Author?," *Partisan Review* 42 (1975): 603–14. David Bromwich, "The Uses of Biography," *Yale Review* 73 (1984): 161, tries to mediate the "prejudice" against examining lives and works. On earlier approaches to the doctrine of sincerity, see Henri Peyre, *Literature and Sincerity* (New Haven: Yale Univ. Press, 1963), and Lionel Trilling, *Sincerity and Authenticity* (Cambridge: Harvard Univ. Press, 1972), p. 6, who says that to call a work sincere in the twentieth century is to award it no higher aesthetic or intellectual admiration. Roy Park, quoting John Stuart Mill's statement that motives have nothing to do with action, says the

doctrine of sincerity reflects anti-utilitarianism, *Hazlitt and the Spirit of the Age* (Oxford: Clarendon, 1971), p. 166. Hazlitt declared, "Sincerity has to do with the connexion between our words and thoughts, and not between our belief and actions" ("On Cant and Hypocrisy," 1828).

48. Keats's well-known dichotomy, the Wordsworthian "egotistical sublime" and the Shakespearian "camelion Poet," appears in his 27 October 1818 letter to Richard Woodhouse. *The Letters of John Keats,* ed. Hyder Edward Rollins (Cambridge: Harvard Univ. Press, 1958), I: 386–87. Coleridge and Hazlitt set up similar categories using different examples. In 1817 Coleridge categorized Shakespeare and Milton: "The former darts himself forth, and passes into all the forms of human character and passion, the one Proteus of the fire and the flood; the other attracts all forms and things to himself, into the unity of his own IDEAL" (*Biographia,* II: 27). In the essay on Byron in *The Spirit of the Age* (1825), Hazlitt introduced the dichotomy, "Sir Walter Scott is the most *dramatic* writer now living; and Lord Byron is the least so."

49. Johnsonian apologists have fostered the misconception of Johnson as one who altogether rejected connections between life and works: Richard Altick, *Lives and Letters* (New York: Knopf, 1966), p. 57, says it is unfair to reproach Johnson for failing to do what no one else at his time did, "to bring the biography of a man to bear on the criticism of his works"; Folkenflik, *Johnson,* p. 10, warns against judging biography from a modernist perspective and thus downgrading Johnson for failing to take an "interest in the connections between life and works"; Lipking, p. 420, says Johnson did not trust connections between life and works and thus "the *Lives* achieve no perfect formal solution to the structural hiatus between life and works."

50. Boswell, III: 251.

51. Boswell, IV: 46. "To write *con amore,* with fondness for the employment, with perpetual touches and retouches, with unwillingness to take leave of his own idea, and an unwearied pursuit of unattainable perfection, was, I think, no part of his character" (*Dryden*). The term arises with increasing frequency in the later eighteenth century.

52. "It is not possible to read, without some contempt and indignation, poems of the same author, ascribing the highest degree of 'power and piety' to Charles the First, then transferring the same 'power and piety' to Oliver Cromwell; now inviting Oliver to take the Crown, and then congratulating Charles the Second on his recovered right" (*Waller*).

53. Hazlitt, review of Spence's *Anecdotes* (1820).

54. The *Lives* in some sense tells the story of the Age of Pope, England's literary history surveyed over two generations, the first represented by Pope's boyhood visit to see Dryden, and the second by the passing of the mantle to Pope, who established himself in the coffee-house where Dryden had presided. One narrative precedent for viewing the *Lives* as culminating in the figure of Pope is Vasari's *Lives of the Most Eminent Painters, Sculptors, and Architects* (1550), which culminates in the longest life, that of his friend Michelangelo, whose conduct (unlike any of Johnson's *Lives*) is presented as a model of how to live and how to practice art. The

same archetypes of youthful precocity and exceptional dedication attach themselves to both figures; even Johnson's use of Garth's account of Pope pretending to
alter his translation of the *Iliad* to please the critical pretensions of Halifax is a
variant of Vasari's account of Michelangelo pretending to modify the nose of
David to please Soderini by filtering dust through his fingers instead of working
the chisel.

55. *Pope* references Dryden, Cowley, Rochester, Milton, Walsh, A. Philips,
Addison, King, Savage, Prior, Fenton, Broome, Mallet, Halifax, Congreve,
Garth, Swift, Tickell, Parnell, Gay, Lyttelton, Waller, and Rowe. Pope is alluded to
throughout the *Lives;* indeed, figures are even assessed in terms of their acquaintance with Pope—Broome must be a worthy man because he is one "whom Pope
chose for an associate."

56. See, for example, Folkenflik, *Johnson*, p. 32; Lipking, p. 455; William C.
Dowling, *Language and Logos in Boswell's Life of Johnson* (Princeton: Princeton
Univ. Press, 1981), pp. 82–84, notes Boswell's avoidance of this cynical theme.

57. The prosperity of Parnell "did not last long. His end, whatever was its cause,
was now approaching. He enjoyed his preferment little more than a year." Prior's
health declines having finally possessed "what wits and philosophers have often
wished, the power of passing the day in contemplative tranquility. But it seems
that busy men seldom live long in a state of quiet." West becomes "sufficiently rich,
but wealth came too late to be long enjoyed; nor could it secure him from the
calamities of life." Thomson finally finds himself "at ease, but was not long to enjoy
it" before death. Lyttelton marries happily "but human pleasures are short; she
died in childbed." Fenton secures a patron and "there was now a prospect of ease
and plenty . . . but the small-pox suddenly put an end to the pleasing expectation."
Escaping poverty with a legacy which he "could scarcely think exhaustible, and
which he did not live to exhaust," Collins suffers "more dreadful calamities,
disease and insanity," of which Johnson observes, "Man is not born for happiness."

58. Eighteenth-century treatises on the term genius include: Addison, *Spectator*
160 (1711); William Sharpe, *A Dissertation Upon Genius* (1755); Joseph Warton, *An
Essay on the Genius and Writings of Pope* (1756–82); Edward Young, *Conjectures on
Original Composition* (1759); William Duff, *Essay on Original Genius* (1767); Duff,
Critical Observations on the Most Celebrated Original Geniuses in Poetry (1770);
Alexander Gerard, *Essay on Genius* (1774); Reynolds, *Discourse* II (1782). The word
genius in the title of many of the nineteenth-century discussions of creativity
signaled a continuing dialogue: Hazlitt, "On Genius and Originality" (1814), "On
Genius and Common Sense" (1821), and "Whether Genius is Conscious of Its
Powers" (1826); Lamb, "Sanity of True Genius" (1826); Isaac D'Israeli, *Essay on the
Manners and Genius of The Literary Character* (1795, rev. 1818 as *The Literary
Character, Illustrated by the History of Men of Genius*); chapter two of Coleridge's
Biographia Literaria (1817) on "men of Genius." See below, Chapter III, note 27,
and Chapter IV, notes 75 and 76. On the changing concept of creativity, see W. J.
Bate, *From Classic to Romantic* (Cambridge: Harvard Univ. Press, 1946); James
Engell, *The Creative Imagination* (Cambridge: Harvard Univ. Press, 1981);

Thomas McFarland, *Originality and Imagination* (Baltimore: Johns Hopkins Univ. Press, 1985).

59. For example, Johnson's long biography of Swift, where we might well expect it, does not mention genius.

60. See "Memoirs of Frances Reynolds," in *Johnsonian Miscellanies,* ed. G. B. Hill (Oxford: Clarendon, 1907), II: 287; Boswell, V: 35.

61. Boswell, V: 35, had argued that "'one man will naturally do the one better than the other. A hare will run up a hill best, from her fore-legs being short; a dog down.'"

62. In *Pope,* notable achievement results from invention, imagination, and judgment; in *Addison,* from "what perhaps every human excellence must be, the product of good-luck improved by genius"; in *Milton,* from "the united force of study and genius." Johnson is concerned with the mind of genius, rather than, in the manner of William Duff's *Critical Observations of the Writings of the Most Celebrated Original Geniuses in Poetry,* searching poems for isolated lines that best exercise genius.

In *Idler* 55 (1759), Johnson parodied the dilettante who thinks to become an author by cataloging traits (very similar to those listed in *Cowley*): "having been long a student, I thought myself qualified in time to become an author. . . . not finding my genius directing me by irresistible impulse to any particular subject, I deliberated three years which part of knowledge to illustrate by my labours. Choice is more often determined by accident than by reason: I walked abroad one morning. . . ." Although self-assessments of talent are generally ridiculed in the *Lives* (Stepney "apparently professed himself a poet" and Somerville "writes very well for a gentleman"), the youthful Pope, "as he confesses, 'thought himself the greatest genius that ever was.' Self-confidence is the first requisite to great undertakings . . . it was the felicity of Pope to rate himself at his real value."

63. D'Israeli declares, "Ask the man of genius if he [has] written all that he wished to have written?" (*Literary Character,* 1818–40). Hazlitt says of Johnson in "On the Conversation of Authors" (1820), "Dr. Johnson's conversation in Boswell's Life is much better than in his published works: and the fragments of the opinions of celebrated men, preserved in their letters or in anecdotes of them, are justly sought after as invaluable for the same reason." De Quincey, in the posthumously published "Conversation and S. T. Coleridge," remarks that to have heard Coleridge talk has become a "great distinction" like a Shakespeare autograph; but in "Southey, Wordsworth, Coleridge" (*Literary Reminiscences,* 1839) he notes that often "the *personal* interest in the author is not in the direct ratio of that which belongs to his works."

64. Johnson's letter to Lord Chesterfield, refusing his patronage, itself represented a breakdown of old cultural alliances; Alvin B. Kernan calls Johnson a "Caliban of literature," *Printing Technology, Letters and Samuel Johnson* (Princeton: Princeton Univ. Press, 1987), p. 131. Johnson's image of a marginalized community of authors was prefigured in the review of Ralph Church's edition of Spenser (*Critical Review,* 1759), formerly attributed to Oliver Goldsmith: "There is a strong similitude between the lives of almost all our English poets. The Ordinary of

Newgate, we are told, has but one story, which serves for the life of every hero that happens to come within the circle of his pastoral care; however unworthy the resemblance appears, it may be asserted that the history of one poet might serve with as little variation for that of any other. . . . Spenser, in short, lived poor, was reviled by the critics of his time, and died at last in utmost distress."

65. Known collectively as the "Newgate Calendar," some collective biographies of criminals were produced "officially" from court records, but many more were by private hands. Transcripts of the sessions papers circulated widely and were collected and expanded in the 1730, 1735, and 1742 *Select Trials*. Other entrepreneurial ventures, which often capitalized on firsthand interviews with the condemned, included: *Tyburn Calendar* (1700), apparently the first; Captain Alexander Smith, *Complete History of the Lives and Robberies of the Most Notorious Highwaymen, Foot-Pads, Shop-lifts and Cheats* (1714); Captain Charles Johnson, *General History of the Lives and Adventures of the Most Famous Highwaymen, Murderers, and Street Robbers, and Accounts of the Voyages and Plunders of the Most Notorious Pyrates* (1734); *Lives of the Most Remarkable Criminals* (1735); *The Bloody Register* (1764), which initiated the "Newgate Calendar" appellation; *Tyburn Chronicle* (1768); J. Cooke's *The Newgate Calendar, or the Malefactor's Bloody Register* (1773); prison ordinary James Villette's *Annals of Newgate* (1776); *Malefactor's Register: New Newgate and Tyburn Calendar* (1796); George Borrow's *Celebrated Trials* (1825); Andrew Knapp and William Baldwin's *Newgate Calendar* (1809–10, 1826).

66. The popularity of gentleman criminals such as Claude Du Vall [Duval] and the witty escape artist Jack Sheppard preceded fictionalizations such as Gay's *Beggar's Opera* and Fielding's *Jonathan Wild*. Fredric Jameson calls this kind of literary appropriation the action of an enfeebled high culture rejuvenating itself through the fertility of popular culture, *The Political Unconscious: Narrative as a Socially Symbolic Act* (Ithaca: Cornell Univ. Press, 1981), p. 87. However, the appropriation seems to have been mutual, since a number of the criminal biographies communicate with the mainstream literary tradition. Captain Alexander Smith's *Complete History,* one of the earliest and most famous collections, adapts episodes from the *Decameron* as events in the lives of eighteenth-century criminals, and uses the alchemical confidence trick of Chaucer's *Canon's Yeoman's Tale* in the life of Claude Du Vall (appropriations further indicating structural links between collective biography and medieval and Renaissance linked storytelling). See Frank Wadleigh Chandler, *The Literature of Roguery* (Boston: Houghton Mifflin, 1907), I: 172–74.

Benjamin Boyce shows how elements of Defoe's *Roxana* were mixed into Savage's pretensions to noble kinship, and how later editions of *Roxana* appear to incorporate sympathies prepared by elements of Savage's tale. "Johnson's *Life of Savage* and Its Literary Background," *Studies in Philology* 53 (1956): 576–98. In the eighteenth and nineteenth centuries particularly, biographical narrative demonstrates what Jacques Derrida calls the impurity of genres, which requires us to view every text as participating in multiple genres. "The Law of Genre," in *On Narrative,* ed. W. J. T. Mitchell (Chicago: Univ. of Chicago Press, 1981), p. 61. Generic exchanges are evident in Boswell's representation of conversation as a playscript ("BOSWELL. . . . JOHNSON. . . . BOSWELL"), and Mason's epistolary biography, which, like the epistolary novel, consisted wholly of sequenced letters. Novels, conversely, often pretended to be autobiographies and biographies (*Moll Flanders . . . Written from her own Memorandums; The History of Tom Jones*).

67. Jean-Paul Sartre, *Saint Genet* (Paris: Gallimard, 1952).

68. Here again, *Savage* contains a rhetorical concealment: Johnson does not explain how it is that Savage and his two companions are "treated with some distinction" and are confined "not among the common criminals" in Newgate, but in the far more expensive cash-only "Press-yard" for the wealthy.

69. Boswell styles Johnson as more favorably disposed to booksellers, "for whom he uniformly professed much regard," I: 438; "He considered them as the patrons of literature," who sponsored the *Dictionary* without certainty of its success, I: 305. Johnson's praise of the generosity of booksellers in backing the *Dictionary* and paying him more than he had asked for the *Lives* may lie in his filial relations—as he tells us, he owes the stories of the large sales of *Absalom and Achitophel* and the humility and popularity of Sprat, to "my father, an old bookseller."

70. Johnson tells how Pope declined the patronage of Halifax, who sought to win prestige from the *Iliad* by making "some advances of favour and some overtures of advantage to Pope, which he seems to have received with sullen coldness. All our knowledge of this transaction is derived from a single letter," which Johnson prints. Boswell, I: 259–63, in turn, prints Johnson's aloof letter rejecting Lord Chesterfield's belated sponsorship of the *Dictionary,* saying Johnson "despised the honeyed words, and was even indignant that Lord Chesterfield should, for a moment, imagine, that he could be the dupe of such an artifice." Boswell was eager to quote Johnson's letter directly, and pestered Johnson for a copy, "till at last in 1781 . . . he was pleased to dictate it to me from memory." The timing seems to suggest the letter was on Johnson's mind as he was finishing the *Life of Pope,* although Boswell's image may also have in mind his remark in *Halifax,* "He was, as Pope says, 'fed with dedications.'"

71. Hill's note, Boswell, III: 19, attributes this to Walpole and Hawkins.

72. D'Israeli's introduction to the *Calamities of Authors* observes, "The title of Author still retains its seduction among our youth, and is consecrated by ages. Yet what affectionate parent would consent to see his son devote himself to his pen as a profession? . . . Most Authors close their lives in apathy or despair, and too many live by means which few of them would not blush to describe."

73. George Granville, Lord Lansdowne; Charles Montagu, Earl of Halifax, and John Sheffield, Duke of Buckingham; Stepney was the schoolmate and satellite of Halifax.

74. Scott ironically added, "But it was always Walpole's foible to disclaim a professed pursuit of public favor" ("Walpole," *Lives of the Novelists,* 1821–24). Walpole begins with royalty and tellingly moves downward through a hierarchy of gender and ethnicity: nobles, peeresses, Scottish lairds, Irish lords.

75. "'Secondly, he was as vain as any of his readers; thirdly, men are very prone

to believe what they do not understand; fourthly, they will believe any thing at all, provided they are under no obligation to believe it; fifthly, they love to take a new road, even when that road leads no where; sixthly, he was reckoned a fine writer and seems [seemed] always to mean more than he said. Would you have any more reasons?'" (*Gray*).

76. Virginia Woolf quotes Johnson's *Gray*, "'I rejoice to concur with the common reader . . .'" as the epigraph of the first series of *The Common Reader* essays (London: Hogarth, 1925), and explains the term in the prefatory essay.

77. Johnson ironically observes that Savage "contented himself with the applause of men of judgement, and was somewhat disposed to exclude all those from the character of men of judgement who did not applaud him." In the *Lives* the public view is most often accurate in perceiving poor writing, as in its lukewarm response to Gay and rejection of Thomson's *Liberty*. Leopold Damrosch, *The Uses of Johnson's Criticism* (Charlottesville: Univ. of Virginia Press, 1976), pp. 38–57, summarizes modern critical speculations on the term common reader.

78. Overruling Addison's judgment in *Smith,* Johnson declares, "The voice of the people, when to please the people is the purpose, deserves regard."

79. D'Israeli, saying Johnson called his the "Age of Authors," concurred with many of his contemporaries in naming theirs the "Age of Criticism" (*Literary Character,* 1795); Hazlitt, "On the Periodical Press" (1823); Allan Cunningham, *Biographical and Critical History* (1833).

CHAPTER III

1. On Romantic literary pilgrimages and the public image of authors (including the incident of a London workman stopping Charles Lamb "to point in awe to Sir Walter Scott as he crosses the street"), see Altick, *Lives,* pp. 136–37. In the twentieth century, T. S. Eliot tried to prohibit any authorized biography; James and Hardy burned letters; and Auden called biography "always superfluous" and "usually in bad taste." On Victorian and modern opposition to biography, see Altick, pp. 117, 161, and Edel, "Figure Under the Carpet," p. 21. On Carlyle, see Cross, p. 28, and Marc Pachter, "Introduction," *Telling Lives,* p. 10.

2. Arbuthnot reported that the bookseller Edmund Curll, "who is one of the new terrors of death, has been writing letters to everybody for memoirs of Gay's life." Hill's note, *Lives,* III: 155. Also quoted by De Quincey in his *Encyclopaedia Britannica* biography of Pope (1837).

3. Boswell, I: 433. See above, Chapter I, note 66.

4. Folkenflik, *Johnson,* p. 81.

5. James Clifford's article, "How Much Should a Biographer Tell?" (in *Biography,* ed. Daghlian), sets the date too late, however, in saying that the question started with Boswell; see p. 90 on the *English Review* (1786) and other contemporary complaints. Altick's chapter of the same title, pp. 146–80, discusses similar concerns in the nineteenth century.

Johnson's undervaluing of figures such as Milton and Gray raised objections but, unlike Boswell, the *Lives* generally did not stir complaints about impropriety (even for such revelations as Pope's padded garments and Thomson's sloth). On responses to Mason, see Draper, pp. 272–75; to Piozzi's *Anecdotes*, see Sherbo's introduction, pp. xi–xii; to Johnson, see Courtney and Smith, pp. 135–39; to Boswell's *Hebrides*, see Frank Brady, "Boswell's Self-Presentation and His Critics," *Studies in English Literature* 12 (1972): 551. Boswell had been warned early on; he says of Andrew Erskine, "He gave me a very sensible advice against repeating what people said, which may do much harm. I have an unlucky custom of doing so" (9 December 1762), *London Journal*, p. 72; yet shortly after he met Johnson, the Tobermory Boswell was writing, "This little specimen of social pleasantry will serve me to tell as an agreeable story to literary people" (14 July 1763), p. 303. At the end of the *Hebrides*, V: 414, Boswell stoutly denied, "It may be objected by some persons, as it has been by one of my friends, that he who has the power of thus exhibiting an exact transcript of conversations is not a desirable member of society." But Clifford, "How Much?," p. 91, discusses evidence that "Boswell was in later years not received in certain circles with the same pleasure as formerly."

6. Freud's letter to his aspiring biographer Arnold Zweig, quoted by Steven Weiland, "The Humanities, the Professions, and the Uses of Biography," in *The Biographer's Gift*, ed. Veninga, p. 51. Biographer Arnold Rampersad observes that artists, at least, usually "have little to fear from their biographers, who tend to champion them," but warns that biographers may well be the unwitting agents of cultural institutions—and we might add, publishing institutions—that surround them. "Biography, Autobiography, and Afro-American Culture," *Yale Review* 73 (1983): 9–12.

7. Such distinctions represent not merely a nineteenth-century phenomenon, or a concern only for the reputation of literary heroes: twentieth-century anxiety about the propriety of reconstructing Thomas Jefferson's sexual relations with his slaves, and the long belated postwar accounting of fascist materials in the lives of authors as diverse as Ezra Pound and P. G. Wodehouse, result from the same fear of damaging literary reputation that stirred, for example, contemporary readers' complaints about the indiscretion of Lockhart's already reticent treatment of Scott's financial downfall.

8. Lockhart, *Scott*, V: 433, III: 186. Safely a decade beyond the biography of Scott, Lockhart again praised Boswell in a letter to John Murray (7 November 1845), regretting that Croker's edition had not kept "Boswell's text entirely undisturbed" and calling for "*saving Boswell entire* in his own station & dignity." See Alan Lang Strout, "Some Unpublished Letters of John Gibson Lockhart," *Notes and Queries* 189 (1945): 34–37.

9. Carlyle refutes these criticisms in his review of Lockhart's *Scott* (1838), and praises *Scott* for fulfilling the dutiful task of the biographer; for Carlyle, the massiveness of the biography is itself a tribute illustrating "'the perpetual fact of hero-worship,'" the "primary . . . and final creed of mankind," an idea he was later to develop in Lecture V of *On Heroes, Hero-worship, and the Heroic in History*, delivered in 1840 and later printed as a collective biography (London: Fraser, 1841).

10. H. N. Coleridge, *Specimens of the Table Talk of the late Samuel Taylor Coleridge* (London: Murray, 1835).

11. Boswell replied, " 'Sir,' said I, 'that is next best to speaking myself.' 'Nay,' said he, 'but you do both' " (1 July 1763), *London Journal,* p. 288.

12. Lockhart, *Scott,* I: 1–2. The fragment begins with this passage. It was left unfinished after a few dozen pages.

13. Although Leigh Hunt, evidently unacquainted with the fragment, used the example of Scott in connecting psychological and physiological maladies of artists in his *Sketches of the Living Poets* (1821), Lockhart ignores the tacit implications of the pathology of the artist in Scott's statement. Like Boswell's quotation of *Rambler* 60 at the beginning of the *Life of Johnson,* Lockhart's quotation of Scott's testimony appropriates the subject's own words to justify his methodology, without putting into effect the implications of the quote.

14. Wordsworth, "The Tables Turned" (1798), "A Poet's Epitaph" (1800).

15. Wordsworth, "My Heart Leaps Up" (1807), reprinted as the epigraph to "Immortality" ode (beginning in 1815). For various appropriations of Wordsworth, see for example, Carlyle's second review of Croker's Boswell (1832); De Quincey's "Infant Literature" (revised *Autobiographic Sketches,* 1853); D'Israeli says, "Man is a continuation of the child" (*The Literary Character,* 1818); Hazlitt, "On Personal Character" (1821), "Character of Mr. Canning" (1824).

16. Post-Boswellian exposés had rendered Mason's *Gray* tame and sage.

17. Tennyson is quoted by Maurois, p. 15, Altick, *Lives,* p. 158. There are very few studies of comparative biography; on biographies of Burns, see the chapter on Burns in Hart, *Lockhart,* pp. 77–129; on biographies of Savage, see Benjamin Boyce, "Johnson's Life of Savage," pp. 576–98. Doris Langley Moore's *The Late Lord Byron* (London: Murray, 1961), offers a history of biographies of Byron, but there has been no analytical work on the texts.

18. Hazlitt, "Mr. Wordsworth and the Westmoreland Election" (1818); "Burns" (*Lectures on the English Poets,* 1818). Wordsworth's attitude represents a striking contrast to the dominant Romantic curiosity about the life of the author. Carlyle's review of Lockhart's *Life of Burns,* for example, declared the preeminence of the life over the works: "True and genial as his poetry must appear, it is not chiefly as a poet, but as a man, that he interests and affects us" (*Edinburgh Review,* 1828). Prioritizing of the life of the author lingers in the modern attitude of finding the *Life of Johnson* more compelling than Johnson's own works, and in the suggestion that Boswell had more of a hand in Johnson's reputation than Johnson. Regarding the joint popular reputation of Johnson and Boswell, see Donald J. Greene, "Reflections on a Literary Anniversary," *Queen's Quarterly* 70 (1963): 198–202; Schwartz, p. 100; and F. A. Pottle's comment that the *Life* is one of the ten greatest English prose works, but Boswell not one of the ten greatest authors, "The Life of Boswell," *Yale Review* 35 (1946): 446.

19. Reviewing Croker's Boswell (1831), Lockhart exclaims, "On what principle Mr. Wordsworth should conceive that 'nothing of this applies' to such authors as the moralist or the poet, who, by his single pen, exercises perhaps wider and more lasting sway over the tone of thought and feeling throughout whole nations, than a regiment of kings and ministers put together;—this indeed is what we cannot pretend to understand."

20. De Quincey, "Stewart, Irving, Wordsworth" (*Literary Reminiscences,* 1840); Shelley, *Defence of Poetry* (1821); Kris, p. 80.

21. Hill's note, *Lives,* I: 85.

22. Although Wordsworth notes that in biography, as in fiction, "restraints may be thrown off" as time passes (*Burns*).

23. Coleridge is here borrowing Lessing (*Biographia,* II: 109n).

24. Coleridge assumes that there are "Those, who by biography or by their own experience are familiar with the general habits of genius." *Biographia,* II: 32, I: 48, 63–65.

25. According to Coleridge, poetry is by definition produced by the "poetic genius itself, which sustains and modifies the images, thoughts, and emotions of the poet's own mind. . . . He diffuses a tone, and spirit of unity, that blends, and (as it were) *fuses,* each into each, by that synthetic and magical power, to which we have exclusively appropriated the name of imagination." *Biographia,* II: 15–16.

26. Coleridge, *Biographia,* I: 224.

27. Horace's term (*Epistles,* II.ii.102) has been translated by various biographers as the touchy, sensitive, or irritable race of poets. In chapter two of the *Biographia,* I: 33–37, subtitled "Supposed irritability of men of Genius," Coleridge declares, "Through all the works of Chaucer there reigns a chearfulness, a manly hilarity, which makes it almost impossible to doubt a correspondent habit of feeling in the author himself. . . . In Spenser indeed, we trace a mind constitutionally tender . . . additionally saddened by the unjust persecution . . . and the severe calamities, which overwhelmed his latter days. These causes have diffused over all his compositions 'a melancholy grace.'"

28. Coleridge, *Biographia,* I: 62–63. See above, Chapter II, note 63.

29. "On the Spirit of Modern Biography," *The Friend* No. 21 (25 January 1810, rev. ed. 1818), I: 356–59, II: 285–87. See above, Chapter I, note 5. Coleridge does not name any particular biographers in calling them garrulous scandal bearers, time-killers, and gossips. See Coleridge's translation of his sobriquet "Satyrane" as "Idoloclast" in *The Friend* No. 14 (23 November 1809), II: 185.

30. Francis Bacon, *The Advancement of Learning* (1623), II: 7. Coleridge's text discredits the common late eighteenth- and early nineteenth-century Baconian justification of biography. D'Israeli, Stanfield, and Adolphus, for example, all paraphrase Bacon in theorizing about biography. Henry Fielding's pseudo-biography, *Jonathan Wild,* also opens with a paraphrase of Bacon, as does the Romantic anthology of autobiographies, *A Collection of the Most Amusing and Instructive Lives Ever Published.*

31. Geoffrey Little concludes Wordsworth annotated Field's *Memoirs* in 1839; *Barron Field's Memoirs of Wordsworth* (Sydney: Sydney Univ. Press, 1975), pp. 16–17; on De Quincey and Hazlitt, pp. 28, 36–37.

32. "My acquaintance with him was the result of a letter of his own volunteered to me. He was 7 months an inmate of my house; and by what breach of the laws of hospitality, that kindness was repaid, his performance, if rightly represented to me, sufficiently shows. A man who can set such an example, I hold to be a pest in society, and one of the most worthless of mankind. They who know me best could

testify, did they think it worth while to notice the thing, that my fault was only that of bearing with him his character and proceedings far more tenderly than I ought to have done."

33. On Wordsworth to Henry Crabb Robinson, see Mary Moorman, *Wordsworth, The Later Years* (Oxford: Clarendon, 1965), p. 237; on *Tait's,* George McLean Harper, *William Wordsworth* (London: Murray, 1923), II: 408; on Crabb Robinson to Wordsworth, John E. Jordan, *De Quincey to Wordsworth* (Berkeley: Univ. of California Press, 1962), p. 347, and Grevel Lindop, *The Opium-Eater: A Life of Thomas De Quincey* (London: Dent, 1981), p. 333. Southey blusteringly recounted to Carlyle his recommendation that Hartley Coleridge cudgel the "calumniator, cowardly spy, traitor, base betrayer of the hospitable social hearth." The Coleridges later tried to get Joseph Cottle to leave out of his *Early Recollections* his account of De Quincey's loan of £300 to Coleridge. Jordan, p. 336.

34. Leslie A. Marchand, *Byron, A Biography* (New York: Knopf, 1957), II: 620.

35. Lindop, pp. 253–54. In *Lord Byron and Some of his Contemporaries* (1828), Leigh Hunt apostrophizes, "O Truth! what scrapes of portraiture have you not got me into!" and protests of some unnamed excess of Byron's, "I would not say anything about it, nor about twenty other matters. . . . It is fortunate there are some which I can omit" (although in the Preface to the second edition, he threatens in another case, "I have something very awful to say on that point, in case it is forced from me").

36. "Vaudracour and Julia" appears as part of the 1805 *Prelude* (IX: 555–935), later deleted; published separately in 1820.

37. Byron, Dedication to Canto IV of *Childe Harold.*

38. On the burning of Byron's memoirs see G. Wilson Knight, *Lord Byron's Marriage* (London: Routledge, 1957), pp. 97–107, 149–55; Marchand, *Byron,* III: 1245–53; Doris Langley Moore, "The Burning of Byron's Memoirs," *Atlantic Monthly* 204 (1959): 27–37, and *The Late Lord Byron,* pp. 1–56.

39. Byron's letter to D'Israeli, 10 June 1822. *Byron's Letters and Journals,* ed. Leslie A. Marchand (London: Murray, 1976), IX: 172. See below, Chapter IV, note 73.

40. Byron's letter to Moore, 9 June 1820 (*Letters,* VII: 117), refers to a biographical sketch prefacing the Paris edition of Moore's works.

41. Review of Leigh Hunt's *Lord Byron and Some of his Contemporaries* (*New Monthly Magazine,* 1828).

42. Johnson had raised the same issue in *Idler* 65 (1759): "He who sees himself surrounded by admirers, and whose vanity is hourly feasted with all the luxuries of studied praise, is easily persuaded that his influence will be extended beyond his life."

43. Boswell, IV: 97.

44. Byron's letter to John Murray, 1 August 1819 (*Letters,* VI: 192–98, gives full text). Moore, *Byron,* II: 183–84; later editions silently omit many of Moore's asterisks.

45. Asterisks make this the most "scriptible" of texts (to use the language of Roland Barthes), for the collaboration between reader and text determines the

endlessly variable content of the passage. Gérard Genette has said the gap is what defines poetry and makes it "antiprose," but we can see here how the Romantic prose text makes use of the narrative gap to foster uncertainty, "Poetic Language, Poetics of Language," *Figures of Literary Discourse* (New York: Columbia Univ. Press, 1982), pp. 78–79.

The actual text of the letter is strikingly unsuggestive in comparison to Moore's rendition. Readers could object only to their own imaginings, which may have been more likely to preserve the erotic mythologizing of Byron than the implications of prostitution in the unglamorous financial arrangements of the deleted passage.

Hazlitt did not live long enough to witness Moore's suggestive use of letters in the biography, but he criticized Moore's hypocrisy in condemning Rousseau for the libido he allowed to Byron, and for the false heroism of burning the memoirs that had been entrusted to him ("On Old English Writers and Speakers," 1825; "On the Jealousy of Spleen and Party," 1826).

46. Charles Altieri, "An Idea and Ideal of the Literary Canon," *Critical Inquiry* 10 (1983): 37.

47. Percival Stockdale, *Lectures on the Truly Eminent English Poets*, 2 vols. (London: Longman, 1807).

48. The anonymous *A Collection of the Most Instructive and Amusing Lives Ever Published Written by the Parties Themselves with brief introductions and compendious sequels carrying on the course of events to the death of each writer*, 33 vols. (London: Hunt and Clark, 1826–32), includes lives as diverse as Cibber, Cellini, Vidocq, and Gibbon. William Godwin, *Lives of the Necromancers* (London: Mason, 1834).

49. *The Works of the English Poets, with Prefaces, Biographical and Critical, by Dr. Samuel Johnson*, 75 vols. (London: Nichols, 1790). Alexander Chalmers, *The Works of the English Poets from Chaucer to Cowper, including the series edited with Prefaces, Biographical and Critical, by Dr. Samuel Johnson*, 21 vols. (London: Johnson, etc., 1810).

50. Thomas Campbell, *Specimens of the British Poets, with Biographical and Critical Notices and an Essay on English Poetry*, 7 vols. (London: Murray, 1819); Henry Francis Cary, *Lives of English Poets from Johnson to Kirke White designed as a continuation of Johnson's Lives* (London: Bohn, 1846, orig. *London Magazine* 1821–24); Joseph Robertson, *Lives of the Scottish Poets*, 3 vols. (London: Boys, 1821–22); *The British Poets*, 100 vols. (Chiswick: Carpenter etc., 1822).

51. Allan Cunningham, "Biographical and Critical History of the Literature of the Last Fifty Years" (*Athenaeum*, 26 October 1833 to 28 December 1833). Reprinted as *Biographical and Critical History of the British Literature of the Last Fifty Years* (Paris: Baudry, 1834), 368 pp.; with an introductory appreciation, "The author of the present work having, of course, omitted his own name in the list of British authors, it will, no doubt, be agreeable to our readers to have the following details"; plus a tag article on "Oriental Literature" not by Cunningham, but which followed the original article when serialized.

52. The title of Cunningham's *The Lives of the Most Eminent British Painters, Sculptors, and Architects*, 6 vols. (London: Murray, 1829–33), echoes the title of

Giorgio Vasari's *The Lives of the Most Eminent Painters, Sculptors, and Architects*. Horace Walpole, *Anecdotes of Painting in England*, 4 vols. (Strawberry Hill, 1762). Cunningham edited and authored the life of Burns in *The Works of Robert Burns with his life*, 8 vols. (London: Cockrane and M'Crone, 1834).

53. De Quincey, "Literary Novitiate" (*Literary Reminiscences*, 1837).

54. Johnson told Piozzi, p. 93, "'Men and women are my subjects of enquiry; let us see how these differ from those we have left behind'"; in *Milton* he declared, "The innovators whom I oppose are turning off attention from life to nature. They seem to think, that we are placed here to watch the growth of plants, or the motions of the stars." D'Israeli, *Calamities of Authors* (1812). Johnson notoriously discussed the pastoral in *Rambler* 36 and 37; but Robert C. Olson, "Samuel Johnson's Ambivalent View of Classical Pastoral," in *Fresh Reflections on Samuel Johnson: Essays in Criticism*, ed. Prem Nath (Troy, NY: Whitson, 1987), pp. 32–33, notes Johnson's favorable quotation of Virgil's *Eclogues* at times, as in the letter to Lord Chesterfield.

55. Cunningham called his a "connected series of Critical Biographies." He does not use the terms compiled and composed, but he calls attention to the distinction between the "minute account" of the Boswellian "'Life and Times'" and the superior form of Johnsonian critical biography. Johnson sought "to exhibit the genius as well as the persons of the poets; to give us their mental picture along with their bodily, and I know of no writer who has equalled him"; Boswellian biography in contrast, gives raw materials of diaries and letters, compelling readers to "draw our own conclusions from the anecdotes," each "according to his abilities," rather than performing the task of analyzing the subject's character and mind. Whereas Johnson's literary biographies indicated he "knew it was by their intellect that they had purchased the distinction of biography; succeeding biographers, and among them Boswell, have thought differently": Boswellian biographers do not assess the achievements of their subjects, "the crowning glory to the 'Lives of the Poets.'"

56. D'Israeli, "Remarks on the Biographical Accounts of the late Samuel Johnson, LL.D. with an attempt to vindicate his Character from late misrepresentations" (*Gentleman's Magazine*, 1786). *Curiosities of Literature* (London: Murray, 1st series, 1791; 2nd series 1823; entered its 14th edition in 1849, the year after his death, with the memoir written by his son Benjamin Disraeli, "On the Life and Writings of Mr. Disraeli"). Essays on explicitly Johnsonian topics ("On Literary Genius" and "On Literary Industry") also appear in *Miscellanies; or Literary Recreations* (London: Cadell and Davies, 1796; rpt. *Literary Miscellanies*, 1801).

Following is the chronology of the major revisions of D'Israeli's works on literary genius: *A Dissertation on Anecdotes* (London: Kearsley and Murray, 1793, rpt. 1801); *An Essay on the Manners and Genius of the Literary Character* (London: Cadell and Davies, 1795); *Calamities of Authors* (London: Murray, 1812); *Quarrels of Authors* (London: Murray, 1814). *The Literary Character* was revised as *The Literary Character, Illustrated by the History of Men of Genius, Drawn from their own Feelings and Confessions* (2nd ed., London: Murray, 1818; 3rd ed., 1822) and *The Literary Character; or the History of Men of Genius, Drawn from their own Feelings and Confessions* (4th ed., London: Colburn, 1828; 5th ed. with *Literary Miscellanies, Calamities,* and *Quarrels,* 1840). The now standard edition is Benjamin Disraeli's, *The Works of Isaac Disraeli* [*sic*], 7 vols. (London: Routledge, Warnes and Routledge, 1858–59). For a full account of the numerous reprints see James Ogden, *Isaac D'Israeli* (Oxford: Clarendon, 1969), pp. 210–15.

57. D'Israeli, *Literary Character* (1818, rev. from 1795); the 1822 preface added, "The philosophy of biography has rarely been discovered." Bolingbroke had described history as "philosophy teaching by example" (*Letters on the Study and Use of History,* 1752). D'Israeli amasses biographical anecdotes to collectively illustrate by example, "casting philosophy into anecdotes and anecdotes into philosophy."

In contrast, John Nichols's *Literary Anecdotes of the Eighteenth Century,* 9 vols. (London: Nichols, 1812–15), did not attempt any biographical argument. In the Advertisement to Vol. IX he describes the project: "It is a Mine of literary materials, whence future Biographers and Historians will readily and unsparingly collect what may suit their several purposes." Both D'Israeli and Johnson drew from anecdotage supplied by Nichols, who notably printed Johnson's *Lives,* reprinted Thomas Fuller's *Worthies of England* (1811), and assisted Edmond Malone in editing Boswell's *Life.* In the 1840 expansion of the *Calamities,* D'Israeli added Nichols to his sympathetic discussion of the unsung antiquarian tasks of William Oldys and Anthony Wood.

58. Bolton Corney wrote several rebuttals to D'Israeli. His *Curiosities of Literature Illustrated* (London: 1837) rejects Byron's and Scott's praise of D'Israeli, accusing him of writing "the romance of bibliographical history" and his own autobiographical sketch rather than the biography of William Oldys ("a silhouette of D'Israeli; executed by the artist himself").

59. The embryonic version of this appears in the final chapter of the 1818 *Literary Character,* which emphasized the unbroken lineage of genius ("Men of genius . . . seem to be the same persons. . . . In the history of genius there is no chronology"), enlarged in subsequent editions. In 1822 he wrote, "Every man of genius will discover, soon or late, that he belongs to the brotherhood of his class, and cannot escape from certain habits, and feelings, and disorders, arising from the same sympathies, occupying the same situation, and passing through the same moral existence." He had declared earlier in the *Dissertation on Anecdotes* (1793), "In literary biography, a man of genius always finds something which relates to himself." The image of a timeless community of authors (D'Israeli uses the word "immortal") derives ultimately from Johnson's *Lives.* Coleridge's manuscript poem "To William Wordsworth" (1807) envisioned a similar brotherhood in "the archives of mankind": "I viewed thee in the choir / Of ever-enduring men. The truly great / Have all one age, and from one visible space / Shed influence!"

60. These comments first appear in 1822, along with the question, "Was it Machiavel who formed his age, or the age which created Machiavel?" The emphasis on the Johnsonian community of artists in the 1818 *Literary Character* shifts in later editions to the discussion of the relation between the "man of genius" and the age, mirroring larger cultural trends seen in Hegel as well. In England, D'Israeli precedes Hazlitt's *The Spirit of the Age* (1825) in raising these issues:

"Genius is not only the organ of its nation; it is also that of the state of the times" (*Literary Character*, 1822).

61. 1818 *Literary Character;* elsewhere, "Literary History becomes that of the human mind" (*Calamities*); "Literary history itself . . . the mere history of the human mind" (*Quarrels*); "The history of the human mind" is carried through "the genealogical lines of genius" (*Literary Character*, 1840).

62. "From the Grecian *Psyche,* or the soul, the Germans have borrowed this expressive term. They have a *Psychological Magazine.* Some of our own recent authors have adopted the term peculiarly adapted to the historian of the human mind" (*Calamities*).

63. *His Very Self and Voice: Collected Conversations of Lord Byron,* ed. Ernest J. Lovell (New York: Macmillan, 1954), p. 65.

64. Johnson says Dryden fails to exhibit "elemental passions"; Milton's *Lycidas* lacks "the effusion of real passion."

65. Wordsworth's *Essay, Supplementary to the Preface* (1815) appeared in the second edition of *Poems, in Two Volumes;* originally designed to supplement the 1815 Preface, in 1836–37 Wordsworth transferred the reference to the Preface to *Lyrical Ballads.* See W. J. B. Owen and Jane Worthington Smyser, eds., *The Prose Works of William Wordsworth* (Oxford: Clarendon, 1974), III: 55. The "classes of readers" of the *Essay, Supplementary* forms a counterpart to the classes of poetry delineated in the main 1815 Preface. The *Essay, Supplementary* may have been conjoined to the *Lyrical Ballads* Preface to unite their commentaries on Johnson (since both answer issues raised in the *Lives*), as well as to fulfill the second half of the promise of the 1802 Preface, to describe the role of the reader as well as the role of the poet: "What is a Poet? To whom does he address himself?"

66. For two views of the 1,300 copies sold of *Paradise Lost* in two years, see Raymond Williams, *The Long Revolution* (New York: Columbia Univ. Press, 1984), p. 160, and Richard Altick, *The English Common Reader* (Chicago: Univ. of Chicago Press, 1957), pp. 20–21.

67. On the unpopularity of Wordsworth's collected poems, see Owen and Smyser, *Prose,* III: 55–59.

68. Wordsworth's use of the word genius in describing Spenser and Shakespeare and himself confirms D. D. Devlin's comment that Wordsworth sought to associate himself with a tradition of poets ignored or misunderstood by their contemporaries. *Wordsworth and the Poetry of Epitaphs* (Totowa, NJ: Barnes and Noble, 1981), pp. 36–48.

69. See Reynolds's discussion of inspiration, genius, and imitation in *Discourse* 6: "Genius is supposed to be a power of producing excellencies, which are out of the reach of the rules of art." On the difficulty of defining the term, he continues, the "excellence which proclaims *genius* is different, in different times and different places; and what shews it to be so is, that mankind have often changed their opinion upon this matter," and he suggests of the attitude toward preceding genius, "The true and liberal ground of imitation is an open field . . . to pursue his course, you need not tread in his footsteps."

70. Hunt, in *Lord Byron and Some of his Contemporaries,* reports of Byron, "He

was anxious to show you that he possessed no Shakespeare and Milton; 'because,' he said, 'he had been accused of borrowing from them.'"

71. On Wordsworth's distinction between the idealized praiseworthy "People" and the contemptible "Public," see also Patrick Cruttwell, "Wordsworth, the Public, and the People," *Sewanee Review* 64 (1956): 51–80.

72. Piozzi, p. 157.

73. On Scott's role in the original project, see Lockhart, *Scott*, III: 419, 512, and Austin Dobson's introduction to *Lives of the Novelists* (London: Oxford Univ. Press, 1906), pp. i–x (the text of this edition is not reliable). The course of publication of Scott's *Lives of the Novelists* resembles that of Johnson's *Lives* (although Scott's series does not appear ever to have been printed as a linear chronology). Originally published in the form of introductory matter to *Ballantyne's Novelist's Library*, 10 vols. (London: Hurst, Robinson, 1821–24), Scott's collective biography was pirated minus the reprinted novels as soon as the series ended, as *Lives of the Novelists*, 2 vols. (Paris: Galignani, 1825). Perceiving the demand, Scott republished it in Vol. III of *The Miscellaneous Prose Works of Sir Walter Scott*, 6 vols. (Edinburgh: Cadell, 1827; London: Longman, 1827), a project itself conceived to counter his financial collapse of 1826. The collective biography has frequently been reprinted, but lives written by Scott at other times (for example, *Defoe*) have often been erroneously inserted into the sequence by later editors; Scott printed these extraneous biographies separately in Vol. IV of the *Miscellaneous Prose Works*. The order of lives varies in the editions as shown below; the 1827 is the final form published by Scott. Parenthetic listings indicate authors included in the original series for whom no lives were written.

BALLANTYNE'S NOVELIST'S LIBRARY (1821–24)	MISCELLANEOUS PROSE WORKS (1827)
Fielding	Richardson
Smollett	Fielding
(Cervantes)	Smollett
Johnstone	Cumberland
Le Sage	Goldsmith
Goldsmith	Johnson
Johnson	Sterne
Mackenzie	Mackenzie
Reeve	Walpole
Sterne	Reeve
Walpole	Radcliffe
Richardson	Le Sage
Bage	Johnstone
Cumberland	Bage
(Swift)	
Radcliffe	

74. Review of Scott's *Lives of the Novelists* (*Quarterly Review*, 1826).

75. Nevertheless, Scott was willing to appropriate Wordsworthian arguments in

his endeavor to elicit prestige for the novel. In saying that the novelist constructs a representation of events "by the mere force of an excited imagination" ("Fielding," *Novelists*), and "Every successful novelist must be more or less a poet, even although he may never have written line of verse" ("Smollett," *Novelists*), Scott invokes the indistinction between the language of prose and the language of poetry familiar in Wordsworth's criticism. The novelists' fictions are simply narrative poetry in prose. Scott drew from the arsenal of both Johnson and Wordsworth in order to defend and elevate the novel.

76. Printed in Vol. I of *The Works of John Dryden,* ed. Walter Scott, 18 vols. (London: Miller, 1808); rev. ed., John Gibson Lockhart (Edinburgh: Cadell, 1834).

77. Clara Reeve, *The Progress of Romance,* 2 vols. (Colchester: Keymer, 1785).

78. Carlyle's review of Lockhart's *Scott* (1838) also characterized "Scott's career" as "writing daily with the ardour of a steam-engine, that he might make £15,000 a-year, and buy upholstery with it."

79. The first edition, *Attempts in Verse, by John Jones, an old servant . . . and an introductory essay on the lives and works of our uneducated poets, by Robert Southey* (by subscription, London: Murray, 1831), opens with Southey's essay, followed by the author's account of himself, and then the verses. The second edition the same year inverted the title: *Southey's Lives of the Uneducated Poets: To which is added Attempts in Verse by John Jones, an old servant* (London: Murray, 1831). See J. S. Childers's introduction to the modern edition, pp. vii–x.

80. De Quincey, "Wordsworth and Southey" (*Literary Reminiscences,* 1839); Coleridge quoted in "Robert Southey," *The Dictionary of National Biography* (Oxford: Oxford Univ. Press, 1917), XVIII: 696.

81. Southey's other biographies include: *The Remains of Henry Kirke White . . . with an account of his life,* 2 vols. (London: Vernor, etc., 1807–8); *Life of Wesley,* 2 vols. (London: Longman, 1820); *Works of William Cowper,* 15 vols. (London: Baldwin and Craddock, 1835–37), *Life of Nelson,* 2 vols. (London: Murray, 1813), *Lives of the British Admirals,* 5 vols. (London: Longman, 1833). It is difficult to reconstruct the many projects Southey undertook; for bibliography see William Haller, *The Early Life of Robert Southey* (New York: Columbia Univ. Press, 1917).

82. Review of Southey's *Uneducated Poets* (*Quarterly Review,* 1831).

83. Boswell, II: 127.

84. D'Israeli, *Literary Character* (1795).

85. The idea ultimately derives from Horace's *Ars Poetica;* Boswell, II: 351–52, reports, "Johnson repeated the common remark, that 'as there is no necessity for our having poetry at all, it being merely a luxury, an instrument of pleasure, it can have no value, unless when exquisite in its kind.'"

86. Jameson, p. 106.

CHAPTER IV

1. John Kinnaird is the only critic to analyze Hazlitt's essays as collections, *William Hazlitt: Critic of Power* (New York: Columbia Univ. Press, 1978); Ready, p. 22, calls *Table Talk* a collective sequence.

2. *An Essay on the Principles of Human Action* (1805); *Lectures on English Philosophy* (delivered 1812, printed posthumously, 1836). All citations from Hazlitt's works are from the standard edition, *The Complete Works of William Hazlitt,* ed. P. P. Howe, 21 vols. (London: J. M. Dent, 1930–34), with corrections made from the original book publications.

3. Lamb, unpublished review of *Table Talk* in *Lamb as Critic,* ed. Park; De Quincey, review of Thomas Noon Talfourd's biography of Lamb (1848). Henry Crabb Robinson reports that Hazlitt "said he would never take advantage of a slip in a man's conversation.... I said ... 'your distinction amounts to this: I won't lie, I will only violate the confidence of friendship'" (22 December 1816). *On Books and Their Writers,* ed. Edith J. Morley (London: Dent, 1938), I: 200–201. Citations of Robinson's diaries are from this edition.

4. Hazlitt remarked that he found Holcroft's narrative diary "almost as amusing as Boswell's life," but he may have let Holcroft tell his own story as much from eagerness to rid himself of the obligation to Godwin, as from any biographical principles. See *Letters of William Hazlitt,* ed. H. M. Sikes, W. H. Bonner, G. Lahey (New York: New York Univ. Press, 1978), p. 113; Virgil R. Stallbaumer, "Hazlitt's Life of Thomas Holcroft," *American Benedictine Review* 5 (1954): 31; on *Napoleon,* see Kinnaird, pp. 328–29; Robert Robinson, *William Hazlitt's Life of Napoleon Buonaparte* (Paris: Minard, 1959).

5. Hazlitt called Northcote the last survivor of Johnson's age. Crabb Robinson (16 December 1831, I: 397) wrote, "I do not believe that Boswell gives so much good talk in an equal quantity of any part of his *Life of Johnson.*" The series appeared intermittently in several publications: as "Boswell Redivivus" (*New Monthly Magazine,* 1826–27, suspended for personal references); "Real Conversations" (*London Weekly Review,* 1829, emphasizing accuracy: "The Conversations here presented to the reader are *real,* not 'Imaginary' ... they are set down almost exactly as they passed from the lips of the speakers ... entirely unpremeditated, and consequently spoken without the remotest view to anything but their immediate effect on the person addressed"); "Conversations as Good as Real" (*Atlas,* 1829); "Conversations with an Eminent Living Artist" (*Court Journal,* 1830); see Howe, XI: 351, 357.

6. The anonymous *Liber Amoris* (1823) also includes parts of letters written to P. G. Patmore and James Sheridan Knowles. Lamb saw autobiography elsewhere in Hazlitt; reviewing *Table Talk,* he called it "a bold confession," "Hazlitt's own ways of feeling," "a piece of Autobiography."

7. *The Round Table,* 1817 (with Leigh Hunt); *Table Talk,* 1821–22 (many previously unpublished); *The Plain Speaker,* 1826. As with the *Comic Writers* he frequently would write an essay for a periodical, use it in a lecture, then place it in a book sequence; sketches such as those of Pitt and Burke were reinserted into many essays; he periodically warehoused lists of aphorisms which he would later use in essays (e.g., "Common Places," *Characteristics,* "Trifles as Light as Air").

8. "My First Acquaintance with Poets" (1823).

9. "On the Living Poets" (*English Poets*). In "On the Causes of Popular Opinion" (1828), he wrote, "I have been accused of inconsistency, for writing an essay,

for instance, on the Advantages of Pedantry, and another, on the *Ignorance of the Learned,* as if ignorance had not its comforts as well as knowledge." Many essays rely on inversion: "On Good Nature" (1816) redefines those with good nature as selfish, and those with ill nature, altruistic.

10. "On the Periodical Essayists" (*Comic Writers*); "Preface" (*Characters of Shakespear's Plays,* 1817). Johnson, however, opened his *Preface to Shakespeare* (1765) complaining of those who "hope for eminence from the heresies of paradox"; and Boswell, I: 441, reports him saying, "'Rousseau, and all those who deal in paradoxes, are led away by a childish desire of novelty.'"

11. Cunningham, *Biographical and Critical History* (1833); Hunt, *Lord Byron and Some of his Contemporaries* (1828). "On Paradox and Common Place" (1821); "On the Causes of Popular Opinion" (1828).

12. This example of the involuntary subjectivity of the reader occurs in: "On the Works of Hogarth" (*Comic Writers*), "On Hogarth's Marriage A-La-Mode," "Why the Arts are not Progressive," "All's Well That Ends Well" (*Shakespear's Plays*), "Sismondi's Literature of the South," "Fine Arts: Whether they are Promoted by Academies and Public Institutions," *Sketches of the Principal Picture Galleries in England.*

13. "Preface" (*Shakespear's Plays*); "On Shakspeare and Milton" and "On Swift, Young, Gray, Collins" (*English Poets*). P. G. Patmore, *My Friends and Acquaintance* (London: Saunders and Otley, 1854), II: 276, 300. Both Johnson and Hazlitt ironically describe the critical task as one of negation and intimidation: "Censure is willingly indulged, because it always implies some superiority; men please themselves with imagining that they have made a deeper search, or a wider survey, than others, and detected faults and follies, which escape vulgar observation" (*Rambler* 2); "Something of this overbearing manner goes a great way with the public. They cannot exactly tell whether you are right or wrong; and if you state your difficulties or pay much deference to the sentiments of others, they will think you a very silly fellow or a mere pretender. . . . A sharp, sententious cavalier, dogmatical tone is therefore necessary, even in self-defence, to the office of a reviewer" ("On Criticism," 1821).

14. Park, *Hazlitt,* p. 216; R. L. Brett, *William Hazlitt* (London: Longman, 1977), p. 5; review of the 1835 reissue of *The Spirit of the Age* (*Tait's,* 1836). Hazlitt used the biographical term to describe his critical methodology (e.g., *Characters of Shakespear's Plays*), he titled his maxims *Characteristics,* and he also wrote various "characters" in the manner of Theophrastus and Thomas Overbury (e.g., "On the Clerical Character").

15. "Jeremy Bentham" (*Spirit of the Age*); "My First Acquaintance with Poets."

16. Review of Spence's *Anecdotes* (1820); review of Lady Morgan's *Life of Salvator Rosa* (1824).

17. "On Thought and Action" (1821); "Elia, and Geoffrey Crayon" (*Spirit of the Age*). In "On the Knowledge of Character" (1822) he observed, "There are various ways of getting at a knowledge of character—by looks, words, actions. The first of these, which seems the most superficial, is perhaps the safest, and least liable to deceive."

18. "On the Imitation of Nature" (1814); "On the Periodical Essayists" (*Comic Writers*). Johnson said of this portrait of his weak eyes, "'He may paint himself as deaf if he chuses,'" referring to Reynolds's self-portrait, "'but I will not be *blinking Sam*.'" Piozzi, p. 142.

19. "On the Causes of Popular Opinion" (1828): Coleridge "encouraged me to write a book, which I did according to the original bent of my mind, making it as dry and meagre as I could. . . . Finding this method did not answer, I despaired for a time: but some trifle I wrote in the Morning Chronicle meeting the approbation of the Editor and the town, I resolved to turn over a new leaf—to take the public at its word, to muster all the tropes and figures I could lay hands on. . . . the paradoxes may be accounted for in the same way." In the unpublished "A Reply to 'Z'" (1818), Hazlitt recounted, "I attempted a more popular style and succeeded."

Coleridge in the *Biographia* (I: 156) also addressed the mystifications of symbolic representation: "An IDEA, in the *highest* sense of that word, cannot be conveyed but by a *symbol;* and, except in geometry, all symbols of necessity involve an apparent contradiction."

20. "On the Works of Hogarth" (*Comic Writers*).

21. "On Dryden and Pope" (*English Poets*). Hazlitt's paired judgments include: Chaucer's dealings with the world braced his understanding, Spenser's alienated him; Shakespeare and Milton opposites; *Mac Flecknoe* superior to the *Dunciad;* Thomson too slovenly, Cowper too finicky; Bloomfield too much the farmer's boy, Crabbe too much the parish beadle; Collins more of a poetical genius than Gray; Campbell deliberates, Moore is exuberant.

22. Hume writes, "It is impossible to continue in the practice of contemplating any order of beauty, without being frequently obliged to form *comparisons*" (1757); Johnson writes, "Nothing can be styled excellent till it has been compared with other works" (1765). Jean Hagstrum, *Samuel Johnson's Literary Criticism* (Minneapolis: Univ. of Minnesota Press, 1952), pp. 28–29.

23. Hume began translating Plutarch in 1752 according to T. H. Green and T. H. Grose, editors of Hume's *Philosophical Works*, 4 vols. (London: Longmans, Green, 1898), p. 59. All citations of Hume are from this text, with corrections. The volumes on the Stuarts in Hume's *History of England* came out in 1754 and 1757.

24. But Tillinghast cautions not to "suggest too close a relationship nor a thoroughly consistent one"; see above, Chapter I, note 33.

25. On philosophical writing as a genre of nonfictional prose, exhibiting its own tropes and conventions of discourse, see Jacques Derrida, "White Mythology: Metaphor in the Text of Philosophy" (orig. 1971), *Margins of Philosophy*, pp. 209–11, 221; John Richetti, *Philosophical Writing: Locke, Berkeley, Hume* (Cambridge: Harvard Univ. Press, 1985), pp. 189–90.

26. E. D. Hirsch argues from the cases of Hazlitt and Coleridge, that the term literature still had not yet found its special aesthetic connotations by the time of the Romantic era. *The Aims of Interpretation* (Chicago: Univ. of Chicago Press, 1976), pp. 131–32. De Quincey, however, speaking of "that great social organ which, collectively, we call literature," distinguishes it as a particular kind of verbal discourse: "Books . . . do not suggest an idea coextensive and interchangeable

with the idea of Literature," and excludes scientific, oratoric, and didactic uses of language (Review of Roscoe's edition of Pope, 1848; see also Letter III, "Letters to a Young Man," 1823). John Gross discusses the broad term "man of letters," *The Rise and Fall of the Man of Letters* (New York: Collier, 1969), pp. xiiiff. The Romantics' distaste for constraining the imagination by imitating inherited categories of literature did not prevent them from redefining preceding genres (e.g., Wordsworth's epic of the self). See Stuart Curran, *Poetic Form and British Romanticism* (New York: Oxford Univ. Press, 1986), on the myth of radical generic breakdown.

27. The *Quarterly Review* (1818) said Hazlitt preferred "the character of the philosophical reasoner," but substituted "the rapid succession of antic forms in which the same or nearly the same thought is exhibited" in place of accurate reasoning and precise language. What Kinnaird, p. 145, says of "gusto," that Hazlitt sought to infuse conversational terms "with philosophical consistency of meaning," is true of Hazlitt's approach to other belletristic topics. Defining genius, "The Indian Jugglers" (1819) only develops a nomenclature for differentiating non-genius (cleverness, accomplishments, talent) from "the Muses' gift." Comparing the aesthetic essays of Hume and Hazlitt, the distinction in systematization is evident: Hazlitt establishes himself as the critical taster for the public; Hume frames analytical questions, "Where are such critics to be found? By what marks are they to be known? How distinguish them from pretenders?" ("The Standard of Taste," 1757).

28. Park, *Hazlitt*, pp. 15, 97–98; Elizabeth Schneider, *The Aesthetics of William Hazlitt: A Study of the Philosophical Basis of His Criticism* (Philadelphia: Univ. of Pennsylvania Press, 1933), p. 20; W. P. Albrecht, *Hazlitt and the Creative Imagination* (Lawrence: Univ. of Kansas Press, 1965), pp. 7, 10, 14; David Bromwich, *Hazlitt, The Mind of a Critic* (New York: Oxford Univ. Press, 1983), pp. 88, 118.

29. Jerome Christiansen's description of Hume—that in moving from a philosophical to a more popular literary mode, Hume did not plan a career, he made a series of career adjustments—is also true of Hazlitt. *Practicing Enlightenment: Hume and the Formation of a Literary Career* (Madison: Univ. of Wisconsin Press, 1987), p. 135. On Hazlitt's praise of Hume, see the *Lectures on English Philosophy*, the review of Coleridge's *Lay Sermon*, and "My First Acquaintance with Poets," where he refutes Coleridge, who "denied the excellence of Hume's general style, which I think betrayed a want of taste or candour."

30. In his 1776 autobiography "My Own Life," posthumously published and designed as a preface for his works, Hume said his *Treatise of Human Nature* "fell *dead-born from the Press*" (possibly paraphrasing Pope's "Epilogue to the Satires," Dialogue II, "drops dead-born from the Press," 1738). He explained that the unpopularity of the *Treatise of Human Nature* (1739–40) "proceeded more from the manner than the matter," so he recast it as the *Enquiry Concerning Human Understanding* (1748, 1750), after making a trial of the new literary and metaphorical style in the *Essays, Moral and Political* (1741–42). The opening passage of the *Enquiry* observes that "the most durable as well as justest fame" will go to that philosophical writing which borrows "all helps from poetry and eloquence":

"Addison, perhaps, will be read with pleasure when Locke shall be entirely forgotten."

31. Johnson discusses the progress of the arts in *Pope:* "There is a time when nations emerging from barbarity, and falling into regular subordination, gain leisure to grow wise. . . . but repletion generates fastidiousness, a saturated intellect soon becomes luxurious, and knowledge finds no willing reception till it is recommended by artificial diction. Thus it will be found in the progress of learning that in all nations the first writers are simple, and that every age improves in elegance. One refinement always makes way for another, and what was expedient to Virgil was necessary to Pope."

32. To declare in favor of the ancients that the best one can strive for is imitation presupposes that the potential for originality in the arts has declined. See Richard Foster Jones, *Ancients and Moderns: A Study of the Background of The Battle of the Books* (St. Louis: Washington State Univ. Press, 1936); Lois Whitney, *Primitivism and the Idea of Progress in English Popular Literature of the Eighteenth Century* (Baltimore: Johns Hopkins Univ. Press, 1934); John D. Scheffer, "The Idea of Decline in Literature and the Fine Arts in Eighteenth Century England," *Modern Philology* 34 (1936): 159; W. J. Bate, *The Burden of the Past and the English Poet* (Cambridge: Harvard Univ. Press, 1970), pp. 80–84; René Wellek, "The Concept of Evolution in Literary History," in *Concepts of Criticism* (New Haven: Yale Univ. Press, 1963), pp. 37–53. It is helpful to restate in terms of other eighteenth-century positions what Hume's idea of decline is not: it is not a mysterious retrogression; nor caused by a corruption of values, a love of mere novelty or laziness on the part of the poets; nor the effeminate consequence of luxury; nor the result of too rigid a codification of critical principles.

33. Thomas Noon Talfourd's "An Attempt to Estimate the Poetical Talent of the Present Age," *Pamphleteer* (1815), provides an abbreviated canon of living authors with a characterization of their works. Cunningham, *Biographical and Critical History* (1833); Hazlitt, "The Periodical Press" (1823); D'Israeli, *Literary Character* (1795).

34. Hazlitt asks the same question in "Mr. Coleridge" (*Spirit of the Age*): "What *niche* remains unoccupied? What path untried?"

35. The first version is the two-part "Fragments on Art. Why the Arts are not Progressive?" (1814); revised as the last essay "Why the Arts are not Progressive: A Fragment" in the *Round Table* (1817), quoted here; and later partly embedded into "On Shakspeare and Milton," in the *English Poets* (1818). Hazlitt complains of the caprice and incompetence of audiences, and rejects the notion of a gradual improvement in public taste; here and in "Fine Arts: Whether they are Promoted by Academies and Public Institutions," "The Periodical Press," and "What is the People?," his reputed egalitarianism is undercut by critical elitism and contempt for audience.

36. Unlike Hume, Hazlitt distinguishes between the rise of the arts and the rise of the sciences, as Joseph Priestley had (see Scheffer, pp. 174–75), and as Macaulay was to do (1828 review of Henry Neele's *The Romance of History*). "Why the Arts are not Progressive" explains that sciences depend "on mere inquiry and experi-

ment, or on absolute demonstration," and thus mature cumulatively over time, whereas in the arts, the greatest geniuses arise soon after the birth of the arts and then decline ever after.

37. Kinnaird, p. 219.

38. Boswell, V: 35.

39. The original series was: Bentham, Edward Irving, Tooke, Scott, and Eldon. The plural term "spirits" has different connotations; for example, in "On the Cockney School of Poetry" (*Blackwood's,* 1818), Lockhart ridicules Keats for calling Wordsworth, Hazlitt, and Haydon the three greatest "spirits of the age." Isaac D'Israeli spoke of the "geniuses of the age," as well as the "genius of the age," the "state of the times," the "spirit of the times." De Quincey was to speak of the "spirit of the times" and the "temper of the age." For the Shakespearian use of "spirits of the age," see Patrick Story, "Hazlitt's Definition of the Spirit of the Age," *Wordsworth Circle* 6 (1975): 101. Common in British publishing was the journal dedicated to summarizing and reprinting articles from other journals: the eighteenth-century *Magazine of Magazines,* the Victorian *Review of Reviews,* and in the age giving rise to consciousness of the *Zeitgeist,* the *Spirit of the Public Journals* (1797–1813 and 1823–25), in 1825 changing its name to *Spirit of the Times.*

40. Conceived in response to Peacock's 1820 "Four Ages of Poetry," Shelley's *Defence of Poetry,* written in 1821, was intended for publication in Byron and Hunt's *The Liberal* but was printed posthumously in 1840; the passage appears in a similar form in the first chapter of *A Philosophical View of Reform* (written 1819–20, printed 1886). In the "Letter to Maria Gisborne" (1820), Shelley describes Godwin as standing at the last judgment "Among the spirits of our age and land."

41. "Of Refinement in the Arts" was retitled eight years after its original publication in the *Political Discourses* (1752) under the title "Of Luxury." The word "arts" implies the broad sense of mechanical, liberal, and intellectual arts and sciences. Hume uses the term luxury to mean a refinement in development of the arts, not a prodigality in consumption: luxury is pernicious only when associated with indolence, selfishness, and vice. Hume counters the traditional moralist assumption that refinement is intrinsically bad; Kames, for example, says the cause of decline in society is luxury; see Scheffer, p. 161. Johnson observed, "'Many things which are false are transmitted from book to book, and gain credit in the world. One of these is the cry against the evil of luxury. Now the truth is, that luxury produces much good.'" Boswell, III: 55–56.

42. Hume's applause of the progress of refinement in "Of Refinement" implies a relative indifference to the poetic decline which must accompany it (according to "The Rise and Progress"). In "Of Simplicity and Refinement in Writing" (1742) Hume specifically denounces the "excess of refinement" that emerges "after learning has made some progress, and after eminent writers have appeared in every species of composition."

43. Stockdale's comment in the *Lectures on the Truly Eminent English Poets* reflects the currency of the concept of *Zeitgeist* (D'Israeli remarks, "Every work of genius is tinctured by the feelings and often originates in the events, of the times,"

Literary Character, 1822, rev. from 1818), although a similar notion is voiced as far back as Dryden: "Every age has a kind of universal genius, which inclines those that live in it to some particular studies" (*An Essay of Dramatic Poesy*, 1668). Shelley's claim that the poet was "herald, companion, and follower," begged the question of the relation between artist and culture. Later collective biographies, however, argued precise relations between the age and the individual artist, "great man," or "representative man": Carlyle, *On Heroes, Hero-worship, and the Heroic in History* (delivered 1840, printed 1841); Emerson, *Representative Men* (delivered in America 1845–56, in England 1847–48, printed 1850); Arnold, *Essays in Criticism: First Series* (1865); Pater, *The Renaissance* (1873); Strachey, *Eminent Victorians* (1918). Arnold's *Essays in Criticism: Second Series* (1888) and Macaulay's uncollected biographical essays of the 1820s and 1830s deal with similar issues (Macaulay's view of historical inevitability appears in the 1828 review of Dryden's works: "It is the age that forms the man, not the man that forms the age. Great minds do indeed react on the society which has made them what they are; but they only pay with interest what they have received"; not only does the age dictate the direction of genius, it will find expression regardless of its individuals; had Luther been born in a different time he would not have been a church reformer, and had he never been born, there would have been a sixteenth-century schism anyway). Sainte-Beuve's *Portraits contemporains* (collected 1846) established a French tradition that led to Taine's interest in "*la race, le milieu, et le moment*," in *Histoire de la littérature Anglaise* (1864); Taine viewed himself as indebted to Sainte-Beuve, although *race* and *moment* correlate with *Volksgeist* and *Zeitgeist*. Unlike Hume's spirit of the age, Marx sees no direct equation between art and culture: "In the case of the arts, it is well known that certain periods of their flowering are out of all proportion to the general development of society" (*Grundrisse*, 1857).

For modern studies of the relation between the individual and history, see Braudy, pp. 55–59, and Sidney Hook, *The Hero in History* (Boston: Beacon, 1943), pp. 59–62; on terms, see René Wellek, *A History of Modern Criticism* (New Haven: Yale Univ. Press, 1955–86), I: 27, 41, II: 212, III: 37–39, IV: 29–31, 47.

44. Herschel Baker, *William Hazlitt* (Cambridge: Harvard Univ. Press, 1962), p. 433.

45. The *Monthly Magazine*'s panegyrical *Contemporary Authors* series (Baillie's imagery is "superior to Shakespeare") ran intermittently from July 1817 to November 1820. The *Athenaeum*'s sentimental *Sketches of Contemporary Authors* series (authored by F. D. Maurice, according to Kinnaird, p. 302) ran January to July 1828 (Wordsworth "has shown us how precious are the associations connected with the foot-print of the clouted shoe"). Richard Hengist Horne (assisted by Elizabeth Barrett Browning and Robert Bell) in *A New Spirit of the Age*, 2 vols. (1844), added a new generation of names, some more names from Hazlitt's generation (Sydney Smith and Mary Shelley), and reconsidered Hunt and Wordsworth. See the modern edition, ed. Walter Jerrold (New York: Oxford Univ. Press, 1907). George Gilfillian's *A Gallery of Literary Portraits* (1845), originally written as essays in the 1840s for the *Dumfriesshire and Galloway Herald* (*A Second*

Gallery of Literary Portraits, 1850; *A Third Gallery of Portraits,* 1854), included preachers, poets, politicians, and Hazlitt himself, and reconsidered many of the same figures. The narrative originality and critical acumen of writers such as Hazlitt and De Quincey stand out most sharply when seen against the background of such pedestrian sequences.

46. John Scott's *Living Authors* series began with the first issue of *London Magazine* in January 1820 (W. Scott, Wordsworth, Godwin, Byron, and in May 1821, Hazlitt's Crabbe). Leigh Hunt's *Sketches of the Living Poets* ran in the *Examiner* from July through October 1821 (Bowles, Byron, Campbell, Coleridge; references to a projected installment on Wordsworth indicate it was planned as a longer sequence). See the modern edition in *Leigh Hunt's Literary Criticism,* ed. L. H. and C. W. Houtchens (New York: Columbia Univ. Press, 1956). Both were critically more sophisticated than other series on contemporary figures.

47. Longaker, *Contemporary Biography,* p. 11. The belief in *Zeitgeist* is not unique to Europe: Bloch, p. 35, quotes a Middle Eastern proverb, "Men resemble their times more than they do their fathers."

48. Arnold, *Culture and Anarchy* (1869). In "William Godwin" (*Spirit of the Age*), Hazlitt said he would rather live in the age of Scott and *Blackwood's* than in the time of Scott's novels (a considerable concession to the present since *Blackwood's* had been Hazlitt's chief adversary). The republicanism that frequently induced Hazlitt to declaim against the argument of Legitimacy made him unwilling to posit obedience to government and custom as a solution to lawlessness.

49. Hazlitt wrote Walter Savage Landor, "You can hardly suppose the depression of body and mind under which I wrote some of those articles," *Letters,* p. 338. "The Pleasure of Hating" hints a despair of seeing the political ascendancy of his views in his lifetime. Howe, XII: 400, and Story, pp. 99–101, see the essay as a précis for *The Spirit of the Age* because some figures are described in both.

50. In contrast, thematic essays open Virginia Woolf's *The Common Reader* (1925), and close Edmund Wilson's *The Wound and the Bow* (1941).

51. Although *The Spirit of the Age: or, Contemporary Portraits* was published anonymously in England like Hazlitt's other works at the time, P. G. Patmore says his authorship was rapidly known; recounted by W. C. Hazlitt, *Memoirs of William Hazlitt* (London: Bentley, 1867), II: 214. The first edition (London: Colburn, 1825) was slightly modified for the third and final edition (London: Colburn, 1825, labeled second edition); the discarded sequence of the second edition (Paris: Galignani, 1825) foregrounded the most famous of the English writers for its Continental audience; changes were evidently made under Hazlitt's direction. Due to an error of judgment in the standard edition of Hazlitt, however, the sequence most commonly read and reprinted today is a modern version not designed or published by Hazlitt: P. P. Howe substitutes "Character of Mr. Canning" (1824) for the essay on Cobbett (orig. "Character of Cobbett," 1821). Both were added to the Paris edition to compensate for some deletions, but only Cobbett was retained for the final London edition. The three sequences, all printed in 1825, are as follows:

LONDON		PARIS	LONDON
1ST ED.		2ND ED.	3RD ED.
ANON.		2 VOLS.	ANON.
Bentham	*Vol. I:*	Byron	Bentham
Godwin		Scott	Godwin
Coleridge		Coleridge	Coleridge
Irving		Southey	Irving
Tooke		Wordsworth	Tooke
Scott		Campbell-Crabbe	Scott
Byron		Bentham	Byron
Campbell-Crabbe		Godwin	Southey
Mackintosh	*Vol. II:*	Irving	Wordsworth
Wordsworth		Tooke	Mackintosh
Malthus		Mackintosh	Malthus
Gifford		Malthus	Gifford
Jeffrey		Gifford	Jeffrey
Brougham-Burdett		Jeffrey	Brougham-Burdett
Eldon-Wilberforce		Brougham-Burdett	Eldon-Wilberforce
Southey		Eldon-Wilberforce	Cobbett
Moore-Hunt		Canning	Campbell-Crabbe
Elia-Crayon		Cobbett	Moore-Hunt
		Elia	Elia-Crayon

52. Plutarchan pairings surface within chapters ("Mr. Brougham—Sir F. Burdett," "Lord Eldon—Mr. Wilberforce," "Mr. Campbell—Mr. Crabbe," "Mr. T. Moore—Mr. Leigh Hunt," "Elia, and Geoffrey Crayon," Cobbett and Thomas Paine, Edward Irving and Thomas Chalmers) as well as in the adjacent chapter juxtapositions.

53. See, for example, Story, pp. 102–7, and Ralph M. Wardle, *Hazlitt* (Lincoln: Univ. of Nebraska Press, 1971), p. 404.

54. Vytautos Kavolis, "Literature and the Dialectics of Modernism," in *Literary Criticism and Sociology,* ed. Joseph P. Strelka (University Park: Pennsylvania State Univ. Press, 1973), pp. 101, 105; Levin, p. 30; Albrecht, pp. 59–60; M. H. Abrams, "English Romanticism: The Spirit of the Age," in *Romanticism Reconsidered,* ed. Northrop Frye (New York: Columbia Univ. Press, 1963), pp. 26ff.; Park, *Hazlitt,* pp. 235–36; Story, pp. 97, 103, 107; Wardle, p. 404; Wellek, *Modern Criticism,* II: 107; George Levine, ed., *The Emergence of a Victorian Consciousness: The Spirit of the Age* (New York: Free Press, 1967), p. 14.

55. Michel Foucault, *The Archaeology of Knowledge* (London: Tavistock, 1972, orig. 1969), pp. 4–8, 15, 21–22; one might say Foucault attempts to demystify the term spirit through the intellectual unit he calls episteme.

56. *The Order of Things* (New York: Random House, 1973, orig. 1966), Part II, pp. 217ff., posits a major intellectual transformation at the end of the eighteenth century which Foucault declines to give a name; in the English foreword (p. xiv) he denies using the concepts of structuralism, although in the introduction to *The Archaeology of Knowledge* he admits the label (p. 11).

57. Boswell's *Hebrides* justification, V: 414–15, continues, "What pleasure would it have given us, to have known their petty habits, their characteristick manners, their modes of composition, and their genuine opinion of preceding writers and of their contemporaries! All these are now irrecoverably lost"; De Quincey, "William Wordsworth," I (*Literary Reminiscences, 1839*); Hazlitt, review of Spence's *Anecdotes*.

58. "Lord Byron" (*Spirit of the Age*); "On Chaucer and Spenser" (*English Poets*). The latter unwittingly illuminates the risk of such cavalier biographical inferences, for one of the poems Hazlitt discusses is the popularly misattributed "The Flower and the Leaf."

59. Review of Spence's *Anecdotes;* "On Burns, and the old English Ballads" (*English Poets*).

60. "On the Living Poets" (*English Poets*). Wordsworth's "Yarrow Unvisited," written 1803, printed 1807, leaves the river to the imagination; "Yarrow Visited," written 1814, printed 1815, shows how subjective impressions derived from literature are brought to scenery, "I see—but not by sight alone"; "Yarrow Revisited," written 1831, printed 1835, describes how in revisiting the river with Walter Scott, it acquires new associations.

61. Hazlitt did not pursue the theory in writing *The Spirit of the Age* (1825) or other case studies, perhaps cautious after the unfavorable reaction to *Liber Amoris* (1823); he claims the death of Byron in 1824 made him reconsider the criticisms he had begun in the Byron chapter.

62. Sigmund Freud, *Leonardo da Vinci and a Memory of His Childhood* (New York: Norton, 1964, orig. 1910), p. 80.

63. Edmund Wilson, *The Wound and the Bow: Seven Studies in Literature* (Boston: Houghton Mifflin, 1941).

64. Johnson records Pope's statement that he was enfeebled by application to study; D'Israeli describes Collins as a one of "our martyrs to the lyre" (*Calamities*). When Johnson ironically laments the "malady" of writing in *Rambler* 2, he is cautioning against the excessive hope of fame from writing: "I shall, therefore, while I am yet but lightly touched with the symptoms of the writer's malady, endeavour to fortify myself against the infection."

65. "On Paradox and Common Place" (1821).

66. Freud continues, "'What I discovered was the scientific method by which the unconscious can be studied.'" See Meredith Anne Skura, *The Literary Uses of the Psychoanalytic Process* (New Haven: Yale Univ. Press, 1981), p. 1; Lionel Trilling, "Freud and Literature" (1940) and "Art and Neurosis" (1945), reprinted in *The Liberal Imagination* (New York: Viking, 1950). Wordsworth's 1800 note to "The Thorn" declares, "Poetry is passion: it is the history or science of feelings."

67. Freud declares, "Pathography does not in the least aim at making the great

man's achievements intelligible," and explains "if psycho-analysis does not throw light on the fact of Leonardo's artistic power, it at least renders its manifestations and its limitations intelligible to us." Of the psychobiographical task he says, "It does not detract from his greatness if we make a study of the sacrifices which his development from childhood must have entailed." *Leonardo,* pp. 13, 80–81, 86. Later describing *Leonardo,* he repeated, "The layman may perhaps expect too much from analysis in this respect, for it must be admitted that it throws no light upon the two problems which probably interest him the most. It can do nothing towards elucidating the nature of the artistic gift, nor can it explain the means by which the artist works—artistic technique." *An Autobiographical Study* (New York: Norton, 1952, orig. 1925), pp. 122–24. Like Freud and the Romantics, in suggesting "the idea that genius and disease, like strength and mutilation, may be inextricably bound up together," Wilson resists a predictive model of compensation or sublimation.

68. Both papers ran anonymously in the *Examiner*'s column, *The Round Table,* Hazlitt's on 15 October 1815, and Hunt's on 5 November 1815 (and appeared in the same order reprinted in the book *The Round Table* in 1817). Byron gives no sign of recognizing Hazlitt's work, but his letter ends with an additional paragraph apparently referring to Hunt's essay, "I have not had time nor paper to attack your *system,* which ought to be done, were it only because it is a *system.*" Hunt closes the Byron chapter in *Lord Byron and Some of his Contemporaries* with several of Byron's letters to him, this being the last. Neither Hunt nor Leslie Marchand identifies Hazlitt as the author of the paper on Methodism, although Marchand guesses the date of the letter as 4–6 November 1815 (*Letters,* IV: 332; punctuation differs slightly).

69. Hunt in *Lord Byron and Some of his Contemporaries* says Byron tried to conceal his lameness in his preference for riding over walking, and a lounging gait: "It was a shrunken foot, a little twisted. This defect unquestionably mortified him exceedingly, and helped to put sarcasm and misanthropy into his taste of life." Byron answered when someone observed that the street boys recognized him, "Every one knows me—I am deformed," Lovell, p. 53.

70. Compare Byron's earlier formulation of the idea in the 29 November 1813 letter to Annabella Milbanke (*Letters,* III: 179): "I by no means rank poetry or poets high in the scale of intellect—this may look like Affectation—but it is my real opinion—it is the lava of the imagination whose eruption prevents an earthquake—they say Poets never or rarely go *mad*—Cowper & Collins are instances to the contrary—(but Cowper was no poet)—it is however to be remarked that they rarely do—but are generally so near it—that I cannot help thinking rhyme is so far useful in anticipating & preventing the disorder."

Byron's enlargement of this idea in his letter to Richard Belgrave Hoppner, 25 November 1818 (*Letters,* VI: 85), amounts to an extended commentary on Johnson's *Lives:* "We are all heirs to misfortune and disappointments—but *poets* especially seem to be a marked race—who has not heard of the blindness of *Milton*—the wretched life, and still more unhappy death of *Otway*—the long sufferings & unrequited services of *Cowley* and of *Butler*—the struggles against poverty & malice which occupied the life of *Dryden*—the constitutional infirmities which embittered the existence of *Pope*—the lamentable idiocy & madness of *Swift*—the almost unparalleled miseries and unhappy end of *Savage*—the frenzy of *Collins*—the indigence of *Goldsmith*—the morbid melancholy and sullen discontent of *Johnson*—the hypochrondrianism of *Gray* and of *Beattie*—the tragical catastrophe of *Chatterton*—the disappointed hopes and premature death of *Burns*—and the sickness, despondency, and madness of *Cowper*."

71. Byron's letters to John Murray, 24 November 1818 and 9 October 1821 (*Letters*, VI: 83–84, VIII: 237). D'Israeli's 1840 Preface declares Byron's interest was "the immediate cause" of republication of *The Literary Character*. The 1818 Preface explains that having obtained Byron's copy of the 1795 edition, and finding it "had been twice read by him in two subsequent years, at Athens, in 1810 and 1811, instantly convinced me that the volume deserved my attention." In 1822 and 1828 D'Israeli added more of Byron's comments.

72. "—Except such as treat of Turkey" (recounted in the preface to the 1828 *Literary Character*). These annotations appear in Byron's copy of the 1818 *Literary Character*. His marginal notes chiefly arise in response to passages where D'Israeli mentions him. He inscribed and presented the book to Captain J. B. Fyler in Greece shortly before his death (now in the Meyer Davis collection, University of Pennsylvania).

73. The 1828 Preface included Byron's letter of 10 June 1822, written in response to D'Israeli's presentation copy of the 1822 edition. "I really cannot know whether I am, or am not, the genius you are pleased to call me," Byron added. "If there are any questions which you would like to ask me, as connected with your Philosophy of the literary Mind (*if* mine be a literary mind), I will answer them fairly or give a reason for *not*, good—bad—or indifferent" (*Letters*, IX: 172–73, punctuation differs slightly). D'Israeli wrote back welcoming more comments, but Byron was on his way to Greece. See Ogden, *D'Israeli*, pp. 107–9, 116–20. D'Israeli also presented Robert Southey with a copy of the 1822 edition (now in the Princeton University Library).

Byron frequently assessed the physical and mental attributes of genius. Striving to lose weight, he told James Smith (*New Monthly Magazine*, 1827), "No man of genius was ever fat," Lovell, pp. 132–33. In the Ravenna Journal (6 January 1821, *Letters*, VIII: 16) he wrote, "I feel a something, which makes me think that, if I ever reach near to old age, like Swift, 'I shall die at top' first." Later that year he meditated, "Plutarch says in his life of Lysander—that Aristotle observes, 'that in general great Geniuses are of a melancholy turn, and instances Socrates—Plato, and Hercules (or Heracleitus) as examples—and Lysander—though not—*while* young—yet—as inclined to it when approaching towards age.'—Whether I am a Genius or not—I have been called such by my friends as well as enemies—and in more countries and languages—than one—and also within a no very long period of existence.—Of my Genius—I can say nothing—but of my melancholy that it is 'increasing—& ought to be diminished' but how?—" (Detached Thoughts 104, 15 October 1821, *Letters*, IX: 47).

74. Joseph Warton's *Essay on the Genius and Writings of Pope* (Vol. II, 1782) labels

Pope an exception to the norm of *mens sana in corpore sano* and depicts the "grace" and "agility" of Petrarch, and the "elegance and urbanity" of Boccaccio.

75. Lamb's essay "The Sanity of True Genius" (1826) discredits truisms about madness and creativity by observing that madness is the sole analogy ordinary minds can find (originally published in *New Monthly Magazine* under the series heading *Popular Fallacies,* "That great Wit is allied to Madness"). Scott, 1808 autobiographical fragment (published 1837). De Quincey writes in *Suspiria de Profundis* (1845) that only in the "convulsion" of creativity, opium derangement or imminent death can the palimpsest of memory be read: "Everlasting layers of ideas, images, feelings, have fallen upon your brain. . . . have inscribed themselves successively upon the palimpsest of your brain; and, like the annual leaves of aboriginal forests, or the undissolving snows on the Himalaya . . . the endless strata have covered up each other in forgetfulness. But by the hour of death, but by fever, but by the searchings of opium, all these can revive in strength. They are not dead, but sleeping."

76. Chapter 2 of the *Biographia Literaria* (I: 30, 37, 42), subtitled "Supposed irritability of men of Genius," implicitly counters D'Israeli's position by describing the irritable as literary impostors, who have "tempers rendered yet more irritable by their desire to *appear* men of genius." See above, Chapter III, note 27. Byron may lie behind Coleridge's observation that an age may sometimes make a writer more popular than the writings could have done: "Yet even in instances of this kind, a close examination will often detect, that the irritability, which has been attributed to the author's *genius* as its cause, did really originate in an ill conformation of body, obtuse pain, or constitutional defect of pleasurable sensation. What is charged to the *author,* belongs to the *man,* who would probably have been still more impatient, but for the humanizing influences of the very pursuit, which yet bears the blame of his irritability." Hazlitt's denial, "No really great man ever thought himself so" ("Whether Genius is Conscious of its Powers?" 1826) indirectly counters D'Israeli's lists of self-conscious genius; in "On the Literary Character" (1813) on intellectual overexertion and in "On Egotism" (1825) on mistaking irritability for genius, he also revives themes from D'Israeli. Keats's letter to Richard Woodhouse on the chameleon poet begins, like the *Biographia,* by referencing the "'genus irritabile'" (27 October 1818, *Letters,* I: 386).

77. In contrast to Hazlitt's comments on Shelley's "philosophical fanaticism" ("On Paradox and Common Place"), Coleridge rejects the association of poets with "fanaticism," and notes the misconceptions arising from "Dryden's famous line 'Great wit' (which here means genius) 'to madness sure is near allied.'" Reluctant to probe the sources of his own unproductivity, Coleridge traces his creativity or absence of it only to "constitutional indolence, aggravated into languor by ill-health": "It never occurred to me to believe or fancy, that the quantum of intellectual power bestowed on me by nature or education was in any way connected with this habit of my feelings; or that it needed any other parents or fosterers, than constitutional indolence, aggravated into languor by ill-health; the accumulating embarrassments of procrastination; the mental cowardice, which is the inseparable companion of procrastination." *Biographia,* I: 31, 33, 44–45.

78. Coleridge's introduction to "Kubla Khan," "The following fragment is here published at the request of a poet of great and deserved celebrity, and, as far as the Author's own opinions are concerned, rather as a psychological curiosity than on the ground of any supposed *poetic* merits," implies Byron read the poem between its composition in 1797–98 and publication in 1816.

79. The poet/Mariner's death-in-life (immortality through verse but tormented while alive) reappears in Coleridge's autographic epitaph: "He who many a year with toil of breath / Found death in life, may here find life in death!" (1833).

80. Hunt's original paper lists Tasso, Racine, Cowper, Collins, and Alfieri; the exception proves the rule, for Parnell's bad spirits resulted from his widowhood, Chatterton's high spirits were overset by pain, and Kirke White was "a martyr to study." Unlike Hazlitt and D'Israeli, Hunt lists at length poets who enjoyed good health. Hunt particularly argues against Hazlitt's assertion that poets possess "*original* poverty of spirit," saying it is only "*occasional* or *incidental*."

81. Leigh Hunt, *Lord Byron and Some of his Contemporaries; with Recollections of the Author's Life and of his Visit to Italy* (London: Colburn, 1828). The quarto was reissued as octavo later that year, and was pirated in Paris and Philadelphia. All citations here are from the second edition, 2 vols. (London: Colburn, 1828). Hazlitt himself annexed the market for Byron reminiscences by opening his 1826 Northcote conversations with accounts drawn from Hunt's unpublished manuscript (to Hunt's annoyance). Although in "The Modern Gradus Ad Parnassum" (1828) he praises Hunt's book, in "The Ruling Passion" (1829) an unnamed speaker says the book was designed "to satisfy the rabble."

82. In a judgment reflecting the Romantic test of sincerity, Hunt asserts Byron assumed roles (citing the synthesized emotion Byron used to write "the *Farewell*" to Lady Byron, "He sat down to *imagine* what a husband might say, who had really loved his wife") and discarded them when he deemed "the romantic character was not necessary to fame." Yet Hunt astutely denies the favorite agency of biographical mythmaking, last words, by dismissing the sentimental idea that Byron called out "My dear wife!," and devotes many pages to critiquing other Byron memoirists, "compilers," who "drunk with credulity" go on "compiling and believing at a most glorious rate."

83. Hunt's notorious financial irresponsibility was exacerbated by his dependence on Byron. As Shelley's friend, Hunt was transported to Italy by Byron (in 1822) to help edit *The Liberal,* but he was stranded after Shelley's death (1822) and Byron's departure for Greece (1823). The publisher Henry Colburn provided an advance to finance his return from Italy in 1825, although Hunt delayed the project three more years. Hunt had originally planned a book on his own experiences, but Colburn, having had success with other Byron memoirs, wanted it to feature Byron. See Stephen Fogle, *Leigh Hunt's Autobiography, the Earliest Sketches* (Gainesville: Univ. of Florida Press, 1959) and J. E. Morpurgo, *The Autobiography of Leigh Hunt* (London: Cresset, 1949). Crabb Robinson reported that Lady Blessington "thinks Leigh Hunt gave in the main a fair account of Lord Byron" (28 September 1832, I: 412).

84. Hart, "Boswell and the Romantics," p. 55.

85. See Coleridge's note to "Kubla Khan" as a "psychological curiosity," and *Biographia,* I: 187, II: 81; and D'Israeli's plan to paint the "psychological character" in the *Calamities of Authors.* In his *Literary Reminiscences,* De Quincey refers to a "psychological history of man," a "psychological history of human nature" ("Society of the Lakes," IV, 1840) and "as Mr. Coleridge expresses it, a psychological curiosity" ("The Saracen's Head," 1839).

86. De Quincey, "Infant Literature" (revised *Autobiographic Sketches,* 1853), added the Wordsworth quote to earlier formulations from *Suspiria;* Hazlitt, "On the Personal Character" (1821), "Character of Mr. Canning" (1824). See above, Chapter III, note 15. In "The Personal Character," Hazlitt tested an eclectic vocabulary to describe the imprint of character from childhood, paraphrasing Wordsworth, borrowing Pope's "'ruling passion,'" and comparing the "predetermination in the blood" of individual and familial character to a doctrine of the elect and condemned, a Calvinism of the intellect, which, despite its archaic locutions, links him intuitively with Freud.

87. William Harness said Byron would declare "'there always was a madness in the family'" and believed Byron had "a morbid love of a bad reputation . . . a sort of diseased and distorted vanity. The same eccentric spirit would induce him to report things which were false with regard to his family, which anybody else would have concealed, though true," Lovell, p. 44. In *Childe Harold* (IV: 166), Byron echoes *Hamlet:* "We bore / These fardels of the heart."

88. Hunt's statement, "His faults were not his own . . . we must seek the causes of them in mistakes common to us all," has certain affinities with Freud's comment about his task in *Leonardo,* "What psychoanalysis was able to do was to take the inter-relations between the impressions of the artist's life, his chance experiences, and his works, and from them to construct his constitution and the impulses at work in it—that is to say, that part of him which he shared with all men," *Autobiographical Study,* p. 123.

89. For Otto Rank, *Art and Artist,* pp. 428–31, the neurotic may be an "artiste manqué," but the life of art is no solution, for the artist is a neurotic "in the toils of old art-ideologies," seeking salvation in artistic creation rather than personality development.

90. D'Israeli, *Literary Character* (1795); Wordsworth, *Letter to a Friend of Robert Burns* (1816); Shelley, *Defence of Poetry* (1821); De Quincey, "Stewart, Irving, Wordsworth" (*Literary Reminiscences,* 1840). See above, Chapter III, note 20.

91. Lukács objects to the valorization of the artist as a isolated bohemian: "This false attitude . . . implies a personal psychic and moral degeneration" and represents "an abnormality in the artist's relationship to society." *Writer and Critic* (London: Merlin, 1978), pp. 104–5. Freud's assertion in "The Moses of Michelangelo" (1914) that the artist aims "to awaken in us the same emotional attitude, the same mental constellation as that which in him produced the impetus to create," indirectly supports, with a different ideology, Lukács's contention that the poet attempts to impose his or her marginalization on others.

92. Byron here paraphrases Macbeth's speech, III.iv.24, another image of the palace and the prison, heroic lord and transgressor, he styled for himself.

93. Prophetic voice is the poet's compensation; but whether pain is bestowed in punitive response for defiant creativity, or whether creativity is bestowed to assuage pain, is not delineated by either Byron or Wilson.

94. The poet is "amid the alien corn" in society, as well as in nature (Keats's sense in "Ode to a Nightingale"). Byron inverts earlier Romantic idealizations of human and nature united by the poet (e.g., Wordsworth's "A Poet's Epitaph" or Coleridge's "The Nightingale"). Byron asks, "Where are the forms" of art? and answers, "in him [the artist] alone." Art is not a reflection of external nature, nor need it be: Thomson had exclaimed, "but who can paint like nature?" (*Spring*, 1728); Byron cynically responds, "Can nature show so fair?" (IV: 122).

95. In Shelley's "Ozymandias" (also written 1817, printed 1818), the ruins of human reputation and the architectural setting, as in *Childe Harold*, are ambiguously immortal: "A ruin—yet what a ruin!" (IV: 143). Despite the Philoctetes archetype throughout Romantic poetry, Wordsworth's sonnet "When Philoctetes in the Lemnian Isle" (1827) uses a St. Francis archetype. De Quincey (1826–27) translated Lessing's remarks on Philoctetes in *Laocoön*.

96. Hunt added, "His hero in this work was a picture of the better part of his own nature." Discussing Reviews in the 8 April 1814 letter to Lady Melbourne (*Letters*, IV: 90), Byron said he was "not much interested in any criticisms favourable or otherwise.—I have had my day—& have done with all that stuff—& must try something new—politics—or rebellion—or methodism—or gaming—of the 2 last I have serious thoughts." Although inevident in Byron's discussion with Hunt on Methodism, Louis Crompton, *Byron and Greek Love* (Berkeley: Univ. of California Press, 1985), pp. 129, 145, mentions that "ma method" and "methodiste" were code terms for homosexuality in Charles Skinner Matthews's correspondence with Byron in 1809–10.

97. John Stuart Mill, *Autobiography*, "A Crisis in My Mental History," 1873.

98. De Quincey ("Society of the Lakes," IV, *Literary Reminiscences*, 1840) references Byron's comment to Thomas Moore, "[Hogg] and half of these Scotch and Lake troubadours, are spoilt by living in little circles and petty societies" (3 August 1814, *Letters*, IV: 152).

CHAPTER V

1. Johnston, p. 179. Gertrude Stein, *Everybody's Autobiography* (New York: Random House, 1937), preface; *The Autobiography of Alice B. Toklas* (New York: Harcourt Brace, 1933) also demonstrates that prolonged "autobiographies" eventually become biographical sketches of acquaintants.

2. Crabb Robinson, 27 April 1857, II: 767.

3. V. A. De Luca, *Thomas De Quincey: The Prose of Vision* (Toronto: Univ. of Toronto Press, 1980), p. x. E. Michael Thron, "Thomas De Quincey and the Fall of Literature," in *Thomas De Quincey: Bicentenary Studies,* ed. Robert Lance Snyder (Norman: Univ. of Oklahoma Press, 1985), pp. 7, 9. John Whale's comment that "Romantic unity is achieved by a method of fragmentation" rightly suggests that what McFarland (*Romanticism and the Forms of Ruin*) and Levinson (*The Romantic*

Fragment Poem) have said of poetry applies as well to prose. *Thomas De Quincey's Reluctant Autobiography* (Totowa, NJ: Barnes and Noble, 1984), p. 231.

4. "Davy, Godwin, Grant," *Literary Reminiscences* (hereafter to be abbreviated *LR*), 1837; Crabb Robinson, 31 October 1821, I: 275.

5. James Hogg, *De Quincey and His Friends* (London: Sampson, etc., 1895), pp. 240–44. Gillies goes on to affirm that De Quincey had been writing, not just posturing: "His various literary compositions, written in his exemplary hand (the best I ever saw, except Southey's) on little scraps of paper, must have reached to a great extent, but in his own estimation they were by no means 'ready for the press.'"

6. De Quincey traveled to Ireland with Westport in 1800 (in whose company he met King George III); attended Oxford 1803–8; received his patrimony in 1806 and made his £300 gift to Coleridge the following year. In the *Confessions* (subtitled *The Life of a Scholar*) and throughout his autobiographical and philological writings, he invoked the cachet of his aristocratic Oxford education. The prosperity of being able to borrow on his patrimony had allowed him the vagrancy in Wales and London (1802–3) chronicled in the *Confessions;* it was confronted for real only when his fortune, dwindling since 1812, was depleted in 1816.

Indeed, De Quincey's memoirs only infrequently take him past 1821, the year of his first literary success. The subject matter of his writings almost always centers on the experiences of his youthful years of prosperity and gentlemanly choice of exile—the voluntary discomforts endured under the safety valve of patrimony. The literary construct of the bohemian intellectual opium-eater was at odds with the real world of addiction and privation of his later years, and De Quincey was unwilling to cloud the prestige he needed to earn his bread, with the realities of survival.

7. De Quincey first wrote to Wordsworth in 1803 before starting Oxford; while there, he introduced himself to Lamb in 1804, traveled to the lake district in 1805 and 1806 (retreating without a visit), and finally met Coleridge in August 1807 at Nether Stowey, and Wordsworth and Southey in the lake district that November; a year later he had left school to live with the Wordsworths at their new house Allan Bank (November 1808–February 1809), had met John Wilson, and was to move into Dove Cottage, which the Wordsworths readied for him while he saw the *Convention of Cintra* to press in London.

8. A baby was born (1816) before his marriage to Margaret Simpson and a large family followed. He kept terms at the Middle Temple in 1812, and inquired about a London University professorship in 1830, having helped Wilson prepare lectures for the Edinburgh chair he won in 1820 (Lindop, pp. 195, 239, 295).

9. Preface to the *Dictionary,* 1755. De Quincey's own vagabonding on Oxford Street evokes Johnson's bohemian wanderings with Savage in London—as he says in the *Confessions* of his Oxford Street bivouac, "I sate rent free; and, as Dr Johnson has recorded, that he never but once in his life had as much wall-fruit as he could eat, so let me be grateful, that on that single occasion I had as large a choice of apartments in a London mansion as I could possibly desire." See Piozzi, p. 94.

10. He edited the *Westmorland Gazette* from July 1818 to November 1819. Charles

Pollitt says the projected series opened with Donne and Carew in the 19 September 1818 issue. *De Quincey's Editorship of the Westmorland Gazette* (Kendal: Atkinson and Pollitt, 1890), p. 70.

11. The Wordsworths had already broken with Coleridge (1810–12). The friendship with De Quincey appears to have decayed for a variety of reasons: his increasing addiction (1813–16), their disapproval of the downward mobility of his marriage with Margaret Simpson (1817), and his reluctance to permit their proprietary meddling in Dove Cottage (in 1811 there was a dispute over the orchard, in 1813 the housekeeper Mary Dawson stirred up trouble, Lindop, pp. 192, 204).

12. Originally printed in the *London Magazine,* September–October 1821, the *Confessions* was slightly revised as a book (London: Taylor and Hessey, 1822, still anonymously) and vastly expanded for the 1856 British collected edition, *Selections Grave and Gay* (the 1850 opening volume of the American collected edition followed its standard practice of reprinting the original periodical text).

13. Quoted from review biography of Laetitia Hawkins's *Anecdotes* (1823); other biographies included the review of Samuel Parr (1831), the reassembled accounts of Kant (1827) and Richard Bentley (1830), and his personal reminiscences of Walking Stewart (1823), John Wilson (1829), and Hannah More (1833) for publications including the *London Magazine, Blackwood's,* and *Tait's.*

14. In 1851 the American collected edition reprinted the *Sketches of Life and Manners* as *Life and Manners; from the Autobiography of an English Opium-Eater,* inserting the 1838 essay on his brother Pink, "My Brother" (which seems to have been held by *Tait's* in reserve from the earlier series). In expanding the *Autobiographic Sketches* (for Vols. I–II of the British collected edition, 1853–54), De Quincey kept the position of the Pink essay, and opened the revised text with spliced sections of *Suspiria de Profundis* (*Blackwood's,* 1845) and "A Sketch [of] from Childhood" (*Hogg's Weekly Instructor,* 1851–52); the American collected edition issued this revision as a separate volume.

15. "Davy, Godwin, Grant" (*LR,* 1837) concludes, "What had been abundantly right for me as a boy, ceased to be right for me when I ceased to be a boy." The concluding words of the *Sketches of Life and Manners* ("German Literature," 1836), a reference to Henry James Pye, indicate not just the end of his youthful era, but also the end of the callow state of British culture emblematized by the obsolete "Laureate Pye."

16. "Some Thoughts on Biography" (*Posthumous Works*).

17. These papers included the biographical essays he wrote on Goethe, Pope, Schiller, and Shakespeare (*Encyclopaedia Britannica,* 1837–38), and Milton (1838); and the biographical review essays of Gillman's *Coleridge* (1845), Gilfillian's *Literary Portraits* (1845), Wordsworth's poetry (1845), Forster's *Goldsmith* (1848), Roscoe's *Pope* (1848), and Talfourd's *Lamb* (1848).

18. He also wrote the articles on Wilson (1850) and his childhood (1851–52) for *Hogg's Instructor,* and the articles associated with *Suspiria* about the *Mail-Coach* (1849) for *Blackwood's.*

19. The textual confusion surrounding De Quincey's works is exacerbated by

the existence of the two collected editions during his lifetime: the American edition, *De Quincey's Writings,* 23 vols. (Boston: Ticknor, Reed, and Fields, 1850–59); and the subsequent British edition *Selections Grave and Gay, From Writings Published and Unpublished of Thomas De Quincey, Revised and Arranged by Himself,* 14 vols. (Edinburgh: Hogg, 1853–60). The Ticknor and Fields edition continued to be republished throughout the century; the Hogg edition was later taken over, reissued, and expanded as *De Quincey's Works,* 16 vols. (Edinburgh: Adam and Charles Black, 1862–71), until it was replaced by David Masson's edition, *The Collected Writings of Thomas De Quincey,* 14 vols. (Edinburgh: Adam and Charles Black, 1889–90), which mistakenly sought to solve the problem by recombining and synthesizing his writings into unprecedented new texts.

In this book, all quotations of the *Literary Reminiscences* are from the original periodical publication in *Tait's* (1834–41), as are references to the *Sketches of Life and Manners; from the Autobiography of an English Opium Eater* (1834–38). References to the revised versions, *Recollections of the Lakes and the Lake Poets* (1854) and *Autobiographic Sketches* (1853–54), are from *Selections Grave and Gay.* In the chaotic state of De Quincey editions, many writings remain scattered or incorrectly reprinted and sequenced. No current editions of the *Literary Reminiscences* are reliable; the readily available paperback edition *Recollections of the Lakes and the Lake Poets,* ed. David Wright (Harmondsworth: Penguin, 1970), has useful annotations but provides a synthesized and unreliable reading text. Grevel Lindop's *Confessions of an English Opium-Eater and other Writings* (Oxford: Oxford World's Classics, 1985) provides sound texts of the first versions of the *Confessions, Suspiria, The English Mail-Coach.* Miscellaneous essays of De Quincey are taken warily from David Masson's edition, and the supplemental collections of Alexander H. Japp, *The Posthumous Works of De Quincey,* 2 vols. (London: Heinemann, 1891), and Stuart M. Tave, *New Essays by De Quincey* (Princeton: Princeton Univ. Press, 1966).

20. "Coleridge," II (*LR,* 1834).

21. The *Literary Reminiscences* consists of a series of biographical essays published between 1837 and 1841 in *Tait's* magazine, plus the four earlier Coleridge essays published in 1834–35 in *Tait's,* a total of twenty-three essays. The most reliable bound text is the first Ticknor and Fields imprint of 1851 (which like the belated mid-century publication of *The Prelude,* finally made available to the public a high Romantic text in book form). Ticknor and Fields preserved the original periodical text and sequence under the title *Literary Reminiscences* (a conflation of the many running titles of the original series which included "Literary Connexions or Acquaintances," "Lake Reminiscences," "Recollections of Grasmere," and so forth). This largely accurate text has been eclipsed by the cannibalized versions popularized by later editions, notably the Edinburgh abridgment De Quincey printed in 1854 to mollify the families of Wordsworth, Southey, and Coleridge, and the ubiquitous late nineteenth-century edition of David Masson, which randomly deleted and recombined essays under the rubric of reconstructive autobiography. Publication schedule of De Quincey's *Literary Reminiscences* in *Tait's:*

Literary Novitiate	February 1837
Sir H. Davy—Mr. Godwin—Mrs. Grant	March 1837
Recollections of Charles Lamb (Part I)	April 1838
Recollections of Charles Lamb (Part II)	June 1838
Walladmor	September 1838
William Wordsworth (Part I)	January 1839
William Wordsworth (Part II)	February 1839
William Wordsworth (Part III)	April 1839
Wordsworth and Southey	July 1839
Southey, Wordsworth, and Coleridge	August 1839
Recollections of Grasmere	September 1839
The Saracen's Head	December 1839
Society of the Lakes (Part I, Westmoreland and the Dalesmen)	January 1840
Society of the Lakes (Part II, Charles Lloyd)	March 1840
Society of the Lakes (Part III, Elizabeth Smith)	June 1840
Society of the Lakes (Part IV, Professor Wilson)	August 1840
Walking Stewart—Edward Irving—William Wordsworth	October 1840
Talfourd—The London Magazine—Junius—Clare—Cunningham	December 1840
Libellous Attack by a London Journal—Duelling	February 1841

The Ticknor and Fields edition positions the four earlier recollections of Coleridge between "Walladmor" and "Wordsworth":

Samuel Taylor Coleridge (Part I)	September 1834
Samuel Taylor Coleridge (Part II)	October 1834
Samuel Taylor Coleridge (Part III)	November 1834
Samuel Taylor Coleridge (Part IV)	January 1835

Following the death of Coleridge in July, *Tait's* interrupted the serial publication of the *Sketches of Life and Manners* with the four-part sequence of essays on Coleridge. Similarly, during the serialization of the *Literary Reminiscences, Tait's* printed several miscellaneous articles, collected by De Quincey in a separate context: e.g., two articles on "Greek Literature" under his own name (December 1838 and June 1839) and the autobiographical essay "My Brother," Pink (March 1838).

In revising the literary reminiscences for the Edinburgh edition, De Quincey followed the Ticknor and Fields edition in positioning the Coleridge essays in the sequence just before those about meeting Wordsworth (as in rewriting the autobiographic sketches he followed the Ticknor and Fields insertion of the essay on his brother), indicating that he either authorized the sequence or accepted it as his own canon. When De Quincey suggested Thomas Noon Talfourd look into his literary sketches (letter of 5 March 1840, Pforzheimer collection, New York Public Library), he alluded to the Coleridge essays in a group with the rest. Readers also evidently regarded them as a unit: Charles Sumner wrote to George Hillard, 23 January 1839, "You know his articles on Coleridge. Wordsworth's turn has come now." A. H. Japp, *Thomas De Quincey: His Life and Writings* (London: Hogg, 1890), p. 199. De Quincey evidently used the Boston edition as a copy text for all of his Edinburgh revisions, often cutting apart and adding material on pages of the American edition. See, Lindop, pp. 374–75, and *De Quincey at Work,* ed. Willard Hallam Bonner (Buffalo, NY: Airport, 1936), pp. 70–71.

Bonner, p. 60, believes De Quincey liked the American edition and made the Edinburgh revisions only to avoid copyright problems. De Quincey wrote of Ticknor and Fields in the 1853 General Preface to *Selections Grave and Gay,* "To them I owe my acknowledgments, first of all, for that service: they have brought together a great majority of my fugitive papers in a series of volumes now amounting to twelve." De Quincey's daughters, Margaret, Florence, and Emily, assisted him by locating the articles, submitting them to him for verification, and conducting correspondence with the Boston publishers. In 1851 he evidently sent a list of the articles "contributed by me to various periodicals" to the Ticknor and Fields agent, J. C. Donaldson (Bonner, p. 13). Revising his works for the British edition in 1857, he wrote, "It is astonishing how much more Boston knows of my literary acts and purposes than I do myself. Were it not indeed through Boston, hardly the sixth part of my literary undertakings, hurried or deliberate, sound, rotting, or rotten, would ever have reached posterity. . . . Everything, in short, relating to myself is in the keeping of Boston" ("Supplement on the Essenes"; see Masson's note, VII: 231–32). In assembling the Ticknor and Fields edition, De Quincey was concerned about correct attribution of his works (he carefully ascertained that his articles on Milton would not be confused with those on similar topics by other writers at the same time); he remembered quite clearly subjects on which he did not write, but often forgot he had written articles until he was shown them again; many he had not seen since he submitted them, and he complained of the " 'havoc' " made by editors shortening them; others he considered incomplete (Bonner, pp. 16, 18, 32, 35). Once the work of assembling had been done for Ticknor and Fields, he seems to have decided to print a separate edition of palimpsests for Hogg—later thoughts on the same subjects (his habitual revising of his materials led him to add annotations to subsequent editions of the American imprint as well).

Although in 1838, in a prospectus for an unpublished article (Lindop, p. 335), De Quincey complained of Wordsworth's revision of his poems ("half ruined . . . altering them when no longer under the free-flowing movement of the original inspiration"), De Quincey constantly wanted to revise his own writings: Margaret reported in a letter to James Fields, 27 May 1852, that he had to be prevented from trying to revise everything, "He is so dissatisfied with what he has written generally, as to make him wish to rewrite the whole article over again." Ironically, Margaret says she did not like De Quincey's revisions any more than he liked Wordsworth's (Bonner, pp. 13–14, 18).

22. Similarly, after his editorship expired, his articles continued to appear in the *Westmorland Gazette* until January 1820 (Masson, XIII: 373, Pollitt, p. 50). The penultimate installment, published December 1840, makes reference to January 1838 as the immediate past ("my experience on last Sunday night but one"), a reference suggesting that the reminiscences were executed as a unit and, moreover, a reference highly unusual in De Quincey, both because he underscores its temporal immediacy and because he so rarely refers to incidents that late in life or so recent in his career. Kenneth Forward, "'Libellous Attack' on De Quincey," *PMLA* 52 (1937): 245, concurs in dating the composition at the latest 1838. Of greater importance for the purposes of this study, however, is the pattern of narrative unity defined by the internal structure and cross-referencing. The first episode also includes a brief précis of forthcoming subjects (Lamb, Davy, Wilson, Wordsworth).

De Quincey told his early publishers Taylor and Hessey, "I am often obliged to compose the whole almost in my mind before I can write a line" (Lindop, p. 294). He evidently had two working methods, intense bursts of industry or complete lassitude. At times pages had to be coaxed from him in order to complete a whole article (Lindop, pp. 281, 300, 361); at other times he ran into the problem of writing sustained narratives of more pages than could be commercially absorbed in the course of several years from any one contributor, and thus had trouble making ends meet even when he alternated contributions to *Tait's* and *Blackwood's* in the 1830s and 1840s. For example, in 1838 he said of William Tait, "I *have* written more than he can print in two years," and in 1845 John Blackwood would not allow his magazine to be dominated for months by *Suspiria* (Lindop, pp. 330, 358); *Tait's* and *Blackwood's* kept material back for fear of overexposure (Lindop, p. 359), and there is reason to believe much that he submitted was unused and lost (in addition to the materials he left behind on his many moves in Edinburgh and Holyrood). He wrote to James Hogg, 11 January 1858 (Bonner, p. 86), "I am continually buying Note paper to supply the place of that which has either—1. disappeared in the unknown abysses which have swallowed up so many uncounted articles (not always articles in a mere pawnbroker's sense, but sometimes in an Editor's sense)."

On his specific working method for the *Literary Reminiscences,* see Jordan, pp. 349–50, and Lindop, pp. 328, 334. Writing to Thomas Noon Talfourd, 5 March 1840, he declared, "If (*led by interest in the names concerned*) you ever look into my Autob. sketches in Tait, bear in mind that I disown them. They were not written, as will be thought, in monthly successions and with intervals sufficient: but all at once 2 years ago; in a coffee-room of a mail coach inn; with a sheriff's officer lurking near; in hurry too extreme to allow of reading them over even *once;* and with no after revision" (Pforzheimer Collection, New York Public Library). On 17 January he complained that *Tait's* had inserted the words "'in this present year of our Lord 1839'" into the first essay on Wordsworth (January 1839) to conceal it had been written the previous year.

There was evidently some revision permitted (although not as much as he would have liked), as we can see from internal evidence as well as his testimony in letters to his publishers. As is evident from a letter to James Hessey, 26 August 1823, concerning his articles in the *London Magazine,* De Quincey was anxious to see all proofs for revision: "In future send me proofs of all things. I foresee most important additions" (Bonner, p. 107). In working for *Tait's* he evidently expected to be allowed similar revisions, for in a letter to William Tait, 20 February 1839, De Quincey was annoyed that he was discouraged from revising his comments on the Wordsworths and worried about the consequences (Jordan, p. 347; Lindop, p. 334). Asterisks indicate some passages may have been abruptly excised as a result. Yet he told Robert Blackwood in 1840 he refused to correct proof or make revisions in *Tait's* (Lindop, p. 339). His comments on the revisions must be read through several motives: concern with the integrity of the text, the fear of insulting his acquaintances, and the need to reassure competing publishers of his exclusivity in writing for them.

23. In May 1837, *Tait's* printed Dr. William Shepherd's letter of complaint written in March about De Quincey's "erroneous assertions." Shepherd, the last living of the three biographers, declared, "He seems to have been at one period of his life, the slave of a deleterious drug which shakes the nerves, and, inflaming the brain, impairs the memory . . . therefore, my recollection is more likely to be correct than his." An introduction several times the length of the letter (entitled "Mr De Quincey, and the Literary Society of Liverpool in 1801") observes, "Mr De Quincey may be mistaken in these critical opinions: but there is surely no very heinous offence in their expression so many years after the world has had the means of forming an unbiased judgment." The following issue of *Tait's* in June, possibly by way of character defense, opens with a review of Joseph Cottle's *Early Recollections* (1837) of Coleridge, prominently describing De Quincey as "the most munificent" of Coleridge's benefactors. Henry Crabb Robinson, however, described as "wise," De Quincey's "character of 'literary society' arising out of his acquaintance with Roscoe and the other Liverpool literati" (11 April 1850, II: 696). The series was not to be reinstated until the following year with the two essays on Lamb.

24. Sketch of John Wilson for "Our Portrait Gallery" (*Hogg's Instructor,* 1850). In "On Wordsworth's Poetry" (1845), however, De Quincey recognized that the Romantic aesthetic of fragmentation posed problems for posterity, and warned that *The Excursion*'s episodic segments would result in its critical diminution into a text that "will be read by future generations in parts and fragments; and, being thus virtually dismembered into many small poems, it will scarcely justify men in allowing it the rank of a long one."

25. Before De Quincey, the presence of Suetonius had been minimal. Folkenflik, *Johnson,* pp. 97–99, declares, "Plutarch was the biographer *par excellence* for the eighteenth century." G. W. Bowersock says "there is no reason to think Suetonius' name was a household word as Plutarch's was," but suggests Rousseau's confessional revelations are indebted to Suetonius. "Suetonius in the Eighteenth Century," *Biography,* ed. Browning, pp. 34–35, 41.

26. John Stuart Mill, review of De Quincey's *Logic of Political Economy* (*Westminster Review*, 1844), Lindop, p. 353.

27. "Introduction," "Julius Caesar" (1832). As in his earlier improvisatory translation of Lessing's *Laocoön* (1826–27), De Quincey prided himself on bringing to light unfamiliar material (he later was to quote large passages of the unpublished *Prelude*), but he often took upon himself the duty of improving them. Much of his "translation" of *Walladmor* (1825), a German pseudo-Waverly novel, was invention. Of De Quincey's transformation of his sources, Lindop (p. 344) says he wanted to write the "narrative as it should have been rather than as it was." Albert Goldman, in charting De Quincey's practice of appropriating books for articles on Kant, Bentley, Parr, and the Caesars, rather cynically describes De Quincey as "essentially a journalist with extraordinary literary abilities," *The Mine and the Mint* (Carbondale: Southern Illinois Univ. Press, 1965), p. 163.

28. De Quincey agrees with Wordsworth's opinion that epitaphs are "tabooed against the revelations of candour," and accuses Plutarch and Johnson of "the propagation of defamatory anecdotes," not from malice but from "credulity."

29. In *Idler* 84, Johnson identified the same subjectivity: "He that writes the life of another is either his friend or his enemy." In the *Literary Reminiscences* De Quincey repeatedly confesses his present estrangement from Wordsworth's friendship: "I acknowledge myself to have been long alienated from Wordsworth" ("Wordsworth," I, *LR*, 1839; "Stewart, Irving, Wordsworth," *LR*, 1840).

30. De Quincey does not disparage Johnson's abilities as a biographer, but objects to some of his narrative manipulations. In the life of Milton (1838) and its "Postscript" (1859) he complains that Johnson attempted to excite mirth by juxtaposing Milton's revolutionary declarations and his return to England to start a school for boys. Perhaps remembering Wordsworth's objections to a life of Horace written "on the Boswellian plan" (*Letter to a Friend of Robert Burns*), De Quincey parodied the idea of some slavish ancient Boswell, a "too faithful and literal secretary," leaving a record of Hannibal for Johnson to distort by juxtaposing the vow at the altar with a tipsy banquet: "Then would rise Sam in his glory, and, turning back to the vow, would insist that this was its fulfillment."

31. "Something more than chronology" is necessary in biography to give "unity to its parts, and to take away the distraction of a mere catalogue," so "it follows that chronology may be safely neglected in general." "Neglect" of chronology is not merely permitted, not merely "inevitable"; strict adherence to chronology has a "negative" or disruptive value: "being false, it would have upset the story—although, being true, it did not establish that story." The entire introductory discussion on biographical theory in "My Brother" was omitted in the 1853 revision of the *Autobiographic Sketches*. In the "Brevia" (*Posthumous Works*), he called for an "architecturally moulded" biography.

32. The early sketches of Walking Stewart and Hannah More were similarly commemorative; likewise, the memory of sibling deaths motivates *Suspiria* and the autobiographical *Sketches of Life and Manners*.

33. Wordsworth's statement in the 1815 *Essay, Supplementary* was preceded by his declaration to Lady Beaumont, 21 May 1807, that the writer must "create the taste

by which he is to be relished." *The Letters of William and Dorothy Wordsworth: The Middle Years, Part I,* ed. Ernest de Selincourt and Mary Moorman, 2nd ed. (Oxford: Clarendon, 1969), p. 150.

34. "Coleridge," IV (*LR,* 1835).

35. "Coleridge," IV (*LR,* 1835). De Quincey's own estimate of dates in his works, and in dating his works, is often unreliable; he does not even get correct the dates of family deaths, and he is unconcernedly vague about factual verification, as in the following paragraph from "Wordsworth," II (*LR,* 1839): "From this period, therefore—that is, from the year 1794–95—we may date the commencement of Wordsworth's entire self-dedication to poetry. . . . Somewhere about this period, also, (though, according to my remembrance of what Miss Wordsworth once told me, I think one year or so later,) his sister joined him. . . . it was, as I have generally understood, and in the year 1797 or 1798, that Wordsworth first became acquainted with Coleridge; though, possibly, in the year I am wrong; for it occurs to me that, in a poem published in 1796, there is an allusion. . . ." See Jordan, pp. 340–41. Like Johnson, D'Israeli, and other anecdotal biographers, De Quincey distinguished between his elevated role as an interpreter and commentator, and the unimaginative role of the biographical researcher, whom he either corrects or advises (recommending figures such as Dorothy Wordsworth, Charles Lloyd, and the clergyman-poet Joseph Sympson to the notice of biographical dictionaries).

36. "Coleridge," I (*LR,* 1834).

37. "Conversation and S. T. Coleridge" (*Posthumous Works*).

38. The term palimpsest had increasingly been associated with perception: in "On History" (1830) Carlyle called the past a "palimpsest" whose meanings are dimly decipherable, and Lockhart, reviewing Croker's Boswell (1831), longed for an ancient Boswellian biography to surface from some "palimpsest."

39. Like De Quincey, Hume also saw the biographer as making visible the hidden patterns of life: "A biographer who should write the life of Achilles would connect events by showing their mutual dependence and relation. . . . Not only in any limited portion of life a man's actions have a dependence on each other, but also during the whole period of his duration from the cradle to the grave; nor is it possible to strike off one link, however minute, in this regular chain without affecting the whole series of events which follow" (*Enquiry Concerning Human Understanding,* Section III). See Noxon, pp. 21–22.

Contemporary critics, however, tend to favor a vocabulary suggesting the writer imposes a structure rather than illuminating intrinsic patterns. For example, Patricia Spacks, p. 38, says, "The crucial literary problem of autobiography is to articulate a significant form for the relative incoherence of human experience," and Roy Pascal, *Design and Truth in Autobiography* (London: Routledge and Kegan Paul, 1960), p. 9, says that autobiography "imposes a pattern" rather than isolates an innate organic structure. For historiographic discussions on how patterns have been seen to arise from or be imposed upon events, see, for example, Collingwood, pp. 48–50, and Mink, "Narrative Form," pp. 129–49.

40. Review of William Roscoe's edition of Pope (1848).

41. "Coleridge," I (*LR,* 1834); General Preface, British collected edition, 1853.

42. Wordsworth's assertion, "There neither is, nor can be, any essential difference between the language of prose and metrical composition" (1802 Preface to *Lyrical Ballads*), is reiterated from 1800 and expanded in the 1802 Appendix, which concluded, "In proportion as ideas and feelings are valuable, whether the composition be in prose or in verse, they require and exact one and the same language." On Wordsworth's indebtedness to contemporary discussions of meter and prose, see M. H. Abrams, *The Mirror and the Lamp* (New York: Oxford Univ. Press, 1953), pp. 95–97.

43. Wordsworth said of Coleridge, "I should have written many things like the Essay upon Epitaphs out of kindness to him in The Friend but he always put me off by saying—'You must wait till my principles are laid down & then I shall be happy to have your contributions.' But the principles never were laid down & the work fell to the ground. As I never was fond of writing prose & required some incitement to do so, I rather regret having been prevented in this way by my dear Friend." *Barron Field's Memoirs,* p. 62.

44. "Society of the Lakes," IV (*LR*, 1840). George McLean Harper's complaint, II: 165–71, that De Quincey's *Literary Reminiscences* presents "secondary opinions formed in later years" is a misconception, for the narrative significance of De Quincey's text lies in its interplay between primary reactions and "secondary opinions." Gérard Genette, *Narrative Discourse,* p. 235, uses the term "narrative metalepsis" to describe the oscillation between then and now, the double temporality of narrative; it is evident to a lesser degree in Hazlitt's "My First Acquaintance with Poets."

45. Hazlitt's use of personal acquaintances is more surreptitious; in *The Spirit of the Age,* for example, he does not mention anything as direct as having been Bentham's tenant in Milton's house, although he evaluates conversations with comments such as, Godwin's "best moments are with an intimate acquaintance or two" (who but a putative intimate could say?).

Elements of autobiography surface throughout Johnson's *Lives.* Johnson's interest in the literary marketplace and his identification with the financial struggles of Savage and Otway have already been noticed. He takes a particular interest in those literary tasks which he has performed: he discusses dictionary making (*Addison, Pope, Milton*); he sympathizes with Dryden, "the father of criticism," with Pope, the editor of Shakespeare, and Addison, the essayist on life and manners; and, as the writer of "The Vanity of Human Wishes, The Tenth Satire of Juvenal Imitated" and "London, A Poem in Imitation of the Third Satire of Juvenal," it is with some autobiographical self-scrutiny that Johnson inspects and devalues the practice of writing imitations in *Pope* ("What is easy is seldom excellent: such imitations cannot give pleasure to common readers") and *West* ("Such compositions are not to be reckoned among the great achievements of intellect. . . . Works of this kind may deserve praise, as proofs of great industry and great nicety of observation; but the highest praise, the praise of genius, they cannot claim"). There is a kind of ironic autobiography inscribed in Johnson's quoting at length a passage in Blackmore's comic prose concerning the "hero of the club" of literati, "one Mr. Johnson; such a constellation of excellence that his character shall not be suppressed"; Blackmore's literary hero, "the gigantick Johnson," is "'a critick of the first rank. . . . useful. . . . industrious. . . . sagacious. . . . impartial.'"

Although Johnson declines to speak familiarly of Collins, Mallet, or Lyttelton, all of whom he knew, he warmly praises his friends Robert Shiels and Gilbert Walmsley and quotes a letter sent to "my friend Mr. Boswell" (*Gray*). Boswell, reflecting his own desire to be linked with Johnson, was eager to identify instances where Johnson equated himself with his subjects. He notices an "unaccountable prejudice against Swift"; "In drawing Dryden's character, Johnson has given, though I suppose unintentionally, some touches of his own"; "We trace Johnson's own character in his observations on Blackmore's 'magnanimity as an author'" and his refusal to answer his enemies (Boswell, IV: 45, 55, 61, V: 44). In modeling Johnson's letter to Lord Chesterfield on Pope's letter refusing Halifax's patronage, Boswell underscores the relationship between Johnson and his subjects (Boswell, I: 259–60). See above Chapter II, note 70.

Many critics have contemplated the link between Johnson and his subjects; see Raleigh, pp. 134–37, 171, on Johnson's "fellow feeling" and "tendency to interpret the lives and characters of other poets by the likeness of his own" in *Sheffield, Milton, Pope,* and *Savage;* Fussell, *Johnson,* pp. 259–60, for Johnson's "complicity" with Savage; Jeffrey Meyers, "Autobiographical Reflections in Johnson's 'Life of Swift,'" *Discourse* 8 (1965): 37–48, on *Swift* and other lives.

46. See, for example, Bertrand Bronson, *Johnson Agonistes* (Cambridge: Cambridge Univ. Press, 1946), pp. 70–76; Ian Ross, "Boswell in Search of a Father? or a Subject?," *Review of English Literature* 5 (1964): 19–34; Donald Greene, "Reflections," pp. 204–7.

47. "I could not help indulging a scheme of taking it for myself many years hence" (19 July 1763), *London Journal,* p. 311.

48. Boswell, I: 392. The *Hamlet* reference does not appear in the original 16 May 1763 entry in the *London Journal* (p. 260); on Boswell's fear of ghosts, see Pottle's note, p. 214. The construct of Johnson as a kind of literary parent underlies Boswell's ecstatic recounting of Johnson's approval of the journal ("Is there any argument which can outweigh the sanction of Mr. Samuel Johnson?," 16 July 1763, p. 305) in silent contrast to his own father's disapproval of the journal (see Pottle's notes, pp. 275, 324); the Johnson who approved his journal replaces the father who ridiculed it.

49. "Wordsworth," I (*LR,* 1839).

50. Lindop, p. 253.

51. Jeffrey Hart, "Some Thoughts on Johnson as Hero," *Johnsonian Studies,* ed. Wahba, p. 24.

52. Boswell wrote in his journal, 31 March 1772, "I have a constant plan to write the life of Mr. Johnson. I have not told him of it yet, nor do I know if I should tell him. I said that if it was not troublesome and presuming too much I would beg of him to tell me all the little circumstances of his life." *Boswell for the Defence,* ed. W. K. Wimsatt and F. A. Pottle (New York: McGraw-Hill, 1959), p. 83; he left his doubts out of the *Life* entry, II: 166. The *Life* reported Johnson's response to the

project, 11 April 1773: "I again solicited him to communicate to me the particulars of his early life. He said, 'You shall have them all for twopence. I hope you shall know a great deal more of me before you write my Life.'" Boswell, II: 217; see also *Boswell for the Defence*, p. 175. In the *Hebrides*, 14 October 1773, Boswell noted: "I asked him several particulars of his life, from his early years, which he readily told me; and I wrote them down before him. . . . I shall collect authentick materials for THE LIFE OF SAMUEL JOHNSON. . . . I shall be one who will most faithfully do honour to his memory." Boswell, V: 312.

53. "Wordsworth," I (*LR*, 1839).

54. Freud, *Leonardo*, p. 80; Ernst Kris, pp. 64ff.; Erik Erikson, "On the Nature of 'Psycho-Historical' Evidence," *Life History and the Historical Moment* (New York: Norton, 1975), p. 147. On the autobiographical implications of a biographer's choice of subject, see Gay, p. 143; *Introspection in Biography: The Biographer's Quest for Self-Awareness*, ed. Samuel Baron and Carl Pletsch (New Jersey: Analytic Press, 1985); and *Psychoanalytic Studies of Biography*, ed. George Moraitis and George H. Pollock (Madison: International Universities Press, 1987); on transference, Edel, *Writing Lives*, pp. 65–75; on counter-transference, Steven Marcus, "Freud and Dora: Story, History, and Case History" (orig. 1974), *Freud and the Culture of Psychoanalysis* (New York: Norton, 1987), pp. 80–81; Roy Schafer calls the psychoanalyst and analysand (patient) "co-authors," "Narrative and the Psychoanalytic Dialogue," in *Narrative*, ed. Mitchell, p. 34.

55. D'Israeli, "Some Observations on Diaries, Self-Biography, and Self-Characters" (1796).

56. See, for example, W. J. Bate, *The Burden of the Past*, p. 36; Harold Bloom, *Anxiety of Influence*, p. 20; Thomas McFarland, "The Originality Paradox" (orig. 1974), *Originality and Imagination*, pp. 1–30.

57. "Literary Novitiate" (*LR*, 1837); "Talfourd, London Magazine, Junius" (*LR*, 1840).

58. In the 1838 *Encyclopaedia Britannica* biography of Shakespeare, De Quincey admires Thomas Campbell's view of Prospero's autobiographical "farewell to the stage," assumes *Timon of Athens* is drawn from Shakespeare's recollections of his father, and detects in *Twelfth Night* reflections of Shakespeare's marital disparity. In his journal, Boswell says of Rousseau, "He was quite the tender Saint-Preux" (15 December 1764), *Boswell on the Grand Tour*, ed. F. A. Pottle (New York: McGraw-Hill, 1953), p. 264.

59. "Wordsworth," I, II, III (*LR*, 1839); "Lamb," I (*LR*, 1838), "Coleridge," IV (*LR*, 1835); "Stewart, Irving, Wordsworth" (*LR*, 1840).

60. In "Lamb," I (*LR*, 1838), De Quincey says Thomas Noon Talfourd's biography of Lamb is likewise "almost unintelligible to the great majority of readers." Talfourd, veiling "Lamb's chequered life" and Mary Lamb's insanity, remarks only that "On the death of his parents, he felt himself called upon by duty to repay to his sister the solicitude with which she had watched over his infancy." *The Letters of Charles Lamb with a Sketch of his Life* (London: Moxon, 1837), I: 25, 334. De Quincey's later article on Lamb's character "in anagram" is a review of the last, more explicit edition, *Final Memorials of Charles Lamb* (London: Moxon, 1848).

61. De Quincey says interest in the life of a philosopher, scientist, or reformer is different from the "interest which attends the great poets who have made themselves necessary to the human heart" ("Wordsworth," I, *LR*, 1839); in "Coleridge," IV (*LR*, 1835), he declared, "because he was a poet . . . I shall feel myself entitled to notice the most striking aspects of his *character*."

62. "Sketch of Professor Wilson: in a Letter to an American Gentleman" (1829); review of Forster's *Goldsmith* (1848). After the furor over the Wordsworth installments of 1838–39, De Quincey was more cautious about personal accounts. In "On Wordsworth's Poetry" (1845) he reflected: "If, however, it is more difficult to write critical sketches than sketches of personal recollections, often it is much less connected with painful scruples. . . . Of men and women you dare not, and must not, tell all that chance may have revealed to you. Safer, then, it is to scrutinize the works of eminent poets, than long to connect yourself with themselves, or to revive your remembrances of them in any personal record." In "Stewart, Irving, Wordsworth" (*LR*, 1840) he had observed, "Men of extraordinary genius and force of mind are far better as objects for distant admiration than as daily companions," and in "Conversation and S. T. Coleridge" he said of his accusations of plagiarism, "We ourselves having, perhaps, been guilty of too wantonly stirring these waters at one time of our lives." While abridging the literary biographies for the British edition, he wrote a prefatory letter in 1853 for the American edition, which had run the series unexpurgated: "Not that I have any intention, or consciously any reason, expressly to disown any one thing that I have ever published; but some things have sufficiently accomplished their purpose when they have met the call of that particular transient occasion in which they arose; and others, it may be thought on review, might as well have been suppressed from the very first." In "Some Thoughts on Biography" De Quincey says Johnson was lucky that Savage, Pope, Swift, and Young "left no near relations behind to call him to account."

63. "Coleridge," I (*LR*, 1834); "Society of the Lakes," IV (*LR*, 1840).

64. Goldman, p. 168; A. H. Japp, *De Quincey Memorials* (London: Heinemann, 1891), pp. 269–71; Lindop, p. 258.

65. "Coleridge," I (*LR*, 1834); "Laxton" (revised *Autobiographic Sketches*, 1854). Since ancient times, symbolic events have traditionally collected around the biography of the poet (analogous to the miraculous events that surround the devout in hagiography). Plato is said to have died in the act of writing, and there is a superstitious coincidence in the birth and death of Shakespeare on the same day. Often such traditions allegorize the works: Anacreon chokes on a grape stone, Aeschylus is killed by an ironic blow from heaven, an eagle dropping a tortoise, whose shell supplied the lyre.

66. W. J. Bate, *The Achievement of Samuel Johnson* (New York: Oxford Univ. Press, 1955), p. 16. Sartre, *Saint Genet*, pp. 1–2, 11, 17: "It is not unusual for the memory to condense into a single mythical moment the contingencies and perpetual rebeginnings of an individual history." Erikson, *Young Man Luther* (New York: Norton, 1958), pp. 23–25, 37, 138–39.

67. Noxon, pp. 25–26, argues that the static "eighteenth-century conception of

biography . . . prevailed until, in our own time, advances in psychological theory enabled biographers to proceed from depiction to explanation of personality," and invokes A. O. J. Cockshut's opinion that the way nineteenth-century biographers reported events "preserves the mystery of personality." *Truth to Life: The Art of Biography in the Nineteenth Century* (New York: Harcourt Brace, 1974), pp. 19–20. Reed, p. 28, believes that biography was so far silenced by evangelicism that the concepts of Romanticism never even became an issue in its composition. Although Altick, *Lives,* pp. 86–87, senses changes in early nineteenth-century biography, he hurries over what he calls "the prolonged immaturity of biography." Hart, *Lockhart,* pp. 10–11, differentiates the older practice evident in Rousseau and Boswell of depicting life as a static sequence of events in the characterization of an unchanging adult, but undervalues the impact of Romantic poetry on biographical composition by using the relatively undaring biographer Lockhart.

68. "The Saracen's Head" (*LR,* 1839); "Society of the Lakes," IV (*LR,* 1840).

69. Keats's letter to George and Georgiana Keats, 19 February 1819 (*Letters,* II: 67).

70. Freud remarks in *The Psychopathology of Everyday Life,* "It can in fact be said quite generally that everyone is continually practicing psychical analysis on his neighbours" (New York: Norton, 1965, orig. 1901), p. 211. On Freud's use of the literary tradition in devising a metaphoric vocabulary, and his belief that psychoanalysis extended beyond a medical framework, see Bruno Bettelheim, *Freud and Man's Soul* (New York: Knopf, 1982), pp. 11–13, 26–35. Tzvetan Todorov, "The Notion of Literature," p. 8, says of the characters in Freud's case studies, "Their status is exactly that of fiction." When a patient recounts the same story narrated in *Decameron* 8.1, Freud's emphasis, like Boccaccio's, is on the telling rather than the originality of the story (*Psychopathology,* p. 92). The Romantic analogy between reading literary and living texts is evident in "Some Character Types Met with in Psychoanalytic Work" (1916), where Freud uses literary characters to illustrate patient syndromes, and conversely, in "A Childhood Recollection from *Dichtung und Wahrheit*" (1917), where he explains Goethe's narrative by referring to type behavior among his patients.

71. "Brevia" (*Posthumous Works*).

72. In "Infant Literature" (modeled on *The Prelude,* Book V), De Quincey says, "Infancy, therefore, is to be viewed, not only as part of a larger world that waits for its final complement in old age, but also as a separate world itself" (revised *Autobiographic Sketches,* 1853).

73. Assuming De Quincey's usual working method of using a book as an "orange to squeeze" for a review article, the essay was probably written in 1847 or shortly thereafter. De Quincey's comment "Coleridge has now been dead for more than fifteen years" must be regarded with his usual inaccuracy about dates in his and anyone else's life. Japp, *Posthumous Works,* p. 34, supposes the article written in 1850, but there is no reason to assume as he does that De Quincey's statement means sixteen or seventeen years rather than fourteen or fifteen years.

74. Dante, *Convivio,* Book II, and *Epistolam X ad Canem Grandem della Scala.* It is not necessarily fruitful, however, to transpose to Romantic secular culture and

narrative the identical medieval grid of literal, allegorical, tropological, and anagogical levels of meaning.

75. De Quincey may be imitating Wordsworth's use in *The Prelude* of the French Revolution as an allegory of his artistic and intellectual movement. Elizabeth W. Bruss, *Autobiographical Acts* (Baltimore: Johns Hopkins Univ. Press, 1976), p. 97; Spengemann, p. 120, also calls De Quincey an allegorist; Susanna Egan, *Patterns of Experience in Autobiography* (Chapel Hill: Univ. of North Carolina Press, 1984), p. 59, discussing mythic patterns in Romantic autobiography, calls De Quincey's departure from school his "original sin."

76. "Recollections of Grasmere" (*LR*, 1839); "Society of the Lakes," II (*LR*, 1840).

77. "Literary Novitiate" (*LR*, 1837); "Davy, Godwin, Grant" (*LR*, 1837); "Walladmor" (*LR*, 1838).

78. "Wordsworth and Southey" (*LR*, 1839).

79. "Literary Novitiate" (*LR*, 1837); "Lamb," I, II (*LR*, 1838).

80. "Wordsworth," I (*LR*, 1839); "Lamb," I (*LR*, 1838).

81. "Literary Novitiate" (*LR*, 1837). Their then well-known biographical writings were Currie's *Life of Burns* (1800), Shepherd's *Life of Poggio Bracciolini* (1802), and Roscoe's *Life of Lorenzo de' Medici* (1796) and *Life of Leo X* (1805).

82. *A Diary of Thomas De Quincey, 1803*, ed. Horace Ainsworth Eaton (London: Douglas, 1927), p. 182.

83. Lindop, p. 367.

84. Wordsworth's lake guide first appeared as a brief anonymous introduction to Joseph Wilkinson's *Select Views in Cumberland, Westmoreland, and Lancashire* (London: Ackermann, 1810), and was enlarged and reprinted many times. It is most convenient to refer to it after the title of Wordsworth's final revision, *A Guide Through the District of the Lakes* . . . (Kendal: Hudson and Nicholson, 1835).

Three prior important lake guides were: William Gilpin, *Observations Relative Chiefly to Picturesque Beauty . . . Particularly the Mountains and Lakes of Cumberland and Westmoreland* (London: Blamire, 1776); Thomas West, *A Guide to the Lakes* (London: Richardson and Urquhart, 1778), 2nd rev. ed. by William Cockin (1780), with Thomas Gray's journal in an appendix. Wordsworth owned reprints of all of these works; see Chester and Alice Shaver, *Wordsworth's Library* (New York: Garland, 1979).

Other guides: Ann Radcliffe, *A Journey Made in the Summer of 1794 . . . to which are added, Observations During a Tour to the Lakes* (London: Robinson, 1795); Joseph Budworth, *A Fortnight's Ramble to the Lakes* (London: Cadell, 1792, revised 1795, 1810); Thomas Wilkinson, *Tours to the British Mountains* (London: Taylor and Hessey, 1824); William Combe, *The Tour of Doctor Syntax in Search of the Picturesque* (London: Ackermann, 1812, orig. *Poetical Magazine*, 1809); John Wilson, *Letters from the Lakes* (Ambleside: Middleton, 1889, 1901). This last appeared in *Blackwood's* in 1819, purporting to be the correspondence of a tourist Philip Kempferhausen; Middleton identifies the author as Wilson, as does Neil Bauer, *William Wordsworth: A Reference Guide* (Boston: Hall, 1978), p. 45; prior to Middleton's reissue, however, William Cushing, *Initials and Pseudonyms* (New York: Campbell, 1885), identified the pseudonym as R. P. Gillies's in *Noctes Ambrosianae*. On lake travel in general see, Norman Nicholson, *The Lakers: The Adventures of the First Tourists* (London: Hale, 1955); on Coleridge's tour, p. 126.

85. This plan was part of a list De Quincey wrote entitled "Constituents of Human Happiness," 18 April 1805. Wordsworth's letter to De Quincey, 6 March 1804, *The Letters of William and Dorothy Wordsworth: The Early Years,* ed. Ernest de Selincourt and Chester L. Shaver, 2nd ed. (Oxford: Clarendon, 1967), p. 454. See Japp, *Thomas de Quincey,* pp. 75–76, Lindop, p. 118; Horace Ainsworth Eaton, *Thomas De Quincey: A Biography* (New York: Oxford Univ. Press, 1936), pp. 102–3; D. D. Devlin, *De Quincey, Wordsworth, and the Art of Prose* (London: Macmillan, 1980), p. 1.

86. Lindop, pp. 249, 256.

87. See John Edwin Wells, "De Quincey and *The Prelude*," *Philological Quarterly* 20 (1941): 1–24. Emerson reported that De Quincey told him he once had five manuscript books of Wordsworth's unpublished poem; Lindop, pp. 187, 332, suggests De Quincey may have made a copy.

88. On Wordsworth, see Jerome Buckley, "Autobiography in the English Bildungsroman," in *The Interpretation of Narrative,* ed. Morton W. Bloomfield (Cambridge: Harvard Univ. Press, 1976), pp. 93–104.

89. De Quincey was not merely contriving to collect famous acquaintances—we never hear in him any echo of the adult Boswell's exultation at having famous guests as visitors: "I am really the Great Man now. I have had David Hume in the forenoon, and Mr. Johnson in the afternoon, of the same day visiting me. Sir John Pringle, Dr. Franklin, and some more company dined with me today; and Mr. Johnson and General Oglethorpe one day, Mr. Garrick alone another, and David Hume and some more literati another, dine with me next week." Letter to William Temple, 14 May 1768; Mark Longaker, *English Biography in the Eighteenth Century* (Philadelphia: Univ. of Pennsylvania Press, 1931), p. 417. Richard Woodhouse's 1821 diary confirms that De Quincey disapproved of the circumstantial celebrity hunting of Evelyn's diary: "You meet, for instance, with such matters recorded as that he dined with *this* person of quality, or called upon or was visited by *that* man of distinction, *without more*. . . . The purpose of setting the circumstance down at all seems to be merely to give an idea of the consequence which the writer imagines himself to derive from being considered an acquaintance of such men." Hogg, *De Quincey and his Friends,* p. 91.

90. Thomas McFarland, "The Symbiosis of Coleridge and Wordsworth" (orig. 1972), *Romanticism and the Forms of Ruin,* pp. 56–103; F. A. Pottle, "The Eye and the Object in the Poetry of Wordsworth," in *Wordsworth Centenary Studies,* ed. Gilbert T. Dunklin (Princeton: Princeton Univ. Press, 1951), pp. 23–42. In his earliest letter to Wordsworth in May 1803 (Jordan, pp. 30–31), De Quincey longed to connect himself with the lake community: "Your name is with me forever linked to the lovely scenes of nature;—and that not yourself only but that each place and object you have mentioned—and all the souls in that delightful community of your's [*sic*]—to me 'Are dearer than the sun!'" He had already found the habit of glossing his own experience with Wordsworthian sentiments (here, "Ruth").

91. Their intellectual relationship, however, continued to fluctuate. In 1829, Wordsworth was reading De Quincey's articles favorably and told Henry Crabb Robinson, "Whatever he writes is worth reading" (27 January 1829), *The Letters of William and Dorothy Wordsworth: The Later Years, Part II,* ed. Alan G. Hill, 2nd ed. (Oxford: Clarendon, 1979), p. 17. And after the tumult over the *Literary Reminiscences* subsided, Wordsworth wrote John Hudson in 1842, asking for De Quincey's assistance in preparing a glossary of names for the revised lake guide: "I am still of the opinion that it is very desirable they should be looked over by Mr De Quincey" (13 March 1842), *The Letters of William and Dorothy Wordsworth: The Later Years, Part IV,* ed. Hill, 2nd ed. (Oxford: Clarendon, 1988), p. 305.

92. For Wordsworth on the picturesque, see *Select Views,* pp. xxvi, 39, 45; on larches, xxviii–xxxi. His lake guide was firmly in the convention of lake travel literature; its many interim titles, announcing "Topographical Description" in some years (printed with "The River Duddon" as *Topographical Description of the Country of the Lakes in the North of England,* 1820) and "Scenery of the Lakes" in others (*A Description of the Scenery of the Lakes in the North of England,* 1822, 1823), assured the purchaser of the convention of the topographical picturesque. Despite recent critical embarrassment over the picturesque of Wordsworth's lake guide, there is nothing intrinsically wrong with the descriptive prose of the picturesque, which was a valid counterresponse to beliefs such as Johnson's, that "a blade of grass is always a blade of grass," and an attempt to educate the eye to scenes of nature and demonstrate the proper study of mankind was more than merely man.

William Gilpin's *Observations on the River Wye and Several Parts of South Wales, Relative Chiefly to Picturesque Beauty* (London: Blamire, 1782) was being reprinted into the nineteenth century, along with his other picturesque travelogues into parts of Britain; Wordsworth's own copy very likely guided him to Tintern Abbey. On Wordsworth, picturesque travel, and landscape, see: J. R. Watson, *Picturesque Landscape and English Romantic Poetry* (London: Hutchinson, 1970), pp. 76–105; John McNulty, "Wordsworth's Tour of the Wye," *Modern Language Notes* 60 (1945): 291–95; Charles Norton Coe, *Wordsworth and the Literature of Travel* (New York: Farrar Straus, 1979, orig. 1953); John R. Nabholtz, "Wordsworth's Guide to the Lakes and the Picturesque Tradition," *Modern Philology* 61 (1964): 288–97; Russell Noyes, *Wordsworth and the Art of Landscape* (Bloomington: Indiana Univ. Press, 1968), pp. 143–250; John Dixon Hunt, *The Figure in the Landscape* (Baltimore: Johns Hopkins Univ. Press, 1976), pp. 156–57; Walter John Hipple, *The Beautiful, The Sublime, and the Picturesque* (Carbondale: Southern Illinois Univ. Press, 1957), pp. 185ff.; on lake travel as a manifestation of the picturesque, see Elizabeth Wheeler Manwaring, *Italian Landscape in Eighteenth-Century England* (New York: Oxford Univ. Press, 1935), pp. 181–97, and Christopher Hussey, *The Picturesque* (London: Cass, 1967, orig. 1927), pp. 97–127.

93. "Recollections of Grasmere" (*LR,* 1839); "Lamb," I (*LR,* 1838); "Society of the Lakes," III (*LR,* 1840). Preceding travel writers had already established an ongoing dialogue. Gray's biographer, Mason, recommends Gray's lake district descriptions be brought and read to enhance the views. West, in turn, reprints Gray's journal from Mason and checks views, walks, weather, and time of day

against Gray's evaluations. Gilpin, whose *River Wye* was urged to press by Mason and Gray, quotes lines from Virgil and Thomson revealing the picturesque in scenery, "pleasing in life, in painting, and in poetry." To enhance his descriptions of the scenery, Wordsworth quotes West, Gilpin, Spenser, Milton, and his own poetry; later editions also print revised versions of Dorothy's journal recounting several of her walking "excursions"—much in the established manner of West's guide which printed Gray's journal in appendix.

94. Reviewing "The River Duddon," the *British Review and London Critical Journal* (1820) said Wordsworth's "new style of local poetry" joined the tradition of descriptive topographical poetry extending back to "Cooper's Hill"; but distinguished Wordsworth's "thoughtful original delineation" of landscape as scenery "philosophized, and spiritualized, and raised into commerce with the soul." Robert A. Aubin positions "An Evening Walk," "Descriptive Sketches," "The River Duddon," and "Tintern Abbey" within existing categories of topographic poetry (hill, estate, town, river, and foreign and domestic travel). *Topographical Poetry in XVIII-Century England* (New York: Modern Language Assn., 1936), pp. 62, 169, 190, 215, 238, 241. In *The Excursion* Wordsworth is also communicating with the topographical tradition of churchyard poems and poetic town histories.

95. This study confines itself to the biographical dimension of the representation of people in the landscape; on its important ideological ramifications see, for example, Jerome McGann, *The Romantic Ideology* (Chicago: Univ. of Chicago Press, 1983), pp. 86–88; Kenneth R. Johnston, "The Politics of 'Tintern Abbey,'" *Wordsworth Circle* 14 (1983): 6–14; Marjorie Levinson, *Wordsworth's Four Great Period Poems* (Cambridge: Cambridge Univ. Press, 1986), pp. 25–43; David Simpson, "Criticism, Politics, and Style in Wordsworth's Poetry," *Critical Inquiry* 11 (1984): 67–79. H. D. Rawnsley makes clear that locals felt Dorothy Wordsworth and Hartley Coleridge mixed more freely among them, and some concluded they had written the poems. *Reminiscences of Wordsworth among the Peasantry of Westmoreland* (London: Dillon's, 1968, orig. 1882), pp. 23, 29.

96. On the Maid of Buttermere, see N. Nicholson, pp. 71–75, 108. Budworth's "Revisit to Buttermere" (*Gentleman's Magazine,* 1800, reprinted with the third edition of 1810) discusses the "mischief" he has done in advertising her; more was to occur, when the bigamist and forger John Hatfield sought her out, married her and was subsequently executed. The events were popularized in plays, poetry, and magazine articles, many of which (like Wordsworth's *Prelude,* Book VII, and De Quincey's "Coleridge," II, *LR,* 1834) lamented the corruption of the lakes by the contamination of the city; De Quincey says Hatfield arrived (like more innocent tourists) as a "picturesque-hunter"; the third edition of Budworth's *Ramble* quotes Gray, "Happy would it be for many a flower, were they 'Born to blush unseen.'" In 1820 Wordsworth expanded his favorable 1814 reference to Robert Heron's *Observations Made in a Journey through the Western Counties of Scotland,* 2 vols. (Perth: Morison, 1793); see Coe, pp. 88–91.

97. Coleridge mentions "Anecdote for Fathers," "Simon Lee," "Alice Fell," "Beggars," "The Sailor's Mother" (*Biographia,* II: 68–69).

98. Lockhart, *Peter's Letters to his Kinsfolk,* 1st ed. (labeled 2nd ed.), 3 vols.

(Edinburgh: Blackwood, 1819). Hart, *Lockhart,* calls it a "biography of a culture"; p. 268, for publication history. Whereas De Quincey validates his authority by emphasizing his long intimacy with the culture, Lockhart conceals his knowledge under anonymity and simulated first impressions. De Quincey refutes the description of Wordsworth in *Peter's Letters* ("Wordsworth," I, *LR,* 1839). William Howitt's *Homes and Haunts of the Most Eminent British Poets,* 2 vols. (London: Bentley, 1847) set the pattern for succeeding travelogues in the biographical picturesque; Edward Thomas, writing *A Literary Pilgrim in England* (London: Methuen, 1917), called the genre "'omes and 'aunts" from the title his publishers originally wanted to use, "Homes and Haunts of Writers"; William Cooke, *Edward Thomas* (London: Faber, 1970). Howitt, *Visits to Remarkable Places . . . Illustrative of Striking Passages in English History and Poetry,* 2 vols. (Vol. I, London: Longman, 1840; Vol. II, 1842). In addition to *Literary Associations of the English Lakes,* 2 vols. (Glasgow: MacLehose, 1894), Rawnsley wrote many books on the people of the lakes, including one on Charles Gough and his dog (Carlisle: Coward, 1892).

99. The lake guide De Quincey considered Wilson already at work on was probably not the "Letters from the Lakes." *Peter's Letters* appeared in mid-July of 1819; the "Letters" had begun in January; the original plan of Lockhart's work called for the third volume to be written by Wilson. Lockhart later said it had not all been written by one hand. Although Wilson appears to have had no great role in *Peter's Letters,* De Quincey may have had this rumor in mind. Hart, *Lockhart,* p. 268; Lindop, p. 295.

100. Edmund Gosse, *Father and Son* (London: Heinemann, 1907), Chapter V.

101. "The Churchyard Among the Mountains" was the portion of the poem De Quincey and contemporary admirers praised the most. Even in the anomalous essay where he faulted Wordsworth's theory of poetic diction, as well as parts of *The Excursion* ("On Wordsworth's Poetry," 1845), De Quincey maintained his admiration for "The Churchyard Among the Mountains." Lockhart, who was to admire *The Excursion* in *Peter's Letters,* records of De Quincey, "Wilson and he were both as enthusiastic concerning the 'Excursion' as you could wish." Lindop, p. 214; and Andrew Lang, *The Life and Letters of John Gibson Lockhart* (London: Nimmo, 1897), I: 98.

102. Part III. Part I of the *Essay upon Epitaphs* originally appeared in 1810 in *The Friend;* the others were only printed posthumously. Part I was reprinted as a footnote to *The Excursion* (V: 978); Part III ends with one of the epitaphs spoken by the pastor (*Excursion,* VII: 396–481, slight variants). Heralded with the invitation, " 'Pause Traveller!' so often found upon the monuments" (Part I), the lake tourist becomes a contemplative traveler in the journey of life upon encountering a sepulchre set amid "the surrounding images of nature."

103. Whereas Wordsworth's phrase "the vision and the faculty divine," is also favored by Coleridge in the *Biographia* (I: 241, II: 60, 131) for its evocation of "true poetic genius," for De Quincey it takes on special meaning precisely because it avoids the implication of a specifically metrical gift.

Gray, the phantom behind many of Wordsworth's writings (the progenitor of the picturesque, the straw man of poetic diction, the versifier of epitaphs praised in the *Essay*), called attention to the biographic and epitaphic role of the poet in the "Elegy Written in a Country Church-yard." Crabbe, like Wordsworth and De Quincey, also wrote churchyard scenes purportedly based on actual lives. Crabbe's 1807 *The Parish Register* (Book III, "Burials") gives a series of short lives, the "annals of the village poor," and the sequence of poetic letters comprising the 1810 *The Borough* bases its grim lives in "The Poor of the Borough" and "The Almshouse" on actual individuals. Always evident in Crabbe, however, is the reprimand of death, the menacing vanity of human wishes of the Johnson who helped him write *The Village* (1783); Jordan, pp. 363–64, says De Quincey followed Wordsworth in disliking Crabbe.

104. "Coleridge," II (*LR,* 1834); "Some Thoughts on Biography."

105. R. H. Tawney, *Social History and Literature* (Cambridge: Cambridge Univ. Press, 1950), p. 23.

106. Erwin Panofsky observes in "Et in Arcadia Ego: Poussin and the Elegiac Tradition," in *Meaning in the Visual Arts* (Garden City, NY: Doubleday, 1955), p. 295, that Johnson misread the recurring trope of the skull or gravestone amid a landscape as "'I am in Arcadia,'" a shallow elegiac longing to share a past golden age (although his contemporaries Reynolds and George III correctly understood it as a reminder of human mortality and the temporality of all things: the presence of Death is even in Arcadia).

107. "Lamb," I (*LR,* 1838); "Stewart, Irving, Wordsworth" (*LR,* 1840).

108. "Talfourd, London Magazine, Junius" (*LR,* 1840).

109. For the details of the 1824 libel, see Forward, pp. 244–60. Of the short life span of the offending *John Bull Magazine* (which also included an article supposedly by Byron called "My Wedding Night") De Quincey remarks with some satisfaction, "The combined forces of Byron and obscenity failed to save them" ("Libellous Attack," *LR,* 1841).

110. John Taylor, *The Identity of Junius* (London: Taylor and Hessey, 1816, rev. ed., 1818). Tave, pp. 236–76, attributes to De Quincey three additional articles on Sir Philip Francis as Junius (*Edinburgh Saturday Post,* 1827–28).

111. "Talfourd, London Magazine, Junius" (*LR,* 1840); *Barron Field's Memoirs,* p. 28.

112. De Quincey's psychological repositioning of the concept of confession stands alongside his appropriation of biblical language in the title of *Suspiria de Profundis* (Psalm 130) and its description of the action of the dormant layers of memory, "They are not dead but sleeping" (Matthew 9:24). See Chapter I, n. 91.

113. "Libellous Attack" (*LR,* 1841); "Saracen's Head" (*LR,* 1839). The passage in *Suspiria* quoted in the beginning of this chapter depicts the tourist in the lakes as an intellectual traveler whose route should be a meandering speculation. Arden Reed's "'Booked for Utter Perplexity' on De Quincey's *English Mail-Coach,*" in *De Quincey,* ed. Snyder, p. 282, discusses the letters carried by the mail coach as an image for the mind's involuntary relationship to language: "Try as he might, he cannot seize the reins or influence the speed or direction of the horses." In "The Simplon Pass" and throughout *The Prelude* Wordsworth also uses in various ways the figure of the traveler as an image for intellectual movement.

114. J. Hillis Miller, "Thomas De Quincey," *The Disappearance of God* (Cambridge: Harvard Univ. Press, 1975, orig. 1963), pp. 25, 28–29, discusses how De Quincey replaces faith and finite goals with an everlasting "wandering." Robert H. Bell suggests that Rousseau's search for a "secular equivalent for Augustinian spiritual vision" led him to posit sincerity as a justification for autobiography. "Rousseau: the Prophet of Sincerity," *Biography* 3 (1980): 297, 302.

115. "Stewart, Irving, Wordsworth" (*LR*, 1840).

116. De Quincey's use of the "Immortality" ode as a Wordsworthian subtext in describing his first glimpse of the lakes—the "sense of a mysterious pre-existence" that he felt when he arrived, his retreat "like a guilty thing"—further contributes to the text's sense of a golden but fugitive age in De Quincey's past and in literary history. Moreover, even the *genius loci* is ephemeral; see Geoffrey Hartman, "Romantic Poetry and the Genius Loci," in *Beyond Formalism* (New Haven: Yale Univ. Press, 1970), pp. 311–36.

117. "Recollections of Grasmere" (*LR*, 1839).

118. Wordsworth himself hints at a similar situation in the Fenwick note to "The Pet-Lamb" (1800), declaring the error of having named Barbara Lewthwaite: "I . . . will here add a caution against the use of names of living persons. Within a few months after the publication of this poem, I was much surprised, and more hurt, to find it in a child's school-book which . . . had come into use at Grasmere School where Barbara was a pupil. And, alas, I had the mortification of hearing that she was very vain of being thus distinguished." The literature of the lakes contributes to the breakdown of local culture even as it celebrates it.

119. First draft of De Quincey's first letter to Wordsworth (1803), Jordan, p. 28.

120. For a discussion of the green world and pastoral convention see Northrop Frye, "The Argument of Comedy," in *English Institute Essays,* ed. D. A. Robertson (New York: Columbia Univ. Press, 1949), pp. 57–83; Harry Berger, Jr., "The Renaissance Imagination: Second World and Green Worlds," *Centennial Review* 9 (1965): 37–78; Sherman Hawkins, "The Two Worlds of Shakespearean Comedy," *Shakespeare Studies* 3 (1967): 62–80.

121. Panofsky, pp. 295–320.

122. Abrams, *Mirror and the Lamp,* p. 240.

Select Bibliography

Aaron, Daniel, ed. *Studies in Biography*. Cambridge: Harvard Univ. Press, 1978.

Abrams, M. H. *The Mirror and the Lamp*. New York: Oxford Univ. Press, 1953.

Addison, Joseph. *The Works of Joseph Addison*. Ed. Richard Hurd. 6 vols. London: Bohn, 1856.

Adolphus, John L. *Biography: A Prize Essay*. Oxford: Collingwood, 1818.

Albrecht, W. P. *Hazlitt and the Creative Imagination*. Lawrence: Univ. of Kansas Press, 1965.

Allport, Gordon W. *The Use of Personal Documents in Psychological Science*. New York: Social Science Research Council, 1942.

Altick, Richard D. *The English Common Reader*. Chicago: Univ. of Chicago Press, 1957.

———. *Lives and Letters: A History of Literary Biography in England and America*. New York: Knopf, 1966.

Arnold, Matthew. *Essays in Criticism: First Series*. London: Macmillan, 1865.

———. *Essays in Criticism: Second Series*. London: Macmillan, 1888.

———, ed. *The Six Chief Lives from Johnson's "Lives of the Poets."* London: Macmillan, 1878.

Aubin, Robert Arnold. *Topographical Poetry in XVIII-Century England*. New York: Modern Language Assn., 1936.

Aubrey, John. *Letters, Written by Eminent Persons in the Seventeenth and Eighteenth Centuries . . . and Lives of Eminent Men*. Ed. John Walker. London: Longman, etc., 1813.

Auerbach, Erich. *Mimesis: The Representation of Reality in Western Literature*. Trans. Willard R. Trask. Princeton: Princeton Univ. Press, 1974, orig. 1953.

Baker, Herschel. *William Hazlitt*. Cambridge: Harvard Univ. Press, 1962.

Baron, Samuel, and Carl Pletsch. *Introspection in Biography: The Biographer's Quest for Self-Awareness*. New Jersey: Analytic Press, 1985.

Barthes, Roland. *Image-Music-Text*. Trans. Stephen Heath. New York: Hill and Wang, 1977.

Bate, Walter Jackson. *The Burden of the Past and the English Poet*. Cambridge: Harvard Univ. Press, 1970.

———. *From Classic to Romantic: Premises of Taste in Eighteenth-Century England*. Cambridge: Harvard Univ. Press, 1946.

———. *Samuel Johnson*. New York: Harcourt Brace, 1975.

Bates, E. Stuart. *Inside Out: An Introduction to Autobiography*. New York: Sheridan House, 1937.

Bayle, Pierre. *Dictionnaire historique et critique*. 16 vols. Paris: DeSoer, 1820 (orig. 1697, rev. ed. 1702).

Beringer, Richard. *Historical Analysis: Contemporary Approaches to Clio's Craft*. New York: John Wiley, 1978.

Biographia Britannica: or, The Lives of the Most Eminent Persons Who Have Flourished in Great Britain and Ireland, From the Earliest Ages, Down to the Present Times. Ed. William Oldys. 6 vols. London: Innys, 1747–66. 2nd ed. Ed. Andrew Kippis. 5 vols. London: Bathurst, etc., 1778–93.

Bloch, Marc. *The Historian's Craft.* Trans. Peter Putnam. New York: Knopf, 1953.

Bloom, Harold. *The Anxiety of Influence.* Oxford: Oxford Univ. Press, 1973.

Bolingbroke, Henry St. John. *Letters on the Study and Use of History.* London: Millar, 1752.

Boswell, James. *Boswell for the Defence.* Ed. W. K. Wimsatt and F. A. Pottle. New York: McGraw-Hill, 1959.

———. *Boswell on the Grand Tour.* Ed. F. A. Pottle. New York: McGraw-Hill, 1953.

———. *Boswell's Life of Johnson.* Ed. George Birkbeck Hill and L. F. Powell. 6 vols. Oxford: Clarendon, 1934.

———. *The Correspondence and Other Papers of James Boswell Relating to the Making of the Life of Johnson.* Ed. Marshall Waingrow. Vol. II of the Yale Edition of the Private Papers of James Boswell. New York: McGraw-Hill, 1969.

———. *The Life of Samuel Johnson, LL.D.* 1st ed. 2 vols. London: Dilly, 1791 (pirated in 3 vols. Dublin: Chambers, etc., 1792); *Principal Corrections and Additions.* London: Dilly, 1793.

———. *The Life of Samuel Johnson, LL.D.* 2nd ed. 3 vols. London: Dilly, 1793; 3rd ed., 1799.

———. *The Life of Samuel Johnson, LL.D.* Ed. and enlarged by Edmond Malone. 4th ed. 4 vols. London: Cadell and Davies, 1804; 5th ed., 1807; 6th ed., 1811.

———. *The Life of Samuel Johnson, LL.D., including A Journal of a Tour to the Hebrides.* Ed. and enlarged by John Wilson Croker. 5 vols. London: Murray, 1831.

———. *London Journal.* Ed. F. A. Pottle. New York: McGraw-Hill, 1950.

———. *Private Papers of James Boswell, from Malahide Castle.* Ed. Geoffrey Scott. Vol. VI. New York: Rudge, 1929.

Bowen, Catherine Drinker. *Biography: The Craft and the Calling.* Boston: Little, Brown, 1968.

Boyce, Benjamin. *The Theophrastan Character in England to 1642.* Cambridge: Harvard Univ. Press, 1947.

Brack, O. M., and Robert E. Kelley, eds. *The Early Biographies of Samuel Johnson.* Iowa City: Univ. of Iowa Press, 1974.

Braudy, Leo. *Narrative Form in History and Fiction.* Princeton: Princeton Univ. Press, 1970.

Brett, R. L. *William Hazlitt.* London: Longman, 1977.

The British Poets Including Translation. 100 vols. Chiswick: Carpenter, etc., 1822.

Britt, Albert. *The Great Biographers.* New York: McGraw-Hill, 1936.

Bromwich, David. *Hazlitt, The Mind of a Critic.* New York: Oxford Univ. Press, 1983.

Bronson, Bertrand H. *Johnson Agonistes and Other Essays.* Cambridge: Cambridge Univ. Press, 1946.

Browning, J. D., ed. *Biography in the 18th Century.* New York: Garland, 1980.

Bruss, Elizabeth. *Autobiographical Acts: The Changing Situation of a Literary Genre.* Baltimore: Johns Hopkins Univ. Press, 1976.

Buckley, Jerome. *The Turning Key: Autobiography and the Subjective Impulse Since 1800.* Cambridge: Harvard Univ. Press, 1984.

Budworth, Joseph. *A Fortnight's Ramble to the Lakes.* 1st ed. London: Cadell, 1792. 2nd ed., 1795; 3rd ed., 1810.

Butt, John. *Biography in the Hands of Walton, Johnson, and Boswell.* Berkeley: Univ. of California Press, 1966.

Byron, George Gordon. *Byron's Letters and Journals.* Ed. Leslie A. Marchand. 6 vols. London: Murray, 1973–82.

———. *Complete Poetical Works.* Ed. Jerome McGann. 5 vols. Oxford: Clarendon, 1980–85.

Camden, Carroll, ed. *Restoration and Eighteenth Century Literature: Essays in Honor of Alan Dugald McKillop.* Chicago: Univ. of Chicago Press, 1963.

Campbell, Thomas. *Specimens of the British Poets with Biographical and Critical Notices and an Essay on English Poetry.* 7 vols. London: Murray, 1819.

Canary, Robert H., and Henry Kozicki, eds. *The Writing of History: Literary Form and Historical Understanding.* Madison: Univ. of Wisconsin Press, 1978.

Carlyle, Thomas. *Critical and Miscellaneous Essays.* Vols. 26–30 of *The Works of Thomas Carlyle.* Ed. H. D. Traill. 30 vols. London: Chapman and Hill, 1899.

———. *On Heroes, Hero-worship, and the Heroic in History.* London: Fraser, 1841.

Cary, Henry Francis. *Lives of English Poets from Johnson to Kirke White designed as a continuation of Johnson's Lives.* London: Bohn, 1846 (orig. *London Magazine,* 1821–24).

Cassirer, Ernst. *An Essay on Man: An Introduction to a Philosophy of Human Culture.* New Haven: Yale Univ. Press, 1979 (orig. 1944).

Chalmers, Alexander. *The Works of the English Poets from Chaucer to Cowper including the series edited with Prefaces, Biographical and Critical, by Dr. Samuel Johnson.* 21 vols. London: Johnson, etc., 1810.

Christiansen, Jerome. *Practicing Enlightenment: Hume and the Formation of a Literary Career.* Madison: Univ. of Wisconsin Press, 1987.

Cibber, Theophilus. *The Lives of the Poets of Great Britain and Ireland to the time of Dean Swift.* 5 vols. London: Griffiths, 1753.

Clifford, James L. *From Puzzles to Portraits: Problems of a Literary Biographer.* Chapel Hill: Univ. of North Carolina Press, 1970.

———, ed. *Biography as an Art: Selected Criticism 1560–1960.* London: Oxford Univ. Press, 1962.

———, ed. *Johnson, Boswell and Their Circle.* Oxford: Clarendon, 1965.

Cocks, Geoffrey, and Travis L. Crosby. *Psycho/History: Readings in the Method of Psychology, Psychoanalysis, and History.* New Haven: Yale Univ. Press, 1987.

Cockshut, A. O. J. *The Art of Autobiography in 19th and 20th Century England.* New Haven: Yale Univ. Press, 1984.

———. *Truth to Life: The Art of Biography in the Nineteenth Century.* New York: Harcourt Brace, 1974.

Coe, Charles Norton. *Wordsworth and the Literature of Travel.* New York: Farrar, Straus, 1979 (orig. 1953).

Cohen, Ralph, ed. *New Directions in Literary History.* Baltimore: Johns Hopkins, 1979.

Coleridge, H. N. *Specimens of the Table Talk of the late Samuel Taylor Coleridge*. London: Murray, 1835.

Coleridge, Samuel Taylor. *Biographia Literaria*. Ed. James Engell and W. J. Bate. 2 vols. Princeton: Princeton Univ. Press, 1983.

———. *Collected Letters*. Ed. Earl Leslie Griggs. 6 vols. Oxford: Clarendon, 1966–71.

———. *Complete Poetical Works*. Ed. E. H. Coleridge. 2 vols. Oxford: Clarendon, 1912.

———. *The Friend*. Ed. Barbara E. Rooke. 2 vols. Princeton: Princeton Univ. Press, 1969.

A Collection of The Most Instructive and Amusing Lives Ever Published Written by The Parties Themselves. 33 vols. London: Hunt and Clark, 1826–32.

Collingwood, R. G. *The Idea of History*. Oxford: Clarendon, 1946.

Combe, William. *The Tour of Doctor Syntax in Search of the Picturesque*. London: Ackermann, 1812 (orig. *Poetical Magazine*, 1809).

"Contemporary Authors." *Monthly Magazine*, July 1817 to November 1820.

Cottle, Joseph. *Early Recollections, chiefly relating to the late Samuel Taylor Coleridge*. 2 vols. (London: Longman, 1837).

Courtney, William Prideaux, and David Nichol Smith. *A Bibliography of Samuel Johnson*. Oxford: Clarendon, 1915.

Cross, Wilbur L. *An Outline of Biography From Plutarch to Strachey*. New York: Holt, 1924.

Culler, Jonathan. *On Deconstruction*. Ithaca: Cornell Univ. Press, 1982.

Cunningham, Allan. "Biographical and Critical History of the Literature of the Last Fifty Years." *The Athenaeum*, October 1833 to December 1833; rpt. *Biographical and Critical History of the British Literature of the Last Fifty Years*. Paris: Baudry, 1834.

———. *The Lives of the Most Eminent British Painters, Sculptors, and Architects*. 6 vols. London: Murray, 1829–33.

———, ed. *The Works of Robert Burns and his Life*. 8 vols. London: Cockrane and M'Crone, 1834.

Curran, Stuart. *Poetic Form and British Romanticism*. New York: Oxford Univ. Press, 1986.

Daghlian, Philip B., ed. *Essays in Eighteenth-Century Biography*. Bloomington: Indiana Univ. Press, 1968.

Damrosch, Leopold. *The Uses of Johnson's Criticism*. Charlottesville: Univ. of Virginia Press, 1976.

Darnton, Robert. *The Great Cat Massacre and other Episodes in French Cultural History*. New York: Basic Books, 1984.

De Luca, V. A. *Thomas De Quincey: The Prose of Vision*. Toronto: Univ. of Toronto Press, 1980.

de Man, Paul. *The Rhetoric of Romanticism*. New York: Columbia Univ. Press, 1984.

De Quincey, Thomas. *The Collected Writings of Thomas De Quincey*. Ed. David Masson. 14 vols. Edinburgh: Adam and Charles Black, 1889–90.

———. *Confessions of an English Opium-Eater*. London: Taylor and Hessey, 1822.

————. *Confessions of an English Opium-Eater and other Writings*. Ed. Grevel Lindop. Oxford: Oxford World's Classics, 1985.

————. *Confessions of an English Opium-Eater in both the Revised and the Original Texts, with its Sequels Suspiria de Profundis and The English Mail-Coach*. Ed. Malcolm Elwin. London: Macdonald, 1956.

————. *De Quincey at Work: As Seen in One Hundred Thirty New and Newly Edited Letters*. Ed. Willard Hallam Bonner. Buffalo: Airport Publishers, 1936.

————. *De Quincey's Editorship of the Westmorland Gazette*. Ed. Charles Pollitt. Kendal: Atkinson and Pollitt, 1890.

————. *De Quincey's Writings*. 22 vols. (expanded to 23 vols.) Boston: Ticknor, Reed and Fields, 1850–59.

————. *A Diary of Thomas De Quincey*. Ed. Horace A. Eaton. London: Douglas, 1927.

————. *Dr. Johnson and Lord Chesterfield*. New York: Abramson, 1945.

————. *New Essays by De Quincey*. Ed. Stuart M. Tave. Princeton: Princeton Univ. Press, 1966.

————. *The Posthumous Works of De Quincey*. Ed. Alexander H. Japp. 2 vols. London: William Heinemann, 1891.

————. *Selections Grave and Gay, From Writings Published and Unpublished, of Thomas De Quincey, Revised and Arranged by Himself*. 14 vols. Edinburgh: Hogg, 1853–60. Reissued and expanded: *De Quincey's Works*. 16 vols. Edinburgh: Adam and Charles Black, 1862–71.

————. *Uncollected Writings of Thomas De Quincey*. Ed. James Hogg. 2 vols. London: Sonnenschein, 1890.

Derrida, Jacques. *Margins of Philosophy*. Trans. Alan Bass. Chicago: Univ. of Chicago Press, 1982.

Devlin, D. D. *De Quincey, Wordsworth and the Art of Prose*. London: Macmillan, 1983.

————. *Wordsworth and the Poetry of Epitaphs*. Totowa, NJ: Barnes and Noble, 1981.

D'Israeli, Isaac. *Amenities of Literature*. 3 vols. London: Moxon, 1841.

————. *The Calamities of Authors*. 2 vols. London: Murray, 1812.

————. *Curiosities of Literature*. Ed. Benjamin D'Israeli. 14th ed. 3 vols. London: Moxon, 1849 (1st ed. London: Murray, 1791).

————. *A Dissertation on Anecdotes*. London: Kearsley and Murray, 1793; rpt. New York: Garland, 1972.

————. *An Essay on the Manners and Genius of the Literary Character*. London: Cadell and Davies, 1795; rpt. New York: Garland, 1970; 2nd rev. ed. *The Literary Character, Illustrated by the History of Men of Genius, Drawn from their own Feelings and Confessions*. London: Murray, 1818; 3rd rev. ed. 2 vols., 1822; 4th rev. ed. *The Literary Character; or the History of Men of Genius, Drawn from their own Feelings and Confessions*. 2 vols. London: Colburn, 1828; 5th rev. ed. In *Miscellanies of Literature*. London: Moxon, 1840.

————. *Miscellanies, or Literary Recreations*. London: Cadell and Davies, 1796.

————. *The Quarrels of Authors*. 3 vols. London: Murray, 1814.

————. *The Works of Isaac Disraeli*. Ed. Benjamin Disraeli. 7 vols. London: Routledge, Warnes, 1858–59.

Dowling, William C. *The Boswellian Hero.* Athens: Univ. of Georgia Press, 1979.
————. *Language and Logos in Boswell's Life of Johnson.* Princeton: Princeton Univ. Press, 1981.
Draper, John W. *William Mason, A Study in Eighteenth-Century Culture.* New York: New York Univ. Press, 1924.
Duff, William. *Critical Observations on the Writings of the Most Celebrated Original Geniuses in Poetry.* London: Becket, 1770; rpt. William Bruce Johnson, ed. Delmar, NY: Scholars' Facsimiles, 1973.
————. *An Essay on Original Genius.* London: Dilly, 1767; rpt. John L. Mahoney, ed. Gainesville: Scholars' Facsimiles, 1964.
Dunn, Waldo. *English Biography.* New York: Dutton, 1916.
Eaton, Horace Ainsworth. *Thomas De Quincey: A Biography.* New York: Oxford Univ. Press, 1936.
Edel, Leon. *The Age of the Archive.* Middleton, CT: Wesleyan Univ. Press, 1966.
————. *Literary Biography.* Garden City, NY: Anchor Books, 1959.
————. *Stuff of Sleep and Dreams: Experiments in Literary Psychology.* New York: Harper and Row, 1982.
————. *Writing Lives: Principia Biographia.* London: Norton, 1984.
Egan, Susanna. *Patterns of Experience in Autobiography.* Chapel Hill: Univ. of North Carolina Press, 1984.
Ellman, Richard. *Golden Codgers: Biographical Speculations.* New York: Oxford Univ. Press, 1973.
————. *Literary Biography.* Oxford: Clarendon, 1971.
Emerson, Ralph Waldo. *Representative Men: Seven Lectures.* Boston: Phillips, Sampson, 1850.
Engell, James. *The Creative Imagination: Enlightenment to Romanticism.* Cambridge: Harvard Univ. Press, 1981.
————, ed. *Johnson and His Age.* Cambridge: Harvard Univ. Press, 1984.
Erikson, Erik. *Life History and the Historical Moment.* New York: Norton, 1975.
————. *Young Man Luther: A Study in Psychoanalysis and History.* New York: Norton, 1958.
Evelyn, John. *Memoirs.* Ed. William Bray. 2 vols. London: Colburn, 1818.
Field, Barron. *Barron Field's Memoirs of Wordsworth.* Ed. Geoffrey Little. Sydney: Sydney Univ. Press, 1975.
Folkenflik, Robert. *Samuel Johnson, Biographer.* Ithaca: Cornell Univ. Press, 1978.
Forster, John. *The Life and Adventures of Oliver Goldsmith.* London: Bradbury and Evans, 1848.
Foucault, Michel. *The Archaeology of Knowledge.* Trans. A. M. Sheridan Smith. London: Tavistock, 1972 (orig. 1969).
————. *The Order of Things.* New York: Random House, 1973 (orig. 1966).
Freud, Sigmund. *An Autobiographical Study.* Trans. James Strachey. New York: Norton, 1952 (orig. 1925).
————. *Character and Culture.* Ed. Philip Rieff. New York: Macmillan, 1963.
————. *Leonardo da Vinci and a Memory of His Childhood.* Trans. Alan Tyson. New York: Norton, 1964 (orig. 1914).
————. *The Psychopathology of Everyday Life.* Trans. Alan Tyson. New York: Norton, 1965 (orig. 1901).

Friedson, Anthony M., ed. *New Directions in Biography*. Honolulu: Univ. of Hawaii Press, 1981.

Fromm, Gloria G., ed. *Essaying Biography: A Celebration for Leon Edel*. Honolulu: Univ. of Hawaii Press, 1986.

Frye, Northrop. *Anatomy of Criticism*. Princeton: Princeton Univ. Press, 1973 (orig. 1957).

Fuller, Thomas. *The History of the Worthies of England*. Ed. John Nichols. 2 vols. London: Rivington, etc., 1811 (orig. London: I.G.W.L., 1662).

Fussell, Paul. *Samuel Johnson and the Life of Writing*. New York: Harcourt Brace, 1971.

Garraty, John A. *The Nature of Biography*. New York: Random House, 1964.

Gay, Peter. *Style in History*. New York: Basic Books, 1974.

Genette, Gérard. *Figures of Literary Discourse*. Trans. Alan Sheridan. New York: Columbia Univ. Press, 1982.

————. *Narrative Discourse*. Trans. Jane E. Lewin. Ithaca: Cornell Univ. Press, 1980.

Gerard, Alexander. *An Essay on Genius*. London: Cadell, 1774; rpt. Bernhard Fabian, ed. Munich: Fink, 1966.

————. *An Essay on Taste*. 3rd ed. London: Cadell, 1780; 1st ed., 1759; rpt. Walter J. Hipple, ed. Gainesville: Scholars' Facsimiles, 1963.

Gilbert, Felix, and Stephen Grubard, eds. *Historical Studies Today*. New York: Norton, 1972.

Gilfillian, George. *A Gallery of Literary Portraits*. Edinburgh: Tait's, 1845.

————. *A Second Gallery of Literary Portraits*. Edinburgh: Hogg, 1850.

————. *A Third Gallery of Portraits*. Edinburgh: Hogg, 1854.

Gillman, James. *The Life of Samuel Taylor Coleridge*. London: Pickering, 1838.

Gilpin, William. *Observations of the River Wye and Several Parts of South Wales, Relative Chiefly to Picturesque Beauty*. London: Blamire, 1782.

————. *Observations Relative Chiefly to Picturesque Beauty . . . Particularly the Mountains and Lakes of Cumberland and Westmoreland*. 2 vols. London: Blamire, 1776.

Gittings, Robert. *The Nature of Biography*. London: Heinemann, 1978.

Goldman, Albert. *The Mine and the Mint: Sources for the Writings of Thomas De Quincey*. Carbondale: Southern Illinois Univ. Press, 1965.

Graham, Walker. *English Literary Periodicals*. New York: Nelson, 1930.

Gross, John. *The Rise and Fall of the Man of Letters*. New York: Collier, 1969.

Grundy, Isobel, ed. *Samuel Johnson: New Critical Essays*. Totowa, NJ: Barnes and Noble, 1984.

Hagstrum, Jean L. *Samuel Johnson's Literary Criticism*. Minneapolis: Univ. of Minnesota Press, 1952.

Haller, William. *The Early Life of Robert Southey*. New York: Columbia Univ. Press, 1917.

Harper, George McLean. *William Wordsworth*. 2 vols. London: Murray, 1923.

Hart, Francis R. *Lockhart as Romantic Biographer*. Edinburgh: Edinburgh Univ. Press, 1971.

Hartman, Geoffrey. *Beyond Formalism*. New Haven: Yale Univ. Press, 1970.

————. *Criticism in the Wilderness*. New Haven: Yale Univ. Press, 1980.

Hayden, John O. *The Romantic Reviewers*. London: Routledge, 1969.

Hayley, William. *Two Dialogues: Containing a Comparative View of the Lives, Characters and Writings of Philip, the late Earl of Chesterfield, and Dr. Samuel Johnson*. London: Cadell, 1787; rpt. Robert E. Kelley, ed. Gainesville: Scholars' Facsimiles, 1970.

Hazlitt, W. Carew. *Four Generations of a Literary Family*. 2 vols. London: Reoway, 1897.

———. *Memoirs of William Hazlitt*. 2 vols. London: Bentley, 1867.

Hazlitt, William. *The Complete Works of William Hazlitt*. Ed. P. P. Howe. 21 vols. London: Dent, 1930–34.

———. *Lectures chiefly on the Dramatic Literature of the Age of Elizabeth*. London: Stodart and Steuart, 1820.

———. *Lectures on the English Comic Writers*. London: Taylor and Hessey, 1819.

———. *Lectures on the English Poets*. London: Taylor and Hessey, 1818.

———. *The Letters of William Hazlitt*. Ed. Herschel Moreland Sikes, Willard Hallam Bonner, and Gerald Lahey. New York: New York Univ. Press, 1978.

———. *Liber Amoris*. Ed. Gerald Lahey. New York: New York Univ. Press, 1980.

———. *The Plain Speaker: Opinions on Books, Men, and Things*. 2 vols. London: Colburn, 1826.

———. *The Round Table: A Collection of Essays on Literature, Men, and Manners* (with essays by Leigh Hunt). 2 vols. London: Longman, etc., 1817.

———. *The Spirit of The Age: or, Contemporary Portraits*. 1st ed. London: Colburn, 1825; 2nd ed. Paris: Galignani, 1825; 3rd ed. (called 2nd ed.) London: Colburn, 1825.

———. *Table Talk; or, Original Essays*. 2 vols. Vol. I, London: Warren, 1821. Vol. II, London: Colburn, 1822; rpt. Paris: Galignani, 1825 (with additions from *The Plain Speaker*).

Heron, Robert. *Observations Made in a Journey through the Western Counties of Scotland*. 2 vols. Perth: Morison, 1793.

Hill, George Birkbeck, ed. *Johnsonian Miscellanies*. 2 vols. Oxford: Clarendon, 1907.

Hilles, Frederick W., ed. *New Light on Dr. Johnson*. New Haven: Yale Univ. Press, 1959.

Hipple, Walter John. *The Beautiful, The Sublime, and the Picturesque in 18th-Century British Aesthetic History*. Carbondale: Southern Illinois Univ. Press, 1957.

Hirsch, E. D. *The Aims of Interpretation*. Chicago: Univ. of Chicago Press, 1976.

Hoberman, Ruth. *Modernizing Lives: Experiments in English Biography, 1919–1939*. Carbondale: Southern Illinois Univ. Press, 1987.

Hogg, James [Ettrick Shepherd]. *Familiar Anecdotes of Sir Walter Scott* (New York: Harper, 1834); rpt. *The Domestic Manners and Private Life of Sir Walter Scott*. Reid: Glasgow, 1834 (pirated).

———. *Memoirs of the Author's Life and Familiar Anecdotes of Sir Walter Scott*. Ed. Douglas S. Mack. Edinburgh: Scottish Academic Press, 1972; *Anecdotes of Sir W. Scott*. Edinburgh: Scottish Academic Press, 1983.

Hogg, James [publisher]. *De Quincey and his Friends*. London: Sampson etc., 1895.

Homberger, Eric, and John Charmley. *The Troubled Face of Biography*. London: Macmillan, 1988.

Hook, Sidney. *The Hero in History.* Boston: Beacon, 1943.

Hoover, Dwight D., and John Koumoulides, eds. *Focus on Biography.* Muncie, IN: Ball State Univ. Press, 1974.

Horne, Richard Hengist. *A New Spirit of the Age.* 2 vols. London: Smith, 1844.

———. *A New Spirit of the Age.* Ed. Walter Jerrold. London: Oxford Univ. Press, 1907.

Howe, P. P. *The Life of William Hazlitt.* Westport, CT: Greenwood Press, 1972 (orig. 1947).

Howitt, William. *Homes and Haunts of the Most Eminent British Poets.* 2 vols. London: Bentley, 1847.

———. *Visits to Remarkable Places.* 2 vols. London: Longman, etc. Vol. I, 1840; Vol. II, 1842 (orig. *Tait's,* 1839).

Hume, David. *The Philosophical Works of David Hume.* Ed. T. H. Green and T. H. Grose. 4 vols. London: Longmans, Green, 1898.

Hunt, John Dixon. *The Figure in the Landscape: Poetry, Painting and Gardening During the Eighteenth Century.* Baltimore: Johns Hopkins Univ. Press, 1976.

Hunt, Leigh. *The Autobiography of Leigh Hunt.* Ed. J. E. Morpurgo. London: Cresset, 1949.

———. *Leigh Hunt's Autobiography, The Earliest Sketches.* Ed. Stephen F. Fogle. Gainesville: Univ. of Florida Press, 1959.

———. *Leigh Hunt's Literary Criticism.* Ed. Lawrence Huston Houtchens and Carolyn Washburn Houtchens. New York: Columbia Univ. Press, 1956.

———. *Lord Byron and Some of his Contemporaries; with Recollections of the Author's Life and of his Visit to Italy.* London: Colburn, 1828; rpt. 2 vols. London: Colburn, 1828.

———. "Sketches of the Living Poets." *The Examiner,* July 1821 to October 1821.

Hussey, Christopher. *The Picturesque: Studies in a Point of View.* London: Cass, 1967 (orig. 1927).

Jameson, Fredric. *The Political Unconscious: Narrative as a Socially Symbolic Act.* Ithaca: Cornell Univ. Press, 1981.

Japp, Alexander H. *De Quincey Memorials.* London: Heinemann, 1891.

———. *Thomas De Quincey: His Life and Writings with Unpublished Correspondence.* London: Hogg, 1890.

Johnson, Edgar. *One Mighty Torrent: The Drama of Biography.* New York: Stockpole Sons, 1937.

Johnson, Samuel. *Early Biographical Writings of Dr. Johnson.* Ed. J. D. Fleeman. Westmead, England: Gregg International, 1973.

———. *The Idler and the Adventurer.* Ed. W. J. Bate, John M. Bullitt, and L. F. Powell. New Haven: Yale Univ. Press, 1963.

———. *A Journey to the Western Islands of Scotland* (orig. 1775). And James Boswell, *The Journal of a Tour to the Hebrides with Samuel Johnson* (orig. 1785). Ed. Allan Wendt. Boston: Houghton Mifflin, 1965.

———. *The Letters of Samuel Johnson.* Ed. R. W. Chapman. 3 vols. Oxford: Clarendon, 1952.

———. *Lives of the English Poets.* Ed. George Birkbeck Hill. 3 vols. Oxford: Clarendon, 1945.

———. *The Lives of the English Poets; and a Criticism on their Works.* 3 vols. Dublin: Whitestone, etc., 1779–81 (pirated).

———. *The Lives of the Most Eminent English Poets; with Critical Observations on their Works.* 2nd rev. ed. 4 vols. London: Bathurst, etc., 1781.

———. *The Lives of the Most Eminent English Poets.* 3rd rev. ed. 4 vols. London: Bathurst, 1783 (last in Johnson's lifetime).

———. *Lives of the Most Eminent English Poets, with Critical Observations on their Works.* Ed. Peter Cunningham. 3 vols. London: Murray, 1854.

———. *Prefaces, Biographical and Critical, to the Works of the English Poets.* 1st ed. 68 vols. (10 vols. of prefaces, 58 vols. of works and index). London: Nichols, for Bathurst, etc., 1779–81.

———. *The Rambler.* Ed. W. J. Bate and Albrecht B. Strauss. 3 vols. New Haven: Yale Univ. Press, 1969.

———. *The Works of the English Poets, with Prefaces, Biographical and Critical, by Dr. Samuel Johnson.* 75 vols. (6 vols. of lives, including new ones not by Johnson). London: Nichols, 1790.

Johnston, James. *Biography: The Literature of Personality.* New York: Century, 1927.

Jordan, John E. *De Quincey to Wordsworth: A Biography of a Relationship.* Berkeley: Univ. of California Press, 1962.

Keats, John. *The Letters of John Keats.* Ed. Hyder Edward Rollins. 2 vols. Cambridge: Harvard Univ. Press, 1958.

———. *Poems.* Ed. Jack Stillinger. Cambridge: Harvard Univ. Press, 1978.

Kendall, Paul Murray. *The Art of Biography.* New York: Norton, 1965.

Kernan, Alvin B. *Printing Technology, Letters and Samuel Johnson.* Princeton: Princeton Univ. Press, 1987.

Kinnaird, John. *William Hazlitt: Critic of Power.* New York: Columbia Univ. Press, 1978.

Knight, G. Wilson. *Lord Byron's Marriage.* London: Routledge, 1957.

Kris, Ernst. *Psychoanalytic Explorations in Art.* New York: International Universities Press, 1952.

Krutch, Joseph Wood. *Samuel Johnson.* New York: Holt, 1945.

Lamb, Charles. *Lamb as Critic.* Ed. Roy Park. London: Routledge and Kegan Paul, 1980.

Lang, Andrew. *The Life and Letters of John Gibson Lockhart.* 2 vols. London: Nimmo, 1897.

Langbaine, Gerard. *An Account of the English Dramatic Poets.* Oxford: West and Clements, 1691; rpt. John Loftis, ed. 2 vols. Los Angeles: Univ. of California Press, 1971.

Lee, Sidney. *The Perspective of Biography.* London: English Association, 1918.

———. *Principles of Biography.* Cambridge: Cambridge Univ. Press, 1911.

Lejeune, Philippe. *Le pacte autobiographique.* Paris: Seuil, 1975.

Levin, David. *History as a Romantic Art.* Stanford: Stanford Univ. Press, 1959.

Levinson, Marjorie. *The Romantic Fragment Poem.* Chapel Hill: Univ. of North Carolina Press, 1986.

Lifton, Robert J., and Eric Olson, eds. *Explorations in Psychohistory.* New York: Simon and Schuster, 1974.

Lindop, Grevel. *The Opium-Eater: A Life of Thomas De Quincey.* London: Dent, 1981.

Lipking, Lawrence. *The Ordering of the Arts in Eighteenth-Century England.* Princeton: Princeton Univ. Press, 1970.

Lockhart, John Gibson. *Memoirs of the Life of Sir Walter Scott.* 7 vols. Edinburgh: Cadell, 1837–38.

———. *Memoirs of Sir Walter Scott.* 5 vols. London: Macmillan, 1900.

———. *Peter's Letters to His Kinsfolk.* 1st ed. (labeled 2nd ed.). 3 vols. Edinburgh: Blackwood, 1819.

———. *Peter's Letters to His Kinsfolk.* Ed. William Ruddick. Edinburgh: Scottish Academic Press, 1977.

Lodge, David. *The Modes of Modern Writing.* London: Arnold, 1977.

Longaker, Mark. *Contemporary Biography.* Philadelphia: Univ. of Pennsylvania Press, 1934.

———. *English Biography in the Eighteenth Century.* Philadelphia: Univ. of Pennsylvania Press, 1931.

Lovell, Ernest J. *His Very Self and Voice: Collected Conversations of Lord Byron.* New York: Macmillan, 1954.

Lukács, Georg. *Writer and Critic.* London: Merlin, 1978.

Macaulay, Thomas Babington. *Miscellaneous Works of Lord Macaulay.* Ed. Lady Trevelyan. 5 vols. New York: Harper, 1899 (orig. 1866).

MacClintock, William Darnell. *Joseph Warton's Essay on Pope: A History of the Five Editions.* Chapel Hill: Univ. of North Carolina Press, 1933.

Maner, Martin. *The Philosophical Biographer: Doubt and Dialectic in Johnson's Lives of the Poets.* Athens: Univ. of Georgia Press, 1988.

Maniquis, Robert. *Lonely Empires: Personal and Public Visions of Thomas De Quincey.* Madison: Univ. of Wisconsin Press Literary Monographs, 1976.

Manwaring, Elizabeth Wheeler. *Italian Landscape in Eighteenth-Century England.* New York: Oxford Univ. Press, 1935.

Marchand, Leslie A. *Byron, A Biography.* 3 vols. New York: Knopf, 1957.

Marcus, Steven. *Freud and the Culture of Psychoanalysis.* New York: Norton, 1987.

Mason, William. *The Poems of Mr. Gray: to which are prefixed Memoirs of his Life and Writings.* York: Dodsley, 1775.

Maurice, F. D. "Sketches of Contemporary Authors." *The Athenaeum,* January 1828 to July 1828.

Maurois, André. *Aspects of Biography.* Trans. S. C. Roberts. Cambridge: Cambridge Univ. Press, 1929.

McFarland, Thomas. *Originality and Imagination.* Baltimore: Johns Hopkins Univ. Press, 1985.

———. *Romanticism and the Forms of Ruin.* Princeton: Princeton Univ. Press, 1981.

McGann, Jerome. *The Romantic Ideology.* Chicago: Univ. of Chicago Press, 1983.

McKenzie, Gordon. *Critical Responsiveness: A Study of the Psychological Current in Later Eighteenth-Century Criticism.* Berkeley: Univ. of California Press, 1949.

Meyers, Jeffrey, ed. *The Craft of Literary Biography.* New York: Macmillan, 1985.

Miller, J. Hillis. *The Disappearance of God.* Cambridge: Harvard Univ. Press, 1963.

Misch, George. *A History of Autobiography in Antiquity.* Trans. G. Misch and E. W. Dickes. Rev. ed. 2 vols. London: Routledge and Kegan Paul, 1950.

Mitchell, W. J. T., ed. *On Narrative.* Chicago: Univ. of Chicago Press, 1981.

Moore, Doris Langley. *The Late Lord Byron.* London: Murray, 1961.

Moore, Thomas. *Letters and Journals of Lord Byron: with Notices of his Life*. 2 vols. London: Murray, 1830.

Moorman, Mary. *William Wordsworth, A Biography: The Early Years, 1770–1803*. Oxford: Clarendon, 1969. *The Later Years, 1803–1850*. Oxford: Clarendon, 1966.

Moraitis, George, and George H. Pollock. *Psychoanalytic Studies of Biography*. Madison: International Universities Press, 1987.

Mortimer, Thomas. *The British Plutarch*. 6 vols. London: Dilly, 1776.

Nadel, Ira Bruce. *Biography: Fiction, Fact and Form*. New York: St. Martin's, 1984.

Nath, Prem, ed. *Fresh Reflections on Samuel Johnson: Essays in Criticism*. Troy, NY: Whitson, 1987.

Nepos, Cornelius. *De Viris Illustribus*. Trans. J. C. Rolfe. London: Loeb Library, 1929.

Nichols, John. *Literary Anecdotes of the Eighteenth Century*. 9 vols. London: Nichols, 1812–16.

———. *Literary Anecdotes of the Eighteenth Century*. Ed. Colin Clair. Carbondale: Southern Illinois Univ. Press, 1967.

———. *Minor Lives: A Collection of Biographies by John Nichols*. Ed. Edward L. Hart. Cambridge: Harvard Univ. Press, 1971.

Nicholson, Harold. *The Development of English Biography*. London: Hogarth, 1927.

Nicholson, Norman. *The Lakers: Adventures of the First Tourists*. London: Hale, 1955.

North, Roger. *The Lives of the Norths*. Ed. A. Jessop. 3 vols. Farnborough, England: Gregg International, 1972.

Novarr, David. *The Lines of Life: Theories of Biography, 1880–1970*. West Lafayette, IN: Purdue Univ. Press, 1980.

———. *The Making of Walton's Lives*. Ithaca: Cornell Univ. Press, 1958.

Noyes, Russell. *Wordsworth and the Art of Landscape*. Bloomington: Indiana Univ. Press, 1968.

Oates, Stephen B. *Biography as High Adventure: Life-Writers Speak on Their Art*. Amherst: Univ. of Massachusetts Press, 1986.

Ogden, James. *Isaac D'Israeli*. Oxford: Clarendon, 1969.

Olney, James. *Autobiography: Essays Theoretical and Critical*. Princeton: Princeton Univ. Press, 1980.

Overbury, Thomas. *The Overburian Characters*. Ed. W. J. Paylor. Oxford: Blackwell, 1936 (orig. series begins 1614).

Pachter, Marc, ed. *Telling Lives: The Biographer's Art*. Washington, DC: New Republic Books, 1979.

Pagliaro, Harold E., ed. *Studies in Eighteenth-Century Culture*. Cleveland: Case Western Reserve Univ. Press, 1973.

Panofsky, Erwin. *Meaning in the Visual Arts*. Garden City, NY: Doubleday, 1955.

Park, Roy. *Hazlitt and the Spirit of the Age*. Oxford: Clarendon, 1971.

Pascal, Roy. *Design and Truth in Autobiography*. London: Routledge and Kegan Paul, 1960.

Passler, David L. *Time, Form, and Style in Boswell's Life of Johnson*. New Haven: Yale Univ. Press, 1971.

Pater, Walter. *The Renaissance*. London: Macmillan, 1873. Rev. eds. 1877, 1888, 1893.

Patmore, P. G. *My Friends and Acquaintance*. London: Saunders and Otley, 1854.

Peacock, Thomas Love. "The Four Ages of Poetry." *Olliers Literary Miscellany,* 1820.

Pepys, Samuel. *Memoirs.* Ed. Richard Braybrooke. 2 vols. London: Colburn, 1825.

Petric, Dennis W. *Ultimately Fiction: Design in Modern American Literary Biography.* West Lafayette, IN: Purdue Univ. Press, 1981.

Peyre, Henri. *Literature and Sincerity.* New Haven: Yale Univ. Press, 1963.

Phillips, Edward. *Theatrum Poetarum.* London: Smith, 1675.

Piozzi, Hester Thrale. *Anecdotes of the Late Samuel Johnson* (orig. 1786). And William Shaw, *Memories of the Life and Writing of the Late Dr. Samuel Johnson* (orig. 1785). Ed. Arthur Sherbo. London: Oxford Univ. Press, 1974.

Plutarch. *Lives.* Trans. Bernadette Perrin. 11 vols. London: Loeb Library, 1948.

———. *Lives of the Noble Grecians and Romans.* Ed. Arthur Hugh Clough. New York: Modern Library, n.d. (orig. *Plutarch's Lives, the Translation called Dryden's.* Boston: Little, Brown, 1868).

Pottle, F. A. *The Literary Career of James Boswell.* Oxford: Clarendon, 1965 (orig. 1929).

Priestley, J. B. *William Hazlitt.* London: Longman, 1960.

Radcliffe, Ann. *A Journey Made in the Summer of 1794 . . . to which are added, Observations During a Tour to the Lakes.* London: Robinson, 1795.

Raleigh, Walter. *Six Essays on Johnson.* New York: Russell and Russell, 1965.

Rank, Otto. *Art and Artist: Creative Urge and Personality Development.* Trans. Charles Francis Atkinson. New York: Agathon, 1968 (orig. 1932).

———. *The Myth of the Birth of the Hero.* Trans. F. Robbins and Smith Ely Jelliffe. New York: Brunner, 1952 (orig. 1914).

Rawnsley, Hardwicke Drummond. *Literary Associations of the English Lakes.* 2 vols. Glasgow: MacLehose, 1894.

———. *Reminiscences of Wordsworth among the Peasantry of Westmorland.* London: Dillon's, 1968 (orig. 1882).

Ready, Robert. *Hazlitt at Table.* East Brunswick, NJ: Associated Universities Press, 1981.

Reed, Joseph W. *English Biography in the Early Nineteenth Century 1801–1838.* New Haven: Yale Univ. Press, 1966.

Reeve, Clara. *The Progress of Romance.* New York: Facsimile Text, 1930 (orig. 1785).

Reynolds, Joshua. *Discourses on Art.* Ed. Robert R. Wark. San Marino, CA: Huntington Library, 1959 (orig. 1797).

Richetti, John. *Philosophical Writing: Locke, Berkeley, Hume.* Cambridge: Harvard Univ. Press, 1985.

Ricoeur, Paul. *History and Truth.* Trans. Charles A. Kelbley. Evanston: Northwestern Univ. Press, 1965.

Robertson, Joseph. *Lives of the Scottish Poets.* 3 vols. London: Thomas Boys, 1821–22.

Robinson, Henry Crabb. *On Books and their Writers.* Ed. Edith J. Morley. 3 vols. London: Dent, 1938.

Rousseau, Jean Jacques. *Les confessions.* Vol. I of *Oeuvres complètes.* Ed. Bernard Gagnebin and Marcel Raymond. 4 vols. Paris: Gallimard, 1959–61.

Said, Edward W. *Beginnings.* New York: Basic Books, 1975.

Sainte-Beuve, Charles Augustin. *Portraits contemporains*. Rev. ed. 5 vols. Paris: Levy, 1869–71 (orig. 3 vols., 1846).

Sartre, Jean-Paul. *Saint Genet*. Vol. I of *Oeuvres complètes de Jean Genet*. 5 vols. Paris: Gallimard, 1952.

Schneider, Elizabeth. *The Aesthetics of William Hazlitt: A Study of the Philosophical Basis of His Criticism*. Philadelphia: Univ. of Pennsylvania Press, 1933.

Scholes, Robert, and Robert Kellogg. *The Nature of Narrative*. Oxford: Oxford Univ. Press, 1966.

Schwartz, Richard B. *Boswell's Johnson: A Preface to the Life*. Madison: Univ. of Wisconsin Press, 1978.

Scott, John. "Living Authors." *London Magazine,* January 1820 to May 1821.

Scott, Walter. "The Life of John Dryden." In Vol. I of *The Works of John Dryden*. Ed. Walter Scott. 18 vols. London: Millar, 1808. Rev. ed. *The Life of John Dryden*. Ed. John Gibson Lockhart. Edinburgh: Cadell, 1834; rpt. Bernard Kreissman, ed. Lincoln: Univ. of Nebraska Press, 1963.

———. *Lives of the Novelists*. 2 vols. Paris: Galignani, 1825.

———. *Lives of the Novelists*. Ed. Austin Dobson. London: Oxford Univ. Press, 1906.

———. *The Miscellaneous Prose Works of Sir Walter Scott*. 6 vols. Edinburgh: Cadell. London: Longman, 1827.

———, ed. *Ballantyne's Novelist's Library*. 10 vols. London: Hurst, Robinson, 1821–24.

Scriptores Historiae Augustae. Trans. David Magie. 3 vols. London: Loeb Library, 1932.

Sharpe, William. *A Dissertation Upon Genius*. London: Bathurst, 1755; rpt. William Bruce Johnson, ed. Delmar, NY: Scholars' Facsimiles, 1973.

Shelley, Percy Bysshe. *The Complete Works of Percy Bysshe Shelley*. Ed. Roger Ingpen and Walter E. Peck. 10 vols. New York: Scribner's, 1930.

———. *The Letters of Percy Bysshe Shelley*. Ed. Frederick L. Jones. 2 vols. Oxford: Clarendon, 1964.

Shelston, Alan. *Biography*. London: Methuen, 1977.

Siebenschuh, William R. *Fictional Techniques and Factual Works*. Athens: Univ. of Georgia Press, 1983.

———. *Form and Purpose in Boswell's Biographical Works*. Berkeley: Univ. of California Press, 1972.

Smith, David Nichol. *Characters from the Histories and Memoirs of the Seventeenth Century*. Oxford: Clarendon, 1918.

Snyder, Robert Lance, ed. *Thomas De Quincey: Bicentenary Studies*. Norman: Univ. of Oklahoma Press, 1985.

Southey, Robert. *Attempts in Verse, by John Jones, an old servant . . . and an introductory essay on the lives and works of our uneducated poets, by Robert Southey*. London: Murray, 1831 (by subscription); 2nd ed. *Southey's Lives of the Uneducated Poets: To which is added Attempts in Verse by John Jones, an old servant*. London: Murray, 1831.

———. *Life of Nelson*. 2 vols. London: Murray, 1813; rpt. Geoffrey Callender, ed. London: Dent, 1922.

———. *The Life of Wesley and the Rise and Progress of Methodism.* 2 vols. London: Longman, 1820.

———. *The Lives and Works of the Uneducated Poets.* Ed. J. S. Childers. London: Humphrey Milford, 1925.

———. *Lives of the British Admirals.* 5 vols. London: Longman, 1833.

———. *The Remains of Henry Kirke White . . . with an account of his life.* 2 vols. London: Vernor, 1807–8; rpt. Donald H. Reiman, ed. New York: Garland, 1927.

———. *Select Works of The British Poets from Chaucer to Johnson with Biographical Sketches.* London: Longman, 1831.

———. *Specimens of the Later English Poets with Preliminary Notices.* 3 vols. London: Longman, 1807.

———, ed. *Works of William Cowper.* 15 vols. London: Baldwin and Craddock, 1835–37.

Spacks, Patricia. *Imagining a Self.* Cambridge: Harvard Univ. Press, 1976.

Spence, Joseph. *Anecdotes, Observations, and Characters of Books and Men.* Ed. Samuel Weller Singer. London: Carpenter, etc., 1820.

———. *Observations, Anecdotes, and Characters of Books and Men.* London: Murray, 1820.

———. *Observations, Anecdotes, and Characters of Books and Men Collected from Conversation.* Ed. James M. Osborn. 2 vols. Oxford: Clarendon, 1966.

Spengemann, William C. *The Forms of Autobiography.* New Haven: Yale Univ. Press, 1980.

Sprat, Thomas. "An Account of the Life and Writings of Mr. Abraham Cowley: Written to Mr. M. Clifford." In *The Works of Mr. Abraham Cowley.* London: Herringman, 1668.

Stanfield, James Field. *An Essay on the Study and Composition of Biography.* Sunderland, England: Garbutt, 1813.

Stauffer, Donald A. *The Art of Biography in Eighteenth Century England and Bibliographical Supplement.* 2 vols. Princeton: Princeton Univ. Press, 1941.

———. *English Biography Before 1700.* Cambridge: Harvard Univ. Press, 1930.

Stockdale, Percival. *Lectures on the Truly Eminent English Poets.* 2 vols. London: Longman, 1807.

Strachey, Lytton. *Eminent Victorians.* London: Chatto and Windus, 1918.

Suetonius. *The Lives of the Caesars* and *The Lives of Illustrious Men.* Trans. John C. Rolfe. 2 vols. London: Loeb Library, 1951.

Tacitus, Cornelius. *Agricola.* Trans. Maurice Hutter. London: Loeb Library, 1946.

Taine, Hippolyte. *Histoire de la littérature Anglaise.* Rev. ed. 5 vols. Paris: Hachette, 1866–78 (orig. 4 vols., 1864).

Talfourd, Thomas Noon. "An Attempt to Estimate the Poetical Talent of the Present Age." *The Pamphleteer,* 1815.

———. *The Letters of Charles Lamb with a Sketch of his Life.* 2 vols. London: Moxon, 1837. Rev. ed. *Final Memorials of Charles Lamb.* London: Moxon, 1848.

Tawney, R. H. *Social History and Literature.* Cambridge: Cambridge Univ. Press, 1950.

Thayer, William Roscoe. *The Art of Biography.* New York: Scribner's, 1920.

Theophrastus. *Characters.* Trans. J. M. Edmunds. London: Loeb Library, 1953.

Todorov, Tzvetan. *The Poetics of Prose.* Trans. Richard Howard. Ithaca: Cornell Univ. Press, 1977.

Trilling, Lionel. *The Liberal Imagination.* New York: Viking, 1950.

————. *Sincerity and Authenticity.* Cambridge: Harvard Univ. Press, 1972.

Tuveson, Ernest Lee. *The Imagination as a Means of Grace: Locke and the Aesthetics of Romanticism.* Berkeley: Univ. of California Press, 1960.

Vance, John A., ed. *Boswell's Life of Johnson: New Questions, New Answers.* Athens: Univ. of Georgia Press, 1985.

Vasari, Giorgio. *Le vite de' più eccellenti architetti, pittori, et scultori italiani [pittori, scultori, et architettori].* Florence: Torrentino, 1550; 2nd ed. *Reviste et ampliate.* Florence: Giunti, 1568. *The Lives of the Most Eminent Painters, Sculptors, and Architects.* Trans. Gaston du C. De Vere. 10 vols. London: Macmillan, 1912–15.

Veninga, James F., ed. *The Biographer's Gift.* College Station: Texas A&M Univ. Press, 1983.

Wahba, Magdi, ed. *Johnsonian Studies.* Cairo: dist. Oxford Univ. Press, 1982.

Walpole, Horace. *Anecdotes of Painting in England.* 4 vols. Strawberry Hill, 1762.

————. *A Catalogue of the Royal and Noble Authors of England.* 2 vols. Strawberry Hill, 1758.

————. *Memoires of the Last Ten Years of the Reign of George the Second.* 2 vols. London: Murray, 1822.

Walton, Izaak. *The Lives of Donne, Wotton, Hooker, Herbert, Sanderson.* London: Oxford Univ. Press, 1973 (orig. *Donne,* 1640; *Wotton,* 1651; *Hooker,* 1665; *Herbert,* 1670; *Sanderson,* 1678; collectively, 1670–75).

Wardle, Ralph M. *Hazlitt.* Lincoln: Univ. of Nebraska Press, 1971.

Warton, Joseph. *An Essay on the Writings and Genius of Pope.* 1st ed. London: Cooper, 1756. Rev. eds. 1762, 1772. *An Essay on the Genius and Writings of Pope.* Vol. II. London: Dodsley, 1782; rpt. 2 vols. New York: Garland, 1974.

Warton, Thomas. *The History of English Poetry From the Close of the Eleventh to the Commencement of the Eighteenth Century.* 4 vols. London: Dodsley, 1774–81; rpt. 4 vols. London: Tegg, 1824.

Watson, J. R. *Picturesque Landscape and English Romantic Poetry.* London: Hutchinson, 1970.

Wellek, René. *Concepts of Criticism.* Ed. Stephen G. Nichols. New Haven: Yale Univ. Press, 1963.

————. *A History of Modern Criticism.* 7 vols. New Haven: Yale Univ. Press, 1955–86.

————. *The Rise of English Literary History.* Chapel Hill: Univ. of North Carolina Press, 1941.

West, Thomas. *A Guide to the Lakes in Cumberland, Westmorland and Lancashire.* London: Richardson and Urquhart, 1778. Rev. ed. *A Guide to the Lakes,* ed. William Cockin. London: Richardson and Urquhart, 1780.

Whale, John C. *Thomas De Quincey's Reluctant Autobiography.* Totowa, NJ: Barnes and Noble, 1984.

White, Hayden. *Metahistory: The Historical Imagination in Nineteenth-Century Europe.* Baltimore: Johns Hopkins Univ. Press, 1973.

Whittemore, Reed. *Pure Lives: The Early Biographers.* Baltimore: Johns Hopkins Univ. Press, 1988.

Wilkinson, Joseph. *Select Views in Cumberland, Westmorland, and Lancashire*. London: Ackermann, 1810.

Wilkinson, Thomas. *Tours to the British Mountains*. London: Taylor and Hessey, 1824.

Williams, Raymond. *The Long Revolution*. New York: Columbia Univ. Press, 1984 (orig. 1961).

———. *Marxism and Literature*. Oxford: Oxford Univ. Press, 1977.

Wilson, Edmund. *The Wound and the Bow: Seven Studies in Literature*. Boston: Houghton Mifflin, 1941.

Wilson, John. "Letters from the Lakes." *Blackwood's*, January 1819 to March 1819 (anonymous); rpt. *Letters from the Lakes*. Ambleside: Middleton, 1901 (orig. 1889).

Winstanley, William. *The Lives of the Most Famous English Poets*. London: Clark, 1687; rpt. William Riley Parker, ed. Gainesville: Scholars' Facsimiles, 1963.

Wood, Anthony. *Athenae Oxonienses*. 2 vols. London: Bennet, 1691–92.

Woolf, Virginia. *The Common Reader*. London: Hogarth, 1925.

Wordsworth, William. *The Letters of William and Dorothy Wordsworth*. Ed. Ernest de Selincourt, Chester L. Shaver, Mary Moorman, and Alan G. Hill. 2nd rev. ed. 7 vols. Oxford: Clarendon, 1967–88.

———. *The Poetical Works of William Wordsworth*. Ed. E. De Selincourt and Helen Darbishire. Rev. ed. 7 vols. Oxford: Clarendon, 1940–59.

———. *The Prose Works of William Wordsworth*. Ed. W. J. B. Owen and Jane Worthington Smyser. 3 vols. Oxford: Clarendon, 1974.

Xenophon. *Memorabilia of Socrates*. Trans. O. J. Todd. London: Loeb Library, 1979.

Young, Edward. *Conjectures on Original Composition: In A Letter to the Author of Sir Charles Grandison*. London: Millar, etc., 1759; rpt. Edith J. Morley, ed. London: Longman, 1918.

Name Index

221, 254, 263; *Lay Sermon,* 232; *Table
  Talk,* 73, 219; "Ancient Mariner," 143–
  44, 149, 173–74, 242; "Kubla Khan,"
  143, 152, 161, 242, 243; "The Night-
  ingale," 244; "To William Words-
  worth," 225
*A Collection of the Most Instructive and
  Amusing Lives Ever Published,* 24, 85,
  203, 221, 223
Collier, Jeremy, 56, 69
Collingwood, R. G., 195, 200, 253
Collins, William, 36, 40, 44, 50, 60, 91, 98,
  142, 207, 211, 214, 231, 238, 239, 240,
  242, 255
Combe, William, 178, 259
Congreve, William, 56, 69, 89, 196, 207,
  214
Contemporary Authors, 129, 235
Cook, Davidson, 205
Cooke, J. (Newgate writer), 216
Cooke, William, 263
Corbet[t], Elizabeth, 43
Corneille, Pierre, 121
Corney, Bolton, 225
Cottle, Joseph, 222, 251
Courtney, William Prideaux, 206, 219
Cowley, Abraham, 10, 20, 31, 32, 35, 37, 39,
  44–45, 46, 47, 51–52, 56, 59, 68, 88,
  94, 97, 98, 195, 206, 209, 211, 214, 215,
  239; *Sprat's Life,* 22, 44–45, 79, 98,
  202, 211
Cowper, William, 88, 106, 119, 142, 182,
  190, 228, 231, 239, 240, 242
Crabbe, George, 130, 132, 231, 236, 237, 264
Crayon, Geoffrey. *See* Irving, Washington
Crocker, Charles, 109
Croker, John Wilson, 14, 24, 72, 194, 197,
  198, 203, 204, 220, 253
Crompton, Louis, 244
Cromwell, Henry, 42, 57, 211
Cromwell, Oliver, 52, 213
Cross, Wilbur, 4, 11, 193, 195, 218
Cruttwell, Patrick, 227
Culler, Jonathan, 28, 206
Cumberland, Richard, 103, 105, 227
Cunningham, Allan, 94, 109, 187, 248; *Bio-
  graphical and Critical History,* 87–90,
  95, 96, 99, 106, 110, 115–16, 122, 218,
  230, 233; *Burns,* 88, 177, 224; *Lives of
  the Painters,* 87, 223–24
Cunningham, Peter, 36, 87, 195, 196, 208
Curll, Edmund, 218
Curran, Stuart, 232
Currie, James, 78, 177, 259

Cushing, William, 259

Dacier, Anne, 67
Daghlian, Philip B., 205, 218
Damrosch, Leopold, 218
Dante Alighieri, 44, 92, 174, 258
Darnton, Robert, 48, 212
Darwin, Charles, 70
Davies, Tom, 164
Davy, Humphry, 176, 248, 250
Dawson, Mary, 240
Defoe, Daniel, 216, 217, 227
DeLuca, V. A., 152, 244
de Man, Paul, 28, 206
Denham, John, 37, 39, 206–7, 262
Dennis, John, 56, 69, 91
De Quincey, Margaret (Simpson), 178,
  245, 246
De Quincey, Margaret, Florence, and Em-
  ily (daughters), 249–50
De Quincey, Richard "Pink" (brother),
  158, 160, 161, 246, 248, 252
De Quincey, Thomas, 8, 15, 26, 28, 60, 81,
  85, 111, 136, 138, 151–91, 221, 234, 236,
  245–65; letters, 170, 178, 190, 221, 245,
  249, 250, 251, 260, 265; *Autobiographic
  Sketches,* 146, 152, 154, 155, 171, 173, 175,
  187, 220, 243, 246, 247, 248, 250, 252,
  257, 258, 259; "Bentley," 246, 252;
  "Brevia," 172, 252, 258; *Caesars,* 154,
  157, 159, 252; *Confessions,* 25, 152, 153,
  154, 155, 170, 179, 180, 185, 187, 203, 245,
  246, 247; "Conversation and Coleridge," 160, 173–74, 212, 253, 257, 258;
  Encyclopedia Britannica biographies,
  246; of Shakespeare, 78, 167, 246, 256;
  "Essenes," 249; Forster's *Goldsmith,*
  167–68, 170, 246, 257; Gilfillan's *Gallery,* 246; Gillman's *Coleridge,* 246;
  "Greek Literature," 248; "Hannah
  More," 246, 252; Hawkins's *Anecdotes,* 246, 258; "Kant," 246, 252; *Laocoön,* 244, 252; *Letters to a Young
  Man,* 232; *Literary Reminiscences,* 5,
  77, 88, 106, 147, 150, 151–52, 154, 155–
  67, 170, 173, 174–91, 204, 205, 215, 221,
  224, 228, 238, 243, 244–65, 221
  (chart); *Logic of Political Economy,* 252;
  Mail-Coach, 152, 188, 246, 247, 264;
  "Milton," 246, 249, 252; "My
  Brother" Pink, 158–59, 160–61, 246,
  248, 252; "Parr," 246, 252; Preface to
  British edition (*Selections Grave and*

Subject Index